LOUISIANA NOTARY AND LEGAL FORMS

WITH EXPLANATIONS

2024 EDITION

MORE NOTARY EDUCATION RESOURCES
FROM QUID PRO BOOKS

Books

Sold online at Amazon, B&N, etc., and such eBook sites as Kindle, Nook, Apple, and Kobo:

Louisiana Notary Exam Sidepiece to the 2024 Study Guide: Tips, Index, Forms—Essentials Missing in the Official Book, by Steven Alan Childress (2024)

Louisiana Notary Exam Outline to the 2024 Study Guide: A Simpler Summary of the Official Book, by Michele Childress (2024)

Louisiana Notary Exam Sample Questions and Answers 2024: Explanations Keyed to the Official Study Guide, by Steven Alan Childress (2024)

Become a Notary Public in Louisiana: Process and Possibilities, by Steven Alan Childress (2023-2024 ed.)

Louisiana Civil Law Dictionary, by Gregory W. Rome and Stephan Kinsella (2011)

Webinars

Remote education found at *www.ChildressNotary.com*, and registered with the Secretary of State:

"Full Court Prep" full-length weekly classes, live-on-Zoom and recorded

"The Big Picture" introductory seminar

"The Final Lap" review seminar and sample-exam workshop

"I Passed – Now What?" practical seminar

LOUISIANA NOTARY AND LEGAL FORMS
WITH EXPLANATIONS

2024 Edition

Michele Childress

and

Steven Alan Childress

QUID PRO BOOKS
NEW ORLEANS, LOUISIANA

Published in 2024 by Quid Pro Books.

ISBN 978-1-61027-508-8 (hardcover)
ISBN 978-1-61027-511-8 (trade pbk.)
ISBN 978-1-61027-507-1 (mass mkt. pbk.)

QUID PRO BOOKS
427 North Theard St. #221
Covington, Louisiana 70433
www.quidprobooks.com

Publisher's Cataloging-in-Publication

Childress, Michele, et al.

Louisiana Notary and Legal Forms with Explanations / Michele Childress and Steven Alan Childress.

p. cm.

Series: *Sherpa Series*, #15

1. Notaries. 2. Notaries—United States. 3. Notaries—Louisiana. 4. Notaries—Louisiana—Handbooks, Manuals, etc. I. Title. II. Series.

KF8799 .C16 2024

First hardcover edition: June 2024

TABLE OF CONTENTS

Introduction

In our seminars for new notaries and discussions with former law students, we determined there was a need for an affordable and comprehensive collection of forms and examples. Attorney and notary alike want access to valid, up-to-date, and adaptable forms for a wide variety of legal and notarial acts and instruments.

The most complete and detailed collection of notarial forms, *Louisiana Notary Handbook* by Kathy D. Underwood and published by Thomson West in 2023, is very good, but costs $956 in paperback and stretches to 928 pages, says their website. By all means it is a worthy resource to consult in parish law libraries or for law firms to own or subscribe to. But realistically it's not very accessible to small notary and law practices. Collections of forms sold by organizations and practitioners are a good start, but not necessarily complete, formatted, or kept current. Internet searches and legal software are hit-and-miss for finding forms that truly work for Louisiana civil law—some even refer to "counties" or offer testaments with mere initialing at the bottom of pages. Using AI for Louisiana law is an invitation to malpractice.

In sum, it hasn't been easy to create valid acts unless you stitch them together like Frankenstein from various sources and pieces, all with fingers firmly crossed. The result may well fail in its purposes, especially if the suggested clause is Abby Normal.

Having operated a notary practice together near New Orleans ourselves—and having taught between us thousands of law students and notary exam candidates—we realized the profession needs a collection of forms with explanatory notes to guide the user. They had to be adaptable to a wide variety of client situations and reflect current law and court decisions. Only in Louisiana can notary public and attorney alike draft most legal instruments for the public without committing the unauthorized practice of law, so this resource is directed at both of them with the hope that it aids their professional function.

To make this collection as accessible and useful as possible, it is being released in both print editions and as downloadable textual files (in properly formatted Word documents, readily converted for Mac or Google Docs). The downloadable files are found at *ChildressNotary.com*, along with information about our notary prep books and remote-online classes. That site also discusses a discount for buying the book and the download together, as well as discounted licensing for multiple users.

Despite this resource, there's still work to be done, for notary and attorney alike. This collection is no substitute for the knowledge, judgment, and research required to identify the client's precise need — which form is right? — and to adapt it in light of the client's background to successfully accomplish their lawful goal. Clients notoriously suffer from having just enough knowledge to ask for the *wrong* thing: they want a "living will," when a little conversation discloses they're planning for after they die — a will. They want a power of attorney to have the agent deal with their things after they die (but that's a will, not a POA). Or they ask for a "trust" having heard that it saves on estate taxes ... when that only helps estates over $13.61 million (so they should be seeing an estate planning specialist anyway).

You'll have to discuss their goals and needs enough, and keep up with notary law such as with C. Alan Jennings' indispensable *Fundamentals of Louisiana Notarial Law and Practice* (plus our own *Outline* and *Sidepiece* guides), to even begin to pick out the right form. And nonattorney-notaries have to do so without giving legal advice or practicing law. Then the right form has to be turned into a valid and legal instrument, fitted to the client's situation and background, before it gets executed and stamped.

So, a resource like this is part of a larger process that doesn't replace professional expertise and good judgment. It's no shortcut to effective practice, and it doesn't purport to provide every nuance and clause that the act may need. And our most important disclaimer, as stated on the copyright page: this resource is used by applying your own notarial or legal background to the best of your ability, but it is not legal advice, the practice of law, or anything that forms an attorney-client relationship with the user.

The more practical disclaimer is simple advice we give newly commissioned notaries: don't hesitate to "just say No" to any client request that's over your head or makes you uncomfortable in any way. It's tempting to try to solve any problem presented to you, but it's responsible to know your limitations. And it's helpful to the client for you to have some trusted names handy for referrals about specific issues — a public tag agent for sticky car title problems, an estate-planning attorney for complicated trusts or wills likely to wind up in litigation, and a real estate expert for complex purchase-finance situations. You'll actually look good turning down work that is not yet in your wheelhouse; but then you can gain experience along the way by asking those experts, as follow up, to teach you something about the transaction and its solution.

We also caution you not to share these forms. We believe they are priced fairly to provide value to any purchaser, especially given the alternatives or the work a user would have to perform to create this bank of forms for themselves. We ask that the hard work we did be respected by directing others to the website *ChildressNotary.com* to buy them rather than just sharing. We have copyrighted the forms, and we use all available technological resources we can to prevent sharing, such as assigning a unique code for downloads. But we recognize that users can outsmart us and find a way to share with nonpaying users. Please don't. We'd like to be able to justify continuing and expanding this project. (If you'd like to purchase multiple books or downloads at a large discount, to be able to provide wider access within a law firm or notary practice, please contact *quidprolaw@gmail.com* re "bulk sales.")

Another important reminder is to maintain client confidentiality at all times. When you adapt a form for a particular client, be sure to secure where the draft or final product — digitally or on paper — is stored. And of course don't forward that form outside your confidential practice, both to maintain client privacy and to respect the copyright noted above.

We also caution readers who are *not* notaries or attorneys to be especially careful in using these forms. It's possible to adapt a form to your own situation and produce a valid legal instrument, but it may be wiser — and more affordable than you think — to use the services of a professional such as a commissioned civil law notary. We made this book available for non-expert self-help, but that does require more research and context for the individual user with no legal background. And it's especially dangerous to purport to adapt these forms for other people, beyond *self*-help. That probably constitutes the unauthorized practice of law, even if you aren't charging for it, and is taken seriously under Louisiana law. Louisiana notaries can do a lot of "legal" acts that are reserved to attorneys in every other state, so they don't commit the unauthorized practice of law here when they adapt these forms appropriately for others. But non-notaries would. (Consider in that case becoming a civil law notary, such as starting with the books and classes we link on *ChildressNotary.com*.)

In addition to the above general cautions, here's some specific advice about how to adapt each form:

1. Remove any bracketed notes or italicized introductions. These are to guide you in adapting the form to your client's specific situation, but they should not be included in the final instrument (document).

2. Remove any footnotes. They are also explanatory and not part of the final document. But read them as you consider the form, because they clarify some fine points worth considering.

3. Remove the occasional copyright notice we put on a form. On the sample testaments, be sure to leave the testator's name and signature line intact (in footer) while removing anything else.

4. The venue line near the top for "Parish of ______" means to fill in the place of signing, not necessarily the place of the notary's or client's home parish, or even the place it will be filed.

5. Appearance clauses and signature lines need to be adapted to the specific situation of the party(ies), so check out the specific files on those in addition to the instrument being used. For example, incorporate a correct and complete appearance clause (from that chapter) into an Act of Donation (from that chapter).

6. We tend to use the modern way of referring to an affiant or appearer later in the instrument as "they," as long as that's clear (or to be even clearer, you can simply repeat "appearer" or the like). But it is perfectly appropriate, and may be your preference, to replace "they" with "he" or "she" and replace "their" with "his" or "her." If you do that, then do it consistently and completely throughout the document, or you may leave a stray "they" which now would be ambiguous.

7. In acts involving married couples, we use the statistically likely example of a husband and wife. But we recognize that in some cases it's more accurate that the couple share a gender or use different terms for their status. Simply adapt that as appropriate in filling out the form; the key is clarity in all cases.

8. It's always a good idea to search "notary public" without the L because spellcheck won't notice that but your client will.

9. Check the status of current law and civil code articles before finalizing a document. The basic form of a simple affidavit is not likely to change any time soon, but the rules and format of a small succession affidavit, for example, certainly may.

These forms are current and valid under our best understanding of the law as of June 1, 2024. We intend to release a new edition in 2025 which will update these forms and annotations in light of substantive changes in the law. At that time, we'll also expand the available forms even further. The current set covers most of the situations that notaries and lawyers preparing legal documents encounter on a day-to-day basis, so we regard it as reasonably complete — at least, compared to most readily available sources. Nevertheless, we intend to commit to this project for the long haul, with hopes it meets the needs of notaries and lawyers for years to come. Thank you.

MICHELE CHILDRESS
Attorney at Law and Notary Public

STEVEN ALAN CHILDRESS
Professor of Law and Notary Public

New Orleans, Louisiana
June 7, 2024

1 • AFFIDAVITS

AFFIDAVITS: MODEL AND GENERIC BLANK

JURAT

The "jurat" (i.e., the phrase below, with or without the name of the city where signed) is used in a large number of juridical acts. Most obviously it is the conclusion clause of the affidavit and those forms of acknowledgment in the form of affidavit (such as acknowledgment of a witness). But it also can be a workable clause to conclude other acts, such as those forms that need to be verified in some way or are missing a place for the notary to sign.

The jurat is never the appropriate conclusion to a notarial testament; rather, the witness attestation clause of LA CC article 1577 (or specialized ones for less common situations such as a blind testator) must be quoted.

In all juridical acts, signing or stamping with a "Bar Roll #" is only proper for notaries who are also active members of the Louisiana state bar. Be sure any stamp or embosser you purchase does not mention "Bar Roll" unless you are a Louisiana attorney at law.

SWORN TO AND SUBSCRIBED BEFORE ME this ______ day of ___________________, 20____, at _______________________, Louisiana.

____

Notary Name: _______________________________

Notary ID or Bar Roll No.: ________________

My Commission is for Life

AFFIDAVIT, BLANK LINES TO WRITE INTO

STATE OF LOUISIANA

PARISH OF ______________________ [*where signed*]

AFFIDAVIT

BEFORE ME, the undersigned duly commissioned and qualified Notary Public, personally came and appeared the undersigned

____

who, after being first duly sworn, deposed and said:

____

____

____

____

____

____

____
Affiant

SWORN TO AND SUBSCRIBED BEFORE ME this _______ day of __________________, 20____

____

Notary Name: ________________________________
Notary ID or Bar Roll[1] No.: _________________
My Commission is for Life

[1] "Bar Roll #" is only for notaries who are also active members of the Louisiana Bar Association. Be sure any stamp or embosser you purchase does not mention "Bar Roll" unless you are a Louisiana attorney at law.

In all juridical acts, it is required to write, type or print notary full name and ID/Bar Roll number below the signature. "Commissioned for life" is not required but puts out-of-state recipients of the act on notice that Louisiana commissions don't expire (they do in all other states). A stamp providing the notary name and ID is adequate, but it is advisable to add that manually or typed into the document as well.

AFFIDAVIT, BLANK LINES WITH WITNESSES

STATE OF LOUISIANA

PARISH OF ______________________ [*where signed*]

AFFIDAVIT[1]

BEFORE ME, the undersigned duly commissioned and qualified Notary Public, personally came and appeared the undersigned

____

who, after being first duly sworn, deposed and said:

____

____

____

____

WITNESSES:	AFFIANT:
________________________________	________________________________
Print Name	Print Name
________________________________	
Print Name	

SWORN TO AND SUBSCRIBED BEFORE ME this _______ day of _______________, 20____

____

Notary Name: ______________________________

Notary ID or Bar Roll No.: _________________

My Commission is for Life

---

[1] Usually an affidavit does not require witnesses other than the notary, though there is nothing incorrect about adding them if the client or recipient prefers. An exception is those relatively few situations where an authentic act is in the form of an affidavit, in which case the affidavit is required to be in authentic form (having two witnesses and the import of the act impressed upon the signer). For example, a declaration of immobilization of a motor home, when not made as part of an act of sale, may be in the form of an affidavit but requires two witnesses as with any other authentic act. An affidavit of correction by a notary relating to an immovable is also an authentic act.

AFFIDAVIT, MODEL, SIGNED BY 1 AFFIANT ONLY

STATE OF LOUISIANA

PARISH OF ____________________

AFFIDAVIT

BEFORE ME, the undersigned duly commissioned and qualified Notary Public, came and appeared the undersigned

Name of Affiant

who, after being first duly sworn, deposed and said:

Body of affidavit, stating facts, legal declaration, or situation; this may be written in first person ("I," meaning Affiant is speaking), or third person from Notary's POV ("That he is a person over the age of 18 and domiciled in Bossier Parish…").

____
Affiant

SWORN TO AND SUBSCRIBED BEFORE ME this _______ day of __________________, 20____

____
Notary Name: ___________________________
Notary ID or Bar Roll No.: ________________
My Commission is for Life

AFFIDAVIT, MODEL, SIGNED BY 1 AFFIANT & WITNESSES

STATE OF LOUISIANA

PARISH OF ____________________

AFFIDAVIT

BEFORE ME, the undersigned duly commissioned and qualified Notary Public, came and appeared the undersigned

Name of Affiant

who, after being first duly sworn, deposed and said:

Body of affidavit, stating facts, declaration or situation

THUS DONE AND PASSED in the presence of the undersigned witnesses and notary.

____

Affiant

WITNESSES:

____

Print Name

____

Print Name

SWORN TO AND SUBSCRIBED BEFORE ME this _______ day of __________________, 20____, at _______________________, Louisiana.

____

Notary Name: ___________________________

Notary ID or Bar Roll No.: ________________

My Commission is for Life

AFFIDAVIT, MODEL, SIGNED BY 2 AFFIANTS APPEARING SAME TIME

STATE OF LOUISIANA

PARISH OF ____________________

AFFIDAVIT

BEFORE ME, the undersigned duly commissioned and qualified Notary Public, came and appeared the undersigned

Name of Affiant 1 and Name of Affiant 2

who, after being first duly sworn, deposed and said:

Body of affidavit, stating facts, legal declaration, or situation; this may be written in first person ("I," meaning Affiant is speaking), or third person from Notary's POV ("That he is a person over the age of 18 and domiciled in Bossier Parish…").

____
Affiant 1 Printed Name

____
Affiant 2 Printed Name

SWORN TO AND SUBSCRIBED BEFORE ME this _______ day of ___________________, 20____

____

Notary Name: __________________________
Notary ID or Bar Roll No.: ________________
My Commission is for Life

AFFIDAVITS FOR SPECIFIC SITUATIONS

CONSENT FOR MINOR TO TRAVEL WITH ANOTHER PERSON, OFTEN ABROAD

When a minor child needs to travel internationally accompanied by a non-parent adult, the adult needs to carry this permission. This has become especially important at the border and on return to the country where there are concerns about child trafficking. It is executed by the non-traveling parent before a notary

The form is also used, and adapted, when the child is traveling with one parent who is not clearly the custodial parent, or there is a court order or agreement in place not allowing international travel without the other parent's permission. In such case the other, non-traveling, parent needs to have the permission signed and notarized.

Similar forms are found on cruise ship websites for Disney, Carnival, Norwegian, RC and others (search their websites for them), as often a grandparent takes a child on a cruise. Find and use their specific form if so. But it is strongly advised to also execute this more comprehensive one that conforms to U.S. State Department expectations, even for cruise travelers. If the grandparent, for example, has to travel with the child in a way not anticipated, crossing a border rather than just getting back on the ship (for example, leaving early for an emergency), the cruise ship form may be inadequate and cause delays or investigation when returning into the U.S. Clients would be well advised to have this more complete form available. This is especially true if the name of the child does not match the adult's name.

Please be aware that the U.S. State Department notes that certain countries have specific entry and exit requirements, and that if a minor is traveling abroad and is not accompanied by both parents or a legal guardian, you should contact the embassy or consulate of the country you will be visiting and ask about entry and exit requirements for that country.

The form may also protect an adult in certain domestic situations and be useful for some non-international travel, especially in states and situations where concerns about child trafficking may be heightened (e.g., a younger child who could not confirm that the adult is related, or one where the child is potentially uncooperative). In such case the form is adapted by removing "abroad" and any other limitations to international travel.

AFFIDAVIT, CONSENT FOR MINOR TO TRAVEL ABROAD

STATE OF LOUISIANA

PARISH OF ____________________

CONSENT FOR MINOR TO TRAVEL ABROAD

BEFORE ME, the undersigned duly commissioned and qualified Notary Public came and appeared the undersigned Affiant, who after being duly sworn does state the following:

Consent:
I, ____ (name of parent; complete one for each person having parental authority or control over the minor child, or legal tutor), am the ________ (mother/father/legal guardian) of ____________________________________ (child name), aged ___________, and do hereby give my consent for ______ (him/her) to travel with ____ ____ (name/address of traveling adult), who is ________________________ (relationship to child), to ______________________ ____ (destinations), from ______________________ (date of first day of travel) until ________ (last date of travel).

Travel Details:
(Include flight numbers, arrival/departure times, cruise line, tour operator, or attach itinerary.)

____

____

____

____
Affiant, Person giving consent

____
Address of Affiant

____
Phone number of Affiant

SWORN TO AND SUBSCRIBED BEFORE ME this _______ day of _________________, 20____, at ______________________, Louisiana.

____

Notary Name: ____________________________
Notary ID or Bar Roll No.: _______________
My Commission is for Life

AFFIDAVIT FOR VERIFICATION OF ONE LIVING WITH AFFIANT

AFFIDAVIT: VERIFY COHABITATION, NON-SUPPORT & INCOME CONTRIBUTION

STATE OF LOUISIANA

PARISH OF ___________________

AFFIDAVIT

BEFORE ME, the undersigned duly commissioned and qualified Notary Public, came and appeared the undersigned,

____

Affiant

who, after being first duly sworn, did depose and say:

I, the above-named Affiant, reside at my home address:

____

____

The following person(s) reside with me at this address:

____

____

____

If there are any questions, I can be reached at:

Main Telephone Number: ____

Alternate Telephone Number: ____

Signed,

____

Affiant

SWORN TO AND SUBSCRIBED BEFORE ME this ______ day of _____________, 20_____

____

Notary Name: ____________________________

Notary ID or Bar Roll No.: _____________

My Commission is for Life

AFFIDAVIT: LIVING WITH AFFIANT BUT CANNOT PROVE BY BILLS OR MAIL

STATE OF LOUISIANA

PARISH OF ___________________

AFFIDAVIT OF RESIDENCE

BEFORE ME, the undersigned duly commissioned and qualified Notary Public, came and appeared the undersigned:

____

AFFIANT

Who did state that *name of person residing with Affiant* resides with me at *address of Affiant*. The person living with me pays no bills and has no mail that comes to the home at that address.

____

Affiant

SWORN TO AND SUBSCRIBED BEFORE ME this _______ day of __________________, 20____

____

Notary Name: _______________________________
Notary ID or Bar Roll No.: _________________
My Commission is for Life

AFFIDAVIT OF NON-SUPPORT BY FATHER

STATE OF LOUISIANA

PARISH OF ____________________

AFFIDAVIT OF NON-SUPPORT

BEFORE ME, the undersigned duly commissioned and qualified Notary Public, came and appeared the undersigned

____

Affiant (Mother)

____

Affiant(Father)

Who, after being first duly sworn, did depose and state that:

1. Mother and Father are living separately and apart.
2. Mother lives and resides at *mother's residential address, city, state, zip code,* along with
3. *Names of minor children,* minor children, who live with Mother at the above address.
4. Father lives and resides at *father's residential address, city, state, zip code.*
5. Father affirms that he does not provide any support for the minor children.

AFFIANTS:

____

Mother

____

Father

SWORN TO AND SUBSCRIBED BEFORE ME this ______ day of ____________________, 20_____

____

Notary Name: __________________________

Notary ID or Bar Roll No.: ____________

My Commission is for Life

AFFIDAVIT FOR VERIFICATION OF INCOME CONTRIBUTION

STATE OF LOUISIANA

PARISH OF ___________________

AFFIDAVIT FOR VERIFICATION OF INCOME CONTRIBUTION

BEFORE ME, the undersigned duly commissioned and qualified Notary Public, came and appeared the undersigned,

____

Affiant

who, after being first duly sworn, did say:

I, the above-named Affiant, give to ____, the amount of $ _________________ per (circle one): week / month / year, to help towards living expenses.

If there are any questions, I can be reached at:

Main Telephone Number: ____

Alternate Telephone Number: ____

Signed,

____

Affiant

SWORN TO AND SUBSCRIBED BEFORE ME this ______ day of ___________________, 20_____

____

Notary Name: ____________________________

Notary ID or Bar Roll No.: _____________

My Commission is for Life

CERTIFICATION BY NOTARY (NOT AN AFFIDAVIT) OF 'TRUE COPY'

AFFIDAVITS & STATEMENTS TO "CERTIFY" COPIES OF ORIGINAL

STATE OF LOUISIANA

PARISH OF ____________________

CERTIFICATION OF TRUE COPY[1]

I hereby certify the attached document to be a TRUE AND CORRECT COPY of the original of this document, named _______________________________, passed before me on the date of ______________________, 20____.

Signed and so certified on this ______ day of _________________, 20____

____

Name: ___________________________________, Notary Public

Notary ID or Bar Roll No.: _________________

My Commission is for Life

---

[1] Certification of "true copy" by this form, or by stamping or writing the words directly onto a document's copy, turns the exact photocopy into one having the force and effect of the original. See LA C.C. art. 1840. Importantly, even though it is grouped with similar "affidavits," *this certificate is not an affidavit* (which would violate the rule against notarizing one's own signature). It is frequently used for a power of attorney or other instruments that need to be carried around and used in real life, while retaining the original. It is not appropriately used for a testament. It cannot be used to certify official governmental records such as birth certificates.

Note that the ability to make a "true copy" technically is limited to documents in which you yourself prepared the original. Clients frequently bring in some other notary's copy and ask you to make it a true copy, but the above certificate is not appropriate for this request. In such cases it is appropriate, and probably sufficient for their needs, to have the *client* sign an affidavit affirming that the copy is an exact duplicate—and this way is advisable if it meets their needs. Or, without using the procedure of art. 1840 above, a notary may confirm that they have made an accurate copy of the original. The certification would be: "I hereby certify this to be an accurate and exact photocopy of the original of this document given to me for copying and certifying this ____ day of _______, 20___." followed by the notary's signature and name. Note that this also is *not* an affidavit.

The exception to requiring the notary to use "true copy" only for their own originals is the situation in which the notary has succeeded to the practice of another notary and is custodian of their records. Then they can make a true copy for the purposes of establishing executive-process foreclosure, under LA R.S. 13:4102.

CERTIFICATION: NOTARY VERIFYING UNALTERED COPY OF VITAL RECORD

STATE OF LOUISIANA

PARISH OF ____________________

VERIFICATION OF UNALTERED COPY[1]

On this ______ day of ________________, 20____, I certify that the preceding or attached document is an, exact, complete, and unaltered copy made by me, _________________________, Notary Public, of a _________________________[2] presented to me in original by the document's custodian, _________________________;[3] and that, to the best of my knowledge, the photocopied document is neither an official public record nor a publicly recordable document,[4] certified copies of which are available from an official source other than a notary.

____

Notary Name: _______________________________

Notary ID or Bar Roll No.: ______________

My Commission is for Life

---

[1] Although it appears to be an affidavit and is grouped (and named) here as such, technically this form is just a signed statement by the notary, who would not be allowed to notarize their own affidavit. So do not include a jurat. In the alternative, the notary could draft and notarize the document holder's affidavit with jurat that this is an exact copy, which affidavit usually suffices for the purposes noted below. See file "Affidavit, vital records holder's exact photocopy." Presenting it as the holder's affidavit may be preferable to this form, for reasons noted in the alternate file.

[2] Insert type of document, i.e., birth certificate, death certificate, etc.

[3] Insert name of the person for whom you made the copy, or the holder of the document.

[4] This is to clarify that this instrument does not purport to be an officially certified copy of the a document that requires governmental certification (such as a filed land record), but instead is a notary's photocopy of one (e.g., a birth certificate, which can be used for many less-formal purposes such as a child's sports league permission or by request from a school).

AFFIDAVIT BY HOLDER OF VITAL RECORD THAT IT IS EXACT PHOTOCOPY

STATE OF LOUISIANA

PARISH OF ____________________

VERIFICATION OF EXACT PHOTOCOPY OF RECORD[1]

BEFORE ME, the undersigned duly commissioned and qualified notary public came and appeared the undersigned

____

[Affiant name][2]

Who, after being duly sworn, did depose and state that they a person of full legal age and a resident of and domiciled in ______________ Parish, Louisiana;

And that Affiant hereby verifies and affirms before a notary public that the attached record, document, act or legal instrument, namely a ______________________________,[3] is an exact, complete and unaltered photocopy of the original.

SWORN TO AND SUBSCRIBED BEFORE ME this _______ day of __________________, 20____, at _______________________, Louisiana.

____

Notary Name: ____________________________
Notary ID or Bar Roll No.: ________________
My Commission is for Life

---

[1] Unlike the notary's verification of unaltered copy, and perhaps in preference to that, this is an affidavit made by the holder of the official record or other document, verifying a photocopy is exact. It involves no statement confirming that by the notary, and yet it usually is accepted for the purposes—a school or sports league requesting a "notarized copy of birth certificate." A notary making a *certified* copy of a vital record such as a birth certificate is not permissible, but note that this attachment to such a record does not purport to be certified by a state agency. Yet it often meets the client's needs.

This is an affidavit by the holder of the document. Normally the notary has no independent duty to verify that factual assertions of a client, even in an affidavit drafted by the notary. In this situation, however, it is advisable to expect the holder to present the original for copying or comparison by the notary and not just a copy. This is because, though this is the holder's affidavit, it is treated as a "notarization of the copy" by the ultimate recipient—and the notary may be uncomfortable notarizing the affidavit if there is no original to view.

Because this form is attached to the copy and the copy is part of the assertion herein, to assure the recipient that there really is an "attachment" and not just a second page clipped on, it is acceptable to use the embosser on both pages by embossing once, onto both, by having the photocopy immediately behind it.

[2] The person asserting the claim or their representative.

[3] Insert type of document, i.e., birth certificate, death certificate, etc.

AFFIDAVIT FOR STOLEN CHECKS

AFFIDAVITS RE LOST, STOLEN, OR FORGED ACCOUNTS & CHECKS

STATE OF LOUISIANA

PARISH OF ________________

AFFIDAVIT REGARDING STOLEN CHECKS

BEFORE ME, the undersigned notary public, duly commissioned and qualified in the parish and state aforesaid, appeared the undersigned Affiant, MARCUS G. NOONAN,

Who, after being first duly sworn, deposed and stated:

That an order of bank checks *[or adapt for one check]* on checking account number 2000224725 with Chase Bank was stolen. I do not know the number series of these checks or how many checks were provided to me by the bank; it was the initial order sent to me after I opened the account.

These checks were stolen from a home in which I lived in Morgan City. I had roommates at that time who had access to these checks. Their names are Cindy Cassiton, William Shore, and Stuart Lionel Jones.

Under penalty of law, I declare that at no time did I ever write or cause to be written any check on the above referenced account. Any check presented on that account to any party purported to be signed by me is a forged check, such check being tendered by persons unknown to me without my knowledge or consent.

I have received notification from merchants or their collection agents who advise that they have in their possession one or more checks drawn on that account. I declare that none of the following items were ever written or presented by me since I never wrote nor issued any check on that account.

Check No:	Amount:	Dated:	Payee:

Further, I have been shown copies of check #231 payable to Cleco Electrical Co. which I understand is being processed as worthless checks by the Caddo Parish District Attorney.

I declare that all checks described in this affidavit are forgeries, having been neither written, issued, authorized, nor presented by me or any person with my approval or consent. I further

AFFIDAVIT FOR STOLEN CHECKS

declare that I have received no benefit nor proceeds from any of the checks itemized or otherwise described in this affidavit.

This affidavit is made for the purpose of inducing Chase Bank to reimburse me, Affiant, for any and all amounts paid on these stolen and forged checks, to induce the St. Mary Parish District Attorney to dismiss any charges which may be pending against me for allegedly issuing these checks, to notify the aforementioned merchants and any other merchants who have or may have received, or may receive in the future, any checks drawn on the above referenced account, that I have no liability to them for these checks which are stolen and forged, and to induce and direct said merchants to delete any unfavorable credit reporting made or caused by their agents to be made against my name on the substance of their original belief that they had any claim against me for these checks.

I declare under penalty of law that all parties may rely on this sworn affidavit to restore my good name in their files and records, and that I will fully cooperate in the prosecution of the individual or individuals who have issued or presented any one or several of the checks described herein.

____
Print name, Affiant

SWORN TO AND SUBSCRIBED BEFORE ME this ______ day of __________________, 20____

____
Notary Name: ___________________________
Notary ID or Bar Roll No.: ____________
My Commission is for Life

AFFIDAVIT OF FORGERY

STATE OF LOUISIANA

PARISH OF ____________________

AFFIDAVIT OF FORGERY

BEFORE ME, the undersigned authority, a Notary Public commissioned and qualified in and for the Parish above and the State of Louisiana, personally came and appeared

____
Affiant

who, after being by me first duly sworn, did depose and say:

That the following check payable to ______________________________ *[name of payee]* was not endorsed by the payee; that the payee did not authorize or instruct anyone to endorse his or her name to said check; did not receive any benefit therefrom; and that the endorsement thereto is a forgery, to-wit:

Check Number ___________ dated ____________ in the amount of $_____________, and

payable to: ______________________________________.

The said check above referred to, on which payee's endorsement has been forged, is attached hereto.

Affiant hereby agrees to assist law enforcement in any criminal proceedings and prosecution. All statements made are voluntary for the purposes of establishing that the indicated signature on the check is a forgery.

____
[Print Name], Affiant

SWORN TO AND SUBSCRIBED BEFORE ME this ______ day of _________________, 20____, at ______________________, Louisiana.

____
Notary Name: ____________________________
Notary ID or Bar Roll No.: ________________
My Commission is for Life

AFFIDAVIT FOR LOST C.D.

STATE OF LOUISIANA

PARISH OF ___________________

AFFIDAVIT FOR LOST CERTIFICATE OF DEPOSIT

BEFORE ME, the undersigned notary public, duly commissioned and qualified in the parish and state aforesaid, appeared the undersigned Affiant, who after being first duly sworn, deposes and says:

Affiant is named ____, and resides at the address of ____, Louisiana.

Affiant is the Purchaser and/or Payee of the Certificate of Deposit drawn by bank or financial institution name of ____, CD number__________ dated ________________, year _________, in the amount of $ ______________________, payable to ____.

Affiant has lost the Certificate of Deposit and is therefore unable to produce the certificate. In order to induce bank and branch ____ to issue a substitute certificate to Affiant, the Affiant warrants that:

1. Affiant has not negotiated or endorsed the certificate listed above,

2. Affiant will indemnify the above-named bank or financial institution and hold it and its officers and directors harmless for any costs, damages and expenses of every nature whatsoever, including attorneys' fees which may sustain at any time as the result of the appearance of any person or persons claiming to be the owner of such certificate or in any way connected with or arising out of Affiant's failure to produce the certificate

3. In case of recovery of the original certificate, Affiant will return said certificate to the above-named bank or financial institution for their retention.

____

Affiant

SWORN TO AND SUBSCRIBED BEFORE ME this ______ day of __________________, 20_____

____

Notary Name: ______________________________

Notary ID or Bar Roll No.: ____________

My Commission is for Life

AFFIDAVIT OF ONE AND THE SAME NAME

AFFIDAVITS OF NAME & IDENTITY

STATE OF LOUISIANA

PARISH OF CADDO

AFFIDAVIT OF ONE AND THE SAME NAME[1]

BEFORE ME, the undersigned notary public, duly commissioned and qualified in and for the parish and state aforesaid, personally came and appeared the undersigned

RICHARD TIFFANY GERE, who is of the age of majority and is domiciled in Bossier Parish, Louisiana, and who, after being first duly sworn, deposes and says:

RICHARD TIFFANY GERE, RICHARD T. GERE, RICHARD GERE, and DICK GERE are one and the same person. This affidavit may be attached to an Act of Donation of immovable property found in the public records under one of these names to identify Affiant for purposes of donating the said property[2] under his currently used and legal name, RICHARD TIFFANY GERE.

____
RICHARD TIFFANY GERE, Affiant

SWORN TO AND SUBSCRIBED BEFORE ME,
This ______ day of ___________________, 20____

____
[*print name*], Notary Public
Notary ID or Bar Roll No.: _____________
My Commission is for Life

[1] This form is often used to reconcile varying names used (often just two), especially on matters in title records (as in this example) or with the OMV. For example, a car's certificate of title may have a slightly different name for "Owner" than is found in GEICO's records when totaling a car. This situation is especially common after a woman marries (and seeks to sell a car, for example), but is even useful when the name varies such as GEICO using Richard Gere but the title adds his actual middle name, Tiffany.

[2] This version is intended to be attached to a specific act (to reconcile earlier title records with the new name), so the language here connects that up and states the purpose. But it can be omitted or adapted when the form is used for a more generic announcement that varying names are used, not tied to a specific transaction.

AFFIDAVIT OF CORRECTION OF NAME ON MARRIAGE LICENSE

STATE OF LOUISIANA

PARISH OF ___________________

AFFIDAVIT OF CORRECTION FOR MARRIAGE LICENSE[1]

BEFORE ME, the undersigned notary public, duly commissioned and qualified in the parish and state aforesaid, appeared the undersigned Affiant,

JOHN WILLIAM MACDONALD

Who, after being first duly sworn, did depose and say:

That his surname is incorrectly spelled as "McDonald" on his marriage license issued _________________, 20____, and that the correct spelling of his surname is "MacDonald," as shown on his ____ *[document proving correct name, such as driver's license; attach copy]*, a copy of which is attached to this affidavit.

Affiant further states that he executes this affidavit for the purpose of correcting the spelling of his name on public records of the State of Louisiana and declares under oath that the information set forth herein is true and correct, and requests that the Clerk of Court for the Parish of _____________________ make all necessary corrections on his marriage license.

____

Affiant

SWORN TO AND SUBSCRIBED BEFORE ME this ______ day of __________________, 20_____

____

Notary Name: ___________________________

Notary ID or Bar Roll No.: ___________

My Commission is for Life

[1] This form can be readily adapted to begin the process of correcting a misspelling or other error (age, birthdate, place of birth, etc.) that finds its way onto various official records, not just marriage licenses. Documentation should be attached proving the correct spelling, or otherwise correct information.

AFFIDAVIT OF NAME CHANGE BY MARRIAGE

STATE OF LOUISIANA

PARISH OF ________________

AFFIDAVIT OF NAME CHANGE BY MARRIAGE

BEFORE ME, the undersigned notary public, duly commissioned and qualified in the parish and state aforesaid, personally CAME AND APPEARED

____

Affiant *[enter original name above]*

Who, after being first duly sworn, deposes and says:

Pursuant to Article 100 of the Louisiana Civil Code, that Affiant does by these presents hereby adopt the surname of Affiant's spouse, ________________________________ *[spouse full name]*, whom Affiant married on __________________, 20_____, and is, therefore, one and the same person as ____ *[married name]*, and signs both signatures below for identification.

____

Print name 1

____

Print name 2

SWORN TO AND SUBSCRIBED BEFORE ME this ______ day of __________________, 20_____

____

Notary Name: __________________________

Notary ID or Bar Roll No.: ___________

My Commission is for Life

AFFIDAVIT & CERTIFICATION OF IDENTITY (OF ANOTHER PERSON)

This is different from the similarly named statutory "Affidavit of Identity" and the related "Affidavit of Distinction" that are used for financial purposes and involve creditors. For example, the "Affidavit of Distinction" is used to deny that the affiant is the same-named person who owes a debt. It is submitted to creditors to prevent actions including foreclosure against the affiant that should rightly be directed at someone else. That one needs witnesses and has many more clauses, and is set out by statute.

This version is a much simpler form used for the specific purpose of establishing identity to obtain documents from the state—of vouching for someone else's identity rather than establishing one's own.

STATE OF LOUISIANA

PARISH OF ________________

AFFIDAVIT AND CERTIFICATION OF IDENTITY

BEFORE ME, the undersigned notary public, duly commissioned and qualified in the parish and state aforesaid, appeared the undersigned Affiant, MARK N. GRANT,

Who, after being first duly sworn, deposed and stated:

That for the purpose of assisting Janet Harley Thompson, a/k/a Janet Rebecca Thompson, who is his aunt, in obtaining identification documents, Affiant does hereby certify that the signature of his aunt, which appears below, is true and genuine; and was affixed hereunder by his aunt in Affiant's presence for the purposes of identification;

And that the photograph affixed below is a photograph made recently of Affiant's aunt for obtaining identification documents issued by the State of Louisiana.

____

Print name, Affiant

SWORN TO AND SUBSCRIBED BEFORE ME this ______ day of ____________________, 20_____

____

Notary Name: ______________________________

Notary ID or Bar Roll No.: ____________

My Commission is for Life

____

Signature of Janet Harley Thompson for Identification [and affix photo]

AFFIDAVIT OF DISTINCTION AND ACKNOWLEDGMENT

STATE OF LOUISIANA

PARISH OF ____________________

AFFIDAVIT OF DISTINCTION
PURSUANT TO LA R.S. 9:5501 *et seq.*

BEFORE ME, the undersigned duly commissioned and qualified Notary Public, came and appeared the undersigned:

____, whose mailing address is

____, and whose marital status is

_____________, who after being duly sworn, deposed as follows:

I, ____, being of sound mind, acknowledge and understand that any intentional falsification of information I am about to provide shall subject me to penalties for the crime of injuring public records and false swearing.

My full name is ____ (including maiden name if applicable). I am _____ years old and was born on the _____ day of __________________, _______ in (city/parish/county and state of birth): ____.

The last 4 digits of my social security number are __________.

I presently reside at ____, and my previous addresses for the preceding 10 years were:

____

____

____

____.

The name and address of my employer is: ____, ____, and the name and address of location of employment is: ____, ____, and my occupation is ___________________________________.

My marital status is ____________________, and (if married), the full name of my spouse is ____ (provide maiden name if spouse is female). The last 4 digits of my spouse's social security number are __________.

I HEREBY AFFIRM AND ATTEST, under penalty of law, that I am not the same person as the debtor or debtors named in the following described recorded judgments, liens or privileges:

A ______________ (lien, judgment, etc.) in favor of: ____; in the amount of $ _____________, dated ______________, filed on ________________; recorded in Mortgage Office Book _____ Folio _______, Instrument number ______________.

AFFIDAVIT OF DISTINCTION AND ACKNOWLEDGMENT

A ______________ (lien, judgment, etc.) in favor of: ______________________________________; in the amount of $ ____________, dated _____________, filed on ________________; recorded in Mortgage Office Book _____ Folio _______, Instrument number ______________.

A ______________ (lien, judgment, etc.) in favor of: ______________________________________; in the amount of $ ____________, dated _____________, filed on ________________; recorded in Mortgage Office Book _____ Folio _______, Instrument number ______________.

I HEREBY FURTHER AFFIRM AND ATTEST that on the _____ day of ________________, 20____, I mailed a copy of the affidavit to each judgment creditor listed in the affidavit at their last known address by registered mail and hereby submit proof of said certified mailing (mail slip or postal confirmation).

I HEREBY AFFIRM AND ATTEST that the judgment creditor has failed to comply with Louisiana R.S. 9:5501, and I hereby execute this affidavit of identity to establish that I am not the same person identified as the debtor in the said recorded judgment, lien or privilege or other such documents itemized above.

Thus done, read and signed at ___________________, Louisiana, this _____ day of ____________________, 20_____.

WITNESSES: AFFIANT:

_____________________________ _______________________________

Print Name Print Name

____

Print Name

____

Notary Name: ______________________________

Notary ID or Bar Roll No.: _____________

My Commission is for Life

AFFIDAVIT OF DISTINCTION AND ACKNOWLEDGMENT

JUDGMENT CREDITOR ACKNOWLEDGMENT

I (we), ____ (name of judgment creditor), hereby acknowledge that the above named affiant is not the same person identified or named in the above identified or described _________________________________ (type of document: judgment, lien, privilege or mortgage), and that the property of the affiant is not subject to the judicial mortgage resulting from the judgment.

Thus done, read and signed at __________________, Louisiana, this _____ day of ___________________, 20_____.

Judgment creditor:

____
Signature

____
Printed Name

Title: ___________________________________

Company Name: ____________________________

____
Notary Name: ______________________________
Notary ID or Bar Roll No.: _____________
My Commission is for Life

AFFIDAVIT OF DISTINCTION, FORM BY LA SUPREME COURT

AFFIDAVIT OF DISTINCTION
(R.S. 9:5503)

State of Louisiana)
Parish of)

BEFORE ME, the undersigned authority, personally came and appeared:

______________________________, who being duly sworn, deposed as follows:

I, being of sound mind acknowledge and understand that any Intentional falsification of information I am about to provide shall subject me to penalties for the crime of inquiring public records and false swearing.

My full name is ______________________. I am ______years old and I was born on _____________________ at _________________. My social security number is xxx-xx-___. I presently reside at ____ and my previous address is ____. Name and address of my employer _______________; Name and address of location of employment________________; Occupation _____________________; Marital status, _________. If married full name of spouse ____________________________, spouse's social security number is xxx-xx______.

I HEREBY AFFIRM AND ATTEST, under penalty of law, that I am not the same person as the debtor or debtors named in the following described recorded judgment, lien, privilege, or mortgage:

Judgment Registry Number _______________ filed _________________
Suit ______________ Judgment rendered on the ______day of ____________ 20____ in favor of ______________________ and against _________________________ in the full sum and true sum of $___________________.
and
Amended Judgment Registry Number ____________ filed _______________ Suit__________
_________________________________ vs. ________________________________, et al against _____________________ $____________. The default Judgment previously rendered on the _____day of ________, 20______ in favor of ___________________________, and against the Defendant, ___________________, be set aside and annulled on basis of Defendant's answer to the Petition.

THUS DONE, READ AND SIGNED at _________________, State of Louisiana, this ______day of _____________, 20_____.

WITNESSES:

____

Name typed:

____

Affiant:

____

Name typed:

____
Notary Public
Print name: _________________________
LA Bar #: __________________________
My commission expires: _______________

AFFIDAVIT OF DISTINCTION, FORM BY LA SUPREME COURT

ACKNOWLEDGMENT

I (we), ____________________________attorney for ______________________ hereby acknowledge that the above-named affiant is not the same person identified or named in the above-identified or described encumbrance and that the property of the affiant is not subject to the lien resulting from the encumbrances.

THUS DONE, READ AND SIGNED at _____________________, State of Louisiana, this _______day of _____________, 20____.

____
Attorney Signature

____
Notary Public

Print name: _________________________

LA Bar #: __________________________

My commission expires: ______________

R-2000 (7/12)

STATE FORM FOR IDENTITY (I.D.) THEFT

LOUISIANA
DEPARTMENT *of* REVENUE

Louisiana Identity Theft Affidavit

Louisiana Department of Revenue
Criminal Investigations Division
P.O. Box 2389
Baton Rouge, LA 70821-2389
Email: fraud.mailbox@la.gov

PLEASE PRINT OR TYPE

Please check one of the following boxes:

☐ I am a **victim of identity theft** and I believe this incident **is affecting** my tax records (*Provide a short explanation of the tax impact*)

☐ I am a **victim of identity theft** and believe I may be at risk for **future impact** to my tax account

☐ I am a **potential victim** of identity theft and believe I may be at risk for future impact to my tax account. (You should check "*potential victim*" if you have not experienced identity theft but are at risk due to a lost/stolen purse or wallet, questionable credit card or credit report activity, etc.)

Tax year(s) impacted and/or date the incident occurred *(if applicable or known)*	Last tax return filed *(year) (Enter NRF if not required to file)*

Taxpayer's last name	First name	MI	Provide the last 4 digits of your Social Security Number (SSN) or your complete Individual Taxpayer Identification Number (ITIN)

Taxpayer's current mailing address

City	State	ZIP

Address on last tax return filed *(Check here ☐ if you are not required to file a tax return)*

City	State	ZIP

Telephone Number ☐ Home ☐ Work ☐ Cell ( )	Best time(s) to call

Primary language ☐ English ☐ Spanish ☐ Other - specify ____________________

Under penalty of perjury, I declare that, to the best of my knowledge and belief, the information entered in this form is true, correct, complete, and made in good faith.

Signature of Taxpayer ____________________ Date Signed *(mm/dd/yyyy)* ____________________

Please submit this completed form and a photocopy of at least one of the following documents to verify your identity.
(Check the box next to the document you are submitting)

☐ a) Passport
☐ b) Driver's license
☐ c) Social Security Card
☐ d) Other valid U.S. Federal or State government issued identification*

* Please do not submit photocopies of federally issued identification where prohibited by 18 U.S.C. 701 *(e.g., official badges designating federal employment)*.

Please submit the photocopies required above with this form to the address listed at the top of the form.

LIEN AFFIDAVIT

AFFIDAVITS OF LIENS & DEBT

STATE OF LOUISIANA

PARISH OF ___________________

LIEN AFFIDAVIT

BEFORE ME, the undersigned duly commissioned and qualified Notary Public, came and appeared the undersigned

Name, address and marital status of the affiant[1]

Who, after being first duly sworn, did depose and say that *Affiant* is a person of the age of majority and a resident of and domiciled in _________________ Parish, Louisiana; and that *Affiant*, doing business as *Name of company or type of business*, entered into an agreement to perform certain services including but not limited to labor and providing materials, in the construction repair, improvement, building, and/or renovation of a building or piece of immovable property located at *address*, for the *owner/contractor/occupant*. The particulars shall be set forth in detail below:

1. *A reasonable identification of the immovable with respect to which the work was performed, or movables or services were supplied or rendered; last date of service was what date;*
2. *The dollar amount and nature of the obligation giving rise to the claim or privilege and reasonably itemize the elements comprising it including the person for whom or to whom the contract was performed, material supplied, or services rendered; and*
3. *Identification of the owner who is liable for the claim under R.S. 9:4806(B), but if that owner's interest in the immovable does not appear of record, the statement of claim or privilege may instead identify the person who appears of record to own the immovable.*

There is an outstanding balance due in the amount of $ *dollars and cents* which amount represents materials delivered to the property for use in and were actually used in construction and/or repair of the above described immovable property. This debt includes all costs and all just credits have been allowed.

---

[1] The affiant may be the representative of a company; if so, the affidavit should be changed to reflect the entity seeking the lien. It is the company that is appearing, but appearing by and through the representative, who signs their own name in that capacity.

LIEN AFFIDAVIT

This affidavit is to preserve the lien and privilege granted to affiant, by law, on the buildings and above described property.

____
Affiant Printed Name

SWORN TO AND SUBSCRIBED BEFORE ME this _______ day of __________________, 20____

____

Notary Name: ___________________________________
Notary ID or Bar Roll No.: _________________
My Commission is for Life

LIEN AFFIDAVIT, ALTERNATE

STATE OF LOUISIANA

PARISH OF ____________________

LIEN AFFIDAVIT

BEFORE ME, the undersigned duly commissioned and qualified Notary Public, came and appeared the undersigned

____
Affiant name[1]

Who, after being duly sworn, did depose and state that they are a person of the legal age of majority and a resident of and domiciled in _________________ Parish, Louisiana; and that affiant, doing business as *name of company*, entered into an agreement to perform certain labor and services and/or furnish certain materials in the construction, repair, and/or improvement of a building for the owner, *name of owner of building or owner's representative*, and/or contractor and/or occupant of the following described property: *description of property*.

Which labor and/or material furnished are more particularly described as: *more detail*

The last services, labor, and/or furnishing of materials were on *date*.

There is a present balance past due and outstanding in the amount of $ *dollars and cents*, which amount represents materials delivered to the property for use in and were actually used and/or labor actually performed in the construction and/or repair described above on the immovable property located at municipal no. *municipal address if available; if none then legal description.* That the debt includes interest and costs and all just credits have been allowed.

This affidavit is to preserve the lien and privilege granted to affiant, by law, on the buildings and property above described.

[Recite social security numbers and municipal numbers where applicable]

This affidavit is made for the purpose of preserving the lien and privilege granted by law under Louisiana R.S. 9:4801 *et seq.*, or as amended, in the above described property; that said debt, plus costs of filing this lien.[2]

____
Affiant Printed Name[3]

[1] The person asserting the claim or their representative.

[2] This lien must be filed timely; filing deadlines may differ depending on the category of contractor.

[3] If the affiant is appearing in a capacity such as corporate representative, signature line should reflect this.

LIEN AFFIDAVIT, ALTERNATE

SWORN TO AND SUBSCRIBED BEFORE ME this _______ day of __________________, 20____

____

Notary Name: ___________________________________

Notary ID or Bar Roll No.: _______________

My Commission is for Life

AFFIDAVIT VERIFYING CORRECTNESS OF DEBT

STATE OF LOUISIANA

PARISH OF ___________________

AFFIDAVIT OF CORRECTNESS OF DEBT

BEFORE ME, the undersigned duly commissioned and qualified Notary Public, came and appeared the undersigned representative/agent of ______________________ *(company)*,

____ *(person appearing)*,

who, after being first duly sworn, deposed and said:

That affiant is personally familiar with the account at issue in this litigation; that all information above and below is true and correct; and that the promissory note and/or security agreement attached hereto and made part of hereof are the instruments upon which this action is based.

1. NAME OF DEBTOR____
2. SOCIAL SECURITY NO. (last 4 digits): ____________________________
3. ADDRESS: ____
4. DATE OF NOTE: ____
5. ORIGINAL AMOUNT: ____
6. TERMS OF PAYMENT: ____
7. UNPAID BALANCE: ____
8. REBATED BALANCE: ____
9. DATE LAST PAID: ____
10. CONTRACT INTEREST RATE:_____________________________________
11. CONTRACT MATURITY DATE: ___________________________________
12. INTEREST AFTER MATURITY: ____________________________________
13. SECURITY (IF APPLICABLE): _____________________________________

____
Affiant

SWORN TO AND SUBSCRIBED BEFORE ME this _______ day of _________________, 20____

____

Notary Name: ____________________________
Notary ID or Bar Roll No.: ________________
My Commission is for Life

STOCK TRANSFER AFFIDAVIT

AFFIDAVITS OF AUTHORIZATION & AUTHORITY

STATE OF LOUISIANA

PARISH OF ____________________

STOCK TRANSFER AFFIDAVIT

BEFORE ME, the undersigned duly commissioned and qualified Notary Public, came and appeared the undersigned

____
Affiant

Who, after being first duly sworn, deposed and said:

That Affiant resides at *address*, and that Affiant is the surviving spouse of the decedent, who died on *date*; that at the time of decedent's death, the domicile of the decedent was at ______________ Parish, Louisiana; that the decedent had resided at that domicile for _________ years and was a registered voter in the same domicile and showed the same as decedent's legal residence on federal and state income tax returns and had not within 3 years prior to the date of death resided in any other state; that the Affiant and all heirs have been placed in possession pursuant to a Judgment of Possession in the decedent's estate, attached to this affidavit, and that all debts, taxes, legacies, and claims against the estate have been paid.

This affidavit is for the purpose of securing the transfer or delivery of property owned by the decedent at the time of decedent's death, to the persons legally entitled thereto pursuant to the attached Judgment of Possession.

____
Affiant

SWORN TO AND SUBSCRIBED BEFORE ME this _______ day of __________________, 20____

____

Notary Name: ____________________________
Notary ID or Bar Roll No.: _______________
My Commission is for Life

AFFIDAVIT AUTHORIZING USE OF MOVABLE

STATE OF LOUISIANA

PARISH OF ________________

AUTHORIZATION FOR USE OF A MOVABLE

BEFORE ME, the undersigned notary public, duly commissioned and qualified in the parish and state aforesaid, appeared the undersigned Affiant, registered owner of a vehicle,

Who, after being first duly sworn, deposes and says:

I, ________________________, of address ____,

Louisiana, certify that I am the registered owner of a vehicle model ____________________________

with VIN No. ____ and license plate #______________,

state of __________________.

And that I have authorized, and do by these presents, authorize ________________________________ *[name],* my ______________________ *[relationship],* to be the authorized principal driver of this vehicle, as my agent and attorney in fact, to recover this vehicle from impound, and to otherwise do any act necessary to protect my interest in this vehicle, including, but not limited to, actions required to properly register this vehicle in any jurisdiction where he may be required in order to drive this vehicle, or to release and receive acquittance in my name and stead, for any just charge incurred in the operation of said vehicle.

And further, I declare that a photocopy or facsimile of this authorization shall be as valid as the original.

____

Affiant

SWORN TO AND SUBSCRIBED BEFORE ME this ______ day of __________________, 20_____

____

Notary Name: ______________________________

Notary ID or Bar Roll No.: ____________

My Commission is for Life

AFFIDAVIT: AUTHORITY OF MINISTER FOR MARRIAGES

STATE OF LOUISIANA

PARISH OF ________________

AFFIDAVIT OF MINISTER OR PASTOR

BEFORE ME, the undersigned notary public, duly commissioned and qualified in the parish and state aforesaid, appeared the undersigned Affiant, is HALEY BETH JONES,

Who, after being first duly sworn, deposed and stated:

That she is authorized by the authorities of the Southern First Eastern Orthodox Church which registered office for the State of Louisiana is at 123 Plymouth Rd. E., Covington, Louisiana 70433, to perform marriage ceremonies. She further declares that her lawful name is as set forth above; her denomination is Eastern Orthodox; and her current mailing address is 999 W. Maple St., Bush, Louisiana 70431.

____

Print name, Affiant

SWORN TO AND SUBSCRIBED BEFORE ME this ______ day of __________________, 20_____

____

Notary Name: __________________________

Notary ID or Bar Roll No.: ___________

My Commission is for Life

REGISTRATION OF MARRIAGE OFFICIANT

Registry Number ______________

Louisiana Marriage Officiant Registration Affidavit

Parish Where Marriages Principally Performed ______________________________

BEFORE ME, the undersigned notary, personally came and appeared

______________________________, who being first sworn by my deposed and stated:

That he/she is a priest, minister, rabbi, clerk of the Religious Society of Friends, or any

clergyman of ____,
(Name of church, denomination, and location)

that he/she is a resident of ______________________________,
(Street Address)

______________________________, ______________________, ________________,
(City) (State) (ZIP)

And, that he/she makes this affidavit for the purpose of registering as a person authorized

to celebrate marriages in the State and Parish as required by LSA-R.S. 9:204.

Signature of Officiant:____

Sworn and subscribed before me this ______ day of __________________, ______________.

My Notary State Registration Number ________________ expires on __________________.

Notary State (if not Louisiana): ____.

REQUIRED ATTACHMENTS:

[ ] Photocopy of ID or Driver's License
[ ] Photocopy of Ordination Certificate

Return completed form by mail to Clerk of Court in parish where marriages will be principally performed. If Orleans Parish, return form to:
Center for Records and Statistics ATTN: Marriage Office
P.O. Box 60630 New Orleans, LA 70160

Rev 1/15
M3

AFFIDAVIT OF TRANSLATION

MISCELLANEOUS & HOLD HARMLESS AGREEMENT

STATE OF LOUISIANA

PARISH OF ____________________

AFFIDAVIT OF TRANSLATION

BEFORE ME, the undersigned duly commissioned and qualified Notary Public came and appeared the undersigned

____

who, after being first duly sworn, deposed and said:

I, ____________________________________, am fluent in English and the ______________________ language. I hereby certify that I have translated and verified the following document(s) which is/are attached to this affidavit:

Description of document(s): (title or type, document date, number of pages)

____

____

____

____

____

I further certify that, to the best of my knowledge, the attached document(s) written in ________________________ is/are a true and accurate translation of the attached document(s) written in that language.

____

Affiant

SWORN TO AND SUBSCRIBED BEFORE ME this _______ day of __________________, 20____

____

Notary Name: ______________________________

Notary ID or Bar Roll No.: _____________

My Commission is for Life

HOLD HARMLESS AGREEMENT

STATE OF LOUISIANA

PARISH OF ____________________

HOLD HARMLESS AGREEMENT

BEFORE ME, the undersigned duly commissioned and qualified Notary Public, came and appeared the undersigned,

____

Appearer

who does voluntarily and knowingly appear before me and agrees to hold *Company name or other entity for whom appearer is doing work* harmless for any and all accidents or injuries incurred while performing the duties and acts of *scope of work being done* on the property located at *address or location of work being done.*

Appearer does understand that this act has the legal effect and consequence of waiving any rights to file lawsuit or claims for any accidents or injuries sustained while performing said duties. Appearer further declares as follows:

This hold harmless agreement is intended to be as broad in nature as possible. I agree not to sue *Company or entity for work which is being done*, and release each of their insurers, officers, agents, representatives, independent contractors, successors, assigns and volunteers from any and all liability, claims, demands, actions and causes of action whatsoever arising out of or related to any loss, damage, or injury, including death, that may be sustained by me, or to any property belonging to me, while working or while on the premises. It is my expressed intent that this release and Hold Harmless Agreement shall bind the members of my family, spouse, heirs, assigns and personal representatives, and shall be deemed by them as a release waiver, discharge and agreement not to sue the above named company or entity.

I hereby further agree that this Hold Harmless Agreement shall be construed in accordance with the laws of the state of Louisiana. If any one or more of the provisions contained in this release and Hold Harmless Agreement are held to be invalid, the invalidity of such clause or provision shall not otherwise affect the remaining provisions of this agreement, which shall otherwise continue to be enforceable.

APPEARER:

____

Print Name

SWORN TO AND SUBSCRIBED BEFORE ME this ______ day of __________________, 20____

____

Notary Name: ___________________________

Notary ID or Bar Roll No.: ___________

My Commission is for Life

2 • ACKNOWLEDGMENTS AND PRIVATE ACTS

ACT UNDER PRIVATE SIGNATURE (PRIVATE ACT): WITNESSES, NO NOTARY

STATE OF LOUISIANA

PARISH OF ____________________

ACT UNDER PRIVATE SIGNATURE[1]

BE IT KNOWN BY ALL THESE PRESENTS

That I, *state your name and the body of the private act here.*

In witness whereof, I have signed hereunto at *name of city,* Louisiana, this *date, month,* 20____, in the presence of the two undersigned witnesses:

WITNESSES:	NAME OF PRINCIPAL:
______________________________	______________________________
Print Name	Print Name
______________________________	
Print Name	

[1] Certain legal acts ("act under private signature" or just "private act") do not require a notary and are valid when simply signed by the parties—though it still may be advisable to have the document executed before a notary. The above assumes one person signing (for example, a principal setting forth powers of an agent, or settlor creating a trust). But the form can be adapted to have two or more parties signing (e.g., a contract or matrimonial agreement).

This document is a private act but one witnessed at the time of signing by the party or parties. The advantage of doing a private act this way is not only that it may be taken more seriously if witnessed (e.g., certain lien releases are acceptable without notarization if signed by two witnesses). It is also that signing before two witnesses later allows one of them, or a party, to take the act to a notary and execute an acknowledgment. It then becomes an "act under private signature" or "acknowledged act." Doing this has certain evidentiary advantages (it is self-proving in court on its face, without calling witnesses). But it also is *required* for some legal acts if they are not done by authentic act, notably creation of an inter vivos trust, and matrimonial agreements (acknowledged by the spouses before a notary after originally signing, as above, before the wedding with two witnesses).

ACKNOWLEDGMENTS AND ACKNOWLEDGED ACTS

STATE OF LOUISIANA

PARISH OF ____________________

PERSONAL ACKNOWLEDGMENT[1]

BEFORE ME, the undersigned duly commissioned and qualified Notary Public in and for the State and Parish aforesaid, and in the presence of the undersigned competent witnesses, came and appeared the undersigned appearer known to me to be the person described, and who, after first being duly sworn, did say and acknowledge that appearer subscribed their name to the foregoing instrument as a party thereunto, and acknowledged that they executed it as their own free act and deed for the uses, purposes and considerations therein expressed.

In witness whereof the appearer does hereunto affix their hand and seal in the presence of the undersigned competent witnesses who sign together with appearer and me, notary, at ____________________ *[city]*, Louisiana, this ______ day of __________________, 20____.

WITNESSES: APPEARER:

______________________________ ______________________________

Print Name Print Name

____

Print Name

____

Notary Name: ________________________________

Notary ID or Bar Roll No.: ________________

My Commission is for Life

---

[1] To be used when a party is acknowledging their own signature under LA C.C. article 1836. This method of acknowledgment does not require that there be two witnesses at the original signing of the act ("the foregoing instrument"), but instead has two witnesses observe the *current* signing. This acknowledgment takes an act under private signature and, with this attachment, makes it acknowledged and self-proving in court.

An alternative version is on the next page, and more specifically is named as "by original appearer" to clarify that the appearer was a party to the previously signed act. Either version is effective for its purposes, and stand in contrast to acknowledgments by a witness to the previous signing, or by a grantor/vendor in the original transaction.

PERSONAL ACKNOWLEDGMENT BY AFFIDAVIT OF ORIGINAL APPEARER

STATE OF LOUISIANA

PARISH OF ____________________

PERSONAL ACKNOWLEDGMENT BY ORIGINAL APPEARER

BEFORE ME, the undersigned duly commissioned and qualified Notary Public in and for the Parish and State aforesaid, and the undersigned competent witnesses, personally came and appeared the affiant, known to me to be the person described, and who, after first being duly sworn, deposed and stated that the affiant executed the foregoing instrument,[1] and further acknowledged that such instrument was executed as their own free act and deed for the uses, considerations and purposes contained therein.

WITNESSES:	AFFIANT:
______________________________	______________________________
Print Name	Print Name
______________________________	
Print Name	

SWORN TO AND SUBSCRIBED BEFORE ME this _______ day of __________________, 20____

____

Notary Name: ______________________________

Notary ID or Bar Roll No.: ______________

My Commission is for Life

[1] Attach instrument. With this affidavit, the original signed act becomes acknowledged and self-proving in court. This form of acknowledgment is appropriate for when the original act was not signed in front of witnesses or one of the witnesses to a witnessed act (or a vendor or grantor in it) is not available to execute an acknowledgment. Note: although an acknowledged act shares the self-proving evidentiary quality with the authentic act, it is not sufficient to make an act complete and valid if the act is *required* by law to be an "authentic act" or in "authentic form." Acknowledgment is an inadequate substitute for such authentic acts.

ACKNOWLEDGMENT BY A WITNESS

STATE OF LOUISIANA

PARISH OF ____________________

PERSONAL ACKNOWLEDGMENT BY A WITNESS[1]

BEFORE ME, the undersigned duly commissioned and qualified Notary Public in and for the State and Parish aforesaid, personally came and appeared the undersigned Affiant known to me to be the person described, and who, after first being duly sworn, deposed and stated that Affiant executed the ________________________[2] as an attesting and subscribing witness[3] thereto, and acknowledged that they executed the same as their own free act as such witness.

And Affiant, being duly sworn, did depose and say that such instrument was executed by the parties in the presence of Affiant and the other subscribing witnesses, and by all parties of their own free act for the uses, purposes and considerations therein expressed.

AFFIANT:

____

Print Affiant Name

SWORN TO AND SUBSCRIBED BEFORE ME this _______ day of _________________, 20____

____

Notary Name: ________________________________

Notary ID or Bar Roll No.: _______________

My Commission is for Life

[1] Form for an acknowledgment of an act under private signature, made under LA RS 13:3720, purporting to have been attested by two or more witnesses and accompanied by an affidavit of the witness that the same was signed or executed by the witness previously. This must have been *properly witnessed* at the time of the execution of the original instrument. If no witnesses at the time of the original signing, use the acknowledgment made under LA CC Art 1836, which is for a party *currently* signing in front of two witnesses and the notary.

[2] Insert caption or name of act, for example, "Contract to Sell" or "Boundary Agreement."

[3] Subscribing witness means one of the original witnesses to the instrument. This witness acknowledgement is attached to the original instrument, making it become an acknowledged act and therefore self-proving in court.

ACKNOWLEDGMENT BY AGENT

STATE OF LOUISIANA

PARISH OF ____________________

PERSONAL ACKNOWLEDGMENT BY A VENDOR[1]

BEFORE ME, the undersigned duly commissioned and qualified Notary Public in and for the State and Parish aforesaid, came and appeared the undersigned Affiant known to me to be the person described, and who, after first being duly sworn, deposed and stated that they are the vendor[2] who executed the foregoing instrument,[3] and who acknowledged that such instrument was executed as their own free act and was executed by the parties in the presence of the Affiant and the subscribing witnesses, of their own free act for the uses, purposes and considerations contained therein.

____

Print Affiant Name

SWORN TO AND SUBSCRIBED BEFORE ME this _______ day of _________________, 20____

____

Notary Name: ________________________________

Notary ID or Bar Roll No.: ______________

My Commission is for Life

---

[1] Form for an acknowledgment of an act under private signature, made under LA RS 13:3720, purporting to have been attested by two or more witnesses and accompanied by this affidavit of the vendor or grantor, that the same was signed or executed by them. This must have been *properly witnessed* at the time of the execution of the original instrument.

[2] Or "grantor," for example when the original private act was not a sale but some other instrument granting an interest. In this case the heading should be "Personal Acknowledgment by a Grantor."

[3] The instrument should be attached

ACKNOWLEDGMENT BY AGENT

STATE OF LOUISIANA

PARISH OF ____________________

PERSONAL ACKNOWLEDGMENT BY AN AGENT[1]

BEFORE ME, the undersigned duly commissioned and qualified Notary Public in and for the State and Parish aforesaid, and in the presence of the undersigned competent witnesses, came and appeared the undersigned appearer known to me to be the person described, and who declared and acknowledged that appearer executed the foregoing instrument as a duly authorized agent and attorney in fact for ___ ____________________,[2] one of the parties described therein, pursuant to a Power of Attorney dated ____________________, and that appearer acknowledges that they executed this instrument[3] as the free act and deed of ____________________[4] for the uses, purposes and considerations expressed therein.

In witness whereof the appearer does hereunto affix their hand and seal in the presence of the undersigned competent witnesses who sign together with appearer and me, notary, at ____________________ *[city]*, Louisiana, this _____ day of __________________, 20_____.

WITNESSES:	APPEARER:
______________________________	______________________________
Print Name	Print Name
______________________________	
Print Name	

____

Notary Name: ______________________________

Notary ID or Bar Roll No.: ______________

My Commission is for Life

[1] To be used when an agent must acknowledge an act on behalf of a principal, corresponding to LA CC Art 1836. Witness acknowledgments under RS 13:3720 cannot be done via an agent, but this *witnessed* version can be.

[2] Insert the principal's name.

[3] Attach instrument. With this form, the original instrument becomes acknowledged and is self-proving in court.

[4] Insert the principal's name.

ACKNOWLEDGMENT BY CORPORATE REPRESENTATIVE

STATE OF LOUISIANA

PARISH OF ____________________

CORPORATE ACKNOWLEDGMENT[1]

BEFORE ME, the undersigned duly commissioned and qualified Notary Public in and for the State and Parish aforesaid, and in the presence of the undersigned competent witnesses, came and appeared the undersigned appearer known to me to be the person described, and who acknowledged and declared that appearer executed the foregoing instrument as a duly authorized agent for ____________________ ____________________,[2] one of the parties described therein, pursuant to a Corporate Resolution[3] dated ____________________, and that appearer executed this instrument[4] as the free act and deed of _ ________________________________[5] for the uses, purposes and considerations expressed therein.

In witness whereof the appearer does hereunto affix their hand and seal in the presence of the undersigned competent witnesses who sign together with appearer and me, notary, at ____________________ *[city]*, Louisiana, this _____ day of __________________, 20____.

WITNESSES:	APPEARER:
________________________________	________________________________
Print Name	Print Name
________________________________	
Print Name	

____

Notary Name: ________________________________

Notary ID or Bar Roll No.: ______________

My Commission is for Life

---

[1] Can be modified for LLC, Partnership, or other form of business enterprise, see LA RS 35:511.

[2] Insert Corporation's name [or LLC, Partnership etc.].

[3] Can be modified to the appropriate authorizing document; or if no resolution is necessary, omit.

[4] Attach instrument, such as a lease or act of sale.

[5] Insert Corporation's name [or LLC, Partnership, etc.]

ACKNOWLEDGMENT BY CORPORATE REPRESENTATIVE WITH SEAL

STATE OF LOUISIANA

PARISH OF ____________________

CORPORATE ACKNOWLEDGMENT WITH SEAL[1]

BEFORE ME, the undersigned duly commissioned and qualified Notary Public in and for the State and Parish aforesaid, and in the presence of the undersigned competent witnesses, came and appeared the undersigned appearer known to me to be the person described, and who, after first being duly sworn, did depose and did state that he is the President[2] of ____________________________ Corp., and that the seal affixed to said instrument is the corporate seal of said corporation,[3] that the instrument was signed and sealed on behalf of the corporation by authority of its Board of Directors,[4] and that appearer acknowledged the instrument to be the free act and deed of the corporation.

WITNESSES:	APPEARER:
______________________________	______________________________
Print Name	Print Name
______________________________	
Print Name	

SWORN TO AND SUBSCRIBED BEFORE ME this _______ day of __________________, 20____

____

Notary Name: ______________________________

Notary ID or Bar Roll No.: ______________

My Commission is for Life

[1] Can also be modified for "joint stock associations," see LA RS 35:511. This is an alternative, in the form of an affidavit, to "Acknowledgment, Personal by a corporate representative," in this case when the entity used a seal on the original document.

[2] Or other officer or agent of the corporation or association.

[3] Or association. If so, replace "corporation" in the next two lines with "association."

[4] Or trustee, for a joint stock association.

3 • AUTHENTIC ACTS

<u>AUTHENTIC ACTS ("AUTHENTIC FORM"), INCLUDING MULTI-PARTY SIGNINGS</u>

STATE OF LOUISIANA

PARISH OF ____________________ *[where signed]*

AUTHENTIC ACT *[generic blank form]*

BEFORE ME, the undersigned notary, duly commissioned and qualified in the state and parish aforesaid, and in the presence of the two witnesses whose names are hereunto subscribed, PERSONALLY CAME and appeared:

Appearance clause(s), which may vary depending on the nature and content of the act.

Who declared unto me:

Body of act, what the act intends to do, convey, etc.

THUS DONE, SIGNED AND PASSED on the _____ day of _________________, 20____, in ____________, Louisiana, in the presence of the undersigned competent witnesses who have signed their names together with the party(ies) and me, notary, after due reading of the whole.

WITNESSES:	PARTIES:
______________________________	______________________________
Print Name	Print Name
	[APPEARER 2, if a second party signs]:
______________________________	______________________________
Print Name	Print Name
	[APPEARER 3, if a third party signs, etc.]:
	______________________________
	Print Name

____

Notary Name: ______________________________

Notary ID or Bar Roll No.: _______________

My Commission is for Life

AUTHENTIC ACT: PARTIES SIGN AT DIFFERENT TIMES, SAME NOTARY

STATE OF LOUISIANA

PARISH OF ____________________ *[where signed; here, before the same notary]*

AUTHENTIC ACT

BEFORE ME, the undersigned notary, duly commissioned and qualified in the state and parish aforesaid, and in the presence of the witnesses whose names are hereunto subscribed, PERSONALLY CAME and appeared:

Appearance clause for Appearer 1 and Appearer 2, etc., which may vary depending on the nature and content of the act.

Who declared unto me:

Body of act, what the act intends to do, convey, etc.

THUS DONE AND PASSED on the _____ day of ________________, 20____, in ____________________, Louisiana, in the presence of the undersigned competent witnesses who have signed their names together with the appearing parties and me, notary, after due reading of the whole.

WITNESSES:	APPEARER 1:
______________________________	______________________________
Print Name	Print Name
______________________________	
Print Name	

____

Notary Name: ______________________________

Notary ID or Bar Roll No.: ________________

My Commission is for Life

THUS DONE AND PASSED on the _____ day of ________________, 20____, in ____________________, Louisiana, in the presence of the undersigned competent witnesses who have signed their names together with the appearing parties and me, notary, after due reading of the whole.

AUTHENTIC ACT: PARTIES SIGN AT DIFFERENT TIMES, SAME NOTARY

WITNESSES: APPEARER 2:

_________________________________ _________________________________

Print Name Print Name

____

Print Name

____

Notary Name: _________________________________ *[same as above]*

Notary ID or Bar Roll No.: ________________

My Commission is for Life

AUTHENTIC ACT: PARTIES SIGN BEFORE DIFFERENT NOTARIES

This form is appropriate when the parties appear and sign before two or more notaries, at different times—and sometimes (as below) in different parishes (or states, where allowed). The form can be simplified when the signings are in the same parish; in that case, use that parish in the venue clause immediately below and delete the extra venue clauses added below the body of act; the preamble should omit "and hereunder stated."

Such multi-party signings (execution "in counterparts") may also be done with separate pages for each signator and notary, and executed by mailing the whole instrument to each party but having them sign only the page for them. All pages are collected and filed together, if required. If the below is used as structured, with signings on one document, it is allowed to pass the document forward for each party's signing (then returned to whoever is responsible for filing), or have multiple originals signed and collected into one valid authentic act, especially combined for filing, if required.

This form can be adapted to three or more parties by repeating the venue clause, conclusion, and signature blocks for each subsequent appearer.

If this act may be signed in another state, the venue should reflect a different state and a "County of"; and the signature block for the notary should omit "or Bar Roll" and state its final line as "My commission expires __________."

AUTHENTIC ACT

STATE OF LOUISIANA

PARISH OF ______________________ *[parish where relevant appearer signs; or if done on one document, insert Appearer 1's parish of signing; or adapt accordingly if the order of signing changes]*

BEFORE ME, one of and each of the undersigned notaries public, duly commissioned and qualified in the state and parishes aforesaid and hereunder stated, and in the presence of the witnesses whose names are hereunto subscribed for each party, PERSONALLY CAME and appeared:

Appearance clause for Appearer 1 and Appearer 2, etc., which may vary depending on the nature and content of the act.

Who declared unto me:

Body of act, what the act intends to do, convey, etc.

As declared and executed, personally and physically, before the following witnesses and notaries.

STATE OF LOUISIANA

PARISH OF ______________________ *[where Appearer 1 signs]*

THUS DONE, SIGNED AND PASSED on the _____ day of ________________, 20____, in __________________, *[city or place of signing, located in parish of venue above]*, Louisiana, in the presence of me, ________________________, *[insert notary 1's name]*, the undersigned competent witnesses who have signed their names together with the appearing party and me, after due reading of the whole.

WITNESSES: APPEARER 1 *[or "Party," no number]*:

____________________________ ____________________________

Print Name Print Name

____

Print Name

____

Notary Name: ____________________________

Notary ID or Bar Roll No.: ______________

My Commission is for Life

STATE OF LOUISIANA

PARISH OF ______________________ *[where Appearer 2 signs]*

THUS DONE, SIGNED AND PASSED on the _____ day of ________________, 20____, in ____________________, Louisiana, in the presence of me, ________________________, *[insert notary 2's name]*, and the undersigned competent witnesses who have signed their names together with the appearing party and me, after due reading of the whole.

WITNESSES: APPEARER 2 *[or just "Party" or omit]*:

____________________________ ____________________________

Print Name Print Name

____

Print Name

____

Notary Name: ____________________________

Notary ID or Bar Roll No.: ______________

My Commission is for Life

4 • APPEARANCE CLAUSES AND SIGNATURE LINES

Appearance Clause Worksheet

The appearer in an act of sale, mortgage, donation, and many authentic acts must be identified by full name, capacity (i.e., being of legal age, and also in *what* capacity if appearing as a representative), parish of domicile, marital status, and permanent mailing address.

What is a "full name" is defined in LA R.S. 35:12(A)(1). Essentially it is *not* using nicknames (Bud, Sissy), "initials alone" (E.E. Cummings), or middle name without first: use at least first initial (Edgar Hoover should at least be J. Edgar Hoover). While technically just first and last qualifies as a full name (and is presented that way frequently in this book), there may be many situations where it makes sense to include a middle initial or middle name too, especially for more common names (John Rogers is better presented as John Philip Rogers). Keep in mind that the more complete the appearance clause, the easier it will be for later title researchers or people using the act (such as those asking for the power of attorney document) to understand the transaction or honor the authority.

In addition, if the act transfers an immovable (sale, donation, exchange, dation en paiement, timber sale, etc.), the transferor must disclose whether there has been a change in marital status, or no change, since acquiring the property originally. That may be done within the appearance clause, or as a separate sentence (often its own paragraph) further down in the document.

A mortgagor/borrower in an act of mortgage or credit sale, or similar instrument giving a security interest in an immovable, must also disclose the last four digits of social security number (or full taxpayer identification number if mortgagor is a juridical person). Certain business filings with the Secretary of State and a statement of authority also require the number, and both parents to an acknowledgment of paternity must, by federal law, include their full number.

For these reasons, creating a proper juridical act often requires collecting sufficient information from the parties, and keeping it private under federal law. This worksheet is a useful checklist of what is needed in an appearance clause and what information to ask for or research.

For each Appearer, complete below:

Appearer No. 1 of ____

Full Name: _________*[First]*, _________*[Middle]*, _________*[Maiden]*, _________*[Last]*

Marital Status:

( ) Married but once, and then to _________, with whom Appearer is presently living and residing and from whom Appearer has never been judicially separated or divorced.

( ) Married, but _________ times, first to: _________, which marriage was terminated by:

APPEARANCE CLAUSE WORKSHEET

( ) Divorce, and if so from whom: ____________________

[Usually just the fact of divorce or being divorced, and from whom, suffices. Four further details are needed if the act is especially about marital history where establishing the divorce matters. In some acts all about the history, a certified copy of the decree is needed.

Court _________ Docket No. _________ Location _________ Date _________]

( ) Death of Spouse; if so, widowed from whom: ____________________

[If act is specifically about marital history or being widowed, such as an affidavit of death and heirship or an application for death benefits or retirement funds, include:

Date of Death _________ Place of Death _________]

… and secondly to: _________, with whom Appearer is presently living and residing at municipal address: _________*[street]*, _________*[city]*, _________*[state]*, ______*[zip]*

Social Security No./TIN: _________ *[but only for mortgagor or other situations noted above]*

Parish of Domicile (permanent home, where voting, etc.): _________

Mailing Address: ____________________

Appearer No. 2 of ____ *(and so on, if more appearers)*

Full Name: _________*[First]*, _________*[Middle]*, _________*[Maiden]*, _________*[Last]*

Marital Status:

( ) Married but once, and then to _________, with whom Appearer is presently living and residing and from whom Appearer has never been judicially separated or divorced.

( ) Married, but _________ times, first to: _________, which marriage was terminated by:

( ) Divorce, and if so from whom: ____________________

[Usually just the fact of divorce or being divorced, and from whom, suffices. Four further details are needed if the act is especially about marital history where establishing the divorce matters. In some acts all about the history, a certified copy of the decree is needed.

Court _________ Docket No. _________ Location _________ Date _________]

( ) Death of Spouse; if so, widowed from whom: ____________________

[If act is specifically about marital history or being widowed, such as an affidavit of death and heirship or an application for death benefits or retirement funds, include:

APPEARANCE CLAUSE WORKSHEET

Date of Death _________ *Place of Death* _________ *]*

… and secondly to: _________, with whom Appearer is presently living and residing at municipal address: _________*[street]*, _________*[city]*, _________*[state]*, ______*[zip]*

Social Security No./TIN: _________ *[but only for mortgagor or other situations noted above]*

Parish of Domicile (permanent home, where voting, etc.): _________

Mailing Address: ____

Appearance Forms in fill-in-the blank format *(completed examples found in pages to follow):*

1. Natural Person/Single:

_________*[Name of appearer]*, a person of the full age of majority domiciled in _______ Parish, Louisiana, who declared that Appearer is not now and has never been married and that Appearer's permanent mailing address is: _________; and further that … *[+ possibly change in marital status clause, and last 4 digits of social—see introduction above]*

2. Wife and Husband Appearing Together:

_________*[Name of appearer]*, born _________*[maiden name]*, wife of/and _________*[name of other appearer]*, both persons of the full age of majority domiciled in _______ Parish, Louisiana, who declared that they have been married but once and then unto each other and that they have not been judicially separated or divorced; and their mailing address is: _________ … *[+ possibly change in marital status clause, and last 4 digits of social*

3. Widow/Widower:

_________*[Name of appearer]*, a person of the full age of majority domiciled in _______ Parish, Louisiana, who declared that Appearer has been married only once and then to _________*[name of appearer's deceased spouse]*, who died in _________*[parish or county]*, _________*[state]* on _________*[date]*; the said Appearer has not remarried; and Appearer's permanent mailing address is _________; and further that … *[+ possible additional information]*

4. Divorced Appearer:

_________*[Name of appearer]*, a person of the full age of majority domiciled in _______ Parish, Louisiana, who declared that Appearer has been married _________ times; first to _________ from whom Appearer was divorced on _________*[date of divorce judgment] [+ possibly more court information and attaching judgment—see above]*; and second to

APPEARANCE CLAUSE WORKSHEET

_________ with whom Appearer is presently living and residing and from whom Appearer has never been judicially separated or divorced; and Appearer's mailing address is _________. *[+ possible additional information]*

5. Appearing through Power of Attorney:

_________*[Name of appearer/principal]*, a person of the full age of majority domiciled in _______ Parish, Louisiana, who has been married once to _________ with whom Appearer is presently living and residing and from whom Appearer has never been judicially separated or divorced; whose mailing address is: _________ *[and whose social security number ends in _____, if mortgagor; and possibly change of marital status if transferor]*, appearing through and represented by _________*[Name of appearer/agent]*, as Appearer's duly authorized and appointed agent, mandatary, and attorney in fact by virtue of the attached power of attorney; this Agent further declared that to the best of Agent's knowledge, the said power of attorney has never been revoked, that Agent's principal is alive and that the principal has never been judicially interdicted.

6. Corporate Appearer:

_________*[Name of appearer]*, a corporation organized under the laws of _________*[state]*, whose taxpayer identification number is _________,[1] having its principal place of business at _________*[corporate address]*, appearing by and through _________*[name]*, its _________*[corporate representative's title or position]*, duly authorized by resolution of the Board of Directors of said corporation, adopted at a meeting held on _________*[date of meeting]*, a certified copy of which is attached hereto.

7. Partnership Appearer:

_________*[Name of appearer]*, _________ a general *[or* in commendam, *if so]* partnership organized under the laws of _________*[state]*, whose taxpayer identification number is _________, having its principal place of business at _________, appearing by and through _________*[name]*, its general partner, duly authorized by partnership resolution, a certified copy of which is attached.

8. Limited Liability Company (LLC) Appearer:

_________, LLC *[Name of appearer]*, a limited liability company organized under the laws of _________*[state]*, whose taxpayer identification number is _________, having its principal place of business at _________, appearing by and through _________*[name]*, its managing member, duly authorized by resolution of the members, a certified copy of which is attached.

[1] For items 6, 7, and 8, the TIN or EIN is technically only mandatory when the act is a mortgage or similar security device, or certain filings with the Secretary of State, but it typically is included in other acts by business entities as it is not private the way a social security number is.

SAMPLE APPEARANCE CLAUSES AND SIGNATURE LINES

Appearance Clauses and Related Signature Lines

Most juridical acts, especially those that will be filed in the public records like transfers of immovables, require a sufficient appearance clause to be able to understand the background of the appearer relevant to the transaction or action and establish their capacity to make the act. They vary with the marital status of the appearer, or whether they appear in a representative capacity rather than just as an individual.

Some acts, such as most affidavits and acts of correction, do not need an expansive appearance clause because the marital situation of the affiant or appearer is not relevant to the matter (such as an affidavit stating what happened in an accident). Often the appearance need only state that the affiant is of the age of majority and where they are domiciled (or even less in a barebones affidavit that establishes simple facts from someone who obviously has capacity to make it). Or the statement of capacity (being 18+) and domicile can be in the *body* of the affidavit rather than in the appearance clause. But a complete appearance clause is still proper for such acts if there is a reason disclosing marital status matters to the statement or transaction.

Transfers of immovables (or an interest in an immovable such as a usufruct) require — in addition to a statement of current marital status and information about that (spouse's name including maiden name) — a statement of whether there has been a *change* in the transferor's marital status (or not) since the property was originally acquired. Basically this puts into the public record for this new act that the previous recorded act's statement of marital status no longer holds. It helps title researchers understand whether the property might be community or separate. They can't follow proper ownership without knowing the change in marital status or confirming there hasn't been any. This change/no-change clause can be part of the appearance clause or a separate sentence elsewhere in the document.

In addition, the last four digits of a social security number (or full taxpayer identification number of a juridical person) are required for the mortgagor/borrower when the transaction involves a financing or security interest, such as a mortgage or a credit sale. For transactions without a security interest, such as an act of sale or an act of donation, this disclosure is no longer required, despite older forms using it (or even the entire number). In such cases without financing, it is no longer good form to ask the client any part of their social security number, unless you understand the transaction to include financing in some way (e.g., a credit sale is effectively owner-financed), and even then only for the borrower. Full TIN is also required for certain business filings by juridical persons with the Secretary of State, and for both parents in acts acknowledging paternity.

When a natural or juridical person openly appears through a representative (such as an LLC appearing through its member, an estate through its executor, or a principal through its agent for the transaction), the appearance clause should disclose both roles, i.e., the appearance of the actual actor (the LLC, the estate, or the principal in these examples) and that of the signer (in what capacity the natural person signing it is appearing). In such situations, we also include here the accompanying "signature line" used later in the act; it should match up with the appearance clause. This is commonly referred to as "signature line," though more accurately it is the stated name *below* the signature line, because the signature line itself is simply the signature of the natural person signing it *for* the LLC, estate, principal, etc. In other words, the way the actual signature used is the representative's own (*not* handwriting the name of the principal, but rather signing their own name). The name printed or typed below that is what repeats the representative capacity of the signer as in the appearance clause, or uses "BY" to suggest representation.

Earlier in this chapter, we included a worksheet by which the notary can gather sufficient information and "build" a complete and appropriate appearance clause for most situations.

Husband and wife in community, appearing together (both involved in transaction)

John W. Smith and Jane J. Smith, born Jones, husband and wife, who declare they are living together in community, both of the full age of majority and domiciled in Jefferson Parish, Louisiana, whose mailing address is 123 Main St., Harahan, LA 70123, and both appearing herein …

Husband and wife in community (for a mortgage or other instrument with security interest; and other clauses below should add the borrower's last 4 digits (or full EIN of a company, etc.) if they similarly involve the mortgagors)

John W. Smith (xxx-xx-1234 *[keeping x's as x's]*) and Jane J. Smith, born Jones (xxx-xx-6789 *[keeping x's as x's]*), husband and wife appearing together, who declare they are living together in community, both of the full age of majority and domiciled in Jefferson Parish, Louisiana, whose mailing address is 123 Main St., Harahan, LA 70123, …

Husband and wife appearing together, alternate (each in their first marriage)

Mr. Husband and Mrs. Wife, born Maiden Name, both of legal age and domiciled in Houma, Terrebonne Parish, Louisiana, who declare that they have been married but once and then to each other, that they are living together in community, and that their permanent mailing address is 111 Grand Caillou Rd., Houma, LA 70363, and both appearing herein …

Husband and wife, separate property regime

James L. Baker and Cathy P. Miller, born Perez, husband and wife, who entered into a separate property regime on *day, month, year*, prior to marriage, both of the full age of majority. James L. Baker is a resident of and domiciled in Jefferson Parish, Louisiana, and whose mailing address is 888 Veterans Blvd., Metairie, LA 70003. Cathy P. Miller is a resident of and domiciled in Clark County, Nevada, and whose mailing address is 3570 S. Las Vegas Blvd., Paradise, NV 89109.

Single person never married

Mary Mia Chicon, a resident of the full age of majority and a domiciliary of the Parish of St. Tammany, State of Louisiana, declaring herself a single woman never having been married, and declaring her mailing address to be 123 Hwy. 190, Mandeville, LA 70471, …

Single person having been widowed

Bernard L. Grant, widower of Mary Sue Grant, of legal age and domiciled in Avoyelles Parish, Louisiana, who declared that he resides at 111 Shelton Rd., Marksville, LA 71351, …

SAMPLE APPEARANCE CLAUSES AND SIGNATURE LINES

Husband and wife appearing together (multiple marriages)

Janet Smith, wife of/and Jack Smith, both persons of the full age of majority, residents and domiciliaries of the Parish of Orleans, State of Louisiana. The said Janet Smith declared that she has been married three times, first to David Jones, from whom she is divorced, second to Brian Miller, from whom she is divorced, and third to Jack Smith, with whom she presently lives and resides. The said Jack Smith declared that he has been married three times, first to Mary Lane, from whom he is widowed, second to Victoria Hemingway, from whom he is divorced, and third to Janet Smith with whom he presently lives and resides. Their present mailing address is 6300 St. Charles Avenue, New Orleans, LA 70118.

Wife appearing separately (the one appearing is in her first marriage)

Cynthia Anne Franklin, born Lee, a married woman, of legal age and domiciled in Houma, Terrebonne Parish, Louisiana, who declared that she has been married but once and then to Timothy R. Franklin, and that her permanent mailing address is 111 Shelton Rd., Houma, LA 70363, …

Husband's [or adapt to wife's] change/no-change in marital status, as transferor of interest in immovable (when stated as a separate sentence in act)

Husband's marital status has changed since acquiring the property; it has changed from single to married on or about August 22, 2021.

or

Husband's marital status has not changed since acquiring the property.

Wife's [or adapt to husband's] change/no-change in marital status, as transferor of interest in immovable (when included within larger appearance clause)

Maxine R. Jones, born Ngyuen, hereinafter "Seller," a married woman, who is of legal age and domiciled in Caddo Parish, Louisiana, who declared that she resides with her husband Robert T. Jones at 111 Dilton Ln., Shreveport, LA 71104, and further declares that that her marital status has changed since she acquired the immovable property described below and donated herein, with the death of her first husband, Fred B. Thimble on June 20, 2014, and then by her marriage to Robert T. Jones on January 4, 2018.

or

Maxine R. Jones, born Ngyuen, hereinafter "Seller," … who further declares that that her marital status has not changed since she acquired the immovable property described below and transferred herein.

Judicially emancipated minor

Billy J. Minor, domiciled in Avoyelles Parish, Louisiana, whose permanent address is 711 Paragon Pl., Marksville, LA 71351, an unmarried minor child judicially emancipated on *insert date of emancipation and court/judgment information*, to which reference is hereby made and a certified copy of judgment annexed hereto and made a part hereof. …

Minor emancipated through notarial act of emancipation

Janie Rona Junior, a domiciliary of the Parish of St. Charles, State of Louisiana, whose permanent mailing address is 160 West Campus Dr., Destrehan, LA 70047, an unmarried minor child acting herein under the provisions of an Act of Limited Emancipation, a certified copy of which is attached hereunto and made a part hereof. …

Minor emancipated through marriage

Faith Faraway, a married person domiciled in the Parish of Orleans, whose permanent mailing address is 1500 Sugar Bowl Dr., New Orleans, LA 70112, a minor over the age of sixteen years, duly emancipated by marriage solemnized on *day, month, year*, in the Parish of St. Bernard. …

Parent acting for a minor (where parental authority exists)

Bill Son Name, an unmarried minor domiciled in the parish of St. John the Baptist, State of Louisiana, whose permanent mailing address is 118 West 10th St., Unit C, Reserve, LA 70084, herein represented by Dad Name and Mom Name appearing together as the persons having parental authority over the said minor, …

or

Susan Daughter Name, an unmarried minor domiciled in the parish of Jefferson, State of Louisiana, whose permanent mailing address is 999 Westbank Expressway, Gretna, LA 70056, herein represented solely by Mom Name appearing as the person having parental authority over the said minor, and declaring that Mom Name is acting without the other parent because of the mental incompetence [*or interdiction, imprisonment, absence, etc.*] of the other parent, …

Tutor acting for a minor

Robert Young, an unmarried minor domiciled in the Parish of West Baton Rouge, State of Louisiana, whose permanent mailing address is 420 N. Lobdell Hwy., Port Allen, LA 70767, herein represented by Father Name, appearing in his capacity as the duly qualified Tutor of the minor child, Robert, said Tutor appearing under and by virtue of Order of Court rendered and signed by the Honorable Judge Greatness, Judge of the 18th Judicial District Court, for the Parish of West Baton Rouge, State of Louisiana, on *date*, a certified copy of which is attached hereto and made a part hereof.

ROBERT YOUNG

By: ______________________________

Tutor Name here

or

SAMPLE APPEARANCE CLAUSES AND SIGNATURE LINES

____
Robert Young, by & through Tutor Name

or

____
Tutor Name, as tutor for Robert Young, minor

Curator (assuming they are single; otherwise add marital status and spouse name)

Nancy Lessabled, an unmarried resident of an domiciled in the Parish of West Baton Rouge, State of Louisiana, whose permanent mailing address is 111 South Lobdell Hwy., Port Allen, LA 70767, herein represented by Curator Name, appearing in his capacity as the duly qualified curator of the Nancy Lessabled, said curator appearing under and by virtue of Order of Court rendered and signed by the Honorable Judge Greatness, Judge of the 18th Judicial District Court, for the Parish of West Baton Rouge, State of Louisiana, on *date*, a certified copy of which is attached hereto and made a part hereof.

NANCY LESSABLED

By: ______________________________
Curator Name here

or

____
Nancy Lessabled, by & through Curator Name

or

____
Curator Name, as curator for Nancy Lessabled

Executrix (and similarly for Executor—and you can always use Executor for either gender to avoid having to adjust form in future)

Sunshine James, appearing herein in her capacity as the duly authorized and qualified Executrix of the estate of Dearly Departed, pursuant to and by virtue of order of court rendered and signed by Judge Fairness of 24th Judicial District Court, in and for the Parish of Jefferson, State of Louisiana, *date*, a certified copy of said order being attached hereto and made a part hereof. …

Succession of Dearly Departed

By: ______________________________
Sunshine James, Executrix

SAMPLE APPEARANCE CLAUSES AND SIGNATURE LINES

Succession representative

Lorenzo K. Washington, appearing herein in his capacity as the duly qualified executor [or administrator, if intestate] of the Succession of Recently M. Departed, Probate No. [number], 21st Judicial District Court, Parish of Livingston, State of Louisiana, and authorized by order of said Court, a certified copy of which is attached hereto and made a part hereof, …

Succession of Recently M. Departed

By: ___________________________

Lorenzo K. Washington, Administrator

Independent executor or administrator

Chazz Stanford Smith, appearing herein in his capacity as the duly qualified independent administrator of the succession of Dexter Jones, Probate No. [number], 22nd Judicial District Court, Parish of St. Tammany, State of Louisiana and authorized by Letters of Independent Administration issued by said court, a certified copy of which is attached hereto and made a part hereof, …

Succession of Dexter Jones

By: ___________________________

Chazz Stanford Smith, Administrator

Agent authorized to act for principal under power of attorney

Jack Jones, Principal, a person of the age of majority and domiciliary of Grant Parish, and whose permanent mailing address is 805 Hooper Rd., Pineville, LA 71360, appearing herein through his duly authorized representative, agent, and attorney in fact Kelly McDonald, by virtue of that certain Power of Attorney dated *day, month, year*, and which was passed before Jane Wonderkind, Notary Public, a notary public in and for the parish of Grant, state of Louisiana, an original *[or true copy]* of which is attached hereto and incorporated herein by reference…

or

Roxanne Smith, a person of the age of majority and domiciliary of Orleans Parish, and whose permanent mailing address is 6500 Magazine St., New Orleans, LA 70118, appearing herein through her duly authorized representative, agent, and attorney in fact, Nick Rob Martin, by virtue of that certain Power of Attorney dated *day, month, year*, and which was passed before James I. McNotary, a notary public in and for Orleans Parish, Louisiana, recorded at *COB/MOB Folio and folio number* in the *conveyance or mortgage* records of Orleans Parish, State of Louisiana and incorporated herein by reference…

Roxanne Smith

By: ___________________________

Nick Rob Martin, Agent

SAMPLE APPEARANCE CLAUSES AND SIGNATURE LINES

Trustee

Jennifer Colleen Edwards, appearing as trustee of the Edwards-Toms Family Trust…

Edwards-Toms Family Trust

By: ____________________________
Jennifer Colleen Edwards

Louisiana LLC (as mortgagor, or for certain filings with Secretary of State)

The Dexter Morgan Fan Club Limited Liability Company (TIN 73-112233), a Louisiana limited liability company whose articles of organization were filed with the Secretary of State on January 1, 2020, having a permanent mailing address of 1155 Arno St., Metairie, LA 70003, appearing herein and through, represented by Alex Timmons, sole member, duly authorized by Unanimous Written Consent of the Sole Member, an original of which is attached hereto and made a part hereof, …

The Dexter Morgan Fan Club, LLC

By: ____________________________
Alex Timmons, Member

LLC (or similarly for Corporation or Partnership)

Big Giant Company, LLC, an LLC organized under the laws of the State of Louisiana, having its principal place of business at 509 S. Carrollton Ave., New Orleans, LA 70118, appearing by and through William E. Meany, duly authorized by Articles of Organization filed with the Louisiana Secretary of State on *day, month, year*, and a statement that William E. Meany may act on behalf of the LLC, a certified copy of which is attached hereto and made a part hereof. …

Big Giant Company, LLC

By: ____________________________
William E. Meany

Corporation, alternative form

Teeny Tiny Corporation, a corporation organized under the laws of the state of Louisiana, having its principal place of business at 9999 Main St., Houma, LA 70363, herein appearing by and through Mary J. E. Carlton, its vice president, duly authorized by a resolution of the Board of Directors of said corporation, adopted at a meeting held on June 12, 2020, a certified copy of which is attached hereto. …

Teeny Tiny Corporation

By: ____________________________
Mary J. E. Carlton

SAMPLE APPEARANCE CLAUSES AND SIGNATURE LINES

Unincorporated association

The Louisiana Avenue Garden Club, an unincorporated association domiciled in Ascension Parish, with its permanent mailing address being 601 Railroad Ave., Donaldsonville, LA 70346, herein represented by its treasurer, Marc Adam Howell, as authorized by a statement of authority[1] filed in the conveyance records of Ascension Parish there designated as *COB*, *Folio*, a certified copy of which is attached hereto and made a part hereof. …

Louisiana Avenue Garden Club

By: ____________________________
Marc Adam Howell, Treasurer

Foreign corporation

Drive Through Poutine, Inc., a Delaware Corporation authorized to do business in the state of Louisiana, herein represented by its duly authorized President, Jason North, by a resolution of the Board of Directors of said corporation, adopted at a meeting held on March 7, 2023, a certified copy which is attached hereto.

Drive Through Poutine, Inc.

By: ____________________________
Jason North, President

[1] A statement of authority for an unincorporated association is an authorizing document much like that used for an LLC (certificate of authority) or corporation (corporate resolution), but it must be in authentic form and include the entity's tax identification number, if it has one. It is particularly used when the unincorporated association is donating, selling, or encumbering immovables in its own name. Then the statement of authority should be filed in the parish where the property is located, LA R.S. 12:505, and referenced in the act, as above.

5 • MATRIMONIAL AGREEMENTS AND SEPARATE PROPERTY

MATRIMONIAL AGREEMENTS TO OPT OUT OF COMMUNITY PROPERTY REGIME

This is the matrimonial agreement, also called a marriage contract (or, often, a "pre-nup"), used to declare prospective spouses, before the wedding, to be entering into a separate property regime (the "contractual regime"). By this, they opt out of the default rule that couples share a community and are in a community property regime ("legal regime"). This version is entered into by a couple domiciled in Louisiana before the wedding takes place. The below is in the form of an authentic act, with two witnesses. To be valid, the agreement must be an authentic act or a private act acknowledged by the parties (both spouses, both signed and acknowledged before the wedding). The form below may be adapted if the acknowledgment method is used.

The agreement is effective upon execution and notarization (after the witnesses sign, or by the acknowledgment of the spouses before a notary). It becomes effective as to third parties, such as creditors, when properly filed—often in the conveyance records of multiple clerks of court. It should be filed in the parish of domicile of the spouses (for movables), including two parishes if each spouse is domiciled in a different parish; and the parish where any property is located (for immovables).

If this agreement is properly executed before marriage, it does not have to be approved by a court (meaning that a valid pre-nup may be enforceable when only done with a notary). A couple is also allowed, even after they marry, to enter into the following matrimonial agreement before a notary (again in authentic form or as acknowledged), but it then must be approved by a court to be valid. A notary is allowed to draft and notarize such a contract, and the below form can be adapted for that purpose, with the caveat that it is not binding on anyone until a court approves.

A different form (also found in this collection) is used when a couple moves into Louisiana from another state. Within one year from the date of establishing domicile in Louisiana, a married couple may execute a matrimonial agreement establishing a separate property regime, which agreement is effective upon execution or acknowledgment and need not be approved by a court. It is a "post-nup" allowed for a couple moving into the state, without court approval, similar to the "pre-nup" for Louisiana residents, below.

The following is one simple version. Other versions are available as well in this collection, with more detail. These can be adapted to account for the backgrounds and different appearance clauses of the individuals. This exemplar assumes that each party has not married before.

When one of the parties is old enough to marry but too young to sign a valid contract, such as age 16, their parent must concur to an agreement in writing and the agreement must be approved by petition to the court. Other limits on the contractual freedom (what terms are disallowed or permissible in a pre-nup) are found in LA C.C. art. 2330, such as forbidding changing the marital portion, and art. 116, allowing fixing of any spousal support post-divorce. (Matters of mutual assistance, fidelity and support during the marriage may not be altered.) The form can be adapted to specify any such permissible terms.

MATRIMONIAL AGREEMENTS: SEPARATE PROPERTY (VERSION 1)

In all such cases, the parties should be given the opportunity to consult with legal counsel before signing, to understand the financial implications of the agreement as to their individual situation. The agreement must be freely entered into, with full understanding of what is lost or changed.

STATE OF LOUISIANA

PARISH OF ____________________

MATRIMONIAL AGREEMENT

BEFORE ME, the undersigned Notary Public, duly commissioned and qualified in and for the parish and state aforesaid, and before the undersigned competent witnesses, personally came and appeared

Jack Jones, a single man never having been married, of the age of majority and a domiciliary of New Orleans, Orleans Parish, Louisiana, whose permanent mailing address is 214 Royal St., New Orleans, LA 70130;

and

Kristie Kris, a single woman never having been married, of the age of majority and a domiciliary of Algiers, Orleans Parish, Louisiana, whose permanent mailing address is 545 Patterson Rd., New Orleans, LA 70114;

who declared that they intend to be joined in the bonds of matrimony on or about December 25, 2024 in Orleans Parish, Louisiana and desire to alter the legal regime of acquets and gains provided by the laws of the State of Louisiana as follows:

Appearers intend to be separate in property and all property and effects owned by either of them, either at the time of the celebration of their marriage or acquired after their marriage, shall be the separate property of the spouse who acquired same, each appearer specifically reserving the administration of their separate estate and each appearer reserving for himself all civil and natural fruits and revenues, including all minerals, bonuses, delay rentals, royalties, and shut-in payments arising from mineral leases.

Thus done and signed at ___________________, Louisiana, this _____ day of _________________, 20____, in the presence of the undersigned competent witnesses and me, notary, after due reading of the whole.

WITNESSES:

______________________________	______________________________
Print witness name	Print name of prospective spouse
______________________________	______________________________
Print witness name	Print name of prospective spouse

____

Notary Name: ______________________________

Notary ID or Bar Roll No.: _______________

My Commission is for Life

MATRIMONIAL AGREEMENTS: SEPARATE PROPERTY (VERSION 2)

STATE OF LOUISIANA

PARISH OF ____________________

MATRIMONIAL AGREEMENT

BE IT KNOWN that on this _______ day of _________________, 20____, before me, a Notary Public qualified in and for the Parish and State aforesaid, and in the presence of the two undersigned competent witnesses, personally came and appeared *future spouse 1* and *future spouse 2*, both residents of the Parish of Avoyelles, State of Louisiana, of full age of majority, who declared that:

A promise of marriage exists between the parties to this Agreement; and, the parties expect to be married on or about the 12th day of July, 2025 in the Parish of Orleans, State of Louisiana, and

The parties intend their domicile to be in the Parish of Orleans, State of Louisiana, and

The parties desire that the existing provisions of the laws of the State of Louisiana affecting property rights of married persons, in their marriage, be excluded or modified; and that a regime of separation of property be established.

The parties do stipulate and agree as follows:

I.

The community of acquets and gains ordinarily provided for by the laws of the State of Louisiana to subsist between married persons shall not exist between parties in any manner whatsoever, the parties hereto renouncing the pertinent provisions of the Louisiana Civil Code which establish such community estate and community property regime. Without limitation of these objectives. but in furtherance of them, the parties hereby stipulate and agree that:

II.

All property now owned by either of said parties shall remain the separate property of that one of the parties to whom such property belongs, and all revenues, fruits and increases arising from such respective properties shall also be considered, and remain, the separate property of the respective parties to whom belongs the property from which such revenues, fruits and other increases arise. Further, any property hereafter acquired by either party from said revenues, fruits, or increases of such separate property, or by the disposition or encumbrance of the original separate property itself, whether by sale, exchange, mortgage, pledge, or otherwise, shall be considered, and remain. the separate property of that party, out of whose revenues, fruits, increases or property the later property shall be acquired.

III.

The provisions of the preceding paragraph shall apply regardless of which of the parties shall administer or manage the revenues, fruits. increases, property or proceeds in question; that is to say, the question as to which party administered or managed, or is administering or managing the revenues, fruits, increases, property, or proceeds of any property, shall in no way affect or modify the provisions of the preceding paragraph, and in no way create a community interest; the fact that either party may assist the other in the administration or management of the property of the other shall not create the presumption of a claim for remuneration in favor of that party assisting the other, but all such services shall be considered and held as gratuitously rendered to each other.

IV.

All property hereafter acquired in the name of either of said parties shall be and remain the separate property of that party in whose name said property is acquired; and the preceding provisions shall apply in all particulars to this property hereafter to be acquired by either party, regardless of the manner of acquisition.

V.

Any increase or improvement of the separate property of either party, as separate property is set forth in this agreement, arising or made during the marriage of the parties through the result of the common labor, expense, or industry of the parties, shall not create any right to a reward in favor of that party, or the legal representatives of that party, to whom the property which has been increased or improved does not belong.

VI.

Nothing in this agreement shall be construed as changing the nature of property which the law generally would regard as the separate property of the parties, it being the intention of the foregoing provisions to add to and enlarge what shall be considered separate property, and not to establish any community between the parties.

THUS DONE AND SIGNED at ____________________, Louisiana, this _____ day of ____________________, 20____, in the presence of the undersigned witnesses and me, notary, after due reading of the whole.

WITNESSES:

______________________________	________________________________
Print witness name	Print name of prospective spouse
______________________________	________________________________
Print witness name	Print name of prospective spouse

____

Notary name: __________________________

Notary ID or Bar Roll No.: ______________

My Commission is for Life

MATRIMONIAL AGREEMENTS: SEPARATE PROPERTY (VERSION 3)

STATE OF LOUISIANA

PARISH OF ____________________

MATRIMONIAL AGREEMENT

This **Agreement** is entered into on this *enter date*, by and between *enter [Prospective] Spouse 1* and *enter [Prospective] Spouse 2*.

1. Purpose. The parties intend to marry each other on July 5, 2025, in Kenner, Louisiana. In advance of their marriage, the parties wish to provide for their rights and obligations in and to each other's assets and property including that which each of the parties currently and separately own, that which each will acquire separately during the marriage and that which both will acquire together during the marriage, in the event the marriage is terminated.

2. Current Circumstances. With respect to current circumstances:

(a) *Spouse 1* currently resides at *Spouse 1 address*. *Spouse 1* represents that she was previously married. *Spouse 1* has 3 children.

(b) *Spouse 2* currently resides at *Spouse 2 address*. *Spouse 2* represents that he was not previously married. *Spouse 2* has 2 children.

3. Effective Date. This Agreement will be effective on July 5, 2025, the date of marriage. If we do not marry each other by such date, this Agreement will be null and void and its provisions unenforceable.

4. Disclosure. The parties have made full, fair, and reasonable disclosure to each other of his or her financial information regarding net worth, assets, income, holdings, liabilities, and debts and agree to a verbal Agreement. *Spouse 1* acknowledges and has understanding of *Spouse 2*'s financial information prior to signing this Agreement. *Spouse 2* acknowledges and has understanding of *Spouse 1*'s financial information prior to signing this Agreement.

5. Legal Representation. *Spouse 1* and *Spouse 2* represent that they had the opportunity to consult with legal counsel but, however, chose not to engage legal counsel in the drafting and negotiation of this Agreement. The failure to consult legal counsel constitutes a waiver of such right. Both parties represent that they understand the contents of this Agreement, acknowledge this Agreement is fair and reasonable, and have chosen to freely and voluntarily enter into this Agreement.

6. Premarital Property. With respect to premarital property:

(a) All of *Spouse 1*'s property that is separately owned including contents prior to the marriage will remain as *Spouse 1*'s non-marital, separate, and individual property during and after the marriage. Any increase in the value relating to the separate property will also remain as the non-marital, separate, and individual property of *Spouse 1*. *Spouse 1* has the full right and authority to manage, sell, gift, transfer or otherwise dispose of *Spouse 1*'s separate property.

(b) All of *Spouse 2*'s property that is separately owned including contents prior to the marriage will remain as *Spouse 2*'s non-marital, separate, and individual property during and after the marriage. Any increase in the value relating to the separate property will also remain as the non-marital, separate, and individual property of *Spouse 2*. *Spouse 2* has the full right and authority to manage, sell, gift, transfer or otherwise dispose of *Spouse 2*'s separate property.

7. Property Acquired During Marriage. With respect to property acquired during marriage:

(a) Property earned, acquired, and given to *Spouse 1* individually during marriage will be treated as *Spouse 1's* own and remain *Spouse 1*'s non-marital, separate, and individual property. Any increase in the value relating to the separate property will also remain as the non-marital, separate, and individual property of *Spouse 1*. *Spouse 1* has the full right and authority to manage, sell, gift, transfer or otherwise dispose of *Spouse 1*'s separate property.

(b) Property earned, acquired, and given to *Spouse 2* individually during marriage will be treated as *Spouse 2*'s own and remain *Spouse 2*'s non-marital, separate, and individual property. Any increase in the value relating to the separate property will also remain as the non-marital, separate, and individual property of *Spouse 2*. *Spouse 2* has the full right and authority to manage, sell, gift, transfer or otherwise dispose of *Spouse 2*'s separate property.

(c) All assets and property that are earned and acquired by both parties through their joint efforts or given to both parties will be treated as marital property and owned equally by *Spouse 1* and *Spouse 2* or as otherwise designated in a writing signed by both parties.

(d) In the event the marriage is terminated, the marital property is subject to division as determined by the jurisdiction whose law governs the construction of this Agreement.

8. Premarital Debts. With respect to premarital debts:

(a) *Spouse 1*'s pre-existing debts or obligations that exist prior to the marriage will remain as *Spouse 1*'s sole responsibility during and after the marriage. Any increase in the value of *Spouse 1*' s pre-existing debts or obligations will also remain the sole responsibility of *Spouse 1*.

(b) *Spouse 2*'s pre-existing debts or obligations that exist prior to the marriage will remain as *Spouse 2*'s sole responsibility during and after the marriage. Any increase in the value of *Spouse 2*'s pre-existing debts or obligations will also remain the sole responsibility of *Spouse 2*.

(c) In the event the marriage is terminated, the marital debt is subject to division as determined by the jurisdiction whose law governs the construction of this Agreement.

9. Debts Acquired During Marriage. With respect to debts acquired during marriage:

(a) Any debts or obligations incurred by *Spouse 1* during the marriage will be *Spouse 1*'s sole responsibility. *Spouse 1* will not assume or become responsible for the debts or obligations due to the marriage without *Spouse 1*'s written consent.

(b) Any debts or obligations incurred by *Spouse 2* during the marriage will be *Spouse 2*'s sole responsibility. *Spouse 2* will not assume or become responsible for the debts or obligations due to the marriage without *Spouse 2*'s written consent.

(c) In the event the marriage is terminated, the marital debt is subject to division determined by the jurisdiction whose law governs the construction of this Agreement.

10. Taxes. With respect to taxes:

(a) During their marriage, the parties may elect to file a joint federal and state income tax return, but each party will continue to be liable for any and all taxes associated with their separate property.

(b) In the event the marriage is terminated, tax returns shall be separately filed.

11. Binding. This Agreement will inure to the benefit of and be binding upon the parties, their successors, heirs, executors, administrators, assigns and representatives.

12. Severability. In the event that any provision of this Agreement is held to be invalid, illegal or unenforceable in whole or in part, the validity, legality and enforceability of the remaining provisions shall not be affected and the remaining provisions shall be construed, to the extent possible, to give effect to this Agreement without the inclusion of such invalid, illegal or unenforceable provision.

13. Governing Law. The terms of this Agreement shall be governed by and construed in accordance with the laws of the State of Louisiana, not including its conflicts of law provisions.

14. Further Assurances. At the written request of either party, the other party shall execute and deliver such other documents and take such other actions as may be reasonably necessary to effect the terms of this Agreement.

15. Headings. The section headings herein are for references purposes only and shall not otherwise affect the meaning, construction, or interpretation of any provision in this Agreement.

16. Entire Agreement. This Agreement which does not include any Exhibits attached hereto contains the entire verbal understanding between the parties and supersedes and cancels all prior agreements of the parties, whether oral or written, with respect to such subject matter.

17. Amendment or Revocation. This Agreement may be amended or modified only by a written agreement signed by both of the parties. This Agreement may be revoked if both parties sign a written agreement before the presence of a notary public or other authorized official. Revocation shall become effective when properly recorded as required by state and local laws.

18. Signatures. The signatures of the parties to this Agreement represent the parties' acknowledgment that they have been informed of their legal rights, given an adequate amount of time to consider entering into this Agreement, read and understood the Agreement, agree with the contents of the Agreement, had sufficient time to review the Agreement and believe it to be fair, have not been pressured or coerced into signing the Agreement and chosen to freely and voluntarily enter into this Agreement.

THUS DONE AND SIGNED, in the presence of the undersigned competent witnesses, and me, notary, at ____________________, Louisiana, this ____ day of __________________, 20____, after due reading of the whole.

WITNESSES:

______________________________	______________________________
Print witness name	Print name of prospective *Spouse 1*
______________________________	______________________________
Print witness name	Print name of prospective *Spouse 2*

____

Notary name: ______________________________

Notary ID or Bar Roll No.: _____________

My Commission is for Life

MATRIMONIAL AGREEMENTS: SEPARATE PROPERTY (VERSION 4)

STATE OF LOUISIANA

PARISH OF ____________________

MATRIMONIAL AGREEMENT

BE IT KNOWN, that on this _____ day of ________________, 20____:

BEFORE ME, a Notary Public duly commissioned and qualified in and for the state and parish aforesaid, and in the presence of the undersigned competent witnesses:

PERSONALLY APPEARED

Prospective Spouse 1, a single man having never been married and a resident and domiciliary of the City of New Orleans, Parish of Orleans, and whose mailing address is 123 Royal St., New Orleans, LA, 70116; and

Prospective Spouse 2, a single woman, having been married but once, to Brian Jones, from whom she was judicially divorced, and has not since remarried, and who is a resident and domiciliary of the city of Harahan, Parish of Jefferson, and whose mailing address is 345 Hickory Ave. Apt. C, Harahan, LA 70123;

who each separately declared that they intend to be joined in the bonds of matrimony on or about *state future date* at ______________ Parish, Louisiana, and in order to fix the property rights and obligations between them, they do agree and contract as follows:

Article 1

The intended husband and wife hereby establish a regime of separation of property as allowed by Civil Code Article 2329. Accordingly, they expressly renounce all provisions of law which establish a legal community of acquets and gains between husband and wife, whether now or later enacted.

Article 2

All property of the intended husband and wife, whether owned at the time of the ceremony of marriage or acquired during the marriage is declared to be separate property. The separate property of an intended spouse consists of, but is not limited to, the following: Property acquired by a spouse through the effort, skill, or industry of that spouse; property donated to the spouses either separately or jointly; and property acquired by a spouse through inheritance.

Article 3

All things in the possession of a spouse, or in the name of one spouse, during the existence of this separation of property regime are presumed to be the separate property of the spouse whose name the property is in or who is in possession of the thing.

MATRIMONIAL AGREEMENTS: SEPARATE PROPERTY (VERSION 4)

Article 4

All natural and civil fruits and revenues of the separate property of each intended spouse, as well as minerals produced from or attributable to a separate asset, and bonuses, delay rentals, royalties, and shut-in payments arising from mineral leases are declared to be and are reserved as the separate property of the intended spouse who owns the thing.

Article 5

All damages, insurance, or indemnity collected due to personal injury, property damage, or other cause are the separate property of the spouse who sustained the injury or damage, whether before or during the marriage.

Article 6

Each spouse acting alone may manage, alienate, encumber, control, or dispose of his or her separate property without the consent or concurrence of the other spouse.

Article 7

An obligation incurred by a spouse before or during the existence of the marriage is a separate obligation of the spouse who incurred it. A spouse who does not personally incur an obligation shall not be liable for the other spouse's obligations.

Article 8

An alimentary obligation imposed by law on a spouse shall be a separate obligation of that spouse.

Article 9

An increase during the marriage in the value of the separate property of a spouse inures to the benefit of that spouse, whether the increase is due to the uncompensated labor or industry of the spouses or not. Buildings, other constructions permanently attached to the ground, component parts, and plantings made on the land of one spouse belong to the owner of the ground. Upon termination of the marriage the spouse whose assets were used to improve the separate property of the other spouse is not entitled to any reimbursement unless otherwise agreed in writing.

Article 10

It is the intention of each party to this agreement that neither will have an economic claim on the other at the termination of this marriage, including without limitation, claims for reimbursements of donations, loans, or expenses of the marriage unless otherwise agreed in writing.

Article 11

Each spouse shall contribute to the expenses of the marriage in proportion to his and her means.

Article 12

This separation of property regime may not be terminated except by authentic act signed by each spouse or act under private signature duly acknowledged by each spouse.

Article 13

This agreement is entered into with the full knowledge on the part of each party as to the extent and value of the patrimony of each party and the rights conferred by law under the legal community property regime, but it is the desire of each party that their respective rights to each other's estate shall be fixed by this agreement, which shall be binding on their respective heirs and legal representatives. Each party admits that they have had the opportunity of benefit of their own legal counsel and are satisfied with the terms of this agreement.

Thus done and signed at ________________, Louisiana, this ____ day of ________________, 20___, in the presence of these competent witness and me, notary, after due reading of the whole.

WITNESSES:

______________________________	______________________________
Print witness name	Print name of prospective spouse 1
______________________________	______________________________
Print witness name	Print name of prospective spouse 2

____

Notary name: ______________________________

Notary ID or Bar Roll No.: ______________

My Commission is for Life

MATRIMONIAL AGREEMENTS: MOVE INTO STATE WITHIN 1 YEAR

This is the matrimonial agreement, also called a marriage contract (or, in this case, a "post-nup") used to declare spouses, within one year of moving into Louisiana, to have and maintain a separate property regime (the "contractual regime"). By this, they fully opt out of the default rule that couples share a community and are in a community property regime ("legal regime"). This version is entered into by a couple already married, who becomes domiciled in Louisiana. They have one year to opt out of the legal regime without needing court approval (whereas any other post-nup requires petition to a court).

The below is in the form of an authentic act, with two witnesses. To be valid, the agreement must be either an authentic act or a private act acknowledged by the parties (both spouses, both signed <u>*and acknowledged*</u> *before the one year grace period ends). The form below may be adapted if the acknowledgment method is used.*

The agreement is effective upon execution and notarization (after the witnesses sign, or by the acknowledgment of the spouses before a notary). It becomes effective as to third parties, such as creditors, when properly filed—often in the conveyance records of multiple clerks of court. It should be filed in the parish of domicile of the spouses (for movables), including two parishes if each spouse is domiciled in a different parish; and the parish where any property is located (for immovables).

A different form (also found in this collection) is used before a couple marries, when they are already Louisiana residents at the time of the wedding.

The following is one simple version (a more detailed version is also found in this collection). It can be adapted to account for the background and different appearance clauses of the individuals. This exemplar assumes that each party has not married before. Other, even more detailed, versions of the marital agreement in this collection may be adapted to this situation, in which the parties move into Louisiana and sign this within the first year.

When one of the parties is old enough to marry but too young to sign a valid contract, such as age 16, their parent must concur to an agreement in writing and the agreement must be approved by petition to the court. Other limits on the contractual freedom (what terms are disallowed or permissible in a pre-nup) are found in LA C.C. art. 2330, such as forbidding changing the marital portion, and art. 116, allowing fixing of any spousal support post-divorce. (Matters of mutual assistance, fidelity and support during the marriage may not be altered.) The form can be adapted to specify any such permissible terms.

In all such cases, the parties should be given the opportunity to consult with legal counsel before signing, to understand the financial implications of the agreement as to their individual situation. The agreement must be freely entered into, with full understanding of what is lost or changed.

STATE OF LOUISIANA

PARISH OF ____________________

MATRIMONIAL AGREEMENT

BEFORE ME, the undersigned Notary Public, duly commissioned and qualified in and for the parish and state aforesaid, and before the undersigned competent witnesses, personally came and appeared

MATRIMONIAL AGREEMENTS: MOVE INTO STATE WITHIN 1 YEAR

Jack Jones, married man of the age of majority and a domiciliary of Tangipahoa Parish, Louisiana, whose permanent mailing address is 222 Maple St., Hammond, LA 70401;

and

Kristie Kris, born Smythe, a married woman of the age of majority and a domiciliary of Tangipahoa Parish, Louisiana, whose permanent mailing address is 222 Maple St., Hammond, LA 70401;

who declared that they are a married couple who established domicile or permanent residence in the state of Louisiana on or about _________________, 20___ in Tangipahoa Parish, Louisiana, having moved to the state from the state of ______________________; and they desire to alter the legal regime of acquets and gains provided by the laws of the State of Louisiana as follows:

Appearers intend to be separate in property, and all property and effects owned by either of them, either at or before the time of their marriage or acquired after their marriage, shall be the separate property of the spouse who acquired same, each appearer specifically reserving the administration of their separate estate and each appearer reserving for himself all civil and natural fruits and revenues, including all minerals, bonuses, delay rentals, royalties, and shut-in payments arising from mineral leases.

THUS DONE AND SIGNED at _____________________, Louisiana, this ______ day of _____________________, 20____, in the presence of the undersigned competent witnesses and me, notary, after due reading of the whole.

WITNESSES:

______________________________	______________________________
Print witness name	Print name of spouse 1
______________________________	______________________________
Print witness name	Print name of spouse 2

____

Notary Name: __________________________________

Notary ID or Bar Roll No.: ________________

My Commission is for Life

MATRIMONIAL AGREEMENT IF MOVE INTO STATE, ALTERNATE

STATE OF LOUISIANA

PARISH OF ____________________

MATRIMONIAL AGREEMENT

BEFORE ME, the undersigned notary public duly commissioned and qualified in and for the parish and state aforesaid, and before the undersigned competent witnesses, personally came and appeared:

Minnie Anne Smith, born Rodriguez, of the legal age of majority, who declares unto me that she has been married but once, and then to Mickey John Smith, to whom she remains married; and

Mickey John Smith, of the legal age of majority, who declares unto me that he has been married but once, and then to Minnie Anne Rodriguez Smith, to whom he remains married, who declare the following:

Minnie Smith and Mickey Smith were married on July 4, 2020, in Omaha, Nebraska, County of Douglas. They lived and there resided, until July 1, 2024,[1] whereupon they relocated to Louisiana, intending to make their true, fixed, permanent home and domicile to be in Caddo Parish, Louisiana, with a mailing address of 123 Gaylyn Dr., Shreveport, LA 71105.

The spouses seek to avail themselves of Louisiana Civil Code article 2329, and enter into a contractual regime, separating the property of the spouses.

1.

The husband and wife shall be separate in property. Neither of them shall be personally liable for the debts contracted by the other once entering into this contract.

2.

The parties hereto recognize and acknowledge that each of them is the owner of separate property, including but not limited to policies of life insurance, and other accounts. Each desires that the separate property remain separate, and each reserves to themselves the right to administer said property for their sole benefit, including changing beneficiaries. Any property considered separate prior to relocating to Louisiana shall be considered separate. Any property owned jointly shall be considered to be property co-owned in indivision.[2]

---

[1] This date must be within 1 year of the execution as an authentic act of the matrimonial agreement (or a private act acknowledged by the spouses). Out of an access of caution, and to put third parties such as creditors on notice of the contractual regime, it is advised that the agreement be filed in the conveyances of records within 1 year, too. Filing is done in the parish of domicile for movables and where property is located for immovables. In this example, if the only immovable is the home in 71105, then the lone place of filing is in Caddo Parish.

[2] This may be modified if all property can be identified as separate and not jointly owned.

MATRIMONIAL AGREEMENT IF MOVE INTO STATE, ALTERNATE

3.

The provisions of the preceding paragraph shall apply regardless of which of the parties shall administer or manage the fruits, revenues, increases, property or proceeds in question; that is, the question as to which party administered or managed, or is administering or managing the fruits, revenues, increases, property, or proceeds of any property shall in no way affect or modify the provisions of the preceding paragraph, and in no way create a community interest; the fact that either party may assist the other in the administration or management of the property of the other shall not create the presumption of a claim for remuneration in favor of that party assisting the other, but all such services shall be considered and held as gratuitously rendered to each other.

4.

All property hereafter acquired in the name of either of said parties shall be and remain the separate property of that party in whose name said property is acquired; and the preceding provisions shall apply in all particulars to this property hereafter to be acquired by either party, regardless of the manner of acquisition.

5.

Any increase or improvement of the separate property of either party, as separate property is set forth in this agreement, arising or made during the marriage of the parties through the result of the common labor, expense, or industry of the parties, shall not create any right to a reward in favor of that party, or the legal representatives of that party, to whom the property which has been increased or improved does not belong.

6.

Nothing in this agreement shall be construed as changing the nature of property which the law generally would regard as the separate property of the parties, it being the intention of the foregoing provisions to add to and enlarge what shall be considered separate property, and not to establish any community between the parties.

Thus done and signed at ________________, Louisiana, this ____ day of __________________, 20____, after due reading of the whole.

WITNESSES:

________________________________ ________________________________

Print witness name Print name of spouse

________________________________ ________________________________

Print witness name Print name of spouse

____

Notary name: ________________________________

Notary ID or Bar Roll No.: ________________

My Commission is for Life

MATRIMONIAL AGREEMENT TO OPT *INTO* COMMUNITY

This is the matrimonial agreement, also called a marriage contract or a "post-nup," that is used when a couple who had previously declared that they were not a community (that they were in a separate property regime, or were already in one because they moved into Louisiana) now wants to convert their situation to the community property ("legal") regime. This act is best done as an authentic act, but this form can also be modified so that it is done as an act under private signature duly acknowledged by both spouses. It does not have to be approved in court, because the couple is choosing to enter into the default regime: community property. It can be completed at any time during the marriage, not just within the first year.

This act is effective between the parties upon execution and notarization (after the witnesses sign, or by the acknowledgment by the spouses before a notary). It becomes effective as to third parties, such as creditors, when filed in the parish of domicile of the spouses (for movables), including two parishes if each spouse is domiciled in a different parish; and the parish where any property is located (for immovables).

In this act, although the spouses are creating a community and adopting that regime, they can specify individual items of property which will remain separate property. There is a suggested section below to do that, which can be omitted if the couple wants everything to be owned as a community. Or it can be adapted in many ways to alter the resultant community property regime.

There are other background facts of this exemplar that may not be appropriate for the actual clients' situation; for example, this one assumed that the couple had entered into a separate property agreement ("pre-nup") and had specifically reserved some items in it as separate (which may not have been necessary, so this should be adapted as to that agreement's terms). But it instead may be that the clients are in a separate property arrangement not because of a pre-nup but because they moved into the state already having a separate regime. In that case the act should express this, such as date of moving into the state and declaring they had a separate regime. Or if a couple moved into the state, then declared within a year that they were in a separate regime, and now want to un-do that choice to join the community property regime, the statement below should say so and reference the previous post-nup as the marital agreement they are modifying.

The appearance clause below also is appropriate for a couple with two previous marriages (just as an example), but a simpler one may be used if not.

STATE OF LOUISIANA

PARISH OF JEFFERSON

MATRIMONIAL AGREEMENT

Before me, notary public, duly commissioned and qualified in the state and parish aforesaid, and the undersigned competent witnesses, personally appeared:

SPOUSE 1, of the age of majority and domiciled in Jefferson Parish, a married man, husband to *SPOUSE 2*, née *Maiden name*, and was previously married to *Spouse 1's wife 1* and *Spouse 1's wife 2*; and *SPOUSE 2*, of the age of majority and domiciled in Jefferson Parish, a married woman, wife to *Spouse 1*, and was previously married to *Spouse 2's husband 1* and *Spouse 2's husband 2*; intending to declare their union a community and join the legal regime, declare that:

This Agreement is entered into on this _______________, 2024 *[date]*, by and between *SPOUSE 1* and *SPOUSE 2*. They were married January 1, 2020 in Orleans Parish. Previous to their marriage, on December

25, 2019, they entered into a matrimonial agreement declaring their union to be a contractual regime of separate property; they reserved as separate property several specifically listed properties.

They now declare that henceforth they are in the legal regime with all property previously owned separately now being community property, specifically revoking the separate property marriage contract, with the exceptions enumerated below. All money, property, assets, and debts existing previous to their marriage and acquired or accrued during their marriage shall henceforth be considered community property, including but not limited to donations, inheritances, property acquired from separate property, retirement accounts, bank accounts, and fruits of the same.

All future property they acquire individually or together shall be considered community property, however acquired or using whatever sources, except as enumerated below, unless otherwise specifically reserved to be separate property by agreement of both parties in writing and passed before a notary.

Exceptions:

1. The immovable at 1234 Sauve Rd., River Ridge, Louisiana 70123 in Jefferson Parish, previously the separate property of *Spouse 2* including the house and land, shall remain her separate property, for her to own, use, and dispose of as she fits without permission of or accounting to *Spouse 1*.

2. Any rents or other fruits of 1234 Sauve Rd., River Ridge, Louisiana 70123 will remain the separate property of *Spouse 2*, with specific reservation of their character as separate property agreed to by both parties.

3. All jewelry, family heirlooms, paintings, and other artwork owned by *Spouse 2* shall remain her separate property, including but not limited to her wedding/engagement ring and artwork created by relatives of *Spouse 2*; and she may freely donate or sell these items to others without permission of or accounting to *Spouse 1*.

The parties intend to establish a matrimonial domicile in Lafayette Parish and own property as community in that parish, within 30 days, and intend to file this Agreement in the registry of the clerk of court of that parish or cause it to be filed there.

This Agreement shall be effective immediately this day upon execution and passing before a notary and two witnesses, and binds the party regardless of its being filed in the registry of any parish court and before such recordation may occur.

Spouse 1 and *Spouse 2* represent that they have had the opportunity to consult with legal counsel; and chose not to engage legal counsel in the drafting and negotiation of this Agreement. The failure to consult legal counsel constitutes a waiver of such right. Both parties represent that they understand the contents of this Agreement, acknowledge this Agreement is fair and reasonable, and have chosen to freely and voluntarily enter into this Agreement.

This Agreement will inure to the benefit of and be binding upon the parties, their successors, heirs, executors, administrators, assigns and representatives.

In the event that any provision of this Agreement is held to be invalid, illegal or unenforceable in whole or in part, the validity, legality, and enforceability of the remaining provisions shall not be affected and the remaining provisions shall be construed, to the extent possible, to give effect to this Agreement without the inclusion of such invalid, illegal, or unenforceable provision.

MATRIMONIAL AGREEMENT TO OPT *INTO* COMMUNITY

The responsibility for filing will be with the executing notary, as delivered to the notary by the parties.

Thus done and signed at _________________, Louisiana, this ____ day of __________________, 20____.

WITNESSES:

______________________________	____________________________________
Print witness name	Print name of *Spouse 1*
______________________________	____________________________________
Print witness name	Print name of *Spouse 2*

____

Notary Name: _________________________________

Notary ID or Bar Roll No.: _______________

My Commission is for Life

DONATION OF SEPARATE PROPERTY TO COMMUNITY

ACTS TO HANDLE SPECIFIC ITEMS OF COMMUNITY OR SEPARATE PROPERTY

CHANGING SEPARATE PROPERTY INTO COMMUNITY PROPERTY:

The following form is used when a couple is already in a community property regime and one spouse wishes to declare an item or items of property that may be considered their separate property to become community property. It acts like a donation and follows the authentic form of that. If not worded correctly (if it appears to be a donation of the property itself to the other spouse without qualification), the act may instead transfer the property completely to the other spouse as separate property, which is not the intended result. The stipulation that it become community property is important.

Always be careful not to state such transfers in terms of "half the house" (thinking you're accounting for community property being "half"), because the result could be, without further stipulation, that donor transfers half of what they own of the house, which is already half. It is better to write it in terms of "his interest in the property." In this case, donating the "described property" (which can only be his interest in it) is clear, because of the stipulation that it be community. Modifying that to try to state it in terms of his percentage is actually unclear.

This act is valid and final upon acceptance by the donee (Spouse 2 in this example). It may also be filed, to be binding upon third parties such as creditors or lenders. It is advisable to file it where the couple has their domicile for movables or, for an immovable, the parish or parishes where the immovable is located.

The following is arranged assuming that both parties are present. As with any donation, it can instead be adapted to the situation in which the donee is not present but instead appears separately in writing (and not necessarily before a notary) to clearly state their acceptance of the donation. It can be written as a separate statement (statement of acceptance, date, name, and signature) below the notary's signature, or it can be a separate signed document attached to this. In such case the appearances and acceptance clause below should be edited to make clear that the donee is a party but not make it seem as though the donee is immediately present.

STATE OF LOUISIANA

PARISH OF JEFFERSON

DONATION OF SEPARATE PROPERTY TO COMMUNITY

BEFORE ME, a notary public duly commissioned and qualified in the parish and state aforesaid, and in the presence of the undersigned witnesses,

PERSONALLY CAME AND APPEARED:

Spouse 1 and *Spouse 2*, born *maiden name*, both of the full age of majority and domiciled in Terrebonne Parish, Louisiana, and each of whom have been duly sworn, have declared that they have been married but once and then to each other, and are living together in community; and who declared their permanent mailing address is 333 Grand Caillou Rd., Houma, LA 70363; and

Spouse 1, who declared that a community of acquets and gains exists between *Spouse 1* and *Spouse*

DONATION OF SEPARATE PROPERTY TO COMMUNITY

2, and that *Spouse 1* owns certain separate property, and in consideration of the natural love and affection which *Spouse 1* has for *Spouse 2*, and *Spouse 1*'s desire that property classified as their separate property will be considered as community property, *Spouse 1* does, in accordance with Civil Code article 2343.1, by these presents, irrevocably give, grant, and donate, inter vivos, unto *Spouse 2* the following described property, with the stipulation that the thing shall be part of the community:

Enter description of property here, and if the property is immovable, enter legal description and municipal address, if one exists (or attach a copy of legal description and state here that it is attached as an exhibit to this act).

Also appearing herein is *Spouse 2*, who accepts this donation and acknowledges that the property shall be part of the community.

THUS DONE AND SIGNED at ______________________ *[city]*, Louisiana, this _____ day of ____________________, 20____, in the presence of the undersigned competent witnesses and me, notary, after due reading of the whole.

WITNESSES:

______________________________	______________________________
Print witness name	Print name of *Spouse 1*
______________________________	______________________________
Print witness name	Print name of *Spouse 2*

____

Notary name: ______________________________

Notary ID or Bar Roll No.: ________________

My Commission is for Life

CHANGING A COMMUNITY INTEREST INTO SPOUSE'S SEPARATE PROPERTY

The following form is used when a couple is already in a community property regime and one spouse wishes to declare an item or items of property that may be considered community property to become the separate property of the other spouse (donee). It acts like a donation and follows the authentic form of that.

This transfer can also be done by having both parties donate their community interest to the one spouse (both appearing and signing as donors and one as donee). But since article 2343 states that the effect of Spouse 1's donation is to also make Spouse 2's equal interest "transformed into separate property" Having one sign as donor, as below, is simpler and accomplishes the same result. Unless the act below otherwise stipulates, article 2343 also states that the fruits and rents of this now-separate property will remain separate property of the donee (unlike the usual rule).

This act is valid and final upon acceptance by the donee (Spouse 2 in this example). It may also be filed, to be binding upon third parties such as creditors or lenders. It is advisable to file it where the couple has their domicile for movables or, for an immovable, the parish or parishes where the immovable is located.

The following is arranged assuming that both parties are present. As with any donation, it can instead be adapted to the situation in which the donee is not present but instead acts separately in writing to clearly state their acceptance of the donation (and not necessarily before a notary—signing a clear written acceptance is enough). It can be written as a separate statement (statement of acceptance, date, name, and signature) on this form, below the notary's signature, or it can be a separate signed document attached to this. In such case the appearances and acceptance clause below should be edited to make clear that the donee is a party but not make it seem as though the donee is immediately present.

STATE OF LOUISIANA

PARISH OF JEFFERSON

DONATION BY SPOUSE OF INTEREST IN COMMUNITY

BEFORE ME, a notary public duly commissioned and qualified in the parish and state aforesaid, and in the presence of the undersigned witnesses,

PERSONALLY CAME AND APPEARED:

Spouse 1 and *Spouse 2*, born *maiden name*, both of the full age of majority and domiciled in Terrebonne Parish, Louisiana, and each of whom have been duly sworn, have declared that they have been married but once and then to each other, and who are living together in community, and who declared their permanent mailing address is 333 Grand Caillou Rd., Houma, LA 70363,

who declared that a community of acquets and gains exists between *Spouse 1* and *Spouse 2*, and in consideration of the natural love and affection which they have for each other, *Spouse 1* does by these presents irrevocably give, grant, and donate inter vivos unto her, his interest in the following described property:

Enter description of property here, and if the property is immovable, enter legal description and municipal address, if one exists (or attach a copy of legal description and state here that it is attached as an exhibit to this act).

Also appearing herein is *Spouse 2*, who accepts this donation. Appearers recognize that the donated property formerly was community property but by virtue of this donation, it now is the separate property of the donee.

THUS DONE AND SIGNED at ______________________ *[city]*, Louisiana, this _____ day of ____________________, 20____, in the presence of the undersigned competent witnesses, after due reading of the whole.

WITNESSES:

________________________________	________________________________
Print witness name	Print name of *Spouse 1*
________________________________	________________________________
Print witness name	Print name of *Spouse 2*

____

Notary name: ________________________________

Notary ID or Bar Roll No.: _______________

My Commission is for Life

RENOUNCING RIGHT TO CONCUR IN TRANSFER OF COMMUNITY PROPERTY

STATE OF LOUISIANA

PARISH OF ST. JOHN THE BAPTIST

RENUNCIATION OF RIGHT TO CONCUR IN ALIENATION OF COMMUNITY PROPERTY

BEFORE ME, a notary public duly commissioned and qualified in the parish and state aforesaid,

PERSONALLY CAME AND APPEARED:

Spouse 1, born *maiden name,*[1] of the age of majority and domiciled in Jefferson Parish, Louisiana, and who has been duly sworn, has declared that they have been married but once and then to *Spouse 2*, and who are living together in community, and who declared their permanent mailing address is 311 Jefferson Hwy. Apt. G, Jefferson, LA 70121.

Spouse 1 does hereby renounce their right to concur[2] in any act of alienation, lease, encumbrance, or mortgage of the below entitled community property:[3]

Enter description of property here, and if the property is immovable, enter legal description and municipal address, if one exists (or attach a copy of legal description and state here that it is attached as an exhibit to this act).

Thus done and signed at _______________, Louisiana, this ____ day of _________________, 20____.

WITNESSES:

_______________________________ _______________________________

Print witness name Print name of *Spouse 1*

____

Print witness name

_____________________________________[4]

Notary name: _________________________________

Notary ID or Bar Roll No.: ______________

My Commission is for Life

---

[1] If Spouse 1 is a female not using a maiden name as a current surname.

[2] Renunciation may be made irrevocable for a stated term up to 3 years; if so, add such a clause after the property description. Renunciation may also be made of the right to participate in the management of a community enterprise. LA C.C. art. 2348.

[3] Can also be used to renounce all decisions affecting all community property, instead of describing just one singular piece of property; replace the phrase "the below entitled community property" with "any community immovable property owned now or in the future by appearer and Spouse 2," and omit the legal description.

[4] A renunciation must be in writing and formally is not required to be notarized, but it is advisable to do so. And while this act need not be recorded by itself, it often gets filed with the act it relates to (e.g., an alienation or mortgage).

CONCERNING BY SPOUSE IN SALE OF COMMUNITY ENTITY

STATE OF LOUISIANA

PARISH OF JEFFERSON

CONCURRENCE OF SPOUSE IN SALE OF COMMUNITY ENTITY

BEFORE ME, a notary public duly commissioned and qualified in the parish and state aforesaid, and in the presence of the undersigned witnesses, PERSONALLY CAME AND APPEARED:

Spouse 1 name, born *maiden name if applicable*, "Concurring Spouse" or "Appearer," who is of the full age of majority and married to and living with *Spouse 2 name*, "Seller," domiciled in _____________ Parish, and residing at ____,

Who does by these presents concur in and ratify the sale by her husband Seller, on ____________, 20____, of the business known as "______________________," a community entity, business or enterprise, to ________________________, Purchaser.

Appearer does hereby concur in the sale of said entity, confirming, ratifying, and binding herself, her successors and assigns as party to the act of sale and the terms and conditions of the contract executed by Seller and __________________, authorized representative of Purchaser, which act is dated ______________________, 20____, a copy of which is attached hereto and incorporated by reference.

THUS DONE AND SIGNED at _____________________, Louisiana, this _____ day of ____________________, 20____, in the presence of the undersigned competent witnesses and me, notary, after due reading of the whole.

WITNESSES:

________________________________ ________________________________

Print witness name Print name of *Spouse 1*

____

Print witness name

____

Notary name: _________________________________

Notary ID or Bar Roll No.: ______________

My Commission is for Life

RESERVATION OF FRUITS OF SEPARATE PROPERTY

STATE OF LOUISIANA

PARISH OF JEFFERSON

RESERVATION OF FRUITS AND REVENUES OF SEPARATE PROPERTY[1]

BEFORE ME, a notary public, duly commissioned and qualified in the parish and state aforesaid, and in the presence of the undersigned witnesses:

PERSONALLY CAME AND APPEARED:

Spouse 1 (born _______ *maiden name*), of the age of majority and domiciled in Jefferson Parish, Louisiana, who declares that she has been married but once and then to *Spouse 2*, that they are living together in community, and that their permanent mailing address is 111 Westbank Expressway, Gretna, LA 70056.

And who further declares that a community of acquets and gains exists between *Spouse 1* and *Spouse 2*, and that appearer owns separate property, and in accordance with the provisions of Louisiana Civil Code article 2339, appearer stipulates that she reserves as her separate property all natural and civil fruits and bonuses, delay rentals, royalties, and shut-in payments arising from mineral leases, and minerals produced from or attributable to the separate property owned by appearer, including but not limited to the following described property:

Enter description of property here, and if the property is immovable, enter legal description and municipal address, if one exists (or attach a copy of legal description and state here that it is attached as an exhibit to this act).

Appearer has provided *Spouse 2* with a copy of this Declaration of Reservation of Fruits and Revenues of Separate Property prior to filing the original for registry as required by Civil Code article 2339.

THUS DONE AND SIGNED at ____________________ *[city]*, Louisiana, this _____ day of ____________________, 20____.

WITNESSES:

______________________________ ______________________________

Print witness name Print name of *Spouse 1*

____

Print witness name

---

[1] Must be done in authentic form or act under private signature duly acknowledged. This form is written assuming it is an authentic act in front of two witnesses and the notary, but may be adapted to be done by either witness acknowledgment or party acknowledgment. To be effective, it must be recorded (after first providing to the spouse) in the conveyance records of the parish where the property is located (for immovables) or where the declarant (or "appearer," here Spouse 1) is domiciled.

____

Notary name: __________________________________

Notary ID or Bar Roll No.: ________________

My Commission is for Life

COVENANT MARRIAGE FOR ENGAGED COUPLES

<u>COVENANT MARRIAGE: BEFORE MARRIAGE & OPT-IN WITH EXISTING MARRIAGES</u>

This is the form and affidavit for declaring a covenant marriage that is executed before a couple gets married. The complete requirements for filing are found in La. R.S. 9:224(C) and 273(B). It is effectively two documents by the spouses and one by the counselor. The attestation by the counselor may be included on this form or separately. Each should be executed in duplicate original (with one original retained by the spouses). Although the statements on the marriage license application and marriage license may be executed by one party, the accompanying declaration and affidavit must be executed by both.

STATE OF LOUISIANA

PARISH OF ____________________

DECLARATION OF INTENT

"We do solemnly declare that marriage is a covenant between a man and a woman who agree to live together as husband and wife for so long as they both may live. We understand the nature, purpose, and responsibilities of marriage. We have read the Covenant Marriage Act, and we understand that a Covenant Marriage is for life. If we experience marital difficulties, we commit ourselves to take reasonable efforts to preserve our marriage, including marital counseling."

"With full knowledge of what this commitment means, we do hereby declare that our marriage will be bound by Louisiana law on Covenant Marriage, and we promise to love, honor, and care for one another as husband and wife for the rest of our lives."

Signed:

____
Print name of Prospective Spouse 1

____
Print name of Prospective Spouse 2

STATE OF LOUISIANA

PARISH OF ____________________

AFFIDAVIT

BEFORE ME, the undersigned duly commissioned and qualified Notary Public came and appeared the undersigned

[Name of Prospective Spouse 1 and Name of Prospective Spouse 2]

COVENANT MARRIAGE FOR ENGAGED COUPLES

Who after being duly sworn by me, deposed and stated that:

Affiants acknowledge that they have received premarital counseling from a priest, minister, rabbi, clerk of the Religious Society of Friends, any clergyman of any religious sect, or a professional marriage counselor, which marriage counseling included:

-- A discussion of the seriousness of Covenant Marriage;

-- Communication of the fact that a Covenant Marriage is a commitment for life;

-- The obligation of a Covenant Marriage to take reasonable efforts to preserve the marriage if marital difficulties arise; and

-- That the affiants both read the pamphlet entitled "The Covenant Marriage Act" developed and promulgated by the office of the attorney general, which provides a full explanation of a Covenant Marriage, including the obligation to seek marital counseling in times of marital difficulties and the exclusive grounds for legally terminating a Covenant Marriage by divorce after judgment of separation from bed and board.

_______________________________ _______________________________

[signature of Prospective Spouse] *[signature of Prospective Spouse]*

SWORN TO AND SUBSCRIBED BEFORE ME, this ______ day of ________________, 20_____

____

Notary Name: ________________________________

Notary ID or Bar Roll No. : ________________

My Commission is for Life

The following Attestation by a counselor may be a separate document, printed on a separate sheet of paper and included with the couple's documents Or it can be part of the overall form, as here.

ATTESTATION

I hereby attest that the affiants did receive counseling from me as to the nature and purpose of marriage, which included a discussion of the seriousness of Covenant Marriage, communication of the fact that a Covenant Marriage is for life, and the obligation of a Covenant Marriage to take reasonable efforts to preserve the marriage if marital difficulties arise.

____

[print name and title under signature],
Counselor

COVENANT MARRIAGE FOR MARRIED COUPLES

This is the form and affidavit for declaring a covenant marriage that is used when they couple is already married. The complete requirements for filing are found in La. R.S. 9:275. It is effectively two documents by the spouses and one by the counselor. Each should be executed in duplicate original. The attestation by the counselor may be included on this form or separately.

STATE OF LOUISIANA

PARISH OF ____________________

DECLARATION OF INTENT

"We do solemnly declare that marriage is a covenant between a man and a woman who agree to live together as husband and wife for so long as they both may live. We understand the nature, purpose, and responsibilities of marriage. We have read the Covenant Marriage Act, and we understand that a Covenant Marriage is for life. If we experience marital difficulties, we commit ourselves to take reasonable efforts to preserve our marriage, including marital counseling."

"With full knowledge of what this commitment means, we do hereby declare that our marriage will be bound by Louisiana law on Covenant Marriage, and we renew our promise to love, honor, and care for one another as husband and wife for the rest of our lives."

Signed:

____

Print name of Spouse

____

Print name of Spouse

STATE OF LOUISIANA

PARISH OF ____________________

AFFIDAVIT

BE IT KNOWN THAT on this _______ day of ________________, 20___, before me the undersigned notary public, personally came and appeared:

____

and

____

[insert names of spouses]

Who after being duly sworn by me, notary, deposed and stated the following:

COVENANT MARRIAGE FOR MARRIED COUPLES

Affiants acknowledge that they have received counseling from a priest, minister, rabbi, clerk of the Religious Society of Friends, or clergymen of any religious sect, or a professional marriage counselor, which counseling included:

-- A discussion of the seriousness of Covenant Marriage;

-- Communication of the fact that a Covenant Marriage is a commitment for life;

-- The obligation of a Covenant Marriage to take reasonable efforts to preserve the marriage if martial difficulties arise, and

-- That the affiants both read the pamphlet entitled "The Covenant Marriage Act" developed and promulgated by the office of the attorney general, which provides a full explanation of a Covenant Marriage, including the obligation to seek marital counseling in times of marital difficulties and the exclusive grounds for legally terminating a Covenant Marriage by divorce or divorce after a judgment of separation from bed or board.

As signed below by both spouses.

____
Print name of spouse

____
Print name of spouse

SWORN TO AND SUBSCRIBED BEFORE ME this _______ day of __________________, 20____, in __________________________, Louisiana.

____

Notary Name: __________________________________
Notary ID or Bar Roll No.: _______________
My Commission is for Life

ATTESTATION

I hereby attest that the affiants did receive counseling from me as to the nature and purpose of marriage, which included a discussion of the seriousness of Covenant Marriage, communication of the fact that a Covenant Marriage is for life, and the obligation of a Covenant Marriage to take reasonable efforts to preserve the marriage if marital difficulties arise.

____
[print name and title under signature],
Counselor

6 • FAMILY RELATIONSHIPS AND ALTERING THEM

ACKNOWLEDGMENT OF PATERNITY

STATE OF LOUISIANA

PARISH OF ____________________

NOTARIAL ACKNOWLEDGMENT OF A CHILD BORN OUTSIDE OF MARRIAGE

BEFORE ME, the undersigned notary, duly commissioned and qualified in the state and parish aforesaid, and in the presence of the two witnesses whose names are hereunto subscribed, PERSONALLY CAME and appeared:

Appearer's name (SS# ___-__-____ *in entirety*), a domiciliary and resident of St. Bernard Parish, whose permanent mailing address is 1 Battlefield Rd., Chalmette, LA 70043; a single man who has never been married,

Who declared that he is the Father of child's name, a minor child born to Mother, *Mother's name* (SS# ___-__-____ *in entirety*), on *date of birth of minor child.*

Appearer declares that he was not married to Mother at the time of conception of the minor child, and is not married to Mother at this time.

Mother was not married at the time of conception of the child, and the child is not filiated to another man.

Appearer acknowledges that the undersigned notary read aloud to him, and appearer has also read and understands, the following:

1. Either party has the right to request a genetic test to determine if the alleged Appearer is the biological Appearer of the child.
2. The alleged Appearer has the right to consult an attorney before signing an acknowledgment of paternity.
3. If the alleged Appearer does not acknowledge the child, the mother has the right to file a paternity suit to establish paternity.
4. After the alleged Appearer signs an acknowledgment of paternity, he has the right to pursue visitation with the child and the right to petition for custody.

5. Once an acknowledgment of paternity is signed, the Appearer may be obligated to provide support for the child.
6. Once an acknowledgment of paternity is signed, the child will have inheritance rights and any rights afforded children born in wedlock.
7. (a) A party who executed a notarial act of acknowledgment may rescind the act, without cause, before the earlier of the following:
   - (i) Sixty days after the signing of the act, in a judicial hearing for the limited purpose of rescinding the acknowledgment.
   - (ii) A judicial hearing relating to the child, including a child support proceeding, wherein the affiant to the notarial act of acknowledgment is a party to the proceeding.

   (b) Thereafter, the acknowledgment of paternity may be voided only upon proof, by clear and convincing evidence, that such act was induced by fraud, duress, or material mistake of fact, or that the Appearer is not the biological Appearer.
8. All parties to the action have any other rights and responsibilities which may be afforded by law now or in the future.

FURTHER, I/we acknowledge receipt of a copy of this disclosure, and oral notice of the legal rights and responsibilities of acknowledging paternity, and understand this notice.

Thus done and passed, on the ____ day of __________________, 20___, in _______________ ____________, Louisiana, in the presence of the undersigned competent witnesses who have signed their names together with the appearer and me, notary, after due reading of the whole.

WITNESSES:	APPEARER:
____________________________	______________________________
Print Name	Print Name
____________________________	
Print Name	

____

Notary Name: ______________________________

Notary ID or Bar Roll No.: _______________

My Commission is for Life

ACKNOWLEDGMENT OF PATERNITY, ALTERNATE STATE FORM follows this page, and constitutes pages 99-100 of this book.

STATE OF LOUISIANA

ACKNOWLEDGMENT OF PATERNITY AFFIDAVIT

CHILD BORN OUTSIDE OF MARRIAGE

NOTICE: You must read and initial the NOTICE OF ALTERNATIVES, RIGHTS AND RESPONSIBILITIES before you sign the affidavit.

SECTION I. CHILD'S INFORMATION

This is a legal document. Complete in ink and do not alter.

Name of Child - First, Middle, Last (As it appears on birth certificate)		Date of Birth - (Month, Day, Year)
Place of Birth - City, State	Name of Hospital	
Name of Child - First, Middle, Last (As the parents want it to appear on birth certificate)		

SECTION II. MOTHER'S INFORMATION

Name of Mother - First, Middle, Last	(Maiden Name)	Date of Birth - (Month, Day, Year)
Mother's Address		Mother's Phone Number
Mother's Place of Birth - City, State	Race (Circle) American Indian, Black, White, Asian If Other, List:	Mother's Social Security Number
Mother's Employer - Name & Address		Mother's Occupation
Was Mother Married at Time of Birth Circle One: Yes No	If Yes, Name and Address of Husband	
Does Mother Have Health Insurance Circle One: Yes No	If Yes, Name of Insurance Company and Policy No.	State Medicaid: Circle One: Yes No

SECTION III. FATHER'S INFORMATION

Name of Father - First, Middle, Last		Date of Birth - (Month, Day, Year)
Father's Address		Father's Phone Number
Father's Place of Birth - City, State	Race (Circle) American Indian, Black, White, Asian If Other, List:	Father's Social Security Number
Father's Employer - Name & Address		Father's Occupation
Father's Guardian (If Father under age 18) Print Name	Guardian's Address	Guardian's Signature
Does Father Have Health Insurance Circle One: Yes No	If Yes, Name of Insurance Company and Policy No.	

BOTH PARENTS AND FATHER'S GUARDIAN (IF APPLICABLE) MUST SIGN IN FRONT OF THE NOTARY PUBLIC

MOTHER: I certify that I am the MOTHER of the child named above and that all statements made herein are true and correct to the best of my knowledge. I am signing this Affidavit voluntarily and of my own free will. I acknowledge that the man named above is the biological father of my child. I give my consent to have his name appear on the Certificate of Birth of my child. I declare and affirm that at the time of my child's birth, I was not married and had not been married in the 300 days prior to the birth of my child. I further acknowledge that I have received oral and written notice of the legal rights and consequences resulting from my acknowledging the paternity of my child and I understand this notice.

MOTHER'S SIGNATURE DATE:

WITNESS: ____________________

WITNESS: ____________________

NOTICE: NOTARY MUST SEE PHOTO ID

State of Louisiana, Parish of ____________________

Signed and Affirmed before me on this ____________________ day of

____________________, ____________________

Signature, then PRINT name of Notary

State Notary Registration Number My Commission Expires on

FATHER: I certify that I am the biological FATHER of the child named above and that all statements made herein are true and correct to the best of my knowledge. I am signing this Affidavit voluntarily and of my own free will. I acknowledge that I have received oral and written notice of the legal rights and consequences resulting from my acknowledging the paternity of my child and I understand this notice.

FATHER'S SIGNATURE DATE:

GUARDIAN'S SIGNATURE (If Father under age 18) DATE:

WITNESS: ____________________

WITNESS: ____________________

NOTICE: NOTARY MUST SEE PHOTO ID

State of Louisiana, Parish of ____________________

Signed and Affirmed before me on this ____________________ day of

____________________, ____________________

Signature, then PRINT name of Notary

State Notary Registration Number My Commission Expires on

DISTRIBUTION OF COPIES: Original to Registrar of Vital Records, Copies to Child Support, Mother and Father.

VRR-44 2-P (05/10

NOTICE OF ALTERNATIVES, RIGHTS AND RESPONSIBILITIES

This is a legal document. Signing the form is voluntary. Since this form has legal consequences, you may want to consult an attorney before signing.

When this Acknowledgement is properly completed and signed, the biological father's name is entered on the birth certificate in place of the name of the husband of the mother and the man becomes the legal father of the child. This acknowledgement has the same effect as a court order establishing paternity and can be used as a basis for entering a child support order.

If either of you is not sure that this man is the biological father of this child, you should not sign the form. You should have a genetic test.

Mothers who are married to someone other than the biological father when the child was conceived or born, or were divorced for less than three hundred days when the child was born, must use the VRR-44 3P (Three Party) affidavit form, instead of this form.

RIGHTS AND RESPONSIBLITIES OF A PARENT

- Either party has the right to request a genetic test to determine if the alleged father is the biological father of the child.
- The alleged father has the right to consult an attorney before signing an acknowledgement of paternity.
- If the alleged father does not acknowledge the child, the mother has the right to file a paternity suit to establish paternity.
- After the alleged father signs an acknowledgement of paternity, he has the right to pursue visitation with the child and the right to petition for custody.
- Once an acknowledgement of paternity is signed, the father may be obligated to provide child support for the child.
- Once an acknowledgement of paternity is signed, the child will have inheritance rights and any rights afforded children born in wedlock.
- A party who executed a notarial act of acknowledgement may rescind the act, without cause, before the earlier of the following:
    - Sixty days after the signing of the act, in a court hearing for the limited purpose of rescinding the acknowledgment.
    - A court hearing relating to the child, including a child support proceeding, in which the father is involved.

Thereafter, the acknowledgement of paternity may be voided only upon proof, by clear and convincing evidence, that such act was induced by fraud, duress, or material mistake of fact, or that the father is not the biological father.

BENEFITS FOR YOUR CHILD

Every child has the right to know his or her mother and father and benefit from a relationship with both parents.

Both of your names will appear on the child's birth certificate.

It will be easier for your child to learn medical histories of both parents and to benefit from health care coverage available to you.

It will be easier for your child to receive benefits such as dependent or survivor's benefits from the Veteran's Administration or from the Social Security Administration as well as share any estate should you die.

To indicate that you have read and understood this notice of alternatives, rights and responsibilities, please initial below. If you require further assistance you may call us at (504) 593 - 5100

Mother's Initials ______________________________

Father's Initials ______________________________

VRR-44 2-P (05/10)

DESIGNATION OF TUTOR

<u>TUTOR FOR MINOR CHILDREN (ON APPEARER'S DEATH) & TEMPORARY CUSTODY</u>

STATE OF LOUISIANA

PARISH OF ____________________

DESIGNATION OF TUTOR

BEFORE ME, a notary public, duly commissioned and qualified in the parish and state aforesaid, and in the presence of the undersigned witnesses, PERSONALLY CAME AND APPEARED:

Parent's name, of the full age of majority and domiciled in _________________ Parish, Louisiana, who declares that they have been married but once, to *Spouse's name*, with whom they live and reside, and who declared their permanent mailing address is *mailing address*,

Who, after being duly sworn did depose and say:

1. I have ________ *number* minor child(ren): *list minor children's names, and dates of birth*

   ____

   ____

   ____

2. If I am the sole remaining parent and any or all of my children are minors at the time of my death, I hereby appoint my *mother/sister/other relation, etc.*, ______________________ *insert name of relation of person to have tutorship*, to be the tutor of my minor children.
3. It is my intent that this designation remain in full force and effect unless revoked by me in writing.

THUS DONE AND SIGNED at ______________________, Louisiana, this _____ day of ____________________, 20____, in the presence of the undersigned competent witnesses and me, notary, after due reading of the whole.

WITNESSES:

________________________________ ________________________________

Print witness name Print name of parent

____

Print witness name

____

Notary name: ________________________________

Notary ID or Bar Roll No.: ______________

My Commission is for Life

PROVISIONAL CUSTODY BY MANDATE (CUSTODY UP TO 1 YEAR)

STATE OF LOUISIANA

PARISH OF ____________________

PROVISIONAL CUSTODY BY MANDATE[1]

BEFORE ME, the undersigned notary, duly commissioned and qualified in the state and parish aforesaid, and in the presence of the two witnesses whose names are hereunto subscribed, PERSONALLY CAME and appeared:

Mother of child and Father of child, both domiciliaries of Jefferson Parish and of the legal age of majority, each having been married only once and then to each other, and whose present mailing address is 12345 Airline Dr., Apt. B, Metairie, LA 70003,[2] who are the parents or persons having parental authority[3] of the following minor child(ren): *child's or children's names.*

Who, by these presents make, name, constitute, and appoint *(agent's name and mailing address)*, and grant provisional custody of the above named child(ren), to provide for the health, education, and welfare of the child as provided by the law on Provisional Custody by Mandate, specifically including the authority to:

INITIAL ALL APPLICABLE PROVISIONS *[all the principal(s) initial below]*:

____ (1) Consent to and authorize such medical care, treatment, or surgery as may be deemed necessary for the health, safety, and welfare of the child.

____ (2) Enroll the child in such schools or educational institutions as may be deemed necessary for his/her due and proper education.

---

[1] This form is used to temporarily turn over parental authority or tutorship to someone other than the parents or tutors. It allows the mandatary (agent who receives the appointment) to act in the place of the parent, to legally make educational, health care, and discipline decisions for the child. This authority can only be delegated for a year or a lesser-stated term. Although this document is in the form of a POA or mandate, and is properly titled as such, it is a personal document seriously affecting family structure for some time. *Unlike many POAs, it must be an authentic act* (to comply with the statutory form of LA R.S. 9:954). The principal(s) may withdraw this authority at any time, though written and notarized notice is strongly advisable (adapting the form "POA, revocation of agency by principal"), including even filing for registry if there is a possibility that mandatary will continue to act or third parties may rely on the original act. This act is also called "Provisional Custody Affidavit."

[2] Or an alternate appearance clause appropriate to the family situation. An appearance clause for this act should include principal's name, marital status, and mailing address.

[3] Or, in the event of divorce, separation, or illegitimacy, say "the parent(s) and the natural (co)tutor," depending on whether it is one or both. Or "grandparent awarded custody" or similar, if appropriate. The situation of "a natural tutor or cotutors with custody, but not yet judicially qualified, or a grandparent awarded custody of a child" is governed by R.S. 9:961, and its statutory form is in 9:962 rather than 9:954 for married parents (who, after a divorce, no longer have "parental authority" but instead are "natural cotutors").

Under LA R.S. 9:951, which also provides this form in 9:954, "A person having parental authority over a child may delegate the provisional custody of that child by written mandate to any natural person." Thus it appears that even one person having parental authority may make this act. But note that not every "parent" has "parental authority" since in most cases parental authority exists during marriage, and divorced parents have tutorship. Nevertheless, if one parent is incompetent or absent, the remaining parent retains parental authority.

PROVISIONAL CUSTODY BY MANDATE (CUSTODY UP TO 1 YEAR)

____ (3) Discipline the child in such reasonable manner as may be necessary for his/her proper rearing, supervision, and training.

____ (4) Do and perform all other such acts as may be necessary for the shelter, support, and general welfare of the child.

This Provisional Custody by Mandate will continue to be effective until ______________, 20___, or one year from date hereof, whichever period is shorter.

I agree that any third party who receives a copy of this document may rely upon the authority granted the agent as indicated herein and may act in reliance on such authority. Revocation or termination by operation of law is not effective as to a third party until he has actual knowledge thereof. I agree to indemnify and hold harmless the third party for any claims that arise against him because of reliance on this Provisional Custody by Mandate.

The undersigned agent does hereby accept the provisional custody of the children named herein.

THUS DONE AND PASSED at ________________________, Louisiana, this _____ day of __________________, 20____, in the presence of the undersigned competent witnesses who have signed their names together with the said Principal(s) and me, notary, after due reading of the whole.

WITNESSES:	PRINCIPALS/APPEARERS:
____________________________	____________________________
Print Name	Print Name
____________________________	____________________________
Print Name	Print Name
	AGENT/MANDATARY:
	____________________________
	Accepted by agent: Print Name[4]

____

Notary name: ________________________________

Notary ID or Bar Roll No.: ________________

My Commission is for Life

[4] Unlike other mandates or POAs, which allow acceptance of the appointment just in writing, the acceptance here should be part of an authentic act – either signed at this time before the same witnesses and notary (as this form is arranged), or in counterparts in a separate authentic signing in front of two witnesses and a notary. For convenience, and to prevent confusion on the part of recipients who rely on the document, it is usually executed in one act with all parties present.

NON-LEGAL CUSTODIAN'S AFFIDAVIT

STATE OF LOUISIANA

PARISH OF ____________________

AFFIDAVIT

BEFORE ME, the undersigned duly commissioned and qualified notary public, came and appeared the undersigned ______________________________________, Affiant.

INSTRUCTIONS: Completion of items 1 through 4 and the signing of the affidavit are sufficient to authorize educational services and school-related medical services for the named child. Completion of items 5 through 8 is additionally required to authorize any other medical services. Please print clearly.

The child named below lives in my home and I am 18 years of age or older.

1. Name of child:

2. Child's date of birth:

3. My name (adult giving authorization):

4. My home address:

5. [ ] I am a non-legal custodian.

6. Check one or both (for example, if one parent was advised and the other cannot be located):

[ ] I have advised the parent(s) or legal custodian(s) of the child of my intent to authorize the rendering of educational or medical services, and have received no objection.

[ ] I am unable to contact the parent(s) or legal custodian(s) of the child at this time, to notify them of my intended authorization.

7. Affiant's date of birth:

8. Affiant's Louisiana driver's license number or identification card number:

WARNING: Do not sign this form if any of the statements above are incorrect, or you will be committing a crime punishable by a fine, imprisonment, or both.

I declare under penalty of perjury under the laws of Louisiana that the foregoing is true and correct.

Signed: ______________________________________, Affiant

Date: ___________________________, 20____

NON-LEGAL CUSTODIAN'S AFFIDAVIT

SWORN TO AND SUBSCRIBED BEFORE ME this ______ day of _____________, 20____.

____

Notary Name: ____________________________________

Notary ID or Bar Roll No.: _______________

My Commission is for Life

Use of this affidavit is authorized by Louisiana R.S. 9:975.

NOTICES:

1. This declaration does not affect the rights of the child's parent or legal guardian regarding the care, custody and control of the child, and does not mean that the non-legal custodian has legal custody of the child.

2. A person who relies on this affidavit has no obligation to make any further inquiry or investigation.

3. This affidavit is not valid for more than one year after the date on which it is executed.

ADDITIONAL INFORMATION:

TO NON-LEGAL CUSTODIANS:

1. If the child stops living with you, you are required to notify anyone to whom you have given this affidavit as well as anyone of whom you have actual knowledge who received the affidavit from a third party.

2. If you do not have the information in item 8 (Louisiana driver's license or identification card), you must provide another form of identification such as your social security card number.

TO SCHOOL OFFICIALS:

The school district may require additional reasonable evidence that the non-legal custodian lives at the address provided in Item 4.

TO HEALTH CARE PROVIDERS AND HEALTH CARE SERVICE PLANS:

1. No person who acts in good faith reliance upon a non-legal custodian's affidavit to render educational or medical services, without actual knowledge of facts contrary to those stated in the affidavit, is subject to criminal prosecution or civil liability to any person, or subject to any professional disciplinary action, for such reliance if the applicable portions of the form are completed.

2. This affidavit does not confer dependency for health care coverage purposes.

EMANCIPATION OF MINOR (2 LIVING PARENTS)

NOTARIAL EMANCIPATION OF MINOR & PERMISSION TO MARRY

FORM WHEN 2 LIVING PARENTS:

The authentic act of limited emancipation is used when the parents or tutor(s) of a child 16 or 17 years old agree that the child should become emancipated, to be allowed to act as to certain enumerated acts or those acts which one of the majority has capacity to do. This form of emancipation can be performed before a notary and two witnesses without requiring judicial approval.

The executed act is not required to be filed for registry. Often if it is prepared in duplicate originals, or with true copies, so that the minor can have originals to present in situations where their capacity would be questioned, such as leasing an apartment. The parties may terminate or modify the act, but if so, the instrument doing so must be filed, in order to be effective against third parties (whether or not the original act was). The place of filing is in the parish where an immovable is located (to be effective toward third parties regarding the property) and, as to movables, where the minor is domiciled at the time of the revocation or modification. This filing puts the public on notice that the act of emancipation has changed or is no longer valid (where a third party may only know about the apparently valid document possessed by the minor). Acts taking under the emancipation before its effective revocation or modification remain valid.

A similar form, which is the next exemplar, is used when there is one living parent or tutor.

STATE OF LOUISIANA

PARISH OF ____________________

LIMITED EMANCIPATION

BEFORE ME, the undersigned notary, duly commissioned and qualified in the state and parish aforesaid, and in the presence of the two witnesses whose names are hereunto subscribed, PERSONALLY CAME and appeared:

Marianne Jane Smith, born Chilton, resident and domiciliary of St. Bernard Parish, whose mailing address is 613 W St Bernard Hwy, Chalmette, LA 70043, and who declares that she has been married but once, and then to David Wayne Smith, from whom she is divorced; and

David Wayne Smith, resident and domiciliary of St. Bernard Parish, and whose mailing address is 7417 N Peters St, Arabi, LA 70032, and who declares that he has been married but once, to Marianne Jane Smith, from whom he is divorced; and

EMANCIPATION OF MINOR (2 LIVING PARENTS)

Who declared that they are the natural co-tutors *[parents, if instead parental authority exists because they are still married]* of Barnaby Marcus Smith, born on January 1, 2006, and also appeared:

Barnaby Marcus Smith, a minor, age 16, who has never married, and who is a resident of and domiciled in Orleans Parish, whose mailing address is 4330 St Charles Ave, New Orleans, LA 70115,

And who declared unto me:

Availing themselves the laws of the State of Louisiana relative to the emancipation of minors, natural co-tutors *[parents, if parental authority exists]* hereby and by these presents emancipate and authorize the minor to make the following kinds of juridical acts:

All juridical acts except those juridical acts prohibited by law to be executed by a minor emancipated by authentic act.[1]

Except as provided herein, all other effects of minority shall continue.

THUS DONE, PASSED AND SIGNED, on the ______ day of __________________, 20_____, in ____________________, Louisiana, in the presence of the undersigned competent witnesses who have signed their names together with the appearers and me, notary, after due reading of the whole.

WITNESSES:

____________________	____________________
Print Name	MARIANNE JANE SMITH
____________________	____________________
Print Name	DAVID WAYNE SMITH
	____________________
	BARNABY MARCUS SMITH, minor

____

Notary Name: ______________________________

Notary ID or Bar Roll No.: ______________

My Commission is for Life

[1] If only certain acts are to be authorized by this emancipation, list those specifically in this place. Replace the bolded statement with a specific list of authorizations.

EMANCIPATION OF MINOR (1 LIVING PARENT)

STATE OF LOUISIANA

PARISH OF ____________________

LIMITED EMANCIPATION

BEFORE ME, the undersigned notary, duly commissioned and qualified in the state and parish aforesaid, and in the presence of the two witnesses whose names are hereunto subscribed, PERSONALLY CAME and appeared:

Beverly Evelyn Paternostro, born Luffy, resident and domiciliary of Orleans Parish, whose mailing address is 6363 St. Charles Ave., New Orleans, LA 70118, and who declares that she has been married but once, and then to David Wayne Smith, from whom she is widowed; and

Who declared that she is the mother and natural tutor of Cynthia Harmon Paternostro, born on January 1, 2006, and also appeared:

Cynthia Harmon Paternostro, a minor, age 16, who has never married, and who is a resident of and domiciled in Orleans Parish, whose mailing address is 225 Bourbon St., New Orleans, LA 70130,

And who declared unto me that they seek to avail themselves of the laws of the State of Louisiana relative to the emancipation of minors,

And the natural tutor[1] hereby and by these presents does emancipate and authorize the minor to make the following kinds of juridical acts:

All juridical acts except those juridical acts prohibited by law to be executed by a minor emancipated by authentic act.[2]

Except as provided herein, all other effects of minority shall continue.

THUS DONE, PASSED AND SIGNED, on the ______ day of ____________________, 20_____, in ______________________, Louisiana, in the presence of the undersigned competent witnesses who have signed their names together with the appearers and me, notary, after due reading of the whole.

WITNESSES:

---

[1] This form is appropriate when there is one tutor, here because she was widowed from the child's father. If parental authority exists in two parents, for example a married couple, use the form for that situation.

[2] If only certain acts are to be authorized by this emancipation, list those instead, in this place. For example: "Execute leases to be able to live independently in an apartment or similar housing, and to open checking accounts with a bank or similar financial institution."

EMANCIPATION OF MINOR (1 LIVING PARENT)

______________________	______________________
Print Name	BEVERLY EVELYN PATERNOSTRO
______________________	______________________
Print Name	CYNTHIA HARMON PATERNOSTRO

____

Notary Name: ______________________________

Notary ID or Bar Roll No.: ______________

My Commission is for Life

AFFIDAVIT OF PARENTAL CONSENT FOR MINOR TO MARRY

STATE OF LOUISIANA

PARISH OF ____________________

AFFIDAVIT OF PARENTAL CONSENT FOR MINOR TO MARRY[1]

BEFORE ME, the undersigned notary, duly commissioned and qualified in the state and parish aforesaid, and in the presence of the two witnesses whose names are hereunto subscribed, PERSONALLY CAME and appeared:

Husband and *Wife*, born *her maiden name*, both of the full age of majority and domiciled in Terrebonne Parish, Louisiana, and each of whom have been duly sworn, have declared that they have been married but once and then to each other, and who are living together in community, and who declared their permanent mailing address is 3211 Grand Caillou Rd., Houma, LA 70363;

And who declared that they are the parents of their minor child, *minor child's name,* who was born on *date of birth*, and that they give their consent to the marriage of their child to *person whom minor child is marrying*.

Thus done and passed, on the ____ day of ________________________, 20___, in ___ ________________________, Louisiana, in the presence of the undersigned competent witnesses who have signed their names together with the appearers and me, notary.

WITNESSES:	APPEARERS:
___________________________	___________________________
Print Name	Mother Print Name
___________________________	___________________________
Print Name	Father Print Name

SWORN TO AND SUBSCRIBED BEFORE ME, notary:

____

Notary Name: ________________________________

Notary ID or Bar Roll No.: ______________

My Commission is for Life

[1] This form only needs to be in writing, but some clerks may not issue the license without *notarized* permission. The minor child may not be under the age of sixteen. LA C.C. art. 1545 provides:" An officiant may not perform a marriage ceremony in which a minor sixteen or seventeen is a party unless the minor has *judicial authorization and* the written consent to marry of either: (1) Both of his parents. (2) The tutor of his person. (3) A person who has been awarded custody of the minor." This form can be adapted accordingly, with different appearers.

ADULT ADOPTION (NO LIVING PARENT)

<u>NOTARIAL ADULT ADOPTION & ADOPTEES SEEKING BIOLOGICAL PARENT</u>

<u>FORM WHEN NO LIVING PARENT: FOR STEP-PARENT TO ADOPT A STEP-CHILD 18+:</u>

This form is used when the parent of the "child" (an adult offspring/adoptee) is no longer alive. The now-adopting parent must have been married to the original parent at his or her death. Another form, found next in this collection, applies when the adopting parent is the current spouse of a (live) parent.

Both situations essentially allow adopting by notarial act, rather than with court approval, a <u>stepchild</u> who is old enough to have capacity and consent to being adopted. If the adult offspring/adoptee is married, their spouse also appears and consents, as noted below. <u>See the related file</u> (next exemplar) for explanations and the further procedure for a name change. The act must be in authentic form and has immediate effect only when filed for registry (in any parish).

STATE OF LOUISIANA

PARISH OF ____________________

AUTHENTIC ACT OF ADULT ADOPTION

BEFORE ME, the undersigned notary public, duly commissioned and qualified in the parish and state above, and in the presence of the undersigned competent witnesses whose names are hereunto subscribed, PERSONALLY CAME and appeared:

Michael Louis Brady, a single man who is of the age of majority and domiciled in Jefferson Parish, Louisiana, residing at 197 Marywood Court, Kenner, LA 70062 as his permanent mailing address, who declares he has been married twice, first to Ima Missing Brady, deceased, and then to Carol Anne Brady, deceased; and who declares that he hereby adopts Greg Ned Stanfield to be his child for all legal and moral purposes.

Also appearing is Greg Ned Stanfield, a married man, domiciled in Orleans Parish and residing at 191 Chef Menteur Hwy, New Orleans, LA 70126 as his permanent mailing address, who declares he has been married but once, and then to Melissa Sue Stanfield, born Rogers, with whom he resides; and who declares that he is of the age of majority and hereby consents to being adopted.

[Assuming Greg is married, the above has changed his marital status and history, adding her signature below. These additions can be removed if Greg is unmarried.] Also appearing for purposes of concurring in this adoption is Melissa Sue Stanfield, born Rogers, a married

woman who has been married but once, and then to Greg Ned Stanfield, with whom she resides; and who hereby signs this act as a concurrence in this adoption.

Appearers declare that Greg Ned Stanfield is the biological child of Carol Anne Brady, born Atlas, deceased, born of her marriage to Daniel Alan Martin, deceased.

The adoptive parent and the adoptive adult child, each declare their intent to establish the legal relationship of parent and child between them, to which end the adoptive parent does consent to adopt, and hereby adopts, the adoptive child; and the adoptive child does hereby consent to be adopted, and is adopted by the adoptive parent.

It is further declared that the name of Greg Ned Stanfield is changed to Greg Stanfield Brady, which shall be his true and lawful name, having been born on February 14, 1992 in St. Tammany Parish, Louisiana.

THUS DONE, PASSED AND SIGNED, on the _____ day of __________________, 20_____, in ____________________, Louisiana, in the presence of the undersigned competent witnesses, who have signed their names together with the appearers and me, notary, after due reading of the whole.

WITNESSES:

____________________________	____________________________________
Print Name	MICHAEL LOUIS BRADY, Adoptive Spouse
____________________________	____________________________________
Print Name	GREG NED STANFIELD, Adoptive Child
	____________________________________
	MELISSA SUE STANFIELD, Concurring Spouse

____

Notary Name: ____________________________________

Notary ID or Bar Roll No.: ______________

My Commission is for Life

ADULT ADOPTION (ADOPTIVE STEP-PARENT IS MARRIED TO PARENT)

This form is used when the biological parent[1] *of the "child" (an adult offspring/adoptee) is still alive, and married to the now-adopting parent. (Another form, found in this collection, applies when the adopting parent is the surviving spouse of a deceased biological parent.) This permits adopting by notarial act, rather than with court approval, a* <u>*stepchild*</u> *who is old enough to have capacity and consent to being adopted. If the biological parent is still alive, all three parties (biological parent; their spouse/adopting parent; their child/adoptee) must appear and consent. In addition, if the adult offspring/adoptee is married, their spouse also appears and consents, as noted below.*

The act must be in authentic form and has immediate effect only when filed for registry (and is actually effective from the date of signing if it is filed within five days). It is filed with the clerk of court in any parish. Unlike most notarial acts, the notary does not have an affirmative duty to file it; the responsibility falls on the parties. But if the notary undertakes the duty and fails to follow through, significant liability may be incurred.

In the process (and in this act), the adult adoptee may change their name, under R.S. 9:465. In such case, a clause should be added to that effect, declaring the new name. An example of that clause is included below but may be removed if no change is desired. If the adult adoptee wishes to further change their name on their birth certificate, under R.S. 40:75, the registrar of vital records will require an "affidavit of no objection" by the district attorney, and submission to the registrar of both the DA's affidavit and a stamped filed copy of this act.

STATE OF LOUISIANA

PARISH OF ____________________

AUTHENTIC ACT OF ADULT ADOPTION

BEFORE ME, the undersigned notary public, duly commissioned and qualified in the parish and state above, and in the presence of the undersigned competent witnesses whose names are hereunto subscribed, PERSONALLY CAME and appeared:

Michael Louis Brady, a married man who is of the age of majority and domiciled in Jefferson Parish, Louisiana, residing at 197 Marywood Court, Kenner, LA 70062 as his permanent mailing address, who declares he has been married twice, first to Ima Missing Brady, from whom he is widowed, and then to Carol Anne Brady, born McGill, to whom he remains married and resides with her at the above address; and who declares that he hereby adopts Greg Ned Stanfield to be his child for all legal and moral purposes.

Also appearing is Greg Ned Stanfield, a single man having never been married, domiciled in Orleans Parish and residing at 191 Chef Menteur Hwy., New Orleans, LA 70126 as his

---

[1] In these notes, to avoid confusion with the current adoption process, the original parent to the adult-child is called the "biological parent." In fact, the parent may also be a legal parent by adoption, originally, but calling her that in this example is unwieldy. Just to be clear, though, the original parent consenting herein is a parent lawfully either by biology, adoption, or court order.

permanent mailing address, who declares that he is of the age of majority and hereby consents to being adopted.

Also appearing for purposes of concurring in this adoption is Carol Anne Brady, spouse of the adoptive parent Michael Louis Brady, a married woman who has been married but twice, first to James H. Stanfield, from whom she is widowed, and then to Michael Louis Brady, with whom she resides, who declares she is the biological parent of Gred Ned Stanfield; and who hereby signs this authentic act of adoption as a concurrence in the adoption.

[If Greg is married, change his marital status and history above, adding spouse name there; then add the following clause and, below, add a signature line for her to concur.] Also appearing for purposes of concurring in this adoption is Melissa Sue Stanfield, born Rogers, a married woman who has been married but once, and then to Greg Ned Stanfield, with whom she resides; and who hereby signs this act as a concurrence in this adoption.

The adoptive parent and the adoptive adult child, each declare their intent to establish the legal relationship of parent and child between them, to which end the adoptive parent does consent to adopt, and hereby adopts, the adoptive child; and the adoptive child does hereby consent to be adopted, and is adopted by the adoptive parent.

It is further declared that the name of Greg Ned Stanfield is changed to Greg Stanfield Brady, which shall be his true and lawful name, having been born on February 14, 1992 in St. Tammany Parish, Louisiana.

THUS DONE, PASSED AND SIGNED, on the _____ day of __________________, 20_____, in ___________________, Louisiana, in the presence of the undersigned competent witnesses, who have signed their names together with the appearers and me, notary, after due reading of the whole.

WITNESSES:

____________________________	____________________________________
Print Name	MICHAEL LOUIS BRADY, Adoptive Spouse
____________________________	____________________________________
Print Name	CAROL ANNE BRADY, Concurring Spouse
	____________________________________
	GREG NED STANFIELD, Adoptive Child

____

Notary Name: ________________________________

Notary ID or Bar Roll No.: _______________

My Commission is for Life

ADOPTED PERSON SEEKING BIOLOGICAL PARENT

UNITED STATES OF AMERICA
VOLUNTARY ADOPTION REGISTRY
STATE OF ______________________
PARISH/COUNTY OF_______________

FOR THE MATCHING OF PERSONS AFFECTED BY ADOPTION

AFFIDAVIT OF ADOPTED PERSON

BEFORE ME, the undersigned Notary Public, personally came and appeared:

____
(Current Full Name of Adopted Adult)

Who, after being duly sworn and deposed, did say that: He/she is a ________________________ adopted adult
(Race and Sex)

born on_____________________________ at ____
(Month, Day, Year, Hour) (Hospital, If Known)
located in

____, to ____,
(City, State) (Full Name of Biological Father, If Known)

whose race was _______ and whose birthplace was: ____,
(City, State)

and to: ____ whose race was _____________
(Full Maiden Name of Biological Mother, If Known)

and whose birthplace was ____;
(City, State)

That the birth was ________________;
(Single/Plural)

That the adopted person's legal adoptive name was ______________________________________;
(Legal Adoptive Name of Adopted Person)

That the full name of his/her adoptive father was ____
(Full Name of Adoptive Father)

and the full maiden name of his/her adoptive mother was ____;
(Full Name of Adoptive Mother)

That the name of the placement agency handling the adoption, if applicable, was _________________
______________________________ (Name of Placement Agency) located at
____;
(City, State)

ADOPTED PERSON SEEKING BIOLOGICAL PARENT

That the adopted person was adopted by virtue of a judgment rendered in ____________________
(Court)
on ______________________, in ________________________________, Louisiana;
(Date) (City)

That the adopted person does not have a biological sibling under the age of 18 adopted by the same adoptive parents;

That the adopted person desires to be contacted at the following address:

____, and
(Street, City, State, Zip)

telephone (Home) ( ) _______________(Work) ( ) ______________(Other)( ) ____________,

and desires to locate his/her biological parent(s) and/or biological sibling(s) through the Voluntary Adoption Registry.

_________________________________ _________________________________
Witness Signature Adopted Person Signature

____
Witness Signature

SWORN TO AND SUBSCRIBED BEFORE ME,
this ____day of ______________________, 20____, at _________.
(Mo. (Year) (Time)

____
NOTARY PUBLIC

FOR OFFICE USE ONLY

Date Received: ____________________

Affidavit Number: ________________
Form 447-A
Reissued: 10/2010 Replacing: 08/2008

DEPARTMENT OF CHILDREN AND FAMILY SERVICES VOLUNTARY ADOPTION REGISTRY PURSUANT TO LA. CHILDREN'S CODE HANDBOOK ARTICLES 1270-1278

NOTE TO NOTARY: This form may be hand or type written. Please affix your notarial seal.

ADOPTED PERSON SEEKING BIOLOGICAL PARENT

INSTRUCTIONS TO APPLICANT: Unknown items shall be left blank or completed as "Unknown." Do not sign except in the presence of a notary.

ELIGIBLE PERSONS

Eligibility is limited to adoptions that were finalized in Louisiana and to the following persons:

1. The adopted person, if he or she is 18 years of age or older.
2. Any biological sibling, at least 18 years of age, of an adopted person.
3. The biological parent(s) of the adopted person.
4. The parents or siblings of a deceased biological parent.
5. The adoptive parent(s) of a minor or deceased adopted person.
6. Any descendent (or his parents if a minor) of a deceased biological parent or a deceased adopted person.

No registration by an adopted person shall be permitted until all biological siblings who were adopted by the same adoptive parents have reached the age of 18 years.

REGISTRATION – FEES AND PROCEDURES

1. Registration shall be by notarized affidavit submitted to the Department of Children and Family Services at the address below.

2. Parent(s), sibling(s), and descendents (or his parent if a minor) of a deceased biological parent shall provide proof of relationship to the deceased (birth certificates) and proof of death of the deceased (death certificate or obituary).

3. Adoptive parents shall provide proof of relationship to the minor or deceased adopted person (birth certificate or adoption decree) and if applicable, proof of death of the adopted person (death certificate or obituary).

4. A descendent (or his parent if a minor) of a deceased adopted person shall provide proof of relationship to the adopted person (birth certificates) and proof of death of the adopted person (death certificate or obituary).

5. The affidavit must be accompanied by a check or money order payable to the Department of Children and Family Services, (DCFS) in the amount of $25.00. The affidavit and payment are mailed to:

ADOPTED PERSON SEEKING BIOLOGICAL PARENT

DEPARTMENT OF CHILDREN AND FAMILY SERVICES
VOLUNTARY ADOPTION REGISTRY
P. O. BOX 3318
BATON ROUGE, LA 70821

THE MATCH PROCESS AND THE MANDATORY COUNSELING REQUIREMENT

The Registry office enters registrant information into a computer database program in the Registry office (not online) which facilitates the match process. If after registration there should be a match, both parties will be required to complete an hour of counseling with one of the following before they will be put into contact with one another: a licensed clinical social worker, a social worker acting in the employ of a licensed adoption agency, a licensed professional counselor, a licensed psychologist, a medical psychologist, a licensed psychiatrist, or a licensed marriage and family therapist.

Upon receipt of the completed counseling forms (Form 447-J) from both parties, the Registry office will submit a written letter only to the counselor of the adopted person (or the counselor of the adoptive parent or descendent in the case of a minor or deceased adopted person) providing the identifying contact information of the registered parties. This counselor shall then contact the matched parties in a careful and confidential manner to give them the information to contact each other.

NOTIFICATION OF DEATH

In any case where one or both of the birth parents are deceased, or where the adopted person is deceased and when this fact is known by the Registry, this information shall be disclosed by the Registry to any person who has registered.

Form 447-A
Reissued: 10/2010 Replacing: 10/2008

7 • MOVABLES AND VEHICLE TRANSFERS

BILL OF SALE OF A MOVABLE[1]

STATE OF LOUISIANA

PARISH OF ____________________

BEFORE ME, the undersigned Notary Public, duly commissioned and qualified in and for the parish and state aforesaid, personally came and appeared:

____,

Seller, of legal age, who hereby sells and delivers with full and general warranty of title unto:

____,

Buyer, of legal age, the following movable property:

Make: ____

Model: ____

Year: _________________________Color: _________________________

VIN: ____

Vehicle Sale Price: $_________________________[2]

Seller warrants that there are no mortgages, liens or encumbrances of any kind against the movable property sold or any accessories attached thereon.

This movable is sold as-is with no further warranties other than as stated above.

Signed and sold on this _____ day of ___________________, 20____.

______________________________________ ______________________________________

SELLER BUYER

____

Notary Name: ____________________________________

Notary ID or Bar Roll No.: _____________

My Commission is for Life

---

[1] Can be adapted for boats, motors and trailers. Or for boats/motors download an official Wildlife & Fisheries form: https://www.wlf.louisiana.gov/assets/Boating/Files/Title-and-Register-Your-Boat/bill_of_sale_of_boat-motor.pdf

[2] If this price does not appear to be fair market value, the OMV may reject the sale as a "disguised donation." Sales for "$1 and further consideration" are really *donations*, and the Act of Donation should be used instead. If the price seems very low but for good reason, such as significant accident damage, also attach "Affidavit justifying selling price" so that it is clear this is not fraud or a donation.

AFFIDAVIT JUSTIFYING SELLING PRICE

STATE OF LOUISIANA

PARISH OF ________________

AFFIDAVIT JUSTIFYING SELLING PRICE

BEFORE ME, the undersigned notary public, duly commissioned and qualified in the parish and state aforesaid, appeared the undersigned

____, SELLER, and

____, BUYER,

Who, after being first duly sworn, deposed and stated:

Affiant Owner/Seller sold, transferred and conveyed to affiant Buyer, for the true sales price of $_____________________, the following described vehicle:

VIN OR SERIAL #:____

MAKE/MODEL: __________________________ YEAR: ___________

Further, that the reason why this titled vehicle was sold for the above-stated price is due to the following defects:

____

____

____

______________________________ ________________________________

SELLER BUYER

SWORN TO AND SUBSCRIBED BEFORE ME this ______ day of _________________, 20_____

____

Notary Name: ________________________________

Notary ID or Bar Roll No.: ___________

My Commission is for Life

AFFIDAVIT OF CORRECTION, SIMPLE

STATE OF LOUISIANA

PARISH OF ________________

AFFIDAVIT OF CORRECTION

BEFORE ME, the undersigned notary public, came and appeared the undersigned Affiant:

____

Who, after being duly sworn, deposed and said that the following error was corrected by hand on the certificate of title:[1]

MISTAKEN INPUT: ____

____

____ and

The correction by hand to this, writing in the following correct information, is

____

____

____.

____

Affiant[2]

SWORN TO AND SUBSCRIBED BEFORE ME this ______ day of ___________________, 20_____

____

Notary Name: ___________________________

Notary ID or Bar Roll No.: ___________

My Commission is for Life

[1] Or Act of Donation, or other document specified here that is required to be submitted to the OMV.

[2] OMV policy may require that both seller and buyer (or donor and donee) sign this act, so create two signature lines if possible, and label each signator as "buyer," "seller," etc. (An OMV agent is more likely to accept this act signed by only seller or buyer if the error is a mere 'typo.') Alternatively, the affiant may be the original notary who makes the changes on the title and executes this affidavit before a second notary. Never use white-out on a title, bill of sale, or act of donation; instead, cross through the mistaken text and write the correct text above it.

This simple affidavit is best used when there are only one or two errors hand-corrected, as is typical. See also next page for a more complete version, more appropriate to replacing complicated or multiple mistakes.

AFFIDAVIT OF CORRECTION, CHECKLIST

STATE OF LOUISIANA

PARISH OF ____________________

AFFIDAVIT OF CORRECTION

Before me, the undersigned Notary Public, personally came and appeared:

____

Who deposed and said that the erasure/strikeover/correction on the [check one]

( ) Manufacturers Certificate of Origin
( ) Certificate of Title # __________________________
( ) Act of Donation
( ) Title Application
( ) Bill of Sale dated ____________________________

On the following described vehicle:

____

Year Make Model Color VIN

Was due to the following: [check *any* applicable]

( ) Typographical error (explained below)
( ) Buyer's name printed incorrectly; correct name should be ________________________________
( ) Seller's name printed incorrectly; correct name should be ________________________________
( ) VIN was typed/written incorrectly; correct VIN should be ________________________________
( ) Seller assigned title to him/herself
( ) Seller assigned title to wrong party
( ) Seller made strikeover in purchaser's name
( ) Odometer reading is missing, should be ______________________ miles in whole digits
( ) ______________________'s name is misspelled; correct spelling is ________________________
( ) Date is incorrect; correct date is ______________________________
( ) Vehicle donated; "for the sum of $" incorrectly entered on title, correct sum should be "DONATION"
( ) Vehicle selling price incorrectly entered on title, correct selling price (sum) should be $ ___________
( ) Assignment placed in error into dealer's assignment section
( ) Notary signed in wrong place, should have signed ____________________________________
( ) ____________________________ and ___________________________ are one and the same.
( ) Other (or further explanation of other item checked):

____
____
____

NO FRAUD INTENDED

____
Affiant verifying correction

SWORN TO AND SUBSCRIBED BEFORE ME this ____ day of __________________, 20____

____
Notary Name: ________________________________
Notary ID or Bar Roll No.: ______________
My Commission is for Life

AFFIDAVIT OF NON-RESIDENCY

STATE OF LOUISIANA

PARISH OF ____________________

AFFIDAVIT OF NON-RESIDENCY IN LOUISIANA[1]

BEFORE ME, the undersigned notary public, duly commissioned in and for the parish and state aforesaid, personally came and appeared:

____

AFFIANT

Who after being sworn did swear and depose that Affiant is not a resident of the State of Louisiana. The Affiant's present residential address is:

____

____

____

Affiant

SWORN TO AND SUBSCRIBED BEFORE ME this ______ day of _______________, 20____

____

Notary name: ___________________________________

Notary ID or Bar Roll No.: _______________

My Commission is for Life

[1] A form to be submitted to Louisiana OMV when one of the parties to the transaction is from out-of-state. Instead, a photocopy of the out-of-state person's driver's license (front and back) may be substituted for this affidavit.

ODOMETER DISCLOSURE STATEMENT

LOUISIANA DEPARTMENT OF PUBLIC SAFETY
OFFICE OF MOTOR VEHICLES

ODOMETER DISCLOSURE STATEMENT

Federal and State law require that you state the mileage upon transfer of ownership. Failure to complete or providing a false statement may result in fine and/or imprisonment.

I, ____________________ certify that the odometer now reads __________
Seller (Print name) (no tenths)
miles and to the best of my knowledge that it reflects the actual mileage of the vehicle described below, unless one of the following statements is checked.

☐ (1) I hereby certify that to the best of my knowledge the odometer reading reflects the amount of **MILEAGE IN EXCESS OF ITS MECHANICAL LIMITS.**

☐ (2) I hereby certify that the odometer reading is **NOT THE ACTUAL MILEAGE. WARNING - ODOMETER DISCREPANCY.**

Make__________________Model__________________Body Type____________

Year ________________

Vehicle Identification Number ____

SELLER'S Signature ____

Printed Name of Seller ____

Seller's Address ____
(Street)

____
(City) (State) (ZIP Code)

BUYER's Signature ____

Printed Name of Buyer ____

Representative Name (of Company) ___________________________________

Buyer's Address ____
(Street)

____
(City) (State) (ZIP Code)

Date of Statement____

DPSMV 1606 (R 10/94)

ACT OF DONATION OF MOVABLE (ALL PARTIES PRESENT)

ACT OF DONATION OF MOVABLE: ALL PARTIES PRESENT TO SIGN

STATE OF LOUISIANA

PARISH OF ____________________

ACT OF DONATION OF A MOVABLE

BEFORE ME, the undersigned notary public, duly commissioned and qualified in and for the parish and state aforesaid, and before the undersigned competent witnesses personally came and appeared:

____,

DONOR

Donor, of legal age, who hereby donates and delivers with full and general warranty of title unto:

____,

DONEE

Donee, of legal age, who hereby accepts this donation of the following described movable property:

____

MAKE MODEL YEAR VIN

The relationship between Donor and Donee is as follows: ______________________________

The value of the movable property donated herein is $ ____________________.

Donor warrants that there are no mortgages, liens, or encumbrances of any kind against the movable property donated or any accessories attached thereon.

THUS DONE AND SIGNED at ____________________, Louisiana, this _____ day of ____________________, 20____, in the presence of the undersigned competent witnesses, after due reading of the whole.

WITNESSES:

______________________________ ______________________________

Print name DONOR

______________________________ ______________________________

Print name DONEE

____

Notary name: ______________________________

Notary ID or Bar Roll No.: ________________

My Commission is for Life

ACT OF DONATION OF MOVABLE (BY BUSINESS)

STATE OF LOUISIANA

PARISH OF ____________________

ACT OF DONATION OF A MOVABLE

BEFORE ME, the undersigned notary public, duly commissioned and qualified in and for the parish and state aforesaid, and before the undersigned competent witnesses personally came and appeared:

____ (Corp., LLC, Partnership, etc.), appearing through its ________________________________ (representative, member, etc.), whose name is ____, does hereby donate and delivers with full and general warranty of title unto:

____,

DONEE

Donee, of legal age, who accepts donation of the following described movable property:

____

MAKE MODEL YEAR VIN

The relationship between Donor and Donee is as follows: ______________________________

The value of the movable property donated herein is $ __________________

Donor warrants that there are no mortgages, liens, or encumbrances of any kind against the movable property donated or any accessories attached thereon.

THUS DONE AND SIGNED at ________________, Louisiana, this _____ day of ______________, 20____, in the presence of the undersigned competent witnesses, after due reading of the whole.

WITNESSES:

______________________________ ________________________________

Print name Person signing: ________________________________,
authorized representative of ____________________

______________________________ ________________________________

Print name DONEE

____

Notary name: ______________________________

Notary ID or Bar Roll No.: _______________

My Commission is for Life

ACT OF DONATION OF MOVABLE (DONEE NOT PRESENT)

STATE OF LOUISIANA

PARISH OF ____________________

ACT OF DONATION OF A MOVABLE

BEFORE ME, the undersigned notary public, duly commissioned and qualified in and for the parish and state aforesaid, and before the undersigned competent witnesses personally came and appeared:

____,

DONOR

Donor, of legal age, who hereby donates and delivers with full and general warranty of title unto:

____,

DONEE

Donee, of legal age, who upon signature accepts donation of the following described movable property:

____

MAKE MODEL YEAR VIN

The relationship between Donor and Donee is as follows: ______________________________

The value of the movable property donated herein is $ __________________

Donor warrants that there are no mortgages, liens, or encumbrances of any kind against the movable property donated or any accessories attached thereon.

THUS DONE AND SIGNED at ________________, Louisiana, this _____ day of ______________, 20____, in the presence of the undersigned competent witnesses, after due reading of the whole.

WITNESSES:

______________________________ ________________________________

Print name DONOR

____

Print name

____

Notary name: ______________________________

Notary ID or Bar Roll No.: ______________

My Commission is for Life

ACCEPTANCE:

DONEE, ______________________________________, hereby accepts the donation of the above movable, accepting ownership and all terms stated in this Act of Donation, as signed below.

DATED: __________________, 20_____ ________________________________

DONEE

WHAT FOLLOWS IN THIS BOOK ARE:

1. OMV FORM FOR DONATION OF VEHICLE which can be used instead of these forms.
2. OMV FORM FOR AFFIDAVIT OF HEIRSHIP allowing heirs to own car outside of succession.

Louisiana Department of Public Safety and Corrections

OFFICE OF MOTOR VEHICLES

ACT OF DONATION OF A MOVABLE

STATE OF LOUISIANA **PARISH OF** ____________________________

BEFORE ME, the undersigned notary public, duly commissioned and qualified in and for the parish and state aforesaid, and before the undersigned competent witnesses personally came and appeared:

____

DONOR

Donor, of legal age, who hereby donates and delivers with full and general warranty of title unto:

____

DONEE

Donee, of legal age, who hereby accepts the within donation of the following described movable property:

____

MAKE MODEL YEAR VIN

The relationship between Donor and Donee is as follows: ________________________________

The value of the movable property donated herein is $____________________.

Donor warrants that there are no mortgages, liens, or encumbrances of any kind against the movable property donated or any accessories attached thereon.

SIGNED on this ___________day of _____________________, 20____.

____ Witness Signature/Printed Name

____ Donor Signature/ Printed Name

____ Witness Signature/Printed Name

____ Donee Signature/ Printed Name

____

Notary Signature Notary Printed Name Notary ID

DPSMV1699 R0518

LOUISIANA DEPARTMENT OF PUBLIC SAFETY & CORRECTIONS
OFFICE OF MOTOR VEHICLES
Affidavit of Heirship

This form is to be used only when a vehicle is registered in the name of a deceased owner & the heirs desire to confirm their ownership interest.

THIS IS TO CERTIFY THAT ____ (deceased owner),
(Copy of Death Certificate or Published Obituary Attached)
hereinafter referred to as decedent, is the registered owner of the following described vehicle:

____
Year Make Model Vehicle Identification No.

____
Louisiana Title No. Current Louisiana License No.

DECLARATION

Upon my/our oath, I/we solemnly swear that the information on this form and the following statements as checked below are true and correct:

☐ The decedent died intestate (i.e., no will).

☐ The decedent died testate (copy of will or notarized statement by one in lawful possession of the original summarizing the disposition of vehicles contained in the will attached).

☐ Certificate of title attached.

☐ Certificate of title cannot be located and is, therefore, not available.

Under penalties provided for providing false reports, I/we declare that this affidavit (including any accompanying schedules and statements) is to the best of my/our knowledge and belief, a true, correct, and complete identification of death circumstances and legal heir ship of the named decedent.

ENTER NAME & ADDRESS OF **SURVIVING SPOUSE**

Name ______________________________
Address ______________________________
City & State ______________________________
Telephone (________) ______________________________
Signature ______________________________

Sworn and subscribed before me
this __________ day of ___________ , 20 ______

____
Notary Public Signature, Printed Name ID # Parish (County) State

ENTER NAME & ADDRESS OF **HEIR OR LEGATEE**
If Minor, Must List Age

Name ______________________________ Age: ___________
Address ______________________________
City & State ______________________________
Relation to Decedent ______________________________
Signature ______________________________

Sworn and subscribed before me
this __________ day of ___________ , 20 ______

____
Notary Public Signature, Printed Name ID# Parish (County) State

ENTER NAME & ADDRESS OF **HEIR OR LEGATEE**
If Minor, Must List Age

Name ______________________________ Age: ___________
Address ______________________________
City & State ______________________________
Relation to Decedent ______________________________
Signature ______________________________

Sworn and subscribed before me
this __________ day of ___________ , 20 ______

____
Notary Public Signature, Printed Name ID# Parish (County) State

ENTER NAME & ADDRESS OF **HEIR OR LEGATEE**
If Minor, Must List Age

Name ______________________________ Age: ___________
Address ______________________________
City & State ______________________________
Relation to Decedent ______________________________
Signature ______________________________

Sworn and subscribed before me
this __________ day of ___________, 20 ______

____
Notary Public Signature, Printed Name ID# Parish (County) State

Heirs And Legatees Must Be Listed
(If more than four, please attach supplementary list)

If there is only one surviving heir and he/she wishes to title the vehicle in his/her name, this affidavit with attachments will be acceptable. If one of the heirs is a surviving spouse and he/she wishes to transfer the vehicle to a new owner, this affidavit of heirship must be completed by him/her as well as all other heirs, but only the surviving spouse is required to execute a notarized bill of sale or act of donation. If there is no surviving spouse and the sale or donation is to a new owner, a bill of sale or act of donation must be executed by all heirs.

The applicant must surrender the previous title, if available.

Fees are $68.50 for transfer of title, $8.00 service handling fee, and license fees as applicable. If a UCC-1 form is submitted to record a lien, an additional fee of $15.00 must be submitted. If any other type security agreement is submitted, an additional fee of $10.00 must be submitted. If a lien was reflected on the title of the decedent, the original paid note or a release of lien on the lienholder's letterhead is required. If a consideration is expressed in a bill of sale, sales tax must also be computed or paid.

Please send check or money order made payable to Office of Motor Vehicles to cover any fees/taxes due. **PLEASE DO NOT SEND CASH.**

DPSMV 1696 (R 09/15)

BILL OF SALE FOR FIREARMS

FIREARMS[1]

LOUISIANA FIREARM BILL OF SALE

PART 1 - THE PARTIES

SELLER

Full Name: ______________________ Driver's License No: __________

Street Address: ______________________ City: __________

Louisiana, ZIP: __________ Phone: ____ -- ________

BUYER

Full Name: ______________________ Driver's License No: __________

Street Address: ______________________ City: __________

Louisiana, ZIP: __________ Phone: ____ -- ________

PART 2 - FIREARM(S)

1. Cost ($): __________ Make: __________ Model: __________

   Action: ☐ Bolt | ☐ Semi-Automatic | ☐ Pump | ☐ Lever | ☐ Break

   Caliber/Gauge: __________ Serial Number (SN): __________

2. **Cost ($)**: __________ Make: __________ Model:

   ____

   Action: ☐ Bolt | ☐ Semi-Automatic | ☐ Pump | ☐ Lever | ☐ Break

   Caliber/Gauge: __________ Serial Number (SN): __________

3. **Cost ($)**: __________ Make: __________ Model:

   ____

   Action: ☐ Bolt | ☐ Semi-Automatic | ☐ Pump | ☐ Lever | ☐ Break

   Caliber/Gauge: __________ Serial Number (SN): __________

TOTAL COST ($): __________

[1] For La. Concealed Handgun Permit Registration, an extensive packet of 3 forms to be filled out then notarized, download at https://www.lsp.org/media/jnmdvqdt/chapplication.pdf

BILL OF SALE FOR FIREARMS

PART 3 - PURCHASE / TRADE

☐ - Seller accepts monetary funds in the amount of $ ____________________ to be paid on:

- ☐ The date of this bill of sale, known as ____________________ (mm/dd/yyyy)
- ☐ At a future date, no later than ____________________ (mm/dd/yyyy)
- ☐ Other: ___________________________________

☐ - Seller accepts a trade for the firearm(s), described as:

____

PART 4 - BUYER'S DISCLOSURE

Buyer declares the following statements are true and that he/she:

- Is not under the legal age to own a firearm;
- Has never been convicted in any court of a crime punishable by imprisonment for a term exceeding 1 year;
- Is not a fugitive from justice;
- Is not an unlawful user of or addicted to any controlled substance;
- Has never been adjudicated as a mental defective or has been committed to a mental institution;
- Is not an alien illegally or unlawfully in the United States or an alien admitted to the United States under a nonimmigrant visa;
- Has not been discharged from the Armed Forces under dishonorable conditions;
- Having been a citizen of the United States, has never renounced his or her citizenship;
- Is not subject to a court order that restrains the person from harassing, stalking, or threatening an intimate partner or child of such intimate partner;
- Has not been convicted of a misdemeanor crime of domestic violence;
- Can lawfully receive, possess, ship, or transport a firearm; and
- Is not a person who is under indictment or information for a crime punishable by imprisonment for a term exceeding 1 year.

Buyer's Signature: ____

BILL OF SALE FOR FIREARMS

PART 5 - SELLER'S DISCLOSURE

Seller declares the following statements are true and that he/she:

- Has verified that the firearm details are correct and the serial number is legible;
- Is the lawful owner of the firearm and has the legal right to sell the firearm;
- Has no knowledge of defects in the firearm;
- Believes that the firearm is fit to be used for its intended purpose;
- Has never been used in a manner of questionable or certain illegality; and
- Assumes no responsibility after the transfer of ownership has taken place.

Buyer's Signature: ____

PART 6 - SIGNATURES

On __________________ (mm/dd/yyyy), the buyer and seller agreed to the above described terms and conditions for the sale/trade/exchange of the firearm.

Seller's Signature: ____

Printed Name: ____

Buyer's Signature: ____

Printed Name: ____

- -

WITNESS 1 Signature: ____

Printed Name: ____

WITNESS 2 Signature: ____

Printed Name: ____

BILL OF SALE FOR FIREARMS

PART 7 - ACKNOWLEDGMENTS OF NOTARY PUBLIC (IF APPLICABLE)

STATE OF LOUISIANA

PARISH OF____________________

On ____________________________ (mm/dd/yyyy), before me appeared ___________________________________, as **SELLER** on this Bill of Sale who proved to me through government-issued photo identification to be the above-named person; and in my presence executed the foregoing instrument and acknowledged that he/she executed the same as his/her free act and deed.

____

Notary Name: ______________________________

Notary ID or Bar Roll No.: ____________

My Commission is for Life

STATE OF LOUISIANA

PARISH OF____________________

On ____________________________ (mm/dd/yyyy), before me appeared ___________________________________, as **BUYER** on this Bill of Sale who proved to me through government-issued photo identification to be the above-named person; and in my presence executed the foregoing instrument and acknowledged that he/she executed the same as his/her free act and deed.

____

Notary Name: ______________________________

Notary ID or Bar Roll No.: ____________

My Commission is for Life

8 • REAL ESTATE, IMMOVABLES AND USUFRUCTS

CONVEYANCES OF IMMOVABLES (EXCEPT DONATIONS)

STATE OF LOUISIANA

PARISH OF ____________________

ACT OF CASH SALE[1]

BEFORE ME, the undersigned notary, duly commissioned and qualified in the state and parish aforesaid, and in the presence of the two witnesses whose names are hereunto subscribed, PERSONALLY CAME and appeared:

SELLER'S NAME with full appearance clause including marital status and change/no-change in marital status.[2]

Hereinafter referred to as "Seller," who declared that they do by these presents grant, bargain, sell, convey, transfer, assign, setover, abandon, and deliver, with all legal warranties and with full substitution and subrogation in and to all the rights and actions of the warranty which they have or may have against all preceding owners and vendors, unto:

BUYER'S NAME with appearance clause (no need for 'change in marital status' if transferee).

Hereinafter referred to as "Purchaser" or "Buyer," here present, accepting and purchasing for themselves, their successors and assigns, and acknowledging due delivery and possession thereof, all and singular, the following described property, to-wit:

---

[1] This is a simplified version of a Cash Sale. Please consider all of the needs of the client, and modify the form as needed. This conveyance of immovables—and all similar ones in this topic—is presented as an authentic act, as is typically used for such an act of sale. Although a straightforward act of sale is technically only *required* to be an act under private signature, it is advisable to have a closing with a notary and execute it in authentic form. This protects against a later finding that it was a donation in disguise. Making it authentic (or at least acknowledged) makes the instrument self-proving in court, if necessary to prove its contents and the parties' signatures.

[2] Social Security numbers of the parties (or EIN for such entities) are no longer required unless the act has a financing or security aspect to it, as with a credit sale or a mortgage.

A typical "change in marital status clause," required for any transfer of an immovable, is the statement (can be a separate statement from the lengthy appearance clause paragraph) that "Seller's marital status has changed since acquisition of the property; it changed from ______ to ______ due to ______ on or about ______." Or simply "has not changed since..." It is required for transferors of any *interest* in immovables, including usufructs, and for donations. See examples of complete appearance clauses in that chapter.

CASH SALE (ACT OF SALE)

Legal property description, including municipal address if one is available (or add at end as an attachment, and reference here that it is Exhibit A or the like).

This sale is made and accepted subject to the following (reference to which is made for notation only and is not to be construed as a renewal or recreation of same), to-wit:

TO HAVE AND TO HOLD the above described property unto the said Purchaser, themselves, their successors and assigns forever.

This sale is made *with/without any warranties of title whatsoever,*[3] whether express or implied, not even for return of the purchase price, or any part thereof, but with full substitution and subrogation in and to all the rights and actions of warranty which Seller has or may have against all preceding owners and sellers; this sale is made without any warranty whatsoever as to the condition or fitness of the property for any purpose, whether expresses or implied, not even for the return of the purchase price, or any part thereof, including, but not limited to, any warranties against redhibitory defects; and the Purchaser hereby expressly waives the benefit of any and all such warranties.

This sale is made and accepted for and in consideration of the price and sum of $ ___________ U.S. dollars, cash, which said Purchaser has well and truly paid in ready and current money to the Seller who hereby acknowledges the receipt thereof and grants full acquittance and discharge therefor.

All taxes up to and including the taxes due and exigible in 20____ *previous year* are paid, and taxes for the current year have been prorated between the parties hereto.

Seller represents and warrants: (1) that no other sale or grant of interest in said property has been or will be made by Seller, and (2) that the said property is not and will not become subject to any lien or encumbrance by act of omission of Seller or claim against Seller, except as otherwise noted or excepted.

"AS IS" CLAUSE, WITH WAIVER OF REDHIBITION

Purchaser acknowledges that a diligent inspection of the entire property and improvements has been made and Purchaser has taken all deficiencies and defects, if any, into consideration in purchasing the property for the price indicated herein.

Purchaser accepts the property and all of the improvements thereon in whatever condition it exists as of the date herein without any warranty other than as to the validity of title. All improvements, specifically including, but not limited to, all appliances, electrical, plumbing, heating and air conditioning systems, roof, structure, and foundation, are sold and accepted in "AS IS" condition; Purchaser agrees that Seller shall have no responsibility or liability whatever for any repairs.

---

[3] This paragraph should include warranties of title, redhibition, fitness, etc. Modify to achieve the client's needs, including any reservation of mineral rights, property inspections, reservations of servitudes, etc. Typically, however, any sale or conveyance states a full and general warranty of title, else it is essentially a quit claim deed.

Seller has not made, and does not make, any representation or warranties whatsoever as to improvements, nor as to the fitness or suitability of the use of occupancy of the property for any particular purpose, nor as to the square footage of the property or any improvements.

Purchaser expressly waives any and all warranties, expressed or implied, against hidden or latent defects, as provided by the Louisiana Civil Code, specifically including any right Purchaser may have to seek redhibition or rescission of this sale and/or to seek quanti minoris or a reduction of the purchase price or the return of any part thereof. These waivers and stipulations shall survive after the delivery of the title at the closing.

PURCHASER ACKNOWLEDGES THAT THIS WAIVER OF WARRANTY AND "AS-IS" CLAUSE HAS BEEN EXPLAINED TO PURCHASER AND IS UNDERSTOOD BY PURCHASER.

____

PURCHASER[4]

The Seller and Purchaser waive production of mortgage and conveyance certificates and relieve and release me, Notary, from all responsibility and liability in connection therewith.

Notice to tax assessor: The person responsible for all property taxes and assessments and the address to which the tax and assessment notices are to be mailed is *Buyer's name*, at the following mailing address: *address*.

The parties to this act are aware of the fact that no survey has been made in connection with this transaction, and hereby release and relieve me, Notary, from defects which might have been disclosed by a survey of the property. Notary takes no responsibility as to any adverse possessory rights, deficiency of quantity of land, boundary line disputes, unrecorded servitudes, easements or encumbrances, or any such other matters as would be determined by an actual survey and physical inspection of the premises.[5]

THUS DONE, READ AND PASSED on the _____ day of _________________, 20____, in ______________________, Louisiana, in the presence of the undersigned competent witnesses who have signed their names together with the parties to this act and me, notary.

WITNESSES:

__________________________	______________________________
Print Name	SELLER'S NAME, Seller[6]

---

[4] Have each buyer sign this waiver if there is more than one.

[5] Add a similar clause relieving the notary of responsibility for filing this act, if the parties agree that the notary's statutory duty is waived; in that case, this clause should state to whom the act will be delivered and who is responsible for its filing.

Some parishes, notably East Baton Rouge, require zoning certificates, but that can be waived similar to the above: "The parties waive any zoning certificate required by _____ Parish and agree to hold Notary harmless from any liability caused by this waiver." This language can be added for other parishes if zoning may be an issue.

[6] Multiple lines can be added on the right margin if there are more than one seller and/or buyer. If more than one buyer, amend the designation of property tax to be clear which one of them receives tax bill and notices. If signed in counterparts in authentic form, create multiple blocks with conclusion, witnesses, signator, and notary.

Witnesses are not strictly required for an act of sale unless it may be considered a donation in disguise.

CASH SALE (ACT OF SALE)

______________________________ ______________________________

Print Name BUYER'S NAME, Buyer

____

Notary Name: ______________________________

Notary ID or Bar Roll No.: ____________

My Commission is for Life

CASH SALE (ACT OF SALE), ALTERNATE

STATE OF LOUISIANA

PARISH OF ____________________

ACT OF CASH SALE[1]

BEFORE ME, the undersigned notary, duly commissioned and qualified in the state and parish aforesaid, and in the presence of the two witnesses whose names are hereunto subscribed, PERSONALLY CAME and appeared:

SELLER'S NAME with full appearance clause including marital status and change/no-change in marital status.[2]

Hereinafter referred to as "Seller," who declared that they do by these presents grant, bargain, sell, convey, transfer, assign, setover, abandon, and deliver, with all legal warranties and with full substitution and subrogation in and to all the rights and actions of the warranty which they have or may have against all preceding owners and vendors, unto:

BUYER'S NAME with appearance clause (no need for change/no-change in marital status).

Hereinafter referred to as "Purchaser" or "Buyer," here present, accepting and purchasing for themselves, their successors and assigns, and acknowledging due delivery and possession thereof, all and singular, the following described property, to-wit:

Legal property description, including municipal address if one is available (or add at end as an attachment, and reference here that it is Exhibit A or the like).

This sale is made and accepted subject to the following (reference to which is made for notation only and is not to be construed as a renewal or recreation of same), to-wit:

1. The Seller declares that it does by these presents grant, bargain, sell, convey, transfer, assign, set over, abandon, and deliver unto the Purchaser, here present accepting, and purchasing for itself and its successors and assigns, and acknowledging due delivery and possession, all and singular the above described property.
2. To HAVE AND TO HOLD the Property unto the Purchaser, and Purchaser's successors, heirs and assigns forever.

---

[1] This is a Cash Sale. Please consider all of the needs of the client and modify the form accordingly. The conveyances of immovables in this collection are structured as an authentic act, as is typically used for such an act of sale though not legally required.

[2] Social Security numbers of the parties (or EIN for such entities) are no longer required unless the act has a financing or security aspect to it, as with a credit sale or a mortgage.

A typical "change in marital status clause," required for the transferor of an interest in immovables, is the statement (can be a separate statement from the lengthy appearance clause paragraph) that "Seller's marital status has changed since acquisition of the property; it changed from ______ to ______ due to ______ on or about ______." Or simply "has not changed since..." See examples of complete appearances in that chapter.

CASH SALE (ACT OF SALE), ALTERNATE

3. This sale is made without any warranties of title whatsoever,[3] whether express or implied, not even for the return of the purchase price, or any part thereof, except for the acts of the Seller or anyone claiming by, through or under the Seller; and specifically, (a) this sale is made without any warranty whatsoever as to the condition or fitness of the Property for any purpose, whether expressed or implied, not even for the return of the purchase price or any part of it, including, but not limited to, any warranties against redhibitory defects; and (b) the Purchaser expressly waives the benefit of any and all such warranties. Without limiting the foregoing, the Purchaser declares and acknowledges that it has had ample opportunity to examine the Property and all of the improvements located on it in connection with the use to which the Purchaser intends to make of the Property and of such improvements, that it accepts the Property and such improvements "as is," "where is" and "with all faults," including, but not limited to, all environmental vices or defects; and that it specifically relieves and releases the Seller from any and all claims for vices or defects in the Property or in any improvements thereon, whether obvious or latent, known or unknown; and that it specifically and particularly waives any and all claims or causes of action for redhibition pursuant to Louisiana Revised Statutes 9:2520 *et seq.* or diminution of the consideration pursuant to Louisiana Revised Statutes 9:2541 *et seq.*, for concealment and/or any other theory of law. However, the Seller subrogates the Purchaser in and to all rights and action in warranty which the Seller has or may have against previous owners and vendors of the Property, including but not limited to any recourse the Seller has against a title insurance company under the Seller's policy of title insurance on the Property.

PURCHASE PRICE

1. This sale is made and accepted for and in consideration of the price of $*dollars and cents*, which the Purchaser has paid, to the Seller, which acknowledges the receipt of the purchase price and grants full acquittance and discharge.

2. Seller acknowledges that it has received full and adequate consideration for the Property conveyed. Accordingly, Seller waives any vendor's lien it may have and any right to rescind this sale, in whole or in part, for failure to pay the consideration or any part of it.

TITLE MATTERS

1. This conveyance is made and accepted subject to the following restrictive covenants, servitudes, encumbrances, and other matters of public record ("Permitted Exceptions"): *list any exceptions*.

2. By acquiring the Property subject to the Permitted Exceptions, the Purchaser does not acknowledge the validity or enforceability of those matters for any purpose, including, but not limited to, interruption of prescription.

MISCELLANEOUS

1. The parties declare that all taxes up to and including taxes due in *previous year* are paid in full. Taxes for the current year, *year*, have been prorated between the parties. Pursuant to Louisiana Revised Statutes 9:2721(B), the Purchaser is responsible for the property taxes and

---

[3] This paragraph should include warranties of title, redhibition, fitness, etc. agreed to by the parties. Modify to achieve the client's needs, including any reservation of mineral rights, property inspections, reservations of servitudes, etc. Typically, however, any sale or conveyance expresses here a full warranty of good title, or else it is essentially a quit claim deed.

assessments from and after the year *year*. In addition, the parties designate a tax-notice recipient as follows:

Notice to tax assessor: The person responsible for all property taxes and assessments and the address to which the tax and assessment notices are to be mailed is *Buyer*, at mailing address *address*.

2. The Seller and Purchaser waive production of mortgage and conveyance certificates and relieve and release me, Notary, from all responsibility and liability in connection therewith.

3. The captions and headings appearing in this sale are for convenience and reference only and are not intended, to any extent or for any purpose, to limit or define the text of any section or subsection.

4. This sale may be executed in counterparts, which, when taken together, shall constitute one instrument.

"AS IS" CLAUSE, WITH WAIVER OF REDHIBITION

Purchaser acknowledges that a diligent inspection of the entire property and improvements has been made and Purchaser has taken all deficiencies and defects, if any, into consideration in purchasing the property for the price indicated herein.

Purchaser accepts the property and all of the improvements thereon in whatever condition it exists as of the date herein without any warranty other than as to the validity of title. All improvements, specifically including, but not limited to, all appliances, electrical, plumbing, heating and air conditioning systems, roof, structure, and foundation, are sold and accepted in "AS IS" condition; Purchaser agrees that Seller shall have no responsibility or liability whatever for any repairs.

Seller has not made, and does not make, any representation or warranties whatsoever as to improvements, nor as to the fitness or suitability of the use of occupancy of the property for any particular purpose, nor as to the square footage of the property or any improvements.

Purchaser expressly waives any and all warranties, expressed or implied, against hidden or latent defects, as provided by the Louisiana Civil Code, specifically including any right Purchaser may have to seek redhibition or rescission of this sale and/or to seek quanti minoris or a reduction of the purchase price or the return of any part thereof. These waivers and stipulations shall survive after the delivery of the title at the closing.

PURCHASER ACKNOWLEDGES THAT THIS WAIVER OF WARRANTY AND "AS-IS" CLAUSE HAS BEEN EXPLAINED TO PURCHASER AND IS UNDERSTOOD BY PURCHASER.

____

PURCHASER[4]

The parties to this act are aware of the fact that no survey has been made in connection with this transaction, and hereby release and relieve me, Notary, from defects which might have been disclosed by a survey of the property.[5]

[4] Have each buyer sign this waiver if there is more than one.

CASH SALE (ACT OF SALE), ALTERNATE

THUS DONE, READ AND PASSED on the _____ day of _________________, 20____, in ___________________, Louisiana, in the presence of the undersigned competent witnesses who have signed their names together with the parties to this act and me, notary, after due reading of the whole.

WITNESSES:

____________________________	____________________________
Print Name	SELLER'S NAME, Seller[6]
____________________________	____________________________
Print Name	BUYER'S NAME, Buyer

____

Notary Name: ______________________________

Notary ID or Bar Roll No.: ___________

My Commission is for Life

---

[5] May add a clause relieving the notary of responsibility for filing this act, if the parties agree; in that case, this clause should state to whom the act will be delivered and who is responsible for its filing.

In addition, some parishes, notably East Baton Rouge, require zoning certificates, but that can be waived similar to the above: "The parties waive any zoning certificate required by _____ Parish and agree to hold Notary harmless from any liability caused by this waiver." This language can be added for other parishes if zoning may be an issue.

[6] Multiple lines can be added on the right margin if there is more than one seller and/or buyer. If more than one buyer, amend the designation of property tax to be clear which one of them receives tax bill and notices. This act may be signed in counterparts, but if done in authentic form, each signer needs their own witness and notary block, with the same conclusion clause stating the date of that signing.

Witnesses are not strictly required for an act of sale unless it may be considered a donation in disguise. Out of an excess of caution, however, use witnesses if possible. Straightforward cash sales are not required to be in authentic form but are traditionally done that way. An accompanying mortgage often has to be done in authentic form anyway (because they usually contain a confession of judgment), so making the sale authentic is readily accomplished as well.

CASH SALE WITH ASSUMPTION OF MORTGAGE

STATE OF LOUISIANA

PARISH OF ____________________

CASH SALE WITH ASSUMPTION OF MORTGAGE[1]

BEFORE ME, the undersigned notary, duly commissioned and qualified in the state and parish aforesaid, and in the presence of the two witnesses whose names are hereunto subscribed, PERSONALLY CAME and appeared:

Seller's name, of full legal age of majority and domiciled in ____________ Parish, having S.S.# or EIN ending in *[put last 4 digits], then remaining appearance clause including change (or not) in marital status.*

Hereinafter referred to as "Seller," who declared that they do by these presents grant, bargain, sell, convey, transfer, assign, setover, abandon, and deliver, with all legal warranties and with full substitution and subrogation in and to all the rights and actions of the warranty which they have or may have against all preceding owners and vendors unto:

Buyer's name, of full legal age of majority and domiciled in ____________ Parish, having S.S.# or EIN ending in *[put last 4 digits], then remaining appearance clause, though not requiring change/no change in marital status clause.*

Hereinafter referred to as "Buyer" or "Purchaser," here present, accepting and purchasing for themselves, their successors and assigns, acknowledging due delivery and possession thereof, all and singular, the following described property, to-wit:

Legal property description, including municipal address if one is available (or add at end as an attachment, and reference here that it is Exhibit A or the like).

THIS SALE IS SUBJECT TO THE FOLLOWING:

This sale is made and accepted for and in consideration of the price of $*dollars and cents* in part payment and deduction of the amount of $*dollars* received by the seller from the Purchaser to Seller, who hereby acknowledges the receipt thereof and grants full acquittance and discharge.

For the balance of the purchase price, Purchaser assumes, individually and in solido, to pay, in full and to its complete and final discharge, the promissory note ("Note") originally made by Seller on *date* with the original principal amount of $*original amount of note*, with interest accruing at the rate of *original interest rate* % per year, from that date until paid. *Describe original payment terms*. The Note is paraphed for identification with an Act of

[1] This form can only be used if the current mortgagee (lender) allows the assumption of mortgage.

CASH SALE WITH ASSUMPTION OF MORTGAGE

Mortgage ("Mortgage") by Seller in favor of Mortgagee, *mortgagee (lender) name*, dated *date*, and recorded in *city*, in _________ Parish, Louisiana, MOB _____, Folio No. ________.

Purchaser agrees, individually and in solido, to fully comply with and discharge all of the terms and conditions of the Mortgage and the Note, to the same extent as if Purchaser had personally executed those instruments.

Seller transfers to Purchaser all of Seller's right, title and interest in and to any escrow funds or other funds held by the Mortgagee to secure payment of any taxes, insurance, or other charges.

Purchaser expressly waives any and all homestead or other exemptions from seizure.

Seller represents and warrants that: (a) all state, city and parish taxes up to and including the taxes due in *year* are paid; (b) the Property has not been alienated by Seller; and (c) the Property is not subject to any encumbrance whatsoever, except as follows: *list encumbrances on property*.

The parties waive the production of mortgage and conveyance certificates and tax researches, and relieve and release the Notary Public from any liability in connection with them. Taxes for the year *year* have been prorated between the parties. Purchaser is now contractually responsible for the property taxes and assessments from hereinafter after the year *year*.

Notice to tax assessor: The person responsible for all property taxes and assessments and the mailing address to which the tax and assessment notice are mailed are: *Buyer name and address.*

Seller provides a warranty of full and general title to the above-described property. No other warranties are made or provided, and all parties agree that it is sold as-is:

"AS IS" CLAUSE, WITH WAIVER OF REDHIBITION

Purchaser acknowledges that a diligent inspection of the entire property and improvements has been made and Purchaser has taken all deficiencies and defects, if any, into consideration in purchasing the property for the price indicated herein.

Purchaser accepts the property and all of the improvements thereon in whatever condition it exists as of the date herein without any warranty other than as to the validity of title. All improvements, specifically including, but not limited to, all appliances, electrical, plumbing, heating and air conditioning systems, roof, structure, and foundation, are sold and accepted in "AS IS" condition, Purchaser agrees that Seller shall have no responsibility or liability whatever for any repairs.

Seller has not made, and does not make, any representation or warranties whatsoever as to improvements, nor as to the fitness or suitability of the use of occupancy of the property for any particular purpose, nor as to the square footage of the property or any improvements.

Purchaser expressly waives any and all warranties, expressed or implied, against hidden or latent defects, as provided by the Louisiana Civil Code, specifically including any right purchaser may have to seek redhibition or rescission of this sale and/or to seek quanti minoris or a reduction of the purchase price or the return of any part thereof. These waivers and stipulations shall survive after the delivery of the title at the closing.

CASH SALE WITH ASSUMPTION OF MORTGAGE

PURCHASER ACKNOWLEDGES THAT THIS WAIVER OF WARRANTY AND "AS-IS" CLAUSE HAS BEEN EXPLAINED TO PURCHASER AND IS UNDERSTOOD BY PURCHASER.

____

PURCHASER[2]

TO HAVE AND TO HOLD, the said described property herein conveyed unto the said Purchaser, and Purchaser's heirs and assigns forever.

The parties hereto take cognizance that no new survey has been made on the herein described property in connection with this Act and the parties do hereby relieve and release me, Notary, from all and any liability in connection with any encroachments which might appear on such survey.[3]

Filing of this instrument shall be the responsibility of ______________, to whom this Act is hereby delivered for filing.

The masculine pronoun as used herein shall include the feminine; the singular shall include the plural.

THUS DONE AND PASSED on the _____ day of __________, 20____, in _______________, Louisiana, in the presence of the undersigned competent witnesses, who have signed their names together with the parties to this act and me, notary, after due reading of the whole.

WITNESSES:

____________________________ _______________________________

Print Name SELLER'S NAME, Seller[4]

____________________________ _______________________________

Print Name BUYER'S NAME, Buyer

____

Notary Name: _______________________________

Notary ID or Bar Roll No.: ____________

My Commission is for Life

[2] Have each buyer sign this waiver if there is more than one.

[3] A similar waiver may be added for not obtaining a certificate of zoning in East Baton Rouge Parish.

[4] Multiple lines may be added on the right margin if there are more than one seller and/or buyer. You should use two witnesses and treat it as an authentic act. Although the sale itself does not require witnesses, the assumption of mortgage may be seen as involving a security interest, which may have contained a confession of judgment clause, so that it is advisable to have this act be in authentic form, too, as is presented here.

CREDIT SALE (SALE WITH VENDOR'S LIEN)

STATE OF LOUISIANA

PARISH OF ____________________

ACT OF CREDIT SALE[1]

BEFORE ME, the undersigned notary, duly commissioned and qualified in the state and parish aforesaid, and in the presence of the two witnesses whose names are hereunto subscribed, PERSONALLY CAME and appeared:

Seller's name, of full legal age of majority and domiciled in ____________ Parish, having S.S.# or EIN ending in *[put last 4 digits], then remaining appearance clause, including change (or not) in marital status (as explained in "Cash Sale" sample)*

Hereinafter referred to as "Seller," who declared that they do by these presents grant, bargain, sell, convey, transfer, assign, setover, abandon, and deliver, with all legal warranties and with full substitution and subrogation in and to all the rights and actions of the warranty which they have or may have against all preceding owners and vendors, unto:

Buyer's name, of full legal age of majority and domiciled in ____________ Parish, having S.S.# or EIN ending in *[put last 4 digits], then remaining appearance clause (but no need for change/no change in marital status).*

Hereinafter referred to as "Buyer" or "Purchaser," and here present, accepting and purchasing for themselves, their successors and assigns, acknowledging due delivery and possession thereof, all and singular, the following described property, to-wit:

---

[1] This is a Credit Sale (a/k/a "sale with vendor's lien" or "sale with vendor's privilege"). This is so even though the parties are referred to as mortgagor (borrower) and mortgagee (lender, i.e., the owner/seller who is financing part or all of the sale). Framing the sale and financing as a Credit Sale is advantageous to the seller because a vendor's lien primes any conventional mortgage. An owner/financer could possibly use the device of mortgage instead, to secure the debt, but that is not advisable because they would lose the priority of the vendor's lien. In this form, and typically, no external mortgage is obtained—the only lender here is the seller.

In the two-party transaction seen here, the financing arrangement is often called a "mortgage," but the contents must make clear the security provided is a vendor's lien or it may be seen as a conventional mortgage.

Where all of the financing is done external to the parties—where the only source of financing is a mortgage or other security arrangement—the proper instrument for the conveyance is simply a "cash sale" (because from the seller's perspective they receive cash at closing) with an accompanying, but separate, mortgage and promissory note. The latter transaction is a side arrangement at the closing between the buyer/borrower and the financing institution. The transaction is sometimes called "act of cash sale with mortgage" though in reality the act of sale is between seller and buyer while a separate transaction, and documentation, is between the buyer (mortgagor) and an unrelated lender (mortgagee).

This instrument could also combine a credit sale with a mortgage, if part of the financing is obtained external to the seller (e.g., part owner-financed, part bank-financed). The mortgage would be a separate document. In the presnt version, the" mortgagee" is not a bank or lending institution. But if this credit sale also had external financing from a bank, etc., this form should be adapted to reference that and to refer to the "buyer" and "seller" simply that way without using the terms "mortgagor" and "mortgagee" as between them.

CREDIT SALE (SALE WITH VENDOR'S LIEN)

Legal property description, including municipal address if one is available (or add at end as an attachment, and reference here that it is Exhibit A or the like).

THIS SALE IS SUBJECT TO THE FOLLOWING:

1. Said property is sold, conveyed, and accepted subject to any and all valid restrictions, servitudes, easements, rights of way, setback lines, mineral conveyances and/or reservations of record affecting same, if any.

2. The parties are aware that no survey has been made in connection with this transaction and hereby release and relieve undersigned Notary, from any and all liabilities which might have been disclosed by a current survey.

3. The parties agree that Notary takes no responsibility as to any adverse possessory rights, deficiency of quantity of land, boundary line disputes, unrecorded servitudes, easements or encumbrances, or any such other matters as would be determined by an actual survey and physical inspection of the premises.

4. This sale is made without warranties of any kind, other than a warranty of good title.[2]

5. The sale is made as-is, waiving right of redhibition as follows:

"AS IS" CLAUSE, WITH WAIVER OF REDHIBITION

Purchaser acknowledges that a diligent inspection of the entire property and improvements has been made and Purchaser has taken all deficiencies and defects, if any, into consideration in purchasing the property for the price indicated herein.

Purchaser accepts the property and all of the improvements thereon in whatever condition it exists as of the date herein without any warranty other than as to the validity of title. All improvements, specifically including, but not limited to, all appliances, electrical, plumbing, heating and air conditioning systems, roof, structure, and foundation, are sold and accepted in "AS IS" condition; Purchaser agrees that Seller shall have no responsibility or liability whatever for any repairs.

Seller has not made, and does not make, any representation or warranties whatsoever as to improvements, nor as to the fitness or suitability of the use of occupancy of the property for any particular purpose, nor as to the square footage of the property or any improvements.

Purchaser expressly waives any and all warranties, expressed or implied, against hidden or latent defects, as provided by the Louisiana Civil Code, specifically including any right Purchaser may have to seek redhibition or rescission of this sale and/or to seek quanti minoris or a reduction of the purchase price or the return of any part thereof. These waivers and stipulations shall survive after the delivery of the title at the closing.

PURCHASER ACKNOWLEDGES THAT THIS WAIVER OF WARRANTY AND "AS-IS" CLAUSE HAS BEEN EXPLAINED TO PURCHASER AND IS UNDERSTOOD BY PURCHASER.

____

PURCHASER[3]

[2] This stipulation may be amended to add other warranties that the seller provides; it could also be amended to further waive warranty of title, though that essentially would make it a quit claim deed and is not typical.

CREDIT SALE (SALE WITH VENDOR'S LIEN)

This sale is made unto the Purchaser, TO HAVE AND TO HOLD, the above-described property herein conveyed unto the said Purchaser, and Purchaser's heirs and assigns forever.

THIS SALE IS MADE AND ACCEPTED, for and in consideration of the price and sum of ______________________________ dollars ($ ____________), total sales price, and other valuable consideration, in part as follows:

1. The sum of $__________ cash down payment, receipt of which Seller hereby acknowledges.
2. The sum of $_________ for which balance, Buyer gives Seller the following described promissory note ("the Note"):

   [full description of Note including repayment schedule; and method of processing payment, typically with an escrow company if not done directly between the parties]

And I, the undersigned notary public, paraphed the Note *"Ne Varietur"* for identification with this Cash Sale with Mortgage and delivered the Note to the Seller, who acknowledges receipt thereof.

Purchaser/Mortgagor further agrees to pay any state, local or other assessments, specifically including but not limited to, any increase or decrease in the monthly escrow amount collected for payment of taxes and insurances unto ______________ *[typically an escrow company]*, monthly until said indebtedness due Seller is paid in full.

Late Payment: Purchaser/Mortgagor shall have a five (5) day grace period in making a monthly payment; if a monthly payment is more than five (5) days late, borrower shall pay a late charge of ten percent (10%) as a late fee. If Purchaser/Mortgagor is more than thirty (30) days late in making a payment, then said borrower shall be in default.

Attorney Fees: In case it should become necessary to place the Note in the hands of an attorney-at-law for collection or to institute suit for the recovery of the amount of said note or any part thereof, the Purchaser hereby binds and obligates themselves to pay the reasonable fees of the attorney-at-law who may be employed or retained for that purpose.

Insurance: Mortgagor hereby binds themselves to keep the property described above constantly insured against the risk of loss, by fire, windstorm, flood, etc. Mortgagor agrees to maintain hazard, flood, wind & hail, and liability insurances in the full amount of the above-described mortgage note, or an amount agreed upon in writing by Mortgagor and Mortgagee, with a loss payable clause in favor of Mortgagee or any other holder or holders of said note(s). In the event of Mortgagor's default with regard to said insurance, Mortgagor hereby authorizes said Mortgagee, or any future holder(s) of the said note(s), to cause said insurance to be effected at the then current rates; the amount of said premium to be added to the next month's principal payment due. Mortgagor agrees to authorize and direct ______________ Insurance Co. to mail Mortgagee any 30 Day Notice(s) of Cancellation should Mortgagor fail to timely remit any insurance payments due during the term of this Cash Sale. Should Mortgagor fail to maintain insurances, Mortgagor shall be in default.

Taxes: Mortgagor further binds itself to pay punctually when due, all taxes and assessments which may be levied on said mortgaged property. In the event of Mortgagor's

[3] Have each buyer sign this waiver if there is more than one.

default in the payment of such taxes, mortgagor hereby authorize said Mortgagee, or any future holder(s) of said note to pay same; the amount of said taxes to be added to the next month's principal payment due.

Security: In order to secure the full and punctual payment of the said note according to its terms and to secure the faithful performance of all of the obligations contained herein, and the reimbursement and/or payment of attorney fees, taxes, assessments, premiums of insurance, costs, fines, late charges, and all advances and expenses whatsoever, **a vendor's lien and privilege is hereby retained**; and the said Purchaser/Mortgagor does, by these presents, specially mortgage, affect, and hypothecate the above-described property unto and in favor of the Seller/Mortgagee and any future holder of said note, the Purchaser/Mortgagor does hereby confess judgment in favor of the present or any future holder of said note, for the full amount of the said promissory note or obligation, together with all interest, taxes, assessments, premiums of insurance, fines, attorney fees, and all costs, late charges, advances and expenses whatsoever; and the said Purchaser/Mortgagor hereby binds and obligates themselves not to sell, alienate or encumber the said property or to permit or suffer it to be sold, alienated, or encumbered or deteriorated to the prejudice of this Act.

Remedies: In the event the Purchaser/Mortgagor should violate any of the conditions of this Act, or should fail to promptly perform any obligation hereunder, or fails for a period of thirty (30) days to make any payment due to the holder of the note under this Act or upon the application by the Mortgagor to be adjudicated a bankrupt, or the institution of involuntary bankruptcy proceedings against Mortgagor, the holder of the note may, at its option, without making a demand or putting the said Mortgagor in default (demand for payment pursuant to Louisiana C.C.P. articles 2639 and 2721 and a putting in default being expressly waived), declare the entire balance due by the Mortgagor to the holder of the Note immediately due, exigible and payable, together with interest, costs, attorney fees, advances and all expenses and other charges, and to cause the property herein described, together with all the improvements thereon, to be seized and sold **under executory or other process** issued by a competent court, or said holder may proceed to the enforcement of his rights in any other manner provided by law, and the property may be sold with or without appraisement to the highest bidder for cash.

Confession of Judgment: Mortgagor hereby **confesses judgment** in favor of the Mortgagee, or any future holder or holders of said note, up to the full amount of principal, interest and attorney fees and for any sums that the Mortgagee may advance during the life of this mortgage for the payments of premiums of insurance, taxes and assessments or for the protection and preservation of its mortgage as authorized elsewhere in this Act, and does by these present, consent, agree and stipulate that, in the event the Note or any installment of principal or interest thereon not being promptly and fully paid when the same becomes due and payable, or in the event of failure to comply with any of the obligations herein set forth, or the breach of this contract in any of its part by mortgagor, the Note shall, at the option of the holder, become due and payable, anything therein contained to the contrary notwithstanding, and it shall be lawful for the holder or holders of the Note, without making a demand and without notice or putting in default, the same being hereby expressly waived, to cause all and singular the property herein mortgaged to be seized and sold by executory process issued by a competent court or to proceed with enforcement of its mortgage in any other manner provided by law.

Assignment of Leases: Mortgagor herein and hereby assigns unto Mortgagee as security for the payment of the aforesaid Notes all of Mortgagor's right, title and interest in and to the rents, issues and profits accruing and to accrue and due and to become due and payable under and pursuant to all contracts of lease, rental and occupancy now in effect or hereafter entered into by Mortgagor and covering any portion of the Property described above and hereby mortgaged. Unless and until default is made by Mortgagor in the payment of any installment of principal or interest in the Notes secured hereby or in the performance or observance of any of the terms, provisions or conditions of this Mortgage, or of the Note secured hereby, Mortgagor shall have the right to collect and receive the rentals accruing under such leases, rental and occupancies, but not in advance, and to enforce the covenants of said leases.

In the event of any default by Mortgagor in the payment of any installment of principal or interest on the Note secured hereby or in the performance or observation of any of the terms, provisions and conditions of this Mortgage, or of the Notes secured hereby, Mortgagee shall have and is hereby given the right to collect all the rents, issues and profits under or with respect to any and all leases, rentals and occupancies covering any portion or portions of the Property herein and hereby mortgaged, and to continue to do so until all obligations of the Mortgagor under this Mortgage and under the Notes secured hereby have been paid and discharged in full, and Mortgagor hereby makes, constitutes and appoints Mortgagee its attorney-in-fact, giving unto said attorney irrevocable power, either in its own name or in the name of the Mortgagor, to take all necessary steps, by proceedings in court or otherwise to notify any and all lessees of this assignment and to collect all rentals, revenues, issues and profits, to cause the said premises to be vacated and, when vacant, to re-let such premises and to do all such things in such manner and on such terms as said Mortgagee may deem best. Mortgagee shall additionally be entitled to the judicial appointment of a receiver of rents at any time after any such default. Mortgagor further agrees and stipulate that they will keep and will cause to be kept valid and unimpaired the assignment of rents and revenues hereinabove set forth and, to that end, shall execute at any future time or times, and as often as may be deemed necessary, on demand of Mortgagee, all such further instruments and/or assignments in such form and effect as may be deemed proper by Mortgagee to the better carrying out of the true intent and meaning of the assignments hereinabove set forth.

Keeper: Pursuant to Louisiana Revised Statutes 9:5136 *et seq.*, Mortgagor hereby designates Mortgagee, or any employee, agent, or other person named by Mortgagee at the time any seizure of the Mortgaged Property is effected by Mortgagee, to serve as a Keeper of the Mortgaged Property pending the judicial sale thereof. The Keeper shall be entitled to reasonable compensation in an amount to be determined by the court before which the proceedings are pending, and the payment of such fees shall be secured by this mortgage. The failure of the holder of the Note to exercise any of its privileges or options at any time shall not constitute a waiver of its rights to exercise the same at any other time.

Mortgagor declares that they do expressly waive and renounce in favor of the holder of the Note any homestead exemption or claim thereto, under the Constitution and laws of this State with respect to the property herein mortgaged.

The Purchaser herein assumes responsibility for payment of property taxes for the year 20____ and Purchaser assumes responsibility for the payment of the property taxes thereafter. Further tax notices and bills shall be sent to Purchaser.

Notice to tax assessor: The person responsible for all property taxes and assessments and the address to which the tax and assessment notices are to be mailed is: *Buyer name and address.*

CREDIT SALE (SALE WITH VENDOR'S LIEN)

The parties hereto take cognizance that no new survey has been made on the herein described property in connection with this Act and the parties do hereby relieve and release me, Notary, from all and any liability in connection with any encroachments which might appear on such survey or defects which might have been disclosed by a survey of the property.[4]

Filing of this instrument shall be the responsibility of ______________, to whom this act is hereby delivered for filing.[5]

The masculine pronoun as used herein shall include the feminine; the singular shall include the plural, and vice versa.

THUS DONE, READ AND PASSED on the _____ day of __________________, 20____, in ______________________, Louisiana, in the presence of the undersigned competent witnesses, who have signed their names together with the parties to this act and me, notary, after due reading of the whole.

WITNESSES:

____________________________	_______________________________
Print Name	SELLER'S NAME, Seller[6]
____________________________	_______________________________
Print Name	BUYER'S NAME, Buyer

____

Notary Name: _______________________________

Notary ID or Bar Roll No.: ____________

My Commission is for Life

---

[4] In addition, some parishes, notably East Baton Rouge, require zoning certificates, but that can be waived similar to the above: "The parties waive any zoning certificate required by _____ Parish and agree to hold Notary harmless from any liability caused by this waiver."

[5] The default is that the notary is responsible for filing, unless that duty is clearly waived by the parties to the act. This waiver is especially important with a Credit Sale—or, the responsibility of the notary is *crucial*, if notary accepts their duty. This is because the advantages of a vendor's lien are lost if the filing is not done properly and timely. The act including the vendor's lien clearly stated (or it may be a separate document, also filed) must be filed within 7 days after execution if the act is passed in the parish where the property is located, or within 15 days if passed in a different parish from where the property is located. See LA C.C. art. 3274.

Where there is a mortgage as part of the transaction which recognizes the vendor's lien, the mortgage instrument is timely filed in the mortgage records while the act of sale is timely filed in the conveyance records.

[6] Multiple lines may be added on the right margin if there are more than one seller and/or buyer. If more than one buyer, amend the designation of property tax to be clear which one of them receives tax bill and notices. If signed in counterparts in authentic form, create multiple blocks with conclusion, witnesses, signator, and notary.

In a credit sale, 2 witnesses are usually required, because of the typical "confession of judgment" clause.

QUIT CLAIM DEED

STATE OF LOUISIANA

PARISH OF ST. TAMMANY

QUIT CLAIM DEED[1]

BEFORE ME, the undersigned notary, duly commissioned and qualified in the state and parish aforesaid, and in the presence of the two witnesses whose names are hereunto subscribed, PERSONALLY CAME and appeared:

Felicia Campagno, of the full age of majority and a domiciliary of the Parish of St. Tammany, State of Louisiana, a single person never having been married,[2] and who declared their mailing address to be 1234567 Hwy 190, Mandeville, LA 70471, hereinafter "Vendor" or "Seller,"

Who declared unto me, notary public, that they, Vendor, do by these presents, grant, bargain, sell, transfer, quitclaim, release and deliver, **"as is, where is,"** and **without any warranty of title** whatsoever, even for the return of the purchase price, and without any recourse against Vendor whatsoever, but with full substitution and subrogation in and to all the rights and actions of warranty which Vendor has or may have against all preceding owners and sellers, unto:

James C. Thompson, of the full age of majority and a domiciliary of the Parish of St. Tammany, State of Louisiana, a single person never having been married, whose mailing address is declared to be 222 Military Heights Dr., Covington, LA 70433, hereinafter "Vendee" or "Purchaser";

All their right, title and interest, which said Vendor may have in and to the following described property, to-wit:

Legal property description, including municipal address if one is available (or add at end as an attachment, and reference here that it is Exhibit A or the like).

---

[1] A quitclaim or quit claim deed is a transfer from Vendor to Vendee of whatever property interest Vendor *may* have, without any warranty that they even have one. It is appropriate to settle boundary disputes, to clear up title (for example, given by possible heirs or legatees who are relinquishing any claim they may have), and to resolve claims of a possible community interest (e.g., accompanying a refinancing of a property by the other spouse). This act is written in terms of Vendor and Vendee because the transfer is made for a payment like a sale. If instead it is done gratuitously, such as giving up a possible claim on a fence line with a neighbor for no consideration, it is advisable to structure the act in authentic form, as here, especially if it could be interpreted as a donation in disguise. Ultimately, though, a quit claim is an inappropriate substitute for a donation, and clients should use that form and process if a donation is intended or if the consideration is not fair market value.

Nevertheless, it can be structured as a unilateral act without any vendee, consideration, or witnesses if all it states is that appearer makes no claim to owning the property. That is often true for incorporeal movables such as intellectual property, or even with an immovable when appearer is merely denying any interest in it.

[2] If previously or currently married, state marital status, and for seller, a change (or not) in marital status. A quit claim deed is still a transfer of an interest in immovables, so that clause (or a separate statement) is required.

QUIT CLAIM DEED

Subject to all restrictions, mortgages, right of way grants, and servitudes of public records, with any outstanding oil or mineral rights.

This sale is made for the consideration of the sum of _____________ dollars ($_________.__) cash in hand and other good and valuable consideration by which third parties may rely, the receipt of which is hereby acknowledged.

Purchaser shall be responsible for all past due and future year's taxes.

The parties to this act are aware of the fact that no survey has been made in connection with this transaction, and hereby release and relieve me, Notary, from defects which might have been disclosed by a survey of the property. PROPERTY DESCRIPTION WAS PROVIDED BY PARTIES. Notary takes no responsibility as to any adverse possessory rights, deficiency of quantity of land, boundary line disputes, unrecorded servitudes, easements or encumbrances, or any such other matters as would be determined by an actual survey and physical inspection of the premises.[3]

THUS DONE, READ AND PASSED on the _____ day of __________________, 20____, in ______________________, Louisiana, in the presence of the undersigned competent witnesses who have signed their names together with the parties to this act and me, notary.

WITNESSES:

____________________________	____________________________
Print Name	Felicia Campagno, Vendor[4]
____________________________	____________________________
Print Name	James C. Thompson, Vendee

____

Notary Name: _______________________________

Notary ID or Bar Roll No.: ____________

My Commission is for Life

---

[3] Add a clause relieving the notary of responsibility for filing this act, if the parties agree that the notary's statutory duty is waived; in that case, this clause should state to whom the act will be delivered and who is responsible for its filing.

[4] Multiple lines can be added on the right margin if there is more than one vendor or vendee. If signed in counterparts in authentic form, create multiple blocks with conclusion, witnesses, signator, and notary.

DATION EN PAIEMENT (GIVING IN PAYMENT)

STATE OF LOUISIANA

PARISH OF ORLEANS

DATION EN PAIEMENT

BEFORE ME, the undersigned notary, duly commissioned and qualified in the state and parish aforesaid, and in the presence of the two witnesses whose names are hereunto subscribed, PERSONALLY CAME and appeared:

> JOHN SMITH DOW (xxx-xx-1234),[1] a single man, of the age of majority and domiciled in and a resident of Jefferson Parish, whose permanent mailing address is 1234 Main St., Metairie, LA 70003, and who declares unto me that he has been married but once, to Betty Ann Smith Dow, from whom he was divorced in Jefferson Parish, March 7, 2008,

hereinafter DEBTOR, who declared to me, Notary, that he is justly and truly indebted unto:

> MARY FRANCES PEABODY (xxx-xx-5678), a single woman, domiciled in and a resident of Jefferson Parish, whose permanent mailing address is 9987 Goodgirl Ln., Jefferson, LA 70121, and who declares unto me that she has never been married,

hereinafter CREDITOR, in the full sum of One Million Dollars ($1,000,000.00), represented by one certain promissory note in the principal amount of 1,000,000.00 AND NO/100 DOLLARS, made payable at 9987 Goodgirl Ln., or whatever place as may be convenient to the parties, bearing interest at the rate of twelve (12%) PERCENT per annum, payable in forty eight (48) equal monthly installments in the sum of $26,333.84 each, beginning on the first day of January, 2023, and a like installment due and payable on or before the first day of each month thereafter until all are paid and which note is secured by an Act of Sale with Mortgage, dated January 1, 2023, passed before *name of previous notary public*, Notary Public for the Parish of Orleans, and which mortgage is of record in the mortgage records of Jefferson Parish.

That wishing to be released from said indebtedness, but being unable to pay said promissory note in accordance with the terms and provisions thereof availing themselves of La. C.C. arts. 2655 through 2659, inclusive, said DEBTOR does hereby make unto said creditor a dation en paiement by hereby transferring, giving, granting, bargaining, setting over and delivering unto

---

[1] The appearance clauses of a dation en paiement (also called a "giving in payment") may no longer require last 4 digits of social security numbers or EIN like they used to, since it is not *securing* a debt as such. But if the parties are amenable, it makes sense with a document dealing so closely with debt that this identifier would be included. This way, for example, there is no doubt that the particular party is the one relieved of debt rather than a similarly named person.

Because the debtor is a transferor, the act requires a change/no change in marital status clause. That is clear enough in the sample to follow (dating the divorce) or it can be a separate statement from a lengthy appearance clause paragraph, e.g., "Debtor's marital status has changed since acquisition of the property; it changed from ______ to ______ due to ______ on or about ______." Or simply "has not changed since..."

said creditor here present, and accepting and acknowledging due delivery and possession thereof, all and singular, the following property, located in the Parish of Jefferson, State of Louisiana, to-wit:

A commercial office building, municipal address 999 Wish St., Jefferson, LA 70121, more particularly described as follows:

Legal property description (or add to end as an attachment, and reference here that it is Exhibit A or the like).

To have and to hold said property herein described unto said CREDITOR, her heirs, successors, and assigns, forever, with full and general warranty of title,[2] free from any lien, mortgage or encumbrance whatsoever, and with full substitution and subrogation to all the rights and actions of warranty which he has or may have against all preceding owners or vendors.

This dation of said property by said DEBTOR is made and accepted for and in consideration of the promissory note aforesaid and is received by said CREDITOR, who does hereby declare her willingness to receive said property in extinguishment and in full acquittance and discharge by CREDITOR to said DEBTOR of the indebtedness aforesaid.

The CREDITOR thereupon did deliver to me, Notary, as fully paid and acquitted the above described promissory note in the sum of ONE MILLION AND NO/100 dollars ($1,000,000.00), dated January 1, 2023, and declared that the said note having been paid in full, she as the last holder thereof does grant a full and complete release of the mortgage securing the payment of said note, and does hereby authorize and direct the Clerk of Court and Recorder of Mortgages for the Parish of Jefferson to cancel and erase entirely from his records the inscription of said mortgage, recorded as set forth above, and I, Notary, have marked said note paid, and cancelled the signature and paraph on the said note, and have filed same with the Clerk of Court and Recorder of Mortgages for Jefferson Parish.

The parties hereto further declare that the just valuation of said property is fixed at the sum of Eight Hundred Ninety Five Thousand Dollars ($895,000.00).[3]

All state and city taxes up to and including the taxes due and exigible in 2023 are paid.

Notice to tax assessor: The person responsible for all property taxes and assessments and the address to which the tax and assessment notices are to be mailed is Creditor, MARY FRANCES PEABODY, whose permanent mailing address is 9987 Goodgirl Ln., Jefferson, LA 70121.

---

[2] It may be advisable for the parties to spell out what other warranties, besides good title, are/are not included in this transaction. If it is being conveyed as-is, with no further warranties, the act may include an "as-is clause with waiver of redhibition," as is seen in our Act of Cash Sale and similar files. There may also be obligations of the owner that continue if the commercial space is being leased, so clauses may need to spell out and deal with assuming those obligations.

[3] This valuation satisfies the 2/3 rule, meaning that if the value of property is less than 2/3 the value of the debt forgiven, the dation is a donation in disguise and must follow the procedure for an authentic act. That the declared value might be wrong (too high, compared to FMV) is a good reason to do this act in authentic form, as was done here, even if technically a dation may be done as a private act.

DATION EN PAIEMENT (GIVING IN PAYMENT)

The parties hereto waive production of conveyance, mortgage, and other certificates, and relieve and release me, Notary, from any and all responsibility in connection therewith.

The parties to this act are aware of the fact that no survey has been made in connection with this transaction, and hereby release and relieve me, Notary, from defects which might have been disclosed by a survey of the property. Notary takes no responsibility as to any adverse possessory rights, deficiency of quantity of land, boundary line disputes, unrecorded servitudes, easements or encumbrances, or any such other matters as would be determined by an actual survey and physical inspection of the premises.[4]

THUS DONE AND PASSED on the 27 day of October, 2023, at my office in New Orleans, Louisiana, in the presence of the undersigned competent witnesses who have signed their names together with the parties to this act and me, notary, after due reading of the whole.

WITNESSES:

______________________________	______________________________
Print Name	JOHN SMITH DOW, Debtor
______________________________	______________________________
Print Name	MARY FRANCES PEABODY, Creditor

____

Notary Name: ______________________________

Notary ID or Bar Roll No.: ____________

My Commission is for Life

[4] Add a similar clause relieving the notary of responsibility for filing this act, if the parties agree that the notary's statutory duty is waived; in that case, this clause should state to whom the act will be delivered and who is responsible for its filing. See also "cash sale" sample for waiver of zoning certificate, if East Baton Rouge Parish.

EXCHANGE (PARTIES TRADE PROPERTIES)

STATE OF LOUISIANA

PARISH OF ____________________

ACT OF EXCHANGE[1]

BEFORE ME, the undersigned notary, duly commissioned and qualified in the state and parish aforesaid, and in the presence of the two witnesses whose names are hereunto subscribed, PERSONALLY CAME and appeared:

EXCHANGER 1's NAME with full appearance clause[2] including marital status and change/no-change in marital status (see note in "cash sale" examples).

Hereinafter referred to as "Exchanger 1," who declared that, for and in consideration of the transfer as hereinafter set forth, Exchanger 1 does hereby grant, bargain, sell, convey, transfer, assign, setover, abandon, and deliver, with all legal warranties and with full substitution and subrogation in and to all the rights and actions of the warranty which they have or may have against all preceding owners and vendors, unto *name*, Exchanger 2, the following property, situated in ______________ Parish, Louisiana and more particularly described as:

Legal property description of property originally acquired by Exchanger 1, including municipal address if one is available (or add at end as an attachment, and reference here that it is Exhibit A), hereinafter referred to as "Property 1."

And, comes now *name*, hereinafter "Exchanger 2," *with full appearance clause including marital status and also change/no-change in marital status,* who:

In consideration of the transfer as aforesaid, does hereby grant, bargain, sell, convey, transfer, assign, setover, abandon, and deliver, with all legal warranties and with full substitution and subrogation in and to all the rights and actions of the warranty which they have or may have against all preceding owners and vendors, unto *name*, Exchanger 1, the following property, situated in ______________ Parish, Louisiana and more particularly described as:

Legal property description of property originally acquired by Exchanger 2, including municipal address if one is available (or add at end as an attachment, and reference here that it is Exhibit B), hereinafter referred to as "Property 2."

---

[1] This is an exchange—an even trade of properties. It is used when the two parties swap properties rather than one "exchanging" money for the property (which is a cash sale). Because each is both a seller and a buyer, in effect, the parties are kept clear by naming them Exchanger 1 and Exchanger 2. The filing rules follow the same requirements of any conveyance of immovables.

[2] Social Security numbers of the parties (or EIN for such entities) are no longer required unless the act has a financing or security aspect to it, as with a credit sale or a mortgage. In the case of an act of exchange, this would only be raised in this document (as opposed to a separate mortgage document) if there was owner-financing of one of the transactions, e.g., the properties were so different in value that a party must make up the difference in future payments. In such situations, it is appropriate to use two documents: an act of sale and a credit sale.

EXCHANGE (PARTIES TRADE PROPERTIES)

This exchange is made and mutually delivered and accepted by the parties hereto. It is further agreed and understood that the properties exchanged are equal in value, each being of the value of $ ______________. This exchange is made and accepted for and in consideration of the transfer one to the other of the above-described properties, and each party who hereby acknowledges the receipt thereof and grants full acquittance and discharge therefor.

TO HAVE AND TO HOLD the above-described properties unto said parties, respectively, the one exchanger unto the other, their heirs, successors, and assigns forever.

This exchange is made *with/without any warranties of title whatsoever*,[3] whether express or implied, not even for return of the property, or any part thereof, but with full substitution and subrogation in and to all the rights and actions of warranty which each exchanger has or may have against all preceding owners; this sale is made without any warranty whatsoever as to the condition or fitness of the property for any purpose, whether expresses or implied, not even for the return of the purchase price, or any part thereof, including, but not limited to, any warranties against redhibitory defects; and the exchangers hereby expressly waive, one to each other, the benefit of any and all such warranties.

All taxes up to and including the taxes due and exigible in 20____ *previous year* are paid, and taxes for the current year are the responsibility of the party acquiring that property in this transaction.

Notice to tax assessor: The person responsible for all property taxes and assessments for Property 1 and the address to which the tax and assessment notices are to be mailed is *Exchanger 2's name*, at the following mailing address: *address*.

The person responsible for all property taxes and assessments for Property 2 and the address to which the tax and assessment notices are to be mailed is *Exchanger 1's name*, at the following mailing address: *address*.

Each exchanger represents and warrants: (1) that no other sale or grant of interest in their respective property has been or will be made by them, and (2) that their said property is not and will not become subject to any lien or encumbrance by act of omission of said exchanger or claim against exchanger, except as otherwise noted or excepted.

"AS IS" CLAUSE, WITH WAIVER OF REDHIBITION, FOR PROPERTY 1

Exchanger 2 acknowledges that a diligent inspection of the entire property, Property 1, and its improvements has been made and Exchanger 2 has taken all deficiencies and defects, if any, into consideration in valuing the property to be equal, as declared above.

Exchanger 2 accepts the property and all of the improvements thereon in whatever condition it exists as of the date herein without any warranty other than as to the validity of title. All improvements, specifically including, but not limited to, all appliances, electrical, plumbing,

[3] This paragraph should include warranties of title, redhibition, fitness, etc. Modify to achieve the parties' mutual needs, including any reservation of mineral rights, property inspections, reservations of servitudes, etc. Typically, however, any such conveyance states a full and general warranty of title, else it is essentially a quit claim deed.

heating and air conditioning systems, roof, structure, and foundation, are sold and accepted in "AS IS" condition, Exchanger 2 agrees that Exchanger 1 shall have no responsibility or liability whatever for any repairs.

Exchanger 1 has not made, and does not make, any representation or warranties whatsoever as to improvements, nor as to the fitness or suitability of the use of occupancy of the property for any particular purpose, nor as to the square footage of the property or any improvements.

Exchanger 2 expressly waives any and all warranties, expressed or implied, against hidden or latent defects, as provided by the Louisiana Civil Code, specifically including any right Exchanger 2 may have to seek redhibition or rescission[4] of this sale and/or to seek the return of any property. These waivers and stipulations shall survive after the delivery of the title at the closing.

EXCHANGER 2 ACKNOWLEDGES THAT THIS WAIVER OF WARRANTY AND "AS-IS" CLAUSE HAS BEEN EXPLAINED AND IS UNDERSTOOD:

____

EXCHANGER 2

"AS IS" CLAUSE, WITH WAIVER OF REDHIBITION, FOR PROPERTY 2

Exchanger 1 acknowledges that a diligent inspection of the entire property, Property 2, and its improvements has been made and Exchanger 1 has taken all deficiencies and defects, if any, into consideration in valuing the property to be equal, as declared above.

Exchanger 1 accepts the property and all of the improvements thereon in whatever condition it exists as of the date herein without any warranty other than as to the validity of title. All improvements, specifically including, but not limited to, all appliances, electrical, plumbing, heating and air conditioning systems, roof, structure, and foundation, are sold and accepted in "AS IS" condition; Exchanger 1 agrees that Exchanger 2 shall have no responsibility or liability whatever for any repairs.

Exchanger 2 has not made, and does not make, any representation or warranties whatsoever as to improvements, nor as to the fitness or suitability of the use of occupancy of the property for any particular purpose, nor as to the square footage of the property or any improvements.

Exchanger 1 expressly waives any and all warranties, expressed or implied, against hidden or latent defects, as provided by the Louisiana Civil Code, specifically including any right Exchanger 1 may have to seek redhibition or rescission of this sale and/or to seek the return of any property. These waivers and stipulations shall survive after the delivery of the title at the closing.

EXCHANGER 1 ACKNOWLEDGES THAT THIS WAIVER OF WARRANTY AND "AS-IS" CLAUSE HAS BEEN EXPLAINED AND IS UNDERSTOOD:

[4] Rights of return, compensation and rescission are controlled by LA C.C. 2662-2663, which should be taken into account if the values are substantially unequal (if given property less than half the value of the other property, a party can claim rescission by lesion) or one of the parties later evicts the other. It is not clear whether the waiver of rescission or compensation will hold up against these articles, but in any event the document should express the parties' intent (even in waiving warranties, or not), and it is not the drafter's role to impose terms on them.

EXCHANGE (PARTIES TRADE PROPERTIES)

____

EXCHANGER 1

The parties to this act waive production of mortgage and conveyance certificates and relieve and release me, Notary, from all responsibility and liability in connection therewith.

The parties are aware of the fact that no survey has been made in connection with this transaction, and hereby release and relieve me, Notary, from defects which might have been disclosed by a survey of the property. Notary takes no responsibility as to any adverse possessory rights, deficiency of quantity of land, boundary line disputes, unrecorded servitudes, easements or encumbrances, or any such other matters as would be determined by an actual survey and physical inspection of the premises.[5]

This sale may be executed in counterparts, which, when taken together, shall constitute one instrument.

The masculine pronoun as used herein shall include the feminine; the singular shall include the plural, and vice versa.

THUS DONE, READ AND PASSED on the _____ day of _________________, 20____, in _____________________, Louisiana, in the presence of the undersigned competent witnesses who have signed their names together with the parties to this act and me, notary.

WITNESSES:

______________________________	_________________________________
Print Name	EXCHANGER 1's NAME, Exchanger 1[6]
______________________________	_________________________________
Print Name	EXCHANGER 2's NAME, Exchanger 2

____

Notary Name: ________________________________

Notary ID or Bar Roll No.: ____________

My Commission is for Life

[5] Add a similar clause relieving the notary of responsibility for filing this act, if the parties agree that the notary's statutory duty is waived; in that case, this clause should state to whom the act will be delivered and who is responsible for its filing. For waiver of zoning certificate in East Baton Rouge Parish, see "cash sale" sample.

[6] If signed in counterparts in authentic form, create multiple blocks with conclusion, witnesses, signator, and notary.

BOND FOR DEED CONTRACT

STATE OF LOUISIANA

PARISH OF ____________________

BOND FOR DEED[1]

BEFORE ME, the undersigned notary, duly commissioned and qualified in the state and parish aforesaid, and in the presence of the two witnesses whose names are hereunto subscribed, PERSONALLY CAME and appeared:

SELLER'S NAME, with full appearance clause including last 4 digits of social security or EIN, whether Seller is married, and change/no change in marital status after the property was acquired, (hereinafter called "Seller"); and

BUYER'S NAME, with full appearance clause including last 4 of social or EIN and marital status, (hereinafter called "Purchaser"),

Which Seller and Purchaser are herein collectively referred to as "Appearers" or "the parties."

Appearers declare that this Contract is a **Bond for Deed** with each other to the effect that Seller will sell immovable property; and Purchaser will purchase the immovable property as hereinafter described with any and all improvements situated thereon.

NOW IT IS CLEARLY UNDERSTOOD AND AGREED THAT THIS DOCUMENT IS NOT A SALE, TRANSFER OR CONVEYANCE BUT ONLY A WRITTEN AGREEMENT TO SELL, TRANSFER AND CONVEY THE HEREIN DESCRIBED PROPERTY IN THE FUTURE PROVIDED ALL OF THE TERMS, CONDITIONS, PAYMENTS AND OBLIGATIONS SET FORTH HEREIN ARE FULLY, COMPLETELY AND TIMELY MET BY PURCHASER.

TERMS OF SALE: Appearers further declare that contemporaneously with the final payment, a sale is to be executed by the said Seller in favor of the said Purchaser in the standard form for a Louisiana cash sale with full warranty of title. The cost of all necessary certificates and vendor's fee shall be paid by Seller and all notarial fees and other expenses shall be paid by Purchaser.

PROPERTY: If, and only if, Purchaser makes all payments prescribed herein and promptly pays all tax assessments and insurance as set forth hereinafter. Seller will at that time execute a sufficient warranty deed, selling and conveying unto Purchaser the following described real property, to wit:

Legal description including municipal address if any (or attach as a referenced exhibit).

[1] The bond for deed contract should be recorded in both the mortgage records and the conveyance records of the parish where the property is located, to ensure the rights of the bond for deed contract are made effective. If the notary is not going to be the one to file it, a waiver of that duty should be stated in the act.

BOND FOR DEED CONTRACT

The said property is subject to any and all restrictions, conditions and servitudes that may appear in the records of _______________ Parish.

CERTIFICATES: Appearers take cognizance of the fact that no survey, nor title examination has been made on the herein described property examination has been made on the herein described property in connection with this Act, and Appearers do hereby relieve and release me, Notary, from any and all liability in connections with encroachment which might appear on such survey and title defects which might have been disclosed by such title examination.

PUBLIC RECORDS: This Bond for Deed will be recorded in the mortgage and conveyance records of the Parish where the Property is located.

PURCHASE PRICE: The total purchase price for the property and any improvements thereon shall be the sum of

____ ($ _____________) DOLLARS.
Appearers declared that contemporaneously with the execution of this instrument, Purchaser has paid to Seller the sum of

____ ($ _____________) DOLLARS,
cash in hand paid, the receipt whereof and the sufficiency thereof is hereby acknowledged, and Purchaser does hereby bind Purchaser, and assigns, to pay unto Seller the additional sum of

____ ($ _____________) DOLLARS,
with interest at the rate of ________% per annum on the unpaid principal balance, payable as follows:

PAYMENTS: Said payments are to be made beginning _________________, 20____, and on the same day of each succeeding month thereafter until the full principal sum has been paid. All payments are to be made to Seller, or to any banking or financial institution designated by Seller. If such an institution is designated, the Purchaser will pay the collection fees required.

ACCELERATION: Seller may require immediate payment in full of all sums if:

1. Within any consecutive twelve-month period, Purchaser defaults by failing to pay in full any two monthly payments within 30 days of the due date; OR

2. Purchaser defaults by failing to pay in full any principal payment required by this Bond for Deed Contract within 30 days of the due date; OR

3. Purchaser defaults by failing, for a period of thirty days after notice, to perform any other obligations contained in this Bond for Deed contract.

WARRANTY: Seller further declares and warrants that the property is not subject to any liens or encumbrances whatsoever and has not been alienated since its acquisition of the same and transferred to the said Purchaser, execute or permit any mortgages, liens or encumbrances to be placed on the said property and will at the time that the title is transferred, clear any inscriptions appearing on the mortgage and conveyance certificates.

Further, the parties acknowledge that this contract is binding and heritable upon the heirs and assigns of all parties. In the event that the Purchaser must take legal action to cure any title defect, cancel any lien or encumbrance or otherwise incur legal expenses to ensure transfer of the property (e.g., open succession in the event of the Seller's death) those expenses, including attorney's fees, will be paid by the Seller.

TAX DEDUCTION: The interest paid by the Purchaser shall be deductible on the income tax return of Purchaser as allowed by IRS and state taxing authorities.

WAIVER:[2] Purchaser expressly *consents to* a waiver of the requirement of Louisiana Revised Statute 9:2943 that a Louisiana bank be designated as "Escrow" Agent. Seller and Purchaser expressly waive any right that they may have to claim the invalidity of this Bond for Deed Contract because of the noncompliance with the said statute, and all parties agree not to initiate or suggest that any action be taken against Seller under R.S. 9:2947. Purchaser further understands that the said statutes are for the Purchaser's protection.

SPECIAL MORTGAGE: In order to secure the full and faithful performance of the foregoing obligation of Seller to deliver title to the above described property, Seller does by these presents further specially mortgage and hypothecate the hereinabove property unto and in favor of Purchaser and Purchaser's successors, heirs and assigns.

The amount of this special mortgage is equal to the sum of all payments, including but not limited to interest, principal, insurance premiums, taxes, escrow or collection fees, the expenses of maintenance and repairs, and all other payments permitted and/or required by this contract, including reasonable attorney's fees, paid by the Purchaser. This special mortgage shall also secure the loss value to Purchaser, which loss of value is defined to be the difference between the principal purchase price and the market value of the property at the time of foreclosure of this property. The maximum amount of the obligation secured by this special mortgage shall be three (3) times the purchase price.

REPAIRS AND OCCUPANCY: Purchaser is hereby granted the immediate right of exclusive occupancy of the herein described property and agrees to keep the property in good repair, to repair and maintain the improvements, and assume all risk of loss and destruction of said improvements. Purchaser agrees to keep the subject property covered under a termite contract with licensed and bonded pest control contractor.

NO LIENS OR PRIVILEGES: No person shall be entitled to a lien or privilege on the immovable property described hereinabove, nor a claim against Seller as owner, under R.S.

---

[2] The client should consider choosing a licensed institution for bond for deed contracts, but if they choose not to, because fees are too high, they can opt out with this waiver language. If the property is mortgaged, the payments must be made to a third party trustee or bank, so this paragraph must be omitted.

9:4801 or R.S. 9:4802, unless Seller shall have specifically agreed in writing to the price and work of any undertaking by Purchaser or any other person.

TAXES: All taxes assessed against the herein described property up to and including the tax year 20____ have been paid. Taxes for the tax year 20____ have been prorated through the date hereof. All property taxes, any state, local or other assessments, from the date of this Act and thereafter shall be the responsibility of Purchaser, and will be promptly paid by Purchaser when due, prior to the time the same become delinquent.

INSURANCE: Purchaser further agrees to carry, at Purchaser's expense, fire and extended coverage (minimum $___________ personal liability) insurance and flood insurance in the minimum amount required. All necessary insurance policies to protect all parties to be in the names of the respective parties, Seller and Purchaser, as required. Certificates of such insurance shall be delivered to Seller at the time of execution of this agreement. It is understood and agreed that all insurance proceeds that might be paid under said insurance policies will be distributed between Seller and Purchaser as their respective interest may exist at the time of the payment of such insurance proceeds. If the existing insurance is continued, Purchaser agrees to review coverage to ascertain the suitability.

DEFAULT: Appearers further declare that the payment of each installment, plus the payment of all taxes, and any state, local or other assessments and insurance premiums is of the essence of this agreement and that if any of the said installments, taxes, assessments or insurance premiums are not paid when due or if Purchaser shall in any other manner violate the covenants hereunder, them in any of such events, Purchaser shall be in default and Seller shall have the right, at Seller's option:

1. To seek specific performance of this Agreement, and to accelerate all installments due for the unexpired term of this Agreement, and declare said amount immediately due and payable, together with an attorney's fee of 20% of the total amount due by Purchaser, in the event an attorney is employed to protect any interest or enforce any rights of Seller under this Agreement. Upon payment of all such amounts Seller will immediately convey title to the herein described property to Purchaser. Purchaser expressly waives demand and all notices of demand; OR
2. To have this Agreement and the Special Mortgage granted hereinabove canceled in accordance with the provisions of R.S. 2945 and Civil Code article 2017, without the necessity of a judicial dissolution. It is expressly agreed that Seller may serve the required forty-five (45) day notice. Purchaser expressly waives any additional time in which to perform that may be allowed by Louisiana Civil Code article 2013. In such event, all of Purchaser's rights under this Agreement shall be forfeited as hereinafter provided.

FORFEITURE: in the event of such default and cancellation under R.S. 9:2945, the title to the above described property shall be free and clear from any and all claims by Purchaser, and Seller shall be entitled to retain all payments heretofore made by Purchaser and all improvements placed upon the said premises without reimbursing Purchaser therefor.

BOND FOR DEED CONTRACT

It is expressly agreed and stipulated that the initial payment, plus the total installments paid by Purchaser, constitute the stipulated compensatory amount and/or liquidated damages which Seller is entitled to retain to fairly compensate Seller for: (1) the fair and reasonable rental value of the property involved herein which is owed to Seller for Purchaser's use of the property during the term of this Agreement, (2) reasonable compensation owed to Seller for Seller's removal of the said property from the market, and the resulting loss of all opportunities to sell the subject property to a third party during the term of this Agreement, (3) reimbursement of real estate agent's or broker's commission, closing fees and costs, taxes, fees and Federal and State incomes taxes paid or incurred by Seller as a result of this Agreement.

Further, Purchaser covenants and agrees that they and all persons holding possession of the property described herein shall immediately surrender said property and the improvements thereon to Seller upon cancellation of this Agreement.

NO WAIVER: Seller's failure to strictly and promptly enforce his rights under this Agreement shall NOT operate as a waiver of Seller's rights, and said Seller hereby expressly reserves the right to always enforce prompt payment of all installments during the entire term of this Agreement, or to seek cancellation of this Agreement and forfeiture of all payments to the day of such cancellation, regardless of any indulgences or extensions previously granted.

COMPLIANCE: Each party agrees to comply with the reasonable requirements of the taxing and policing authorities having dominion over the property. Seller agrees to take no act which renders performance impossible by the Purchaser and to take all reasonable measures to permit Purchaser to satisfy Purchaser's obligations.

NO SURVEY: The parties to this Act are aware of the fact that no survey has been made in connection with this transaction, and hereby release and relieve me, Notary, from defects which might have been disclosed by a survey of the property.

THUS DONE, READ AND PASSED on the _____ day of __________________, 20____, in ____________________, Louisiana, in the presence of the undersigned competent witnesses who have signed their names together with the parties to this act and me, notary.

WITNESSES:

____________________________	______________________________
Print Name	SELLER'S NAME, Seller
____________________________	______________________________
Print Name	PURCHASER'S NAME, Purchaser

____

Notary Name: ________________________________

Notary ID or Bar Roll No.: ____________

My Commission is for Life

ACT OF MORTGAGE

MORTGAGES & PROMISSORY NOTES

STATE OF LOUISIANA

PARISH OF ___________________

MORTGAGE

BEFORE ME, the undersigned notary, duly commissioned and qualified in the state and parish aforesaid, and in the presence of the two witnesses whose names are hereunto subscribed, PERSONALLY CAME and appeared:

Wes Lee Westley (xxx-xx-1234), a person of the full age of majority and domiciled in Sabine Parish, Louisiana, and Princess D. Buttercup (xxx-xx-5678), a person of the full age of majority and domiciled in Sabine Parish, Louisiana, and whose mailing address is 1111 Cliffs of Insanity Dr., Florien LA 71429, who declare to me that they have been married but once, unto each other,[1] and remain married and reside together (herein referred to collectively as "MORTGAGOR," whether singular or plural),

Who declared that MORTGAGOR is justly and truly indebted unto:

Prince L. Humperdink (xxx-xx-6666), a person of the full age of majority and a domiciliary of Sabine Parish, Louisiana, and whose present mailing address is 99 Fire Swamp Dr., Florien LA 71429, who declares to me that he has never been married (herein "MORTGAGEE," whether singular or plural).

To represent this debt, MORTGAGOR has subscribed his one certain promissory note dated this day to the order of Prince Humperdink in the amount of $100.00 and stipulating to bear interest at the rate of Eight per cent (8%) per annum until paid, said note being payable in four (4) monthly installments of twenty five dollars and 00/100 ($25.00), the first such installment being due and payable on October 12, 2023, and a like installment being due and payable on the first day of each succeeding month thereafter until paid, which ***note was paraphed "Ne Varietur" by me Notary***, for identification herewith, and MORTGAGEE acknowledges its receipt and accepts this mortgage.

In order to secure the full payment of this indebtedness in principal and interest, together with all costs, including attorney's fees of 100 % per cent of the amount due or in suit, if it should be placed in the hands of an attorney for collection, by suit or otherwise, MORTGAGOR specially

---

[1] Even in a mortgage, as with appearance clauses in acts of sale, there must also be a statement of the change (or not) in marital status of any transferor of the property since they acquired it. That does not seem to be necessary where no transferor appears in the particular stand-alone act of mortgage.

mortgages unto MORTGAGEE and such person or persons who may eventually be the holder or holders of the note, the following described property:

Legal description of property including municipal address, if any; or attach as an exhibit but reference here that it is attached, for example as "Exhibit A."

The property shall remain mortgaged until the full payment of the note. It shall not be sold, alienated, or encumbered to the MORTGAGEE'S prejudice. If the debt, or any part of it, is not punctually paid at its maturity and according to its tenor, it shall be lawful for the property mortgaged to be seized and sold under executory process issued by any court of competent jurisdiction, without appraisement, to the highest bidder, payable cash: MORTGAGOR hereby expressly confesses judgment in favor of any holder or the note, for its full amount with interest, and cost including attorney's fees and all other amounts secured hereby. MORTGAGOR further expressly waives citation and all notice and delays, including the three-day notice provided by Article 2639 of the Louisiana Code of Civil Procedure.

MORTGAGOR shall pay all taxes assessed and all liens which may be assessed by any government authorities against the property before they become delinquent and keep the buildings and improvements on it, or which may be passed on it, constantly insured against loss by fire and such other casualties as are covered by the Louisiana Standard Fire Policy in an amount equal to the unpaid balance on the note unless otherwise noted herein, in solvent insurance companies and shall deliver the policies and renewals of such insurance to the holder or holders of the note. If MORTGAGOR fails to do so, any holder is authorized (but not obligated) to pay the taxes or liens, and cause such insurance to be effected, at MORTGAGOR'S expense. Said holder shall become subrogated to all the rights and privileges of the governmental authorities to taxes or liens were due, and all sums expended in paying taxes, liens, fees or insurance shalt bear interest at the maximum rate of legal interest authorized by law from date of disbursement, and be further secured by this mortgage to the additional amount of fifteen (15%) per cent of the original amount of the note.

If MORTGAGOR shall become insolvent, or apply to a bankruptcy court to be adjudged a voluntary bankrupt, or proceedings be instituted to have MORTGAGOR adjudged an involuntary bankrupt, or proceedings be taken against MORTGAGOR looking to the appointment or a receiver or syndic, or any proceedings be instituted for the seizure or sale of the property herein mortgaged by judicial process; or in case MORTGAGOR should fail to pay the note or any sum secured by this mortgage, or any part thereof, or the interest thereon, or the taxes, promptly when due or to effect and keep in force insurance, or to transfer and deliver the policies, as herein provided; then, in such event, all the indebtedness shall, ipso facto, **and without any demand or putting in default, become immediately due** and exigible.

All parties sign the within instrument have declared themselves to be of full legal capacity.

Both MORTGAGOR and MORTGAGOR'S spouse declared that they do expressly waive and renounce in favor of the holders of the note any homestead exemption or claim thereto under the Constitution and laws of this State with respect to the property being mortgaged. The word "note" as used above includes the several notes, if more than one is referred to, and that term includes all indebtedness secured hereby, including principal, interest, attorney's fees and costs.

All the agreements and stipulations herein contained, and all the obligations herein assumed, shall inure to the benefit of and be binding upon the heirs, successors and assigns of the respective parties hereto.

THUS DONE, READ AND PASSED on the _____ day of _________________, 20____, in ___________________, Louisiana, in the presence of the undersigned competent witnesses who have signed their names together with the parties to this act and me, notary, after due reading of the whole.

WITNESSES:

____________________________	____________________________
Print Name	WES LEE WESTLEY, Mortgagor[2]
____________________________	____________________________
Print Name	PRINCESS D. BUTTERCUP, Mortgagor
____________________________	____________________________
Print Name	PRINCE L. HUMPERDINK, Mortgagee

____

Notary Name: ______________________________

Notary ID or Bar Roll No.: ___________

My Commission is for Life

[2] Multiple lines can be added on the right margin if there are more than one or two mortgagors (here, both spouses are taking out the mortgage so both sign). If signed in counterparts in authentic form, create multiple blocks with conclusion, witnesses, signator, and notary.

Witnesses are strictly required for an act of mortgage that contains a "confession of judgment" clause as this one does, and as most do because the mortgagee (which is usually an institution rather than a natural person) insists on having executory process to foreclose.

AMENDMENT OF MORTGAGE

STATE OF LOUISIANA

PARISH OF ____________________

AMENDMENT OF MORTGAGE

BEFORE ME, the undersigned notary, duly commissioned and qualified in the state and parish aforesaid, and in the presence of the two witnesses whose names are hereunto subscribed, PERSONALLY CAME and appeared:

Zane Bluesky, a single man of the age of majority and domiciliary of Natchitoches Parish, Louisiana, whose permanent mailing address is 622 Sexton St., Natchitoches, LA 71457, and who declares unto me that he has never been married (herein "Mortgagor"), and

Jon L. Augustus, a single man of the age of majority and domiciliary of Natchitoches Parish, Louisiana, whose permanent mailing address is 108 Mill St., Natchitoches, LA 71457, and who declares unto me that he has never been married (herein "Mortgagee").

Which said Appearers, Mortgagor and Mortgagee, declared that, by act before *Notary name who notarized original mortgage,* Notary Public, dated *date of mortgage*, recorded in MOB_____, Folio _____, for the Parish of Natchitoches, Zane Bluesky, Mortgagor, mortgaged unto Jon L. Augustus, Mortgagee, certain property known as *legal description including municipal address, if any*, and issued its promissory note in the original sum of *amount* dated *date* payable at the interest rate of *interest rate* per annum to the order of Jon L. Augustus, this note which was paraphed for identification with the aforesaid act of mortgage. The note has been reduced by payments to the present balance of *current balance owing on note*, as of this date.

Whereby the Appearers hereby desire to amend the terms of the mortgage as follows:
List all of the changes being made to the mortgage, length of contract, interest rate, etc.

Now, this note and the mortgage identified herewith are hereby amended, changed and modified in the foregoing respects, and no others, all without novation and without prejudice to the effectiveness, validity, enforceability and priority of the mortgagee pursuant to Louisiana R.S. 9:5390.

Whereupon, the said Mortgagee did present unto me the mortgage note here described, and I, Notary Public, paraphed the same "Ne Varietur" for identification with this act of amendment, and returned the said note to Mortgagee, who hereby acknowledges receipt thereof. The parties agree that Mortgagee is responsible for filing this instrument in the appropriate mortgage records of Natchitoches Parish, and that they hold me, notary, harmless from that obligation.

Thus done and passed, <u>IN DUPLICATE ORIGINALS</u>, on the _____ day of _______________, 20____, in ______________________, Louisiana, in the presence of the undersigned competent witnesses who have signed their names together with the parties to this act and me, notary, after due reading of the whole.

AMENDMENT OF MORTGAGE

WITNESSES:

____________________________	____________________________
Print Name	ZANE BLUESKY, Mortgagor[1]
____________________________	____________________________
Print Name	JON L. AUGUSTUS, Mortgagee

____

Notary Name: ______________________________

Notary ID or Bar Roll No.: ____________

My Commission is for Life

[1] Multiple lines can be added on the right margin if there is more than mortgagor (for example, a married couple). Witnesses are used here because the original act of mortgage very likely was an authentic act.

PROMISSORY NOTE

STATE OF LOUISIANA

PARISH OF TANGIPAHOA

PROMISSORY NOTE

$100.00

FOR VALUE RECEIVED, I, we, or either of us, in solido, promise to pay to the order of Bearer at any such place as the holder of the note may designate, the principal sum of One Hundred Dollars and No Cents ($100.00), with interest from August 11, 2023, until paid at the rate of Eight per cent (8%) per annum; interest and principal payable as follows, to-wit:

> Payable in 120 equal consecutive monthly installments of $.07 each, commencing on August 11, 2023, and due on the 11th of each month thereafter with a final installment of all unpaid principal and interest on August 11, 2033;
>
> Prepayment penalty privilege is reserved to the makers of this note to prepay this note in full prior to August 11, 2024 upon a payment of prepayment premium, as set forth herein;
>
> Five per cent (5%) premium on the outstanding principal if prepaid on or before August 11, 2023. Four per cent (4%) premium on the outstanding principal if prepaid on or before August 11, 2024.

The makers of this note and the endorsers, guarantors and sureties hereon hereby severally waive presentment for payment, demand notice of non-payment, protest, and all pleas of division and discussion, and agree that the time of payment hereof may be extended from time to time, one or more times, without notice of such extension or extensions, and without previous consent hereby binding themselves, in solido, unconditionally and as original promissors, for the payment thereof in principal, interest, cost and attorney's fees. It is hereby expressly agreed that failure to pay this note punctually at maturity shall constitute default hereunder or, if this note be payable in installments, that if default be made in any of the payments of the aforesaid installments when and as the same shall become due and payable, then and in that event, the unpaid balance of the aforesaid principal sum at the option of the holder or holders hereof shall become and be due and payable, and the holder or holders hereof may proceed to have seized and sold the property described in the act with which this note is identified, given to secure the same under the terms and in the manner provided in the said act. Every person at any time liable for the payment of the debt evidenced hereby waives any homestead or exemption right against said debt and waives presentment for payment, demand, protest and notice of non-payment of this note and any or all lack of diligence or delays in collection which may occur and consents that the holder or holders may extend the time of payment or otherwise modify the terms of payment or any part of the whole of the debt at any time at the request of any other person liable, and agrees that should this note not be paid at maturity or when due or demandable, as herein provided, or should it become necessary to employ an attorney to enforce the same or recover the amount hereof or any portion of same, or should this note be placed in the hands of an attorney for collection or compromise or for any other reason to pay the fees of such attorneys, which are hereby fixed at Twenty-five (25%) per cent (minimum fee $200.00) on the amount then due on this note with interest and all costs.

PROMISSORY NOTE

By: ______________________________

SABRINA R. WESTLEY, Member/Manager

It is understood and agreed that if the monthly payments provided for in the note herein issued shall not be received by the holder of the note within fifteen (15) days after said payment is due, the maker(s) of the note herein issued shall pay to the holder a "late charge" of Four per cent (4%) of such monthly installments, to cover the extra expense involved in handling delinquent payments.

"NE VARIETUR"
For identification with an Act of
Credit Sale executed before me
this 12th day of August, 2023.

____

Nancy Tam Salinas, Notary Public
Notary Identification No. 123456

For value received, the undersigned, individually and in solido, hereby guarantees the payment of the within note and any renewal of same, and hereby waive protest, demand, and notice of non-payment thereof and agree to be obligated on said note as maker.

____

SABRINA R. WESTLEY

PROMISSORY NOTE, ALTERNATE

STATE OF LOUISIANA

PARISH OF JEFFERSON

PROMISSORY NOTE

$*total amount of debt*

As of *date of note*,

For value received, the undersigned, *name* ("Maker"), promises to pay to the order of *name* ("Lender" or "Holder"), the amount of $*dollars and cents*, together with interest from the date above until paid at the rate of *interest rate* percent per annum.

This note is payable in *number of payments* consecutive monthly installments of principal and interest in the amount of $*note payment* commencing on *date*, and continuing on the same day of each succeeding month thereafter through and until *date*, when the entire unpaid principal balance and all accrued interest shall be due and payable.

This note may be prepaid in whole or in part at any time without payment of premium or penalty.[1] A partial prepayment will not reduce the fixed monthly installments due.

Both the principal and interest are payable in lawful money of the United States of America at *city where payments are made*, Louisiana, or at such other place as Holder may from time to time designate.

If any payment hereunder is not paid strictly when due and Maker fails to cure the default within *number of days for default* days after receipt of a written notice of default, then Holder, at Holder's option, may without additional notice to Maker declare the entire principal balance, together with all accrued interest, to be immediately due and payable and the entire indebtedness shall be immediately due and payable without presentment, demand, protest, notice of protest, notice of intention to accelerate or other notice of any kind, all of which are expressly waived.

Notwithstanding anything to the contrary in this note, if for any reason the effective rate of interest on the indebtedness evidenced by this note should exceed the maximum lawful rate of interest, the effective rate of interest on the indebtedness will be deemed reduced to and will be the maximum lawful rate. Any amounts of interest that have been collected in excess of the maximum lawful rate will be applied by the holder as a credit against the unpaid principal amount due.

Maker and endorsers, sureties and guarantors severally waive presentment for payment, demand, notice of nonpayment, protest, and agree that a payment may be extended from time to time, one or more times, without notice, binding themselves, solidarily, unconditionally, and as original promisors for the payment in principal and interest, costs and attorney's fees and expenses.

[1] Prepayment penalty can be modified.

PROMISSORY NOTE, ALTERNATE

No delay on the part of Holder in exercising any rights hereunder shall operate as a waiver of such rights.

If this note is placed in the hands of an attorney or attorneys at law for collection, to prosecute claims in bankruptcy, to institute legal proceedings to recover the amount, or any part, in principal or interest, for compromise or other action, or otherwise to protect the interests of Holder, then Maker and endorsers of the note bind themselves, jointly, severally and in solido, to pay the reasonable fees of the attorney(s) who may be employed or retained for that purpose.

This note shall be governed by and construed in accordance with the laws of Louisiana.

By: ______________________________

Maker *(Borrower)*

"NE VARIETUR"
For identification with an Act of Mortgage executed before me this 12th day of August, 2024.

____

Sarah Lane Trahan, Notary Public
Bar Roll No. 26332

GRANT OF USUFRUCT

OTHER ACTS RELATED TO IMMOVABLES

:

STATE OF LOUISIANA

PARISH OF LAFAYETTE

GRANT OF USUFRUCT[1]

BEFORE ME, the undersigned Notary Public, duly commissioned and qualified in and for the Parish and State aforesaid, and before the undersigned competent witnesses, personally came and appeared:

JANET PAULINE SUGGS, born Huff (hereinafter "Grantor" or "Appearer"), a single woman of the age of majority domiciled in Lafayette Parish, whose TIN ends in 2037, who has been married but once, to Thomas R. Suggs, from whom she was divorced before acquiring the property hereafter described, and whose mailing address is 123 Main St., Lafayette, LA 70502,

And who declared and said that she is the owner of the property described as follows:

Legal property description (our example in Breaux Bridge), including municipal address if one is available (or add at end as an attachment, and reference here that it is Exhibit A).

And the said Appearer declared that she does, by these presents, grant, convey, assign, set over, and deliver unto MARTHA LEE MATTHEWS and PHILIP I. MATTHEWS (hereinafter collectively "Grantee"), a married couple each of the age of majority and domiciled in St. Martin Parish, during their natural lives,[2] the usufruct of the property in indivision, hereinabove described and now occupied by said usufructuaries.

This grant is made and accepted for and in consideration of the price of $226,800.00, which the Grantee has paid to Grantor, who acknowledges the receipt of the purchase price and grants full

---

[1] This form, also called "Act of Usufruct," transfers an interest in an immovable from an owner to a usufructuary (though it can also be a movable, if adapted). This one is structured as a sale of the interest, with compensatory terms. The grant may also be done as a donation; in such case, the parties may be "donor" and "donee," though the terms above are fine, as long as the instrument is in authentic form. Even as a sale, it should be done as an authentic act, because it later could be determined to be inadequate payment and thus gratuitous.

Because it transfers an interest in an immovable, appearance clauses should include, in addition to marital status of each party, a status change/no-change clause for the *grantor*. It does not require social security or EIN unless the financing is included in the act (owner financing). It is valid upon signing but must be filed to be effective against third parties. If a party will file it, the act needs to state that the notary is relieved from the duty.

[2] This term can also be stated in terms of years, or upon some lawful condition such as a person's remarrying. This example has two usufructuaries but need not have two. If there is only one, delete the paragraph making the usufructuaries bound jointly.

acquittance and discharge. The parties hereby agree that this is a fair and just price for the value of the interest received herein.

Grantor acknowledges that it has received full and adequate consideration for the Property conveyed. Accordingly, Grantor waives any vendor's lien it may have and any right to rescind this sale, in whole or in part, for failure to pay the consideration or any part of it.

And the said usufructuaries declare that they accept the said usufruct, acknowledge delivery thereof, and bind themselves to pay all taxes upon the property above described and to maintain it in the condition in which it now is, in its entirety, during the existence of the usufruct.

The usufructuaries bind themselves jointly, severally, and in solido to make the usual repairs to the property covered by this usufruct, necessary to keep said house and premises in as good order as they now are.

Grantor waives inventory, appraisement, and security.

Grantee appears herein to accept the usufruct and agrees that during the term of the usufruct they will maintain the property and keep it in good repair, and pay all taxes that may fall due on the property. The entire building, which the usufructuaries are to possess and enjoy as herein stipulated, is to be kept insured by Grantee against damages from fire and windstorm in a solvent company or companies in the full sum of $450,000.00, or current market value, whichever is higher, and the usufructuaries are to promptly pay all premiums therefor. It is agreed and understood that in the case of damage or destruction by fire of the said property, total or partial, through no fault of the usufructuaries, the owner is to repair or rebuild, as the case may require, said house and premises, out of or with the proceeds realized under the insurance herein stipulated, and the right of usufruct herein granted and accorded shall continue and affect the new building, if any, erected in the place of the old; all in substantial compliance with the terms and the spirit of this act. Grantee shall/shall not *[parties choose one]* have the right to dispose of nonconsumables without the consent of Grantor.

Grantee agrees to indemnify and hold harmless Grantor from any liability arising out of Grantee's exercise of this usufruct, and agrees to maintain liability insurance coverage with minimum limits of $500,000.00, and to have Grantor named as an additional insured on such coverage.

The parties to this act are aware of the fact that no survey has been made in connection with this transaction, and hereby release and relieve me, Notary, from defects which might have been disclosed by a survey of the property.

THUS DONE, READ AND PASSED on the _____ day of ___________________, 20____, in ______________________, Louisiana, in the presence of the undersigned competent witnesses who have signed their names together with the parties to this act and me, notary, after due reading of the whole.

GRANT OF USUFRUCT

WITNESSES:

______________________________	____
Print Name	JANET PAULINE SUGGS, Grantor
______________________________	____
Print Name	MARTHA LEE MATTHEWS, Grantee
	____
	PHILIP I. MATTHEWS, Grantee

____

Notary Name: ________________________________

Notary ID or Bar Roll No.: _____________

My Commission is for Life

RELEASE OF USUFRUCT

STATE OF LOUISIANA

PARISH OF ____________________

RELEASE OF USUFRUCT

BEFORE ME, the undersigned duly commissioned and qualified Notary Public, came and appeared the undersigned

Affiant, a widow(er), who has been married [but once, and then to…] [first to … etc.] *appearance clause stating number of marriages and to whom, the last one causing Affiant to be a widow(er)*,

Who, after being first duly sworn, deposed and said:

1. That she is the legatee of a certain usufruct over the property located at *municipal address of property if available, legal description if no municipal address exists* which she was recognized in a Judgment of Possession entered in "The Succession of *Decedent's name (usually spouse)," then enter full title and caption of the probate proceedings here which granted the usufruct, example probate case number, district court number*, and recorded in the public records of _____________ Parish as Original No. ____ Bundle ______;
2. That pursuant to that judgment, the usufruct was a legal usufruct granted by Louisiana Civil Code article 890, and conditioned upon Affiant not remarrying;
3. That on or about *date*, Affiant did remarry and as such relinquished her usufruct back to the naked owners *insert names of naked owners*;
4. Affiant agrees and stipulates that she has abandoned the usufruct and that it has returned to the naked owners stated above.

____

Affiant

SWORN TO AND SUBSCRIBED BEFORE ME this ______ day of ___________________, 20_____

____

Notary Name: ______________________________

Notary ID or Bar Roll No.: ____________

My Commission is for Life

ACT OF PARTITION

STATE OF LOUISIANA

PARISH OF ____________________

ACT OF PARTITION[1]

BEFORE ME, the undersigned notary, duly commissioned and qualified in the state and parish aforesaid, and in the presence of the two witnesses whose names are hereunto subscribed, PERSONALLY CAME and appeared:

Full name of owner #1 and appearance clause including change/no change in marital status, hereafter "Owner 1," and

Full name of owner #2 and appearance clause including change/no change in marital status, hereafter "Owner 2,"

Who declared unto me:

That they are the property owners in indivision of the property described below (hereafter, the "Property"):

Tract 1: Insert legal description, including municipal address if one is available, or attach as Exhibit A and reference to it here as incorporated into this act

Tract 2: Insert legal description, including municipal address if one is available, or attach as Exhibit B and reference to it here as incorporated into this act

Appearers declare that they no longer wish to remain owners in indivision and hereby partition the property as follows:

Owner 1 hereby transfers all interest, rights, title and claims he has to Tract 1 to Owner 2 in full ownership.

Owner 2 hereby transfers all interest, rights, title and claims he has to Tract 2 to Owner 1 in full ownership.

This Act of Partition is made without any warranties as to title, fitness for purpose, redhibition, or any other warranties.
No surveys have been conducted, nor have any mortgage conveyance tax zoning, or flood certificates been requested nor produced. Appearers hereby release the undersigned notary from

---

[1] This is for land that is divided into tracts. If the land is one undivided piece of property, it will have to either be partitioned by licitation, or be divided first at a municipal zoning hearing. The act could also be used for movables, where there is no need to go before a government authority. It could be used without approval for immovables where there are two already separated entities, recognized in the title records. It cannot be used without licitation or zoning approval for merely taking one 80-acre tract and dividing into two 40-acre ones.

any liability in the non-production of any and all documents and certificates in the Act of Partition.

This Act of Partition shall be binding on Appearers, their successors, heirs, and assigns, forever.

Property tax for the current year have been paid, by the Appearers.

Notice to tax assessor: The person responsible for all property taxes and assessments for Tract 1 shall be Owner 2, and the address to which the tax and assessment notices are to be mailed is Owner 2, *address, city, state and zip code.*

Notice to tax assessor: The person responsible for all property taxes and assessments for Tract 2 shall be Owner 1 and the address to which the tax and assessment notices are to be mailed is Owner 1, *address, city, state and zip code.*

The responsibility for filing will be with the executing notary, as delivered to the notary by the parties.[2]

THUS DONE AND PASSED at ______________________, Louisiana, this ____ day of __________________, 20____.

WITNESSES:[3]

________________________________	______________________________________
Print witness name	Print name of *Owner 1,* Owner 1
________________________________	______________________________________
Print witness name	Print name of *Owner 2,* Owner 2

____

Notary Name: ____________________________

Notary ID or Bar Roll No.: ___________

My Commission is for Life

[2] Can be changed to relieve the notary of this duty and have the original delivered to one named party for filing.

[3] The Act of Partition is not necessarily an authentic act, so witnesses are optional. But it is advisable to have the act signed with witnesses and treated as authentic, because the differing values of the two tracts may be enough that one could later allege this is actually a donation and should have been made in authentic form.

ACT OF CORRECTION BY NOTARY (CLERICAL ERRORS)

STATE OF LOUISIANA

PARISH OF ____________________

ACT OF CORRECTION BY NOTARY[1]

BEFORE ME, the undersigned notary, duly commissioned and qualified in the state and parish aforesaid, and in the presence of the two witnesses whose names are hereunto subscribed, PERSONALLY CAME and appeared:

JOHN GOODMAN, Notary Public, of the age of majority and domiciled in Washington Parish, Louisiana ("Appearer"), who after being duly sworn appears, deposes and declares:

That Appearer acted as Notary Public in regard to a certain Act of Sale in the amount of $986,000.00, dated and passed before him June 16, 2018, from Mary Jane Trainor-Smith to Manuel H. Garcia, conveying the property at 123 Main St., Bossier City, LA 71111, and recorded June 22, 2018, in the Parish of Bossier, affecting that property;

That the referenced Act of Sale document incorrectly referenced the said property as being in Section 14 when it should have stated that the property is located in Section 24, so that the property should be described as:

Insert a complete, corrected legal description of the affected property.

Now, wishing to take advantage of Louisiana R.S. 35.2.1 (or as amended) and more particularly that provision allowing a notary to file an act of correction to correct a clerical error, Appearer executes this act to amend the aforesaid Act of Sale to correct the original document as specified above; and Appearer, the notary to that act, further requests that the Clerk of Court for Bossier

---

[1] This is the act of correction made by the notary to a previous act (here, an act of sale), now executed before another notary. The "appearer" is the original notary. This act is limited to clerical errors (such as the misspelling of a party's name, a misstatement of the property address, or inconsistent dates listed in the sale document). It must be in authentic form. It is not crucial who made the error in the first place as long as it is not a substantive error. The appearer may be either the notary before whom it was passed (as it is stated in the above example) or the notary who prepared the original act (in which case the form should be adapted to state that). It may even be the notary who has possession of the records, supporting the correction, of that notary (such as a successor to a notary practice), if the notary is dead, incapacitated, or unable to be located.

Although this act of correction may be made as to both movables and immovables (or related rights such as a usufruct), this particular form contemplates an immovable or valuable movables which have been registered in parish records. A simpler affidavit of correction that need not be in authentic form may be used for OMV filings involving motor vehicles (and see the chapter on movables and titled vehicles for the appropriate form).

When a substantive error was made that is more than a typo or clerical error, but instead affects the material rights of the parties (such as omitting important terms agreed to, or omitting an entire party rather than just misspelling their name, or having a party appear individually when it is their LLC that is the real party), the proper act is "Act of Correction by Party." In any event, "The act of correction shall not alter the true agreement and intent of the parties." LA R.S. 35.2.1(B).

ACT OF CORRECTION BY NOTARY (CLERICAL ERRORS)

Parish, Louisiana make a marginal notation on the original act above-described, making reference to this Act of Correction.

Appearer hereby authorizes the Clerk and Recorder in and for Bossier Parish, Louisiana to record this Act of Correction in the records of his or her office to serve as occasion may require.

THUS DONE, PASSED AND SIGNED, on the _____ day of __________________, 20____, in ____________________, Louisiana, in the presence of the undersigned competent witnesses, who have signed their names together with the appearers and me, notary.

WITNESSES: APPEARER:

____________________________ ______________________________

Print Name JOHN GOODMAN

____

Print Name

____

Notary Name: _________________________________

Notary ID or Bar Roll No.: _______________

My Commission is for Life

ACT OF CORRECTION BY PARTY (SUBSTANTIVE OR CLERICAL ERRORS)

STATE OF LOUISIANA

PARISH OF ____________________

ACT OF CORRECTION BY PARTY[1]

BEFORE ME, the undersigned notary, duly commissioned and qualified in the state and parish aforesaid, and in the presence of the two witnesses whose names are hereunto subscribed, PERSONALLY CAME and appeared:

LOLLIPOPS, INC., A Louisiana corporation represented herein by Sheldon Lollipop, Sr., its duly authorized officer (hereafter referred to as "Appearer"), who after being duly sworn declares that:

Appearer executed Declaration of Covenants and Restrictions for Lollipop Estates, dated March 7, 2024 and recorded as:

Lot 1, Sq 1, of the official records of Jefferson Parish, Louisiana.

An error was committed in the first Paragraph of the document in describing the property subject to said Covenants, Conditions, and Restrictions. It was erroneously written:

"Lots 1 through 200 in Lollipop Estates as shown on the plat by Cotton Candy Engineering entitled 'Final Plat of Lollipop Estates Filings One through Four, filed in the records of the Clerk of Jefferson Parish'."

Appearer hereby agrees to reform the above described Declaration of Covenants, Conditions and Restrictions for Lollipops Estates as follows:

"Lots 1 through 50 in Lollipop Estates as shown on the plat by Cotton Candy Engineering dated March 7, 2024, entitled 'Final Plat of the Lollipop Estates, First Filing, filed in the records of the Clerk of Court of Jefferson Parish, in Original 1, Bundle 2'."

Appearer hereby authorizes the Clerk and Recorder in and for Jefferson Parish, Louisiana to record this Act of Correction in the records of his office to serve as occasion may require, and to notate upon the original act a reference to this Act of Correction.

THUS DONE, PASSED AND SIGNED, on the _____ day of __________________, 20_____, in ____________________, Louisiana, in the presence of the undersigned competent witnesses, who have signed their names together with the appearer and me, notary.

---

[1] This act may be used for substantive errors in the original act, and also mere clerical errors, as long as the correction does not change the original intent. See further notes for the similar Act of Correction by Notary, which is limited to correcting clerical errors such as typos and misspelled parties.

In this version, all parties to the original act appear before a notary (even the same notary they used before) and execute the act of correction. Although this version is not always required to be in authentic form – unless the original act was—it is advisable to do any correction regarding an immovable in authentic form; the preparer of this act may not know for sure whether the original act was an authentic act or should have been.

ACT OF CORRECTION BY PARTY (SUBSTANTIVE OR CLERICAL ERRORS)

WITNESSES:	LOLLIPOPS, INC.
______________________________	______________________________
Print Name	BY: Sheldon Lollipop, Sr., President and CEO
______________________________	
Print Name	

____

Notary Name: ____________________________________

Notary ID or Bar Roll No.: __________________

My Commission is for Life

STATE OF LOUISIANA

PARISH OF ___________________

COUNTERLETTER[1]

BEFORE ME, the undersigned notary, duly commissioned and qualified in the state and parish aforesaid, and in the presence of the two witnesses whose names are hereunto subscribed, PERSONALLY CAME and appeared:

Appearer's name, of full legal age of majority and domiciled in _____________ Parish, *then remaining appearance clause, including change (or not) in marital status if act relates to a transfer of an interest in immovables.*

Hereinafter referred to as "Appearer," who did declare that they did, on *date of notarial act*, before *name of notary they appeared before*, by *type of act [for example Cash Sale]*, did record in the conveyance records for the Parish of ________________, in COB folio number *folio and page number*, the following property:

Legal description, including municipal address, if one exists.

That Appearer has never held any ownership interest in said property; that title was placed in Appearer's name for convenience only; and that the above-described property was purchased for *name of true owner.* Appearer does obligate himself to execute any act necessary such that *true owner* can receive all rights and title to the said property.

Filing of this instrument shall be the responsibility of __________________, to whom this act is hereby delivered for filing.

THUS DONE AND PASSED on the _____ day of ____________, 20___, in _______________, Louisiana, in the presence of the undersigned competent witnesses, who have signed their names together with the parties to this act and me, notary.

WITNESSES: APPEARER:

____________________________ ______________________________

Print Name

____

Print Name

____

Notary Name: ____________________________

Notary ID or Bar Roll No.: ____________

My Commission is for Life

[1] This is a simplified version of a counterletter. Please consider needs of the client and modify the form as needed. This version follows and applies to a transaction that had involved an immovable; other common uses for counterletters involve other types of contracts and operating agreements.

COMMERCIAL REAL ESTATE LEASE

STATE OF LOUISIANA

PARISH OF ____________________

COMMERCIAL REAL ESTATE LEASE

BEFORE ME, the undersigned notary, duly commissioned and qualified in the state and parish aforesaid, and in the presence of the two witnesses whose names are hereunto subscribed, PERSONALLY CAME and appeared:

Name of owner or owner's agent, (referred to "Lessor"), by this agreement leases to *Name of lessee* (referred to as "Lessee"), the following described premises: *address* located at *city*, Louisiana, *zip code* (hereinafter, "premises").

This lease is for the term of _______ months commencing on *date* and ending on *date*.

Section I

(A) This lease is made for and in consideration of a base monthly rental of $*base rent* ("base rental"), payable monthly, in advance without prior written notice, to Lessor, at the office of *place*, on the 1st day of every calendar month of the term of this lease. The obligations of all Lessees being individually and jointly in solido, Lessor may from time-to-time designate other places for the payment of the rent by written notice mailed to Lessee.

(1) In the event that the Lessee fails to pay any rental installment when due, a **delinquency fee** in the amount of $*amount of delinquency fee* will be assessed against the Lessee for each monthly rental installment that is missed or late. This fee will compensate Lessor for damages incurred by Lessor for the additional administrative duties caused by Lessee's failure to render timely payment of the rent.

(2) In addition, for each month thereafter that each rental installment remains unpaid, Lessee must pay an additional fee to compensate Lessor for damages in the amount of $*additional amount*.

It is agreed that this figure must be charged separately for each installment that is late and shall be charged for each and every month that each of those installments are late.

(B) On execution of this Lease Agreement, Lessee must tender *amount of prepaid months* months prepaid rent amounting to $*dollars of prepaid*, that advance to apply to the rent for the first full calendar month of the primary term and the last *number of months* full calendar months of the primary term, or if there be an *(number of months) extension or renewal or exercised option*, then to the last _____ full calendar months of the last _______ *extension or renewal or exercised option* term.

(1) If the lease begins and/or Lessee is given possession of other than the first day of a month, rent from that date until the first of the next succeeding month will be prorated for each day at the rate of one-thirtieth of the base rental payment, payable in advance on the first day of the term of this lease, with similar prorating for a portion of the last month of the lease term, so that rental payments must be made on the first of each month during the term of the Lease.

(2) Any amounts received by Lessor from or on behalf of the Lessee will be applied to the oldest amounts due in point of time, regardless of any instructions received in those payments.
(3) In the event that the Lessor advances any money or pays any bills on behalf of the Lessee, then the Lessee agrees to pay interest on the unpaid balance from the date of disbursement by the Lessor until that amount is repaid by the Lessee, at the rate of 8% in the cause of a private individual, and 15% in the case of a corporation, limited partnership, and/or of an individual who guarantees the obligation of that corporation or limited partnership.

(C) The premises are to be used only for the following purposes: *list purposes*.
(D) The use of the premises must specifically exclude the following:
(1) Any use by Lessee that in any way obstructs or interferes with the rights or comforts of co-tenants, or injures or annoys them, or their use of their space, nor may the premises be used for lodging, sleeping, manufacturing, or for any improper, immoral, unlawful or illegal purpose and Lessee will not carry on, any trade or occupation on the premises which is in violation of the law.
(2) The use of any portion of the premises as an office for the possession, storage, manufacture or sale of liquor, narcotics or controlled dangerous substances; or as an employment bureau. No Lessee may engage or pay any employees on the premises, except those actually working for the Lessee on the premises, nor advertise for laborers giving an address at the premises.
(3) Parking excessively in the event that there is a parking area provided for the subject building. Lessee is allocated only one car for every 600 square feet of the premises and no additional cars are to be parked in the building lot, within the above allocation, and only those cars of employees of tenants, and tenants are allowed to use the parking lot and then only during business hours or as specified in this lease. Any unauthorized vehicles parked on the premises will be towed away by Lessor at the Lessee's expense.

Section II

(A) Lessor reserves the right to reject any and all offers to renew this lease. In the event the Lessee fails to notify the Lessor at least 90 days before the expiration of this lease or of a renewal of it, in writing, of its intention not to retain the premises and provided that Lessor does not give written notice of its intention to not renew this lease, Lessee is deemed to have made a new lease of the premises for a period of one year from the expiration of this lease or of the renewals subject to the following increases in the base rental:
(B)
(1) Cost of Living. There will be an annual revaluation and increase of the monthly rental payable under this lease based on the Cost of Living Index as established by the United States Department of Labor, Consumer Price Index for Urban Wage Earners and Clerical Workers, All Items Group, commonly identified as the CPI-W ("CPI"), or its successor publication, as published as of the commencement date of this lease or the closest subsequent date on which the CPI is published.
(2) It is the intention of the parties to automatically increase the monthly rental stipulated in this agreement in the same ratio as the CPI increased from the above mentioned date of

publication to each anniversary date of that publication through the original term of this lease and through the term of any extensions or renewals of this lease.

(3) Increasing in rent resulting from increases in the CPI referred to above in subparagraph (2) will be effective without written notice of Lessor. Payment of Lease is due within five days after the increase becomes effective and is to continue monthly throughout the term of the lease subject to increase due to other CPI increases.

(C)

(1) Operating Cost Increases. The base rental assumes recurring payment of the same amounts for: (i) real estate taxes imposed on the building and the land on which it is located no greater than the total amount of those real estate taxes payable by Lessor for the first 12 months that taxes are based on full assessment of it as a completed building or the 12 months at full assessment immediately prior to this date, whichever, is later; (ii) "Insurance" charges payable by Lessor as of this date; (iii) all "Other Operating Costs" as of this date. To the extent that during the term of this lease the real estate taxes payable on the building and land, or the "Insurance" charges, or any or all "Other Operating Costs" or all of the above charges, in any 12-month period dating from and including the month in which the lease term commences, exceed the previously set forth respective amounts of real estate taxes and "Insurance" and all "Operating Costs" for the 12-month base period, any such excess amount or amounts must be deemed to constitute "Excess Operating Costs." Lessee agrees to pay its proportionate share of any "Excess Operating Costs" as additional rent, calculated in the ratio which the square footage of floor area of its premises bears to the total rentable square footage of office and business floor area of the building.

(2) Following the end of each 12-month period successively following the 12-month base period determined, Lessor must determine whether or not it has incurred any Excess Operating Costs, and if any, must notify Lessee of the amounts payable by it pursuant to subparagraph (C)(1) of this section, and the basis for those amounts. Lessee agrees and covenants to pay the full amount or full amounts as additional rent with the next succeeding monthly installment of base rental. Lessor's failure to render a bill for Lessee's share of Excess Operating Costs does not act as a waiver of Lessor's right to that share of Excess Operating Costs. The parties recognize that the necessity for payment of additional rent for Excess Operating Costs may be determinable or fairly estimated from periodic billings prior to expiration of a 12-month period. In that event, Lessor, to avoid accumulation of charges, may make a reasonable estimate of the amount of Excess Operating Costs projected for a given 12-month period as against the base period, to be paid with the next monthly installment of fixed rent, with exact adjustment to be made at the end of the particular 12-month period, at which time Lessor must refund any excess collected as additional rent on its estimate and Lessee must pay any deficiency as the case may be. The original records from which determinations or estimates of Excess Operating Costs are made will be available for examination by Lessee at Lessor's office during business hours until expiration of 60 days after the close of the 12-month period involved.

(D) In the event that Lessor elects to accelerate the rent, as set out below, due to a breach of the lease by the Lessee, then the cost of living increases and Excess Operating Costs must be included in calculating the total rent due by Lessee in that accelerated period.

(E) It is further understood that any failure to pay the above described cost of living increases and Excess Operating Costs due to the Lessor by the Lessee constitutes a breach of this lease, and Lessor has the right to exercise its options and remedies as set out in Paragraph 14 of the lease.

Section III

(A) If during the term of this lease, the described building or premises are destroyed by fire or otherwise, or partially destroyed, so as to render the premises wholly unfit for occupancy, and if they are so badly injured that they cannot be repaired with reasonable diligence within 180 days from the happening of that injury, or if the building is so badly damaged that the Lessor decides not to rebuild or reconstruct it, then on notice this lease will cease and become null and void from the date of that damage or destruction.
(B) In the event of the foregoing the Lessee is nevertheless entitled to a credit corresponding to the unexpired term of the lease, and the Lessee must immediately surrender the premises to the Lessor, who at once has the right to take possession of the premises discharged of this lease and to eject all persons and property from those premises.
(C) If the premises are repaired within 180 days from the happening of injury, then this lease will not be null and void but will continue in effect but the rent must not run or accrue to Lessor while the process of repairs is going on. The Lessor must repair the premises with all reasonable diligence, and the rent must recommence immediately after the repairs shall have been completed and the premises are available for occupancy.
(D) If the premises are so slightly injured by fire or otherwise as not to be rendered unfit for occupancy, then the Lessor agrees that they will be repaired with reasonable diligence in which case the rental payments must not cease or diminish.

Section IV

(A) It is understood and agreed between the Lessor and Lessee that no assent or consent to any waiver of any part of this lease by the Lessor, in spirit or letter, is deemed or taken as made, unless that is done in writing and attached to or endorsed on this lease by the Lessor.
(B) This lease contains and exhibits the agreement between the parties, all previous or contemporaneous agreements being merged in and waived by this agreement, and will be null and void on the signing of this lease by both parties.
(C) It is further agreed that any notice to be given under this lease by Lessor to Lessee is considered duly transmitted if made, in writing, addressed to Lessee and mailed to the Lessee at the premises. Any notice to be given under this lease by Lessee to Lessor is considered duly given if made in writing, addressed to Lessor and mailed by registered or certified mail to Lessor at *address*, *city*, Louisiana *zip code* and so received by Lessor. Either party may change the designated place or places to which its written notice is to be sent by advising the other party in writing by certified or registered mail at the place designated in this lease or at another place as may have been subsequently designated in accordance with this paragraph.

COMMERCIAL REAL ESTATE LEASE

Section V

(A) Lessor or Lessor's agents have made no representations or promises with respect to the described building or the premises except as expressly set forth.
(B) The taking possession of the premises by Lessee is conclusive evidence, as against Lessee, that the premises and the building of which they form a part were in good and satisfactory condition at the time possession was so taken.
(C) By so taking possession of the premises and appurtenances, Lessee accepts the locks, keys, plumbing, plate glass, elevators, lifts, machinery, lighting system and heating system, if any, and all other fixtures in their present condition, and Lessee further agrees to and does assume the responsibility for the care, maintenance and repairs of those fixtures, together with all liability or claims for damages.
(D) Except for those repairs and improvements which are written into this lease and except those which may be needed to the roof or rendered necessary by fire or other casualty, not the fault of Lessee, the Lessee is responsible for all repairs and maintenance and is entitled to no other improvements other than those specifically written into this lease. Lessee further agrees that under no circumstances does it have the right to perform any improvements or repairs on the premises and then apply the cost of those improvements and repairs as a set-off or abatement of rent due.
(E) The Lessee agrees to keep the premises in the same order as received, during the term of this lease, and comply at the Lessee's expense with all ordinances and laws, now existing or to the enacted, and at the termination or cancellation of this lease to return the premises broom clean and free from trash, and in like good order as received and must make actual delivery of the keys to Lessor's Agent.

Section VI

(A) As set out above, Lessee assumes responsibility for the condition of the premises and all appliances and appurtenances of those premises. Lessor is not responsible or liable for damage to persons or property by reason of the condition of the building or of the premises or of any appliance or appurtenance of the premises nor for damage or injury caused by leaks in the roof, bursting or leaking of pipes of plumbing work except in the case of positive neglect of the roof where written notice of the defective condition or otherwise has been given by Lessee to Lessor and the latter has failed to correct that condition within 30 days after the described notice, and in the case of Lessee's failure to promptly so notify Lessor in writing of any defects, Lessee will become responsible for any damage resulting to Lessee or other parties.
(B) The Lessee before closing its office, and leaving the premises at any time, shall see that all windows are closed, thus avoiding possible damage from fire, storms, rain or freezing, and Lessor is not responsible for any resulting damages.
(C) The requirements of Lessee will be attended to only on application at the office of the building. Lessor's employees must not perform any work or do anything outside of their regular duties unless under special instruction from the office of the Lessor and Lessee agrees not to request Lessor's employees to perform any work.
(D) Lessee agrees that under no circumstances will Lessor be liable for damages to Lessee or to any third party.

COMMERCIAL REAL ESTATE LEASE

Section VII

(A) Signs displayed in, on or above the premises are a privilege granted by the Lessor to the Lessee and are not a right. Lessee must not display, in, on or above the premises any sign or decoration, the nature of which, in the judgment of the Lessor is dangerous, detrimental or unsightly with regard to the premises.

Lessee is absolutely prohibited from so exhibiting, painting, posting or affixing any signs on the premises without prior written consent of Lessor. Lessee is obligated to promptly remove any and all signs exhibited, painted, posted or placed in or on any part of the premises, to Lessor's satisfaction and may restore the premises to their original condition. If Lessee does not remove the sign within 24 hours, then Lessor may take legal action to enforce this provision, and the parties agree that injunctive relief will be an appropriate legal remedy. Lessee will be obligated to pay for reasonable attorney's fees and/or fees of Lessor's agent, or Lessor may remove the sign without liability, and may charge the expense incurred by that removal to the Lessee or Lessees violating this rule.

(B) In order to insure uniformity and to make the premises a better place for all tenants, no awnings or other projections may be attached to the outside walls of the building without the prior written consent of Lessor. No curtains, blinds, shades or screens may be attached to, hung in or used in connection with any window or door of the premises without the prior written consent of Lessor. Awnings, projections, curtains, blinds, shades, screens or other fixtures will be approved if they are in harmony with the building and are of a quality, type, design, color and the manner in which they are to be attached to the building are acceptable to Lessor.

(C) Curtains, awnings or venetian blinds which are the property of the Lessee must be removed by Lessee when vacating the building but Lessee must not damage the premises in so doing. Any curtain, shades, awnings or venetian blinds left in or on the building more than 15 days after Lessee vacates becomes the property of the Lessor, Lessee expressly assenting to this provision and waiving any claim to such items.

(D) No showcases or other articles may be put in front of or affixed on any part of the exterior of the building nor placed in the halls, corridors or vestibules in any manner without the prior written consent of Lessor.

(E) In addition, Lessee will pay for the door lettering and directory identification, which is prescribed and is considered standard for this building. Lessor will try to be available to assist Lessee in obtaining the described items at Lessee's expense, but does not by this agreement incur an obligation to do so.

Section VIII

(A) Any background music used by Lessee is to be contracted and purchased through the firm which has the exclusive background music contract for the building, and Lessee is prohibited from contracting with or using any other background music firm.

(B) Lessee, their employees and occupants of the premises must not make, nor permit any loud noise, nor use any loud speaker, radio, radio equipment or musical instrument either inside or outside the building nor do anything that will annoy, disturb or interfere in any way with other tenants or those having business with them. PETS: No dogs, cats or other animals will be allowed in the building.

COMMERCIAL REAL ESTATE LEASE

Section IX

Lessor agrees to pay *name of agent* commission of *percentage* on the gross amount on any agreement to sell or exchange the property covered by this agreement to anyone, which is entered into during the existence of this contract.

Section X

(A) Lessor, Lessor's heirs, successors or assigns agree to pay agent, *name*, their successors or assigns, a cash commission of *percentage amount*% on the gross rental of this lease, and a similar commission on any (*number of) extensions or renewals*, if there is a privilege, the rental commission on this lease to be paid in cash for the whole term when this lease is signed by Lessee and Lessor and/or for the whole extension period or periods and/or renewals when those extension period or periods and/or renewal or renewals become effective.
(B) Lessor agrees that all deposits, prepaid rent and rental payments will be turned over to *name of agent*, its successors or assigns in its capacity as agent for the Lessor.
(C) For management services, Lessor must pay monthly *name of manager*, of the gross rentals.
(D) In the event an authorization to rent and/or management contract is entered into between *name* and Lessor and that contract is terminated during the life of the lease, or if contract is on any month to month rental basis, and if *name of manager* shall cease to manage the building and/or collect the rents, then *name of manager* shall be paid by Lessor, payable in cash at the time of cancellation, any and all amounts due *name of manager*, for the unexpired term of the rental and management commission computed on the full basis as above mentioned.
(E)

(1) In the event that the Lessee fails to comply with the terms of this lease, Lessor will be still obligated to pay the rental commission to *name of manager* since the rental services are rendered and completed when the parties sign the lease.
(2) It is further understood and agreed by Lessor and the Lessee that in the event that the Lessee fails to comply with the terms of this lease, and/or this lease is terminated that any and all prepaid rent in the possession of *name of manager* as Lessor's agent will be applied as payment for any real estate commission or management fees owed to *name of manager* by the Lessor, leaving Lessee and Lessor to settle between them any possible reimbursement if any be due under the terms of this lease.

(F) Lessor also reserves the right to keep posted on the premises signs "For sale" or "By auction" at any time during the terms of this lease and also signs "For rent" during the 120 days preceding the expiration of this lease; and lessee must allow parties authorized by Lessor or Agent to visit the premises in view of buying during the term of this lease and in view of renting for 120 days prior to expiration, from 9:00 a.m. to 5:00 p.m. each day.
(G) In the event that Lessor enters into a new lease with a Lessee originally furnished by *name of agent* then Lessor shall be obligated to pay a cash commission of *percentage*% of the gross rentals agreed on in the new lease to *name of agent*, due and payable on execution by both parties of the new lease.

COMMERCIAL REAL ESTATE LEASE

Section XI

(A) Lessor is permitted to assign this lease either for consideration and/or as security for any debt, either with or without the sale of the building.
(B) Lessor has the right and privilege to change the name of the building.
(C) It is understood and agreed that Lessor may sell the building subject to this lease, or may assign this lease, and in either of those events, all of the provisions of this lease must then apply to the purchaser or assignee of the lease, and Lessor must then be divested of all rights and released from all obligations under this lease, at the option of the Lessor.

Section XII

(A) Lessee is not permitted to re-rent or sublet or assign this lease or grant use or possession of the premises to any other party without the written consent of the Lessor, and then only in accordance with the terms of this lease.
(B) Should the permission to re-rent, sublet or assign this lease be given by Lessor to Lessee, that sublease, etc. must be handled by Lessor's Agent, *name*, at the expense of the Lessee, and Lessee agrees to pay Lessor's Agent a commission of *percentasge*% on the gross rental of that sublease, etc.

Section XIII

(A) Lessee is not permitted to sell food, beverages, tobacco, candy, vending items or merchandise of any kind, in person or by machine.
(B) It is agreed by the Lessee that the right to sell the above mentioned items has been or will be given to one company and/or operator who has, or who will have, the exclusive right to sell these items throughout the building, and for any violation of the preceding provisions the Lessee will be liable to the Lessor for any damage it sustains because of the infringement on the above referred to company's or operator's exclusive right to the concession sales for the entire building.
(C) No cooking may be done or permitted by any Lessee on the premises without first obtaining the written consent of the Lessor.
(D) No Lessee must cause or permit any unusual or objectionable odors to be produced on or to permeate from the premises.

Section XIV

(A) Should the Lessee at any time violate any of the conditions, terms, rules, regulations, restrictions or obligations of this lease and/or should the Lessee actually be ejected for any breach of this lease, or should the Lessee vacate, abandon or discontinue the use of the premises for the purpose for which they were rented, or fail to pay the full rent, penalties, utility bills, cost of living increases in the rent, Excess Operating Costs, or other expenses punctually, at maturity, as stipulated, or on the adjudication of Lessee in bankruptcy, receivership or respite petition by the Lessee; or on Lessee's suspension, failure or insolvency to the prejudice of the Lessor's lien, or remove or attempt to remove a substantial portion of Lessee's personal property and/or furniture, whether or not to the prejudice of the Lessor's lien, then the Lessor may elect to exercise any of the following remedies or options, to wit:

(1) Call due and payable at once the rent for the whole unexpired term of this lease, plus all penalties together with attorney fees of 25% on the full amount of that rent, but in no case less than $500, without putting the Lessee in default, and in which case that entire amount must be tendered to the Lessor immediately on demand.
(2) Cancel the lease, collect any past due rent or other amounts plus all penalties owed it by the Lessee together with attorney fees of 25%, but in no case less than $500, and have the Lessee vacate the premises immediately.
(3) Demand that the Lessee cure any breach of the lease, and if the Lessee complies with the demand, then the Lessor may allow the term of the Lease to continue to run.
(4) Without canceling this lease, to sue for all past due rents, penalties and other charges owed by Lessee together with attorney's fees of 25%, with a minimum fee of $500.
(5) The Lessor may prevent such violations from continuing by obtaining injunctive relief in any court of competent jurisdiction.

(B) In the event that the Lessor elects to accelerate the rent as provided by Section A(1) of this paragraph, then Lessor at its option may reenter and relet the premises for the price and terms as may be immediately obtainable, and apply the net amount realized to the payment of the rent.

Section XV

It is further agreed that in the event that the Lessee should vacate, abandon or discontinue the use of the premises, then the Lessor has the right to change the locks to the premises in order to maintain security for the premises and for the building as a whole. Lessee agrees to the changing of locks and agrees that this will not be construed as a disturbance of the Lessee's peaceful possession. Lessor agrees to permit Lessee access to the premises and/or give a key to the new lock on request by Lessee.

Section XVI

(A) Failure to strictly and promptly enforce any of these conditions does not operate as a waiver of Lessor's rights, Lessor expressly reserving the right to always enforce prompt payment of rent or commissions or Lessee's other obligations as provided in this lease, regardless of any indulgences or extensions previously granted.
(B) The receiving by Lessor, or Lessor's representative of any rent in arrears, or after notice or after institution of any suit for acceleration of rents or for cancellation of this lease, will not be considered as a waiver of notice of suit, or of any of the rights of Lessor, but will only entitle Lessee to a credit for the money received.
(C) Lessee in any and all cases, must pay attorney fees assessed pursuant to this agreement as 25% of the total amount due Lessor in enforcing any of the claims or rights arising from the terms of this lease, but in no case will the attorney fees be less than $500.

Section XVII

Lessor is not liable for any loss, injury or damage to person or property sustained by Lessee or Lessee's representatives, agents, servants, clerks, employees, guests or licensees during its occupancy of the building, the risk and all loss, injury or damage is assumed by the Lessee.

COMMERCIAL REAL ESTATE LEASE

Section XVIII

(A) The sidewalks, entries, passages, vestibules, halls and stairways must not be obstructed in any way, nor must any rags, paper, ashes, dust, rubbish, boxes, books, buckets, bicycles or other objects or things be placed there by Lessee, its employees or any occupants of the premises, nor be used by them for any other purpose than ingress and egress to and from their respective rooms or offices.
(B) All damages to the building or elevators caused by the removal or carrying of articles in them will be assessed to and paid for by Lessee.
(C)
 (1) All furniture, safes and other bulky or heavy articles must be carried up or into the premises only at times and only in a manner as expressly specified and approved by the Lessor, after having received due and adequate notice by the Lessee.
 (2) It is further agreed that in no case may any of those articles be received in the building or carried up or down in the elevators during those hours which may be designated by Lessor in the "Rules and Regulations" as set forth on the back of this lease. The "Rules and Regulations" are subject to change by Lessor at any time on notice to the Lessees.
 (3) Lessor expressly reserves the right to prescribe the weight limitation and position of all articles, brought into the building as well as to designate the proper method for distributing the weight of those articles, and in no case may the Lessee bring into the building above the ground floor any object weighing more than 1,200 pounds.
 (4) The persons employed to move the furniture, safes, heavy or other bulky articles must be acceptable to the Lessor, and the Lessee is responsible for all damage to the building, tenants or other persons caused by the moving.

Section XIX

(A) The Lessor specifically reserves the right to regulate both the number of elevators operated and the times during which those elevators can operate together with the right to stop operation of those elevators at any time which Lessor may deem appropriate.
(B) Lessor must designate the normal hours of elevator operation and promulgate them in the "Rules and Regulations" as set forth on the back of this lease, with it being understood that the "Rules and Regulations" are subject to change at a time by the Lessor on notice to the Lessee.
(C) It is further agreed that the Lessor is not responsible for interrupted elevator service, either partial or total, on account of repairs, breakdowns, strikes, lockouts, or on account of any other cause; nor for any claim arising in consequence of the use of the elevator.

Section XX

(A) The bathrooms, water closets and other water fixtures must not be used for any purpose other than those for which they were constructed, and any damage resulting to them from misuse or the defacing or injury of any part of the building, will be borne by the Lessee, whether caused by Lessee or Lessee's employees or any occupant of Lessee's premises.
(B) Any stoppages in the plumbing must be the complete responsibility of the Lessee and must be promptly corrected on discovery by the Lessee.

COMMERCIAL REAL ESTATE LEASE

Section XXI

(A) No electric wires for any purpose may be brought into the building, except with the permission and under the direction of the Lessor.
(B) If Lessee desires telegraphic or telephone connections, Lessor will direct as to where and how the wires are to be introduced and routed throughout the premises.
(C) There will be no boring or cutting for wires of any nature whatsoever without the express permission of the Lessor, and in the event that the Lessor approves the introduction of such wires, any boring or cutting must be directed by Lessor as to where and how the wires are to be introduced.
(D) Spikes, hooks, screws and nails must not be put into walls, or woodwork of the building, without Lessor's prior written consent.
(E) No Lessee may mark, paint, drill into or in any manner deface any party of the premises or the building of which they form a part.
(F) No Lessee may lay carpet, tile or other similar floor coverings unless by permission of Lessor and then only in a manner that does not come into direct contact with the floor of the premises, and an interlining of builder's deadening felt must be first affixed to the floor by a paste or other material soluble in water, the use of cement or other similar adhesive material being expressly prohibited.
(G) Any violation of the preceding provisions in Paragraph 21 constitutes a breach of the lease and Lessor may elect to exercise any of the remedies as set out in Paragraph 14 or at Lessor's option will be required to immediately restore the premises to their original condition or the Lessor is by this agreement authorized to have restoration undertaken at the expense of the Lessee, at the option of Lessor.

Section XXII

(A) Two keys will be furnished by the Lessor, and no duplicate keys may be made without Lessor's consent.
(B) No additional locks or bolts may be placed on any door of the building without the written consent of the Lessor first obtained and endorsed on this lease, and no change must be made in existing locks or their mechanisms.
(C) Each Lessee must, on termination of its tenancy, restore to the Lessor all keys to stores, offices and toilet rooms, either furnished to or otherwise procured by that Lessee, and in the event of loss of any keys so furnished, that Lessee must pay to Lessor the cost of their replacement, and/or forfeit any deposit which was placed with Lessor when key was first obtained.
(D) Any violation of the above constitutes a breach of the lease and gives rise to the Lessor's remedies as set out in Paragraph 14.

Section XXIII

(A) No Lessee may do or permit anything to be done, in or about the premises, or bring or keep anything in them, which will in any way increase the rate of fire insurance of the building or on property kept in it, or obstruct or interfere with the rights of or otherwise injure or annoy other tenants, or conflict with the laws relating to fires or with the regulations of the Fire Departments,

or with any insurance policy on the building, or any other of the departments of the City or Parish or State of Louisiana.
(B) Lessee is responsible for the payment of the full amount of any additional insurance premium or increased amount or amounts of insurance premium, taxes or any other cost or costs which are caused directly or indirectly by Lessee's occupancy of, or Lessee's acts on the premises, including its lawful normal occupancy, regardless of the purpose for which the premises are leased. These increased amounts will be billed to Lessee in lump sums in advance, which billings must be paid on receipt. This agreement is in addition to the agreement of Lessee to pay its pro rata of increased operating costs set out in Paragraph 2 in this agreement.
(C) No Lessee nor any of Lessee's servants, employees, agents, visitors or licensees may put up or operate any steam engines, boilers or machinery or keep or use oils, burning fluids, camphene, kerosene, naphtha, gasoline or any other inflammable, combustible or explosive fluid, chemical or substance for storage, sale or heating, cooking, warming, lighting, or use anything but electricity for illuminating the premises.

Section XXIV

(A) This is a net lease and no services of any kind will be due to Lessee by Lessor, and Lessee agrees to pay all charges for electricity, gas, water, telephone services, janitorial services and all other services. The Lessee is responsible for the cost of repairs, care, maintenance and replacement of the structure, machinery and equipment located on the premises. Lessee further agrees to obtain plate glass insurance together with a single limit liability insurance policy in the amount of $500,000, and in those insurance policies Lessee must designate Lessor as an additional insured and must furnish Lessor with certificates of insurance as evidence that Lessee has obtained the required insurance coverage.
(B)

(1) Lessee further agrees that any interruption in utility or other services including but not limited to water, heating, lighting, electricity and air conditioning is the Lessee's responsibility and interruptions in service at any time does not give Lessee any right to an abatement or reduction in or of the rent.
(2) It is understood that any violation by the Lessee of the preceding provision constitutes a breach of this lease and the Lessor may then elect to exercise any of the options or remedies as set out in Paragraph 14 of this lease.
(3) Lessee further agrees that in the event that Lessor does not perform any of the above services and an interruption occurs that Lessee is not entitled to an abatement or reduction in rent, nor is Lessee entitled to have any repairs to the premises made and charged to the Lessor. In the event that Lessee has any repairs made with Lessor's permission, it is agreed that it will be a gift by Lessee to Lessor.

(C) Lessee agrees to assume the sole responsibility to shampoo, care and maintain all carpeting located on the premises. It is further agreed that the Lessee must shampoo the carpeting at least once a year.
(D) Lessee agrees to assume the sole responsibility for the washing of windows located on the premises and that no window washing services of any kind will be performed by the Lessor. It is further agreed that the windows must be washed at least once a year.
(E) If there are any elevators, lifts, machinery, glass or plate glass on the premises, their care, maintenance and repairs are assumed by Lessee, together with all liability or claims for damages.

(F) Lessee further agrees to pay all bills and charges for services such as water, heating, electricity and air-conditioning and any other utility charges.

Section XXV

(A) Lessee must not install any other method of heating and air conditioning either primary or auxiliary other than any that may already be provided for on the premises, without the express written consent of the Lessor.
(B) Lessor must furnish the initial tubes and/or bulbs for the light fixtures on the premises, however, Lessee must pay for all replacements and service.
(C) In the event that there is a mail chute located in the building within which the premises are located, then the Lessee has the free use of the mail chute, but it is further agreed that Lessor is in no way responsible for any damage or delay which may arise from its use.
(D) The water must not be left running nor the electric lights burning unless in actual use on the premises.

Section XXVI

It is understood and agreed that this lease and the obligation of Lessee to pay rent under it and perform all of the other covenants and agreements under this lease on part of tenant to be performed will in no way be affected, impaired or excused because landlord is unable to supply or is delayed in supplying any service expressly or impliedly to be supplied, or is unable to make or is delayed in making any repairs, additions, alterations or decorations or is unable to supply, or is delayed in supplying any equipment or fixtures if landlord is prevented or delayed from so doing for any reason.

Section XXVII

(A) The Lessor, and its agents, also have the right to enter the premises by pass keys or otherwise, whether vacated or not, at all reasonable hours for the purpose of examining the premises, making repairs, alterations, improvements and additions which they deem necessary for the safety, preservation or improvement of the premises, or building, or to punch the watchman's clock for any station that may be located in the premises.
(B) The Lessor is allowed to take all material into and on premises that may be required to make repairs, improvements and additions or any alterations for the benefit of the building without in any way being deemed or held guilty of any eviction of the Lessee; and the rent must not abate while the repairs, alternations, improvements or additions are being made, and the Lessee is not entitled to maintain a set-off or counterclaim for damages against the Lessor by reason of loss or interruption to the business of the Lessee because of the persecution of any work.
(C) Lessor has this same right of entry to the premises where Lessee has vacated the premises before the termination of the lease, whether Lessee is in default or not, and if in default to move from those premises at Lessee's expense, any furniture, fixtures or other property of the Lessee.
(D) All repairs, decorations, alterations, additions and improvements must be done during ordinary business hours, or if any work is at the request of the Lessee to be done during any other hours the Lessee must pay for all overtime.

COMMERCIAL REAL ESTATE LEASE

Section XXVIII

(A) At the expiration of this lease, or at its termination for cause, Lessee is obligated to immediately surrender possession, and should Lessee fail to do so, Lessee consents to pay any and all damages, but in no case less than five times the regular rent per day, the amount of 25% of the principal claim, for attorney fees and all court costs incurred.
(B) Lessee also expressly waives any notice to vacate at the expiration or termination of this lease and all legal delays and by this agreement confesses judgment with costs placing Lessor in possession to be executed at once.
(C) Should Lessor allow or permit Lessee to remain in the premises after the expiration or termination of this lease, this will not be construed as a reconduction of this lease (unless the renewal clause, as set out above is exercised).

Section XXIX

(A) No auction sales, or any sales of furniture, fixtures, etc., may be conducted on the premises without the written consent of the Lessor or Agent.
(B) Canvassing, soliciting and peddling in the building are prohibited and each Lessee must cooperate to prevent these acts from occurring.

Section XXX

Lessee and Lessor's servants, employees, agents, visitors and licensees, must observe faithfully and comply strictly with the "Rules and Regulations" as set forth on the back of this lease, with it being understood that the "Rules and Regulations" are subject to change at any time by the Lessor on due notice to the Lessee. Lessor is not liable to Lessee for the violation of any of the rules and regulations or the breach of any covenant or condition in any lease by any other tenant in the building.

Section XXXI

(A) Lessor specifically reserves the right to deny any person access to the premises, who, for any reason in Lessor's judgment, should be denied access to the premises.
(B) Lessor further reserves the right to close the building after normal working hours, on Sundays, and on legal holidays. It is further understood that the times during which the building is to be closed shall be designated and promulgated by the Lessor in the "Rules and Regulations" being subject to change at any time on notice to the Lessee.

Section XXXII

It is understood and agreed that this lease does not grant any rights to light, view or air over adjacent property, so that any diminution or shutting off of light, view or air by any structure which may be erected adjacent to the building will in no way affect this lease or impose any liability on Lessor.

COMMERCIAL REAL ESTATE LEASE

Section XXXIII

If there be a taking of the premises by a governmental or quasi-governmental unit exercising the right of eminent domain and this taking prevents Lessee from conducting business but is of a less severe nature, then the amount of this lease will only be reduced proportionately to the amount of space taken In the event all or any portion of the leased space or the building of which the leased space is a part is so taken, Lessor is entitled to the entire award of the condemning authority, and Lessee is not entitled to any portion of that award.

Section XXXIV

(A) If the premises are not ready for occupancy due to noncompletion of the premises, repairs, alterations, renovations or decorative work of any sort or to the holding over of any previous Lessee, or any cause, on the day above fixed for the beginning of the term of this lease, the rent under this lease must not commence on the term and must not begin until the premises are ready for occupancy and Lessee agrees that allowances for rent must be received by Lessee in full settlement of any claim which Lessee might otherwise have reason of the premises not being ready for occupancy. The ending date of this lease, however, will remain the same.
(B) Regardless of the failure of tenant to occupy the premises, the rent begins when Lessor has the premises available for occupancy by Lessee, or in the event repairs, alterations and/or decorations are to be made by Lessor, when those repairs, alterations, and decorations are substantially completed, the rent begins.
(C) It is further agreed that in the event that the Lessee elects to undertake those repairs, alterations, renovations or decorative work, then Lessee will be solely responsible for their timely completion and the rent term begins to run on the day that the premises are made available to Lessee, unless this lease contains a provision otherwise.

Section XXXV

If the premises contain less than 1,000 square feet, the Lessor reserves the right to move the Lessee to another space in the building on 30 days' notice, Lessee having the right within 10 days from the date of that notice to agree with Lessor on the new space. In case Lessor and Lessee do not agree within 10 days on terms of removal, then this lease becomes null and void and of no further effect, after 30 days from the date of above notice. Lessor agrees to pay actual expenses, not to exceed the amount of one month's rental, of moving Lessee to the new space agreed on.

Section XXXVI

This is a Louisiana contract, to be interpreted and enforced under and in accordance with the laws of Louisiana.

Section XXXVII

By signing this Lease, both the Lessee and the Surety(ies) (if any) agree to and each do by this agreement make the Secretary of State for Louisiana, their agent for service of process for legal processes in Louisiana, and written notice by the Secretary of State to Lessee and/or Surety(ies) mailed to the last known business address of the Lessee and/or Surety(ies) will constitute full notice of service of process.

Section XXXVIII

All addenda, attachments or exhibits or rules and regulations attached to this document are made part of this lease by reference. And it is by this agreement agreed by Lessor and Lessee that in the event that any clause or provision of this lease is deemed or adjudged as legally unenforceable, that that clause will be severed from this lease and its remaining provisions, and the legal effect of all other provisions and of the lease as a whole will remain unimpaired, valid and binding. No clause or provision must be interpreted to cause an automatic termination of this lease, since all causes for termination require action on the part of the terminating party.

Section XXXIX

AND NOW COME the persons signed below who are made parties to this contract of lease and are bound with Lessee jointly and IN SOLIDO for the faithful execution of all the obligations to be performed on the part of the Lessee, and furthermore waive all right to a release from this obligation due to Lessor's failure to protest for nonpayment of rent or due granting of any extensions or indulgences to Lessee or any modifications of this lease, or due to the filing of a bankruptcy, receivership or respite petition by or against Lessee or discharge in bankruptcy of Lessee, or on Lessee's suspension, failure or insolvency or to the appointment of a receiver for Lessee by any competent court. Surety and Lessee waive division.

THUS DONE AND PASSED on the _____ day of ___________, 20___, in ________________, Louisiana, in the presence of the undersigned competent witnesses who have signed their names together with the appearers and me, notary.[1]

WITNESSES:

______________________________	______________________________
Print Name	LESSOR
______________________________	______________________________
Print Name	LESSEE

____

Notary Name: ______________________________

Notary ID or Bar Roll No.: ____________

My Commission is for Life

[1] A lease is not required to be an authentic act, or for that matter a notarized one, but it is advisable. By having the Lessee sign before a notary, it impresses on them the seriousness of the act and how it is legally binding. By also doing this in authentic form, the lease is readily introduced in court, if necessary, as a self-proving document. This last feature can also be accomplished by adapting this lease into an acknowledged act (remove references to notary; the parties and witnesses sign privately; a witness or a party (preferably Lessee) goes before a notary and acknowledges execution; that is attached to this lease. Recording makes it effective against third parties.

MOBILE HOME: ACT OF IMMOBILIZATION

MOBILE HOMES (TRAILER HOMES)

STATE OF LOUISIANA

PARISH OF ____________________

ACT OF IMMOBILIZATION

BEFORE ME, the undersigned notary, duly commissioned and qualified in the state and parish aforesaid, and in the presence of the two witnesses whose names are hereunto subscribed, PERSONALLY CAME and appeared:

Sigmund J. Ericson and Moriah Ellie Ericson, born Smith, hereinafter "appearers," both of the full age of majority and domiciled in Jefferson Parish, Louisiana, and each of whom have been duly sworn, have declared that they have been married but once and then to each other, and who are living together in community, and who declared their permanent mailing address is 200 Chateau Latour Dr., Kenner, LA 70065.

Said appearers declared that they are the owners of the following described mobile home, to wit:

One (1) MOBILE HOME bearing the VIN# ______________________________.

Appearers further declared that said mobile home is situated upon the following described immovable property owned by Appearer, to-wit:

Lot 3 sq 3 Chateau Estates Subdivision *[etc.]*

And appearers further declared that under the provisions of Louisiana Revised Statute 9:1149.4, appearers do hereby declare that the aforementioned mobile home shall remain permanently attached to the tract of land described above and shall hereafter be considered as an immovable and as a part of said tract of land.

Appearers do hereby attach to this declaration the Certificate of Title or Manufacturer's Certificate for the said mobile home described herein, all in accordance with the provisions of the aforementioned statute.

THUS DONE AND PASSED on the ____ day of __________, 20____, in ________________, Louisiana, in the presence of the undersigned competent witnesses who have signed their names together with the appearers and me, notary, after due reading of the whole.

MOBILE HOME: ACT OF IMMOBILIZATION

WITNESSES:

______________________________	______________________________
Print Name	SIGMUND J. ERICSON
______________________________	______________________________
Print Name	MORIAH ELLIE ERICSON

____

Notary Name: ______________________________

Notary ID or Bar Roll No.: ____________

My Commission is for Life

MOBILE HOME: ACT OF DEIMMOBILIZATION

STATE OF LOUISIANA

PARISH OF ____________________

ACT OF DEIMMOBILIZATION

BEFORE ME, the undersigned notary, duly commissioned and qualified in the state and parish aforesaid, and in the presence of the two witnesses whose names are hereunto subscribed, PERSONALLY CAME and appeared:

Finley T. Breese and Sarah Elizabeth Breese, born Griswold (hereinafter "appearers"), both of the full age of majority and domiciled in Avoyelles Parish, Louisiana, and each of whom have been duly sworn, have declared that they have been married but once and then to each other, and who are living together in community, and who declared their permanent mailing address is 146 Gin St., Plaucheville, LA, 71362.

Said appearers declared that they are the owners of the following described mobile home, to wit:

One (1) MOBILE HOME bearing the VIN# ______________________________.

Said mobile home being situated on the following described immovable property owned by appearers, to wit:

Lot 1 sq 1 Marble Road Subdivision, Backstep, Avoyelles, LA,

Which mobile home was immobilized by Act of Immobilization dated 01/04/2020, filed and recorded under registry number 123456 Conveyance Book, records of Avoyelles Parish, Louisiana.

Appearers declare that they no longer desire the mobile home to be an immovable and by this act they declare that the mobile home is a movable and subject to all laws concerning movable property.

This act is done in compliance with Louisiana R.S. 9:1149.6 *et seq*.

THUS DONE AND PASSED on the _____ day of __________, 20____, in _______________, Louisiana, in the presence of the undersigned competent witnesses who have signed their names together with the appearers and me, notary, after due reading of the whole.

WITNESSES:

____________________________	______________________________
Print Name	FINLEY T. BREESE

MOBILE HOME: ACT OF DEIMMOBILIZATION

______________________________	______________________________
Print Name	SARAH ELIZABETH BREESE

____

Notary Name: ________________________________

Notary ID or Bar Roll No.: ____________

My Commission is for Life

9 • DONATIONS

STATE OF LOUISIANA

PARISH OF JEFFERSON

DONATION INTER VIVOS

BEFORE ME, a notary public duly commissioned and qualified in the parish and state aforesaid, and in the presence of the undersigned witnesses, PERSONALLY CAME AND APPEARED:

Donor name, Maria Rena Rodriguez, of the full age of majority and domiciled in _______________ Parish, Louisiana, hereafter DONOR, who declares that she has never been married and her permanent mailing address is *mailing address*,

Said DONOR did and by these presents does gift, grant, convey, donate, assign, set over and deliver unto

Donee name, Joseph Thomas Regan, of the full age of majority and domiciled in _______________ Parish, Louisiana, hereafter DONEE, who declares that he has never been married and his permanent mailing address is *mailing address*, here present and accepting with gratitude, for himself, his successors and assigns, and acknowledging due delivery and possession thereof, the following described property.

DONOR declared that, in consideration of the love and affection she bears for DONEE, she donates, sells, transfers and delivers unto the Donee the following described property, to wit ("Property"):

Full property description (for movables or immovables) including municipal address, if any (either as part of this instrument; or attached as a separate exhibit, referenced here and incorporated into act).

DONOR expressly acknowledges that her interest in the Property donated constitutes her separate property, and that DONOR possessed full ownership of the Property prior to this Act of Donation.

DONOR represents and warrants that: (a) all state, city, and parish taxes up to and including the taxes due and exigible in _________ *year* have been paid (if any); (b) the Property has not been alienated by DONOR; and (c) the Property is not subject to any encumbrance whatsoever.

[For immovables] Appearers agree that property taxes henceforth will be the responsibility of DONEE and he is designated to receive tax notices.

ACT OF DONATION OF IMMOVABLE OR MOVABLE, SIMPLE

DONEE accepts the donation of the above-described property for his benefit, as his separate property under separate management and acknowledges due delivery and possession of the Property for himself and for his heirs, successors and assigns.

Thus done and signed at __________________, Louisiana, this _____ day of _________________, 20_____, in the presence of the undersigned competent witnesses and me, notary, after due reading of the whole.

WITNESSES:

____
Print witness name

____
Print name of DONOR

____
Print witness name

____
Print name of DONEE

____

Notary Name: ________________________________

Notary ID or Bar Roll No.: ________________

My Commission is for Life

DONATION OF IMMOVABLE (ALL PARTIES PRESENT)

STATE OF LOUISIANA

PARISH OF JEFFERSON

DONATION OF IMMOVABLE PROPERTY

BEFORE ME, a notary public, duly commissioned and qualified in the parish and state aforesaid, and in the presence of the undersigned witnesses, PERSONALLY CAME AND APPEARED:

Donor name, Maxwell R. Stanton, of the full age of majority and domiciled in Jefferson Parish, Louisiana, hereafter DONOR, who declares that he has never been married, and who declared his permanent mailing address is 111 Westbank Expy., Gretna, LA 70056;

Said DONOR did and by these presents does gift, grant, convey, donate, assign, set over and deliver unto

Donee name, Samantha T. Trajan, of the full age of majority and domiciled in Jefferson Parish, Louisiana, hereafter DONEE, who declares that she has never been married and who declared her permanent mailing address is 10654 Jefferson Hwy., River Ridge, LA 70123, here present and accepting with gratitude, for herself, her successors and assigns, and acknowledging due delivery and possession thereof, the following described property:

Full legal property description, including municipal address, if any (either as part of this instrument; or attached as a separate exhibit, referenced here and incorporated into act).

The parties hereto estimate the value of said donated property in the amount of *put reasonable property value in words* dollars ($ ________), and DONOR declares that the property hereby donated by him does not exceed the disposable portion of his estate.

To have and to hold the said property unto DONEE, her heirs, successors and assigns, in full ownership forever, with full and general warranty of title, and with full substitution and subrogation to all rights and actions of warranty which said DONOR may have against all former owners or vendors of said property.

All taxes due on said property have been paid, as evidenced by tax certificate attached hereto.

The parties agree that henceforth all tax notices including parish property taxes will be sent to DONEE, at 10654 Jefferson Hwy, River Ridge, LA 70123, who is responsible for payment of taxes and is designated to receive such notices and hereby assumes responsibility for their payment.

The parties waive and dispense with the production of any mortgage, conveyance, or other certificates, required by law, and relieve and release me, notary, from any and all connection therewith.

DONATION OF IMMOVABLE (ALL PARTIES PRESENT)

Said DONOR stipulates that the aforesaid property has not been alienated by him and is free of all encumbrances.

This act is passed before me, notary, without a request for examination of title and none was made. The description herein was furnished to me, notary, by the parties, and the parties relieve and release me, notary, from any and all liability in connection therewith, forever holding me, notary, and my heirs and successors harmless from any and all claims forever.

This act of donation, upon execution, is delivered in the original to DONEE, who accepts responsibility for registration and filing in the conveyance records of _____________ Parish, where the property is located; and all parties agree to relieve me, notary, of any duty to file.

Thus done and signed at ________________, Louisiana, this ____ day of ________________, 20____, in the presence of the undersigned competent witnesses and me, notary, after due reading of the whole.

WITNESSES:

____________________________	________________________________
Print witness name	MAXWELL R. STANTON, DONOR
____________________________	________________________________
Print witness name	SAMANTHA T. TRAJAN, DONEE

____

Notary Name: ________________________________

Notary ID or Bar Roll No.: ________________

My Commission is for Life

DONATION OF IMMOVABLE (MULTIPLE PARTIES SIGNING SEPARATELY)

STATE OF LOUISIANA

PARISH OF JEFFERSON

DONATION OF IMMOVABLE PROPERTY

BEFORE ME, a notary public duly commissioned and qualified in the parish and state aforesaid, and in the presence of the undersigned witnesses, PERSONALLY CAME AND APPEARED:

Donor name, Maxwell R. Stanton, of the full age of majority and domiciled in Jefferson Parish, Louisiana, hereafter DONOR, who declares that he has never been married, and who declared his permanent mailing address is 111 Westbank Expressway, Gretna, LA 70056;

Said DONOR did and by these presents does gift, grant, convey, donate, assign, set over and deliver unto

Donee 1 name, Samantha T. Trajan, of the full age of majority and domiciled in Jefferson Parish, Louisiana, hereafter DONEE, who declares that she has never been married and who declared her permanent mailing address is 10654 Jefferson Hwy, River Ridge, LA 70123; and to

Donee 2 name, Helena Y. Marcon, of the full age of majority and domiciled in Jefferson Parish, Louisiana, hereafter DONEE, who declares that she has never been married and who declared her permanent mailing address is 111 St. Charles Ave., New Orleans, LA 70115; donation of

Full and complete ownership, in equal shares[1] and as their separate property, of the property located at the municipal address of 77 Oak Avenue, Harahan, Louisiana 70123, as legally described in full on the property description attached as "Exhibit A," and of all movables and immovables contained therein, to

DONEES, personally accepting this donation in writing, with said donation complete upon both signing acceptance,[2] do by their signatures accept with gratitude, each for herself, and her successors and assigns, and acknowledging due delivery and possession thereof, as a donation, the following described property:

Full legal property description including municipal address, if any (either as part of this instrument; or attached as a separate exhibit, referenced here and incorporated into act).

---

[1] This donation is being made 50-50 to the two donees, but it does not have to be.

[2] Unrelated to the example of having two donees, this version is structured so that the donees may sign later and not be present when the donor executes the authentic act (and may sign separately from each other). The acceptance of donation must be express and in writing, but it does not have to be an authentic act. So, in this version, the donees do not "appear" n the authentic act (nothing is stated in terms of "Now comes Donee"), but instead it is stated that their signatures at the bottom of the act constitute acceptance. In this way the donees can sign at a later time and place, and at that time the donation is complete, awaiting filing (in this case by the designated donee, to relieve notary of the duty).

DONATION OF IMMOVABLE (MULTIPLE PARTIES SIGNING SEPARATELY)

The parties hereto estimate the value of said donated property in the amount of *put reasonable property value in words* dollars ($ _______), and DONOR declares that the property hereby donated by him does not exceed the disposable portion of his estate.

To have and to hold the said property unto DONEES, their heirs, successors and assigns, in full ownership forever, with full and general warranty of title, and with full substitution and subrogation to all rights and actions of warranty which said DONOR may have against all former owners or vendors of said property.

All taxes due on said property have been paid, as evidenced by tax certificate attached hereto.

The parties agree that henceforth all tax notices including parish property taxes will be sent to DONEE Helena Y. Marcon, whose permanent mailing address is 111 St. Charles Ave., New Orleans, LA 70115, who is responsible for payment of taxes and is designated to receive such notices and hereby assumes responsibility for their timely payment.

The parties waive and dispense with the production of any mortgage, conveyance, or other certificates, required by law, and relieve and release me, notary, from any and all connection therewith.

Said DONOR stipulates that the aforesaid property has not been alienated by him and is free of all encumbrances.

This act is passed before me, notary, without a request for examination of title and none was made. The description herein was furnished to me, notary, by DONOR, who along with the DONEES relieve and release me, notary, from any and all liability in connection therewith, forever holding me, notary, and my heirs and successors harmless from any and all claims forever.

This act of donation, upon execution, is delivered in the original to DONEE Samantha T. Trajan, who accepts responsibility for registration and filing in the conveyance records of Jefferson Parish, where the property is located; and all parties agree to relieve me, notary, of any duty to file.

Thus done and signed at _______________, Louisiana, this ____ day of __________________, 20____, in the presence of the undersigned competent witnesses and me, notary, after due reading of the whole.

WITNESSES:

____________________________	________________________________
Print witness name	MAXWELL R. STANTON, DONOR
____________________________	
Print witness name	

____

Notary Name: _________________________________

Notary ID or Bar Roll No.: ________________

My Commission is for Life

ACCEPTANCES:

COMES NOW the DONEE Samantha T. Trajan, who by this signature hereby acknowledges that she has read the foregoing and freely and fully accepts the donation as stated in this instrument.

____

SAMANTHA T. TRAJAN, DONEE

DATE: ____________________, 20____

COMES NOW the DONEE Helena Y. Marcon, who by this signature hereby acknowledges that she has read the foregoing and freely and fully accepts the donation as stated in this instrument.

____

HELENA Y. MARCON, DONEE

DATE: ____________________, 20____

DONATION TO TRUST

STATE OF LOUISIANA

PARISH OF JEFFERSON

DONATION OF IMMOVABLE PROPERTY TO TRUST

BEFORE ME, a notary public duly commissioned and qualified in the parish and state aforesaid, and in the presence of the undersigned witnesses, PERSONALLY CAME AND APPEARED:

Name of Settlor, who by these presents makes known:

That appearer, referred to as "settlor" in this instrument, is the owner of an undivided _______ % interest in and to the community of acquets and gains formerly existing between settlor and ______________________, which includes the following described immovable property, to wit: ____ *[property description]*.

And now, the settlor declares that in consideration for the love and affection which settlor bears for the beneficiary, and with the express condition that the settlor does not reserve or retain any usufruct, including that granted by Louisiana Civil Code article 223, the settlor has given, donated, and delivered, and does by this formal act of donation irrevocably give and donate inter vivos to __________________________, as trustee, to be administered by him as a fiduciary for __________________________, the beneficiary referred to in this instrument, and, in accordance with the provisions of Louisiana Revised Statutes § 9:2352, specifically and expressly relinquishing any and all right settlor may now, or in the future, have to revoke the donation, it being the settlor's intention to make the donation absolutely irrevocable, the property described as: ____ *[list donation for the benefit of beneficiary]*.

The trustee accepts the donation inter vivos made in trust on behalf of the beneficiary, accepts the trust created by this Act of Donation, and acknowledges receipt of the property delivered to him as trustee.

The trustee further accepts the duties and obligations imposed upon him as trustee and agrees to faithfully discharge his office in accordance with the law and the terms of this Act of Donation.

And the settlor, expressly waiving any informality or defect in the giving and receiving of the property by the trustee named, and expressly acknowledging the validity of the trust and the right and capacity of the trustee to act on behalf of the beneficiary, does declare that, if for any reason, the donation to the trust should be ineffective, the property will, for all intents and purposes, be irrevocably considered as having been donated, directly and individually, in full ownership, to the beneficiary of settlor.

Since the settlor has executed a power of attorney authorizing __________________________ as agent to appear before any notary public and to execute an act of sale in the settlor's name,

DONATION TO TRUST

place, and stead, the settlor does irrevocably give to the said agent the instructions to receive any proceeds due to the settlor from the act of sale and to immediately convey the proceeds to the trustee to be administered by him as a fiduciary for the beneficiary.

Thus done, passed and signed at ________________, Louisiana, this _____ day of __________________, 20____, in the presence of the undersigned competent witnesses and me, notary, after due reading of the whole.

WITNESSES:

______________________________	______________________________
Print witness name	Print name of DONOR
______________________________	______________________________
Print witness name	Print name of DONEE

____

Notary Name: ________________________________

Notary ID or Bar Roll No.: ________________

My Commission is for Life

10 • TESTAMENTS AND SUCCESSIONS

APPOINTING NOTARY TO SEARCH FOR TESTAMENT

In place of the usual venue clause, such a petition to be filed into a court record (as opposed to filings into conveyance and mortgage records) typically has a full caption above it with the docket statement, including court name and location, division, case number, docket number, and case name (Succession of [decedent's name]). These are readily adapted from previous court filings in this succession, plus add a space for the date of filing and name of deputy clerk for this particular filing.

This form is essentially a request from petitioner or petitioner's attorney to appoint a notary for this search, and need not be notarized itself. The notary is only involved insofar as it empowers the notary to act under it.

Optional additions to this petition include a statement that keys to the box have not been located among decedent's effects after a thorough search and a request that the notary be authorized to have the box drilled (then an order to allow this, in '3. Additional Relief').

This form is accompanied by an Affidavit of Death, Domicile and Heirship, which is found at end of this chapter ("Miscellaneous"); it is used for many other purposes besides being an attachment to this form.

For the process by which a notary opens a safe deposit box, see the next chapter.

PETITION TO APPOINT NOTARY TO SEARCH FOR TESTAMENT

This Petition of *name of petitioner*, a person of the full age of majority and the only child and legal heir of *name of decedent*, respectfully represents the following:

SECTION I

As appears from the Affidavit of Death, Domicile and Heirship filed with this petition, *name of decedent* (hereafter "decedent") died on *date*, at which time decedent was domiciled in ____________________ Parish, Louisiana.

SECTION II

Petitioner is the only child of the decedent and is, therefore, the decedent's sole legal heir.

SECTION III

Petitioner believes the decedent left a last will and testament. However, Petitioner has been unable to locate the decedent's will after due diligence.

APPOINTMENT OF NOTARY TO SEARCH FOR TESTAMENT

SECTION IV

The decedent maintained a safe deposit box at *name of bank*, located at *street address*, in ____________________, Louisiana, which safe deposit box is identified as Box No. _________.

SECTION V

The Petitioner believes the decedent's last will and testament may be located in the above-described safe deposit box. Accordingly, it is appropriate and necessary that a Notary Public be appointed to search the safe deposit box for any documents purporting to be the last will and testament of the decedent, or codicils to that will, and to remove them from that site.

THEREFORE, the Petitioner prays for an Order:

1. Appointing and authorizing *name of notary,* Notary Public in and for ________________ Parish, Louisiana, to enter safe deposit Box No. __________, maintained by the decedent at *name of bank*, located at *address*, __________________, Louisiana to search for a last will and testament, and codicils of the decedent, and to remove them if found so that they may be filed in Court.

2. Ordering *name of bank* to permit *name of notary,* Notary Public, to enter the above-described safe deposit box and to remove any documents purporting to be a last will and testament or codicil of the decedent.

3. *Any additional relief appropriate to the situation.*

Respectfully submitted,

____

Name
Title (such as Attorney for Petitioner)
Address (and bar roll number)

RETURN OF NOTARY AFTER SEARCH FOR TESTAMENT

In place of the usual venue clause, such a document to be filed into a court record (as opposed to filings into conveyance and mortgage records) typically has a full caption above it with the docket statement, including court name and location, division, case number, docket number, and case name (Succession of [decedent's name]). These are easily adapted from previous court filings in this succession, plus add the date of filing and name of deputy clerk for this particular filing.

This form is essentially an affidavit of the notary who searched for a will, and it must be sworn before a second notary, who also signs.

RETURN OF NOTARY AFTER SEARCH FOR TESTAMENT

NOW INTO COURT comes *name of notary*, a Notary Public duly commissioned and qualified in and for ________________ Parish, State of Louisiana, whose mailing address is *address*, who being duly sworn states the following:

SECTION I

Pursuant to an Order of the Court dated ____________, 20____, the undersigned Notary entered and examined *name of bank* safe deposit Box No. _________, located at *street address*, ______________, Louisiana. The purpose of the examination was to search for any last will and testaments or codicils executed by the decedent and to remove them so that they may be filed with the Court.

SECTION II

Upon inspecting the contents of the above-described safe deposit box, the undersigned Notary located a document purporting to be the last will and testament of the decedent in notarial form, dated ______________, 20____. Undersigned Notary removed the document purporting to be the last will and testament of the decedent from the safe deposit box in order to present it to the Court to be filed and executed in accordance with the law.

____

Affiant, Notary Public ID No. __________

SWORN TO AND SUBSCRIBED BEFORE ME this _______ day of ___________________, 20____, at ______________________, Louisiana.

____

Notary Name: ______________________________

Notary ID or Bar Roll No.: ________________

My Commission is for Life

TESTAMENTARY INTERVIEW FORM

NOTARIAL TESTAMENT: PLANNING, SAMPLE WILLS & TESTAMENTARY CLAUSES

WILL/ESTATE PLANNING QUESTIONNAIRE

Date: ____________________

GENERAL INFORMATION

Full Name:	
Date of Birth:	
Citizenship:	
Residence	
Address:	
Home Ph:	
Work Ph:	
Cell Ph:	
Email:	

Former marital status: How many times were you married? Full names including maiden? Dates of those marriages? Dates of those dissolutions? How were those marriages dissolved (divorce? death of spouse?) Parish of marriage and dissolution? ____

____

____

____

Do you have a will currently in existence? ____ Yes ____ No

If so, in whose custody is the original? ____________________________________

(Please enclose a copy).

Do you have a revocable or irrevocable trust (e.g., a "life insurance trust") in existence?

____ Yes ____ No   If yes, please provide a copy.

CHILDREN

Names of Children	Age	Married? Spouse Name?

GRANDCHILDREN

Names of Grandchildren	Age	Parent?

TESTAMENTARY INTERVIEW FORM

PARENTS

Are your parents living? ____ Yes ____ No

DISABILITY

Are you, your spouse, any of your children or grandchildren (or any other possible beneficiary of your estate) under a disability that will require special provisions in your will or estate plan?

____ Yes ____ No

If yes, please provide information about the individual and his or her disability.

BUSINESS INTERESTS

Do you own an equity interest (stock, partnership, interest, etc.) in any closely-held business?

____ Yes ____ No

If so, please answer the following questions.

Name of business: ____

Type of entity: (*please circle one*) sole proprietorship corporation partnership limited partnership
Percentage of ownership: __________

Other owners and their percentages:

____

____

____

Type of business: ____

PERSONAL REPRESENTATIVES (Executor)

Whom do you desire to be the Personal Representative? ______________________________

Your Personal Representative (the same as "Executor") manages the probate and settlement of your estate. You can name your spouse, adult children, trusted friends or other relatives. And a backup? Please provide the following information:

	Personal Representative	Backup Personal Representative?
Full name		
Address		
Phone Number		
Email		
Age		

GUARDIAN OF MINORS:

A surviving parent of a minor child (i.e., a child under the age of 18) will automatically be the "guardian" or "tutor" of the person of the minor child if the other parent dies (except in cases where the surviving parent has no parental rights). But what if the other parent of your minor child does not survive you? You should identify in your Last Will and Testament individuals whom you would like to serve as guardians for any minor children. Please provide the following information if you have any minor children:

	Guardian to serve if other parent does not survive	Alternate Guardian
Full name		
Address		
Phone Number		
Email		
Age		

If you have designated a married couple in your Last Will and Testament to serve as Guardians of your minor children, does it make a difference to you that they are married at the time they serve as Guardians? In other words, what if the couple gets divorced? Separated? Or one of the persons dies? If it is important to you that a married couple be designated as guardians, then provisions must be made in your Last Will and Testament addressing the possibility that the married couple is no longer a couple at the time they are asked to serve as guardians. You don't need to make a decision on this issue in this questionnaire, but you should think about this possibility and whether you want it addressed in your Last Will and Testament.

ASSETS TO BE DISTRIBUTED TO MINOR BENEFICIARIES

Persons who are under the age of 18 cannot "own" property because of their age. Thus, if there is a possibility (no matter how remote) that someone who is under the age of 18 could be a beneficiary of your estate, then you could specify in the Last Will and Testament how those assets should be handled at the time of distribution to the minor beneficiary. One option is to have the assets distributed to a Uniform Transfers to Minors Act Account (which is easy and inexpensive) but the payout age to the minor can be no later than the age of twenty-one (21) years. Another option is to have the money held in trust for the benefit of the minor beneficiary but with this option, you must consider the cost of creating and maintaining a trust for the benefit of the beneficiary. The simplest (and most common) option is to name the children as a legatee without regard to a trust, and allow the court in a succession to establish who will handle the property for the child until they are of the age of majority (so that the child inherits the property according to the will and the terms of ownership and protection of the child are set by the court). We can discuss the options when we meet. But in the meantime, if you think that you want the assets for a minor beneficiary to be held in trust, then please answer the following questions:

	Trustee	Alternate Trustee
Full name		
Address		
Phone Number		
Email		
Age		

You should consider the age at which you want the beneficiary of the trust to receive his or her inheritance—25, 30, 35, 40? Most people choose to leave the money in trust until the beneficiary reaches what the person believes will be a responsible age. The money is available for the beneficiary's support up until the time for complete distribution and the trust is simply for the protection of the beneficiary.

TESTAMENTARY INTERVIEW FORM

Having assets in trust can provide a good "pre-nup agreement" for the beneficiary, for example, or can protect the beneficiary from unfortunate business investments.

TRUSTEE OF TRUST FOR BENEFICIARIES WITH SPECIAL NEEDS

If a person who is receiving government benefits or a person who cannot handle money might be a beneficiary of your estate, then you may want to have the assets for the person left to a "discretionary trust" or what some people call "a special needs trust." If that is the case for you, then the same questions must be answered, but you should consult a financial planner or lawyer experienced with such a trust.

	Personal Representative	Successor Personal Representative
Full name		
Address		
Phone Number		
Email		
Age		

DISPOSITIVE WILL TERMS

Please specify to whom your assets are to be distributed upon your death:

What if your children (or grandchildren) do not survive you? To whom would you like your assets to pass in that unlikely scenario?

Do you have any tangible personal property items that you would like distributed to certain individuals?

Other specific provisions you desire in your will:

GENERAL POWER OF ATTORNEY (e.g., as a conditional procuration that becomes effective only when the Principal becomes incapacitated to handle their affairs)

It is advisable that we prepare for you a document that grants to another person or persons the authority to handle your financial affairs if you are unable to do so. Below, please indicate the full name, address, and all contact information about the person whom you would like to serve in that capacity and the person who is your second choice if your first choice is unable to serve? (It is best to have two individuals at least and get their verbal agreement to serve.) Please provide full names and addresses, telephone numbers and email addresses, to the extent you have that information:

TESTAMENTARY INTERVIEW FORM

	Agent	Alternate Agent
Full name		
Address		
Phone Number		
Email		
Age		

Do you want this authority to be dependent upon a finding of your disability or do you want this authority to be effective immediately? It can sometimes be difficult to find doctors who are willing to make a determination of incapacity, but on the other hand, a requirement of a doctor's certification of incapacity can provide some protection for you. We can discuss this more fully when we meet.

MEDICAL DIRECTIVE AND LIVING WILL

It is also advisable for you to execute a document whereby you appoint one person, with a successor, to make medical decisions for you if you are unable to express your wishes.

You should get these persons to agree to serve. Also, you might want to prepare what is called a "Living Will," expressing how you wish to be treated in the event you are in an end stage condition and unable to communicate. If you want such a document, please indicate the names, addresses and telephone numbers and email addresses, to the extent known, of the individuals to serve in this capacity.

	Agent	Alternate Agent
Full name		
Address		
Phone Number		
Email		
Age		

DISPOSITION OF REMAINS: Do you have wishes for how your body will be handled at your death? They may not be enforceable but you are allowed to add your wishes to your will.

____

____

____.

And you certainly may name a *PERSON* who will have the legal power to make the decision about this matter. For example, you could name a person who is very likely to honor your wishes above.

____

Consider also doing this in a separate notarized document readily accessible before the will is probated.

TESTAMENT: GENERIC AND BLANK FORM

STATE OF LOUISIANA

PARISH OF ___________________

LAST WILL AND TESTAMENT

OF

[TESTATOR FULL NAME]

BE IT KNOWN that before me, the undersigned authority, duly commissioned and qualified in and for the parish and state aforesaid, and in the presence of the undersigned competent witnesses, personally came and appeared:

> [TESTATOR FULL NAME], of the full age of majority, who declared that s/he lives and resides in the Parish of _______________, Louisiana at the following address: [street address, city, LA, zip code],

who declared to me, Notary, that s/he wishes to take advantage of the provisions of La. Civ. Code art. 1576, *et seq.*, and does hereby make and declare this to be his/her last will and testament:

I, [FULL NAME], being able to comprehend generally the nature and consequences of this act, being able to read and write and sign my name, realizing the precarious and uncertain nature of life, and wishing to dispose of all the property which I may own at the time of my death by Last Will and Testament, declare this to be my final testament. I revoke all of my prior testaments or codicils.

I.

Marriage and children. I, [FULL NAME], have been married [number of times], first to [NAME, if so], from whom I am [divorced/widowed], and second to [NAME, if so], to whom I remain married [or whom I divorced]. My children are: [NAMES, if so; otherwise "No children are born to or adopted by me."].

II.

A) Particular Bequests. [if any] As a specific bequest, I give, will, and bequest the full and complete ownership of my __________________ to [NAME 1], my [relation, if any], and my __________________ to NAME 2], my [relation, if any].

B) As an additional specific bequest, I give the full and complete ownership of the bank accounts and any stocks in my name to [NAME].

C) Residuary Estate: I give, will and bequeath the full and complete ownership all of the rest of my property, whether movable or immovable, to [NAME(S)]. If they should predecease me, then the property should go to [NAME(S)].

III.

A) Executor. I appoint [NAME 1] as Executor of my succession to serve with full seizin

____

[testator name]

[and without bond, if intended]. Should s/he cease or fail to serve, then I name [NAME 3] as successor Executor. [optional: All of my executors may serve as independent administrators, without court supervision.]

B) Compensation. My individual Executors shall serve without compensation, but shall be entitled to recover his or her expenses from my Estate. [or set terms of compensation]

C) Bond. My Executor(s) or administrator(s) shall post reasonable security for the protection of the Estate, as determined by the court [or: I dispense all of my Executors, including any duly appointed dative or provisional executor, from giving bond].

D) Selection of Assets. Pursuant to Louisiana Civil Code article 1572, my Executor has the authority to select assets to satisfy any legacy herein expressed as a quantum or value of my estate, including a fractional share.

E) Common Disaster. Should I die together with any legatee in a common disaster or under such circumstances as to render it doubtful as to who died first, it shall be presumed that I survived.

F) Collation. I dispense all of my heirs from collating any gift received from me whether inter vivos or by reason of my death.

G) Undue Influence. No disposition in this testament has been made by me as a result of hatred, anger, suggestion or captation. I understand the nature and extent of my property and the consequences of the dispositions in this testament.

H) Should any of the provisions of this will be for any reason declared invalid, such invalidity shall not affect any of the other provisions of this will and all invalid provisions shall be wholly disregarded in interpreting this will.

IN WITNESS WHEREOF, I have signed on each page and declared this to be my Last Will and Testament, consisting of two (2) pages, in the presence of the Notary Public and the competent witnesses hereafter named and undersigned, at [city], Louisiana at the date written.

____

[Testator name below signature], Testator

In our presence the testator has declared or signified that this instrument is his/her testament and has signed it at the end and on each other separate page, and in the presence of the testator and each other we have hereunto subscribed our names this ____ day of ________________, 20____ at [city], Louisiana.

WITNESSES:

____________________________________	____________________________________
[Witness #1 name printed or typed here]	[Witness #2 name printed or typed here]

____

[Notary's name printed or typed below signature], Notary Public

Notary Identification or Bar Roll No.: ___________

My Commission is for Life

____

[testator name]

TESTAMENT: EXAMPLE WITH DETAILED NOTES

This a basic template for a testament (will). But it actually is sufficient for most client needs. Other examples and files in this collection have additional provisions and trust clauses, as well as some complications missing here. But this is a good form to meet the needs of most clients, yet still presented professionally.

The font for the caption can be changed back to a more generic one if you prefer. Some clients prefer the gravitas of an "old English" font, and may appreciate the finished product being delivered in a folder.

Each person must have their own will. There's no such thing as a joint will. It is a personal act and cannot be signed by an agent under a power of attorney. But in responsible estate planning, a client often will want some form of power of attorney and a living will, in addition to this testament.

Before drafting a testament for a client, consider giving them the "Testator interview form" (earlier in chapter). It collects info in writing that can be incorporated into a draft, with reduced error over oral interviews. The information they provide isn't the last word on every issue and does not preclude an oral discussion of available options (though not legal advice, for nonlawyer-notaries). But it's a good start.

Technically the testator does not have to sign at the bottom of the same page where they signed at the end of the dispositive portion, so some notaries do not have them sign the last page-bottom thinking it will not need it. But it is actually advisable that you make a habit of having a testator sign at the bottom of each page no matter what; consider that the final draft may have accidentally pushed the notary signature to a final page different from that of the end of the dispositive portion, leaving the will possibly challengeable because one of the pages winds up with no testator signature on it.

Similarly, although notaries often put the number of pages into the text, that habit does require a final proofread to see that it names the actual number of pages in the final printing. We have here included a page tally in the footer because it is readily seen as "off" when it shows for instance "Page 5 of 4," but in actuality there is no rule whatsoever that any page count be given in a testament. The key rule is signature at the bottom of every page — including each <u>side</u> of two-sided paper if the will happens to be printed that way (which is not very presentable but is acceptable).

This example has relatively few complications or added provisions dealing with tutorships, remains, no-content clauses, trust provisions, or disinheriting heirs. Other files discuss those options. Note that unless the testator is specifying a reason to disinherit a child who might be a forced heir, there's no real reason to take into account forced heirship in writing a basic will. It's more something the <u>court</u> deals with in a succession than an important factor in drafting. It will act as a set-aside by the court in which the court will ignore some terms of the will while reserving property to some heirs; but a failure to provide enough property to a forced heir is not a reason to invalidate the will. Put another way, allocations that wind up short of the required forced portion ("legitime") will be adjusted in the succession, and should not overly concern the drafter. And as a basic matter, the testator may not know who will be a forced heir at death.

This is a "notarial testament," whether drafted by lawyer or notary (so named because it is effective once notarized). Notaries have nothing to do with olographic wills and should make clear to clients we do not notarize those. It may be an opportunity to be retained to turn those wishes into a notarial will. Or at most you could, without risk to the rules of olographic wills, have them seal it in an envelope, then date and notarize only their signature on the <u>outside</u>. That is not overly useful but clients are happy. In the process, it is not wise to review the olographic will or give legal advice about it, such as making it valid.

For testamentary changes to an existing will, use our examples of "codicil." Individual edits or modifications to a will must be made in testamentary form, not just by an authentic act, though wholesale revocation of a prior testament can be done either way.

TESTAMENT: EXAMPLE WITH DETAILED NOTES

STATE OF LOUISIANA

PARISH OF AVOYELLES

Last Will and Testament
of
John Martin Smythe

BE IT KNOWN that before me, the undersigned authority, duly commissioned and qualified in and for the Parish of Avoyelles, State of Louisiana, and in the presence of the undersigned competent witnesses, personally came and appeared:

> John Martin Smythe, of the full age of majority, who declared that he lives and resides in the Parish of Rapides, at the following address: 221 Oak Street, Alexandria, LA 71307,

who declared to me, Notary, that he wishes to take advantage of the provisions of La. Civ. Code art. 1576, *et seq*., and does hereby make and declare this to be his last will and testament:

I, John Martin Smythe, being able to comprehend generally the nature and consequences of this act, knowing how and being able to read and write and sign my name, realizing the precarious and uncertain nature of life, and wishing to dispose of all the property which I may own at the time of my death by Last Will and Testament, declare this to be my final testament. I revoke all of my prior testaments or codicils.

I.

Marriage and children. I, John Martin Smythe, have been married twice, first to Doris Nunzia Baker, from whom I am divorced, and second to Sofia Hendricks Smythe, with whom I am married and reside at the address above. Of my marriage to Doris, I have two children, Ruth Anne Smythe Jones and Robert Mark Jones; of my marriage to Sofia, I have one daughter, Becka Ronda Smythe. I have no minor children or forced heirs.[1] No other children were born to or adopted by me.

II.

A) Particular Bequest. As a specific bequest, I give, will, and bequeath the full and complete ownership of my box of files and records to Sofia Hendricks Smythe, my wife, so that she may finalize my estate.

B) As an additional specific bequest, I give[2] my 2020 Honda Accord, or one car that I

[1] If true at the time of the testament, it may clarify intent to point out this fact. But of course whether there will actually be a forced heir at the time of death is not necessarily known when signing the will; some forced heirs will turn 24 and no longer qualify, while others over the age will become forced heirs due to disability.

[2] Using direct statements such as "I give" or "I leave to" is better than using the passive voice or expressing "I wish" terms, which a court may see as advisory rather than clearly intending to donate. Drafters make a mistake if they think it sounds more legalistic to write formally ("I would like Jim to have my watch") rather than directly ("I give").

may have titled to me at my death, to my daughter Becka.

C) To the extent not already provided in the designations of beneficiary on file with banks and other financial institutions, I give and bequeath the full and complete ownership of the bank accounts and any stocks in my name,[3] and the condo at 2046 Beach Blvd., Biloxi, Mississippi, to my wife, Sofia Smythe.[4]

D) I give to LSU-A's department of athletics a gift of $5,000.

E) I leave my ownership interest in the property at 221 Oak Street, Alexandria, in equal shares and per stirpes,[5] to my three children, Ruth, Robert, and Becka; reserving to my wife Sofia a usufruct until such time as she remarries or dies.

F) Residuary Estate. I give, will and bequeath the full and complete ownership all of the rest of my property, in equal shares and per stirpes, to my three children.

III.

A) Executor. I appoint my wife Sofia Smythe as Executor[6] of my succession to serve with full seizin and without bond. Should she be unwilling or unable to serve, I name my granddaughter, Sally Theresa Jones, as successor Executor.[7] All of my executors have my express authority to serve as independent administrators, without court supervision.[8]

---

[3] Bank and similar accounts often have beneficiary appointments which, if used correctly, have the proceeds go directly to a named person instead of being part of the estate. Nonetheless, it is advisable to include them in the testament, naming the *same* recipients, so as to protect against the institution's refusal to honor the beneficiary designation for some reason that will be too late to fix (or sometimes they require a lot of new paperwork).

[4] Drafters sometimes make the mistake of trying to account for community property in the will by giving out the "half" they think the testator owns. But wording it that way ("I leave half my house to my son Jim") actually may leave only half of the half (1/4) to Jim, not what was intended. That is because the testator can only give what they own, and if they own half, that is already captured by saying "my interest in the house" or just "my house" [which necessarily means only their half]). It is better to avoid characterizing property (or drawing legal conclusions in the will) but instead expressly grant whatever they have — and let the court decide what "giving my house" means. The simpler the better, so trying to "legalize" it by assuming it is community property or writing "my half" may lead to error. The above example works whether it turns out the condo is community, separate, or not John's at all.

[5] Leaving this in proportions among legatees may be considered a "general legacy" but acts similarly to a universal legacy where, as here, it gives away the residual estate completely (or if it were the only bequest, giving everything). Specifying that the legacy is "per stirpes" makes sure that the testator's grandchild(ren) are protected if their own parent (the testator's child) predeceases the testator. That "root" is not cut out by losing a child first. That may happen anyway under the rules of accretion, but if the testator's intent is to have their child's surviving descendants "represent" the predeceased child in a succession, saying the legacy is "per stirpes" (or "by root") makes that intent clear with just a few words.

[6] A female executor may be called an "Executrix," though there is no requirement of assigning gender to the role; and a common error made if using that gendered way is that it is mismatched when the draft is used later in a different matter as a template. It may be best to just use "Executor" in all cases. Note: Testators sometimes do not know that they are allowed to appoint a spouse to that role; although they should not be advised what to do, they should be informed of the option.

[7] Although it is often advisable to name a *successor* (back-up) executor, it may not be wise to appoint two co-executors if it means that they will have to consult and agree on all decisions, and sign all checks together. It is also possible to appoint co-executors each with independent authority (stating so in the will), but that presents its own risks of inconsistent actions and disputes. These decisions, however, are for the testator to make.

[8] Whether it is wise to make the executors "independent" (not having to report to court) and/or to dispense with bond (security protection of the assets of the estate, for example by mismanagement or worse by the executor) is a personal decision of the testator. It is not the kind of decision that a nonattorney-notary should advise about,

John Martin Smythe PAGE 2 OF 4

B) Bond. I dispense all of my executors, including any duly appointed dative or provisional executor, from giving bond or other security to serve as executor.

C) Compensation. My individual executor shall serve without compensation, but shall be entitled to recover his or her expenses from my Estate.[9]

D) Selection of Assets. Pursuant to Louisiana Civil Code art. 1572, my Executor has the authority to allocate specific assets to satisfy any legacy herein expressed as a quantum or value of my estate, including a fractional share.

E) Common Disaster. Should I die together with any legatee in a common disaster or under such circumstances as to render it doubtful as to who died first, it shall be presumed that I survived.[10]

F) Collation. I dispense all of my heirs from collating any gift received from me whether inter vivos or by reason of my death.[11]

G) Undue Influence. No disposition in this testament has been made by me as a result of hatred, anger, suggestion or captation. I understand the nature and extent of my property and the consequences of the dispositions in this testament.

H) Should any of the provisions of this testament be for any reason declared invalid, such invalidity shall not affect any of the other provisions of this will and all invalid provisions shall be wholly disregarded in interpreting this will.

IN WITNESS WHEREOF, I have signed on each page and declared this to be my Last Will and Testament, in the presence of the Notary Public and the competent witnesses hereafter named and undersigned, at Marksville, Louisiana, at the date written and after due reading of the whole.

DATE: _______________, 20____[12] ____

JOHN MARTIN SMYTHE

In our presence the testator has declared or signified that this instrument is his testament and has signed it at the end and on each other separate page, and in the presence of the testator and each

---

though the notary may explain the differences. The present example is written in a way that truly places trust in the executor and may not be right for some testators.

[9] Or the testator may state a fixed compensation amount for this service, or one stated in terms of a percentage of the estate. Compensation is especially common when the executor is an unrelated attorney, accountant, or juridical person.

[10] See other ways of dealing with simultaneous death (defined as up to 6 months) in "Testamentary provisions."

[11] This means that any debt owed to the testator is forgiven before assets are distributed rather than being paid as part of the legacy to that person, or having them pay back the debt before the estate is divided.

[12] Drafters of wills often type in the date it is anticipated that the testament is to be signed. Nonetheless, it may be advisable to leave blank spaces, to fill in at the last minute by hand (the notary may do so), because the signing is often postponed in reality. Having it typed in already runs the risk that it will not be the actual date of signing. Even if that happens, it can be corrected by hand before anyone signs. But it's advisable to avoid inconsistencies or errors and just wait to date it. Similarly, it is probably best to leave the witness names blank until they are present.

other we have hereunto subscribed our names this _____ day of _______________, 20____ at Marksville, Louisiana.[13]

WITNESSES:

_______________________________ _______________________________

Name: __________________________ Name: __________________________

____

Notary name: _______________________________, Notary Public

Notary ID or Bar Roll Number: ____________

My Commission is for Life

[13] There is never a good reason to risk invalidity by paraphrasing the attestation clause rather than quoting it verbatim from art. 1577. The only exceptions should be the relatively rare situations in which the testator is unable to read due to illiteracy or vision impairment, unable to sign their name, or deaf. In those cases there are particular procedures and attestation clauses, required by arts. 1578 (physical limitations), 1579 (vision impairment or unable to read), 1580 (reads Braille), or 1580.1 (deaf, or deaf and blind), that must be strictly followed and quoted.

TESTAMENT: EXAMPLE WITH CLAUSES AND PET TRUST

STATE OF LOUISIANA

PARISH OF ST. CHARLES

LAST WILL AND TESTAMENT

OF

KENNETH ALLEN MCKENNETH

BE IT KNOWN, that before me, the undersigned Notary Public, duly commissioned and qualified in and for the parish and state aforesaid, and in the presence of the undersigned competent witnesses, on the 8th day of July, 2024, personally came and appeared:

> KENNETH ALLEN MCKENNETH, of the full age of majority, who declared that he lives and resides in the Parish of Jefferson, Louisiana, at the following address: 7001 Veterans Memorial Blvd., Metairie, LA 70003.

Who declared to me, Notary, that he wishes to take advantage of the provisions of La. Civ. Code article 1576, *et seq.* as is now or as amended, and does hereby make and declare this to be his last will and testament:

I, KENNETH ALLEN MCKENNETH, being able to comprehend generally the nature and consequences of this act, knowing how and being able to read and write, realizing the precarious and uncertain nature of life, and wishing to dispose of all the property which I may own at the time of my death by Last Will and Testament, declare this to be my final testament. I revoke all prior testaments or codicils.

I.

Marriage and children. I, KENNETH ALLEN MCKENNETH, have been married but twice, first to Ellie Sue McBarker, whom I divorced in 1990, and second to Frances McBitterand, to whom I remain married. I have two children, namely Keely McKenneth and Louis McKenneth. Keely McKenneth was born of the marriage to Ellie Sue McBarker, her date of birth is January 1, 1989, and Louis McKenneth was born of the marriage to Frances McBitterand, his date of birth is January 1, 1991. No other children have been born to or adopted by me. At the time of this act, no children are minors or forced heirs.

II.

Particular bequests. I hereby gift the following particular bequests from my estate:

> To my neighbor, Lucinda B. Marquette, I bequeath my quilts and my quilt-making accessories.
>
> To my nephew Huey, I leave my Rolex Submariner watch.

____

Kenneth Allen McKenneth

To my nephew Dewey, I leave my 1964 Ford Thunderbird. If my nephew should predecease me or is otherwise unable to take the Thunderbird, I bequeath this vehicle to my friend, Marcus Ronald George.

If my godson, Joseph "Fire" McIntyre is enrolled in or has graduated from college by the time of my death, I bequeath to him the sum of twenty thousand dollars ($20,000.00) in cash.

I hereby relieve my goddaughter, Emliada Frund, of the fifty thousand dollar ($50,000.00) debt she borrowed from me in 2020 to attend circus school.

Bank accounts, stocks, bonds, CDs, and retirement funds. I give and bequeath in full and complete ownership, all financial, bank, and retirement accounts and stocks and bonds and similar incorporeal investments, of whatever ownership interest I may have, to my wife Frances.

General Legacy and Usufruct. I leave my ownership interest in the house and land at 7001 Veterans Blvd., but not the movables contained in it, to be divided in equal shares to my daughter Keely McKenneth and my brother Michael Strong, reserving to my wife Frances a usufruct to remain until her death. If either Keely or Michael, or both, predecease me, their share shall go to Frances.

Disinherison. I hereby specifically disinherit my son, Louis McKenneth. Louis is not in the military and knows how to contact me, but he has failed to do so for the last 7 years. His last communications to me were a telephone call in 2016 and some texts ending in summer 2017. He is to receive nothing under this testament.

Business. I give and bequeath the ownership, assets, and control of my business Wonderlust Prejean, LLC to Frances, to manage, encumber, sell, or alienate as she pleases.

Residuary Estate. I give and bequeath the remainder of my estate, including all personal property, intellectual property, any other vehicle I may own or have an interest in, and other immovables I may own at the time of my death, to my daughter Keely.

III.

I name and appoint my wife, Frances, to be the executor of my estate, with full seizin, without the necessity of bond, and without the necessity of inventory. In the event that my spouse is unwilling or unable to qualify or serve as my executor, in that event, and only in that event, I name my daughter, Keely McKenneth, as alternate executor with full seizin. I name and appoint Juan LaFonta as attorney for my estate and my executor.

I provide that my succession be processed under independent administration. All administrators or executors for my estate shall serve as independent administrators.

I expressly dispense of my executor, including any successor or duly appointed dative or provisional Executor, from giving bond or similar security to serve in this role.

My individual executor shall serve without compensation, but shall be entitled to recover her expenses from my estate.

Pursuant to La. Civil Code art. 1572, my executor has the authority to select assets to satisfy any legacy herein expressed as a quantum or value of my estate, including a fractional share. I further authorize my executor, in accordance with statutory law, to satisfy all of my just debts, funeral expenses, inheritance and other taxes, and expenses incurred in connection with my death as

____
Kenneth Allen McKenneth

soon as can be done conveniently after my death out of my estate with contributions from no one.

IV.

I give all of my pet(s) to my executor with the direction that the executor deliver my pet(s) to my wife Frances, if she survives me, and my brother Michael, if she does not, with the request that she or he take custody of my pet(s) and provide them with a good home; or, if neither survives me or is able to take custody of them, find and deliver my pet(s) to a suitable person(s) to take custody of them and provide them with a good home and proper care.

V.

If any person shall, in any manner, directly or indirectly, attempt to contest or oppose the validity of this testament, or commences, continues, or prosecutes any legal proceeding to set this it aside, then such person shall forfeit his or her share, cease to have any right or interest in the trust property, and shall, for purposes of this testament, be deemed to have predeceased me.

VI.

Should I die together with any legatee in a common disaster or under such circumstances as to render it doubtful as to who died first, it shall be presumed that I survived. Pursuant to La. Civil Code art. 1521, I specifically provide that if any heir or legatee provided for herein does not survive me by a period of more than thirty (30) days, then any such legatee shall be considered as having predeceased me. If there is not sufficient evidence that any legatee herein named and I have died otherwise than simultaneously, it shall be presumed that I survived such legatee.

VII.

Disposition of remains. I grant to Keely McKenneth the final decision as to the disposition of my remains. I express to her my desire that I be cremated and the ashes distributed upon the sea.

VIII.

No disposition in this testament has been made by me as a result of hatred, anger, suggestion or captation. I understand the nature and extent of my property and the consequences of the dispositions in this testament, including specifically my decision to disinherit my son.

IV.

Should any of the provisions of this will be for any reason declared invalid, such invalidity shall not affect any of the other provisions of this will and all invalid provisions shall be wholly disregarded in interpreting this will.

IN WITNESS WHEREOF, I have signed on each page and declared this to be my Last Will and Testament, consisting of three (3) pages, in the presence of the Notary Public and the competent witnesses hereafter named and undersigned, at Hahnville, Louisiana, at the date written.

____

KENNETH ALLEN MCKENNETH

____

Kenneth Allen McKenneth

TESTAMENT: EXAMPLE WITH CLAUSES AND PET TRUST

In our presence the testator has declared or signified that this instrument is his testament and has signed it at the end and on each other separate page, and in the presence of the testator and each other we have hereunto subscribed our names this 8th day of July, 2024, at Harahan, Louisiana.

WITNESSES:

____

Printed Name

____

Printed Name

____

Name: ___________________________________, Notary Public

Notary Identification or Bar Roll No.: ___________

My Commission is for Life

\- -

Pet trust 1:
Optional simple expansion of paragraph IV to provide funds for care of pets

The executor shall distribute the sum of twenty thousand dollars ($20,000.00) to the person who has custody of my pet(s). If no pet(s) survive me, the executor shall distribute the sum of ten thousand dollars ($10,000.00) or the remainder of the funds, whichever is lower, to a local dog rescue of their choice.

Definition of "Pet(s)". The terms "pet(s)" means my dog(s) presently, Pooches and Spot, and any other dog(s) owned by me and living at the time of my death.

Pet trust 2:
A more expansive structure for care of pets

Trust for Pets. If I am survived by one or more pet(s) of mine, I give and bequeath to Sally Effron, Trustee, the sum of seventy-five thousand dollars ($75,000.00), to set aside and hold such sum in a separate trust to be disposed of for the benefit of my pet(s) (hereinafter "pet," whether singular or plural) that survive me, under the following provisions.

Trust for Pets Provisions:

____

Kenneth Allen McKenneth

The trust property directed to be held in the Trust for Pets in accordance with the provisions of this section shall be disposed of as follows:

A. Distribution until Termination of Trust. Until the death of the last surviving pet of mine,

1. The Trustee may distribute all or any portion of the trust property to the person I appoint to have custody of my pet, or if they are unable or unwilling to take custody of and care for my pet, to the person the Trustee appoints as a suitable person to take custody of and care for my pet; or directly apply such trust property, for the care of any one or more of my pets in such amounts and at such times as the Trustee, in the Trustee's discretion, may determine. Such care shall take into account my pet's living standard at the time of my death, and includes but is not limited to costs for food, veterinary care, medication, grooming, routine expenses, pet sitting and the disposition of my pet's remains.
2. The Trustee shall also distribute the sum of five thousand dollars ($5000.00) per month to the person who has custody of my pets for the time and effort of providing a good home for my pets. This is intended to be compensation and not reimbursement for expenses. The amount stated is fixed regardless of the number of pets under care.

B. Termination of Trust. This trust shall terminate upon the death of the last surviving pet of mine. Upon termination of the trust, the Trustee shall distribute the then remaining trust property to a local dog rescue of their choice.

Definition of "Pet(s)," The term "pet(s)" means my dogs presently, Pooches and Spotify, and any other dog or domesticated animal owned by me and living at the time of my death.

STATE OF LOUISIANA

PARISH OF ____________________

LAST WILL AND TESTAMENT
OF
[TESTATOR]

BE IT KNOWN, that before me, the undersigned notary, duly commissioned and qualified in the parish and state above, and in the presence of the undersigned competent witnesses, on the ____ day of ______________, 20___, personally came and appeared [NAME], who declared that he or she is of full legal age, is able to read and write, and comprehends generally the nature and consequences of this act; and further declares this to be his Last Will and Testament, revoking all previous wills and codicils:

I, [NAME], am domiciled in *name of parish* Parish, Louisiana, residing at this address: *address. Full appearance clause, with current marital status, former marriages, and children born to each marriage:*

Of my marriage to *name of first spouse*, these children were born, *names and ideally adding birth dates; repeat for each spouse, if no children were born of that marriage, indicate none.*

No other child was born to me, and I have filiated no other child, either formally or informally, nor have I ever adopted any other child.

I name and appoint my spouse, *name of spouse*, executor of my estate, with full seizin and without bond. I specifically provide that my succession be processed under independent administration. In the event that my spouse is unwilling or is unable to qualify and serve as executor, then in that event, and only in that event, I name *name of alternate executor* as alternate executor with full seizin. I name and appoint *name of attorney, if one is being used*, attorney for my estate, for my executor, and for the trust created by this document.

I give and bequeath my entire estate to *name of trustee*, as trustee, to hold in trust and as fiduciary for the designated beneficiaries.

The trustee must hold this property in trust for the term and on the conditions set forth below.

TRUST DURING LIFE OF SPOUSE

I name my spouse, *name of spouse*, as the income beneficiary for life of the trust. I name my children as the principal beneficiaries, and their interest shall be equal. Upon my spouse's death, my children shall be the successor income beneficiaries, in equal shares. The trust should provide my spouse with the means necessary to maintain her present reasonable standard of living and with necessary medical and other living expenses. To that end, I direct that the trustee disburse all of the trust income and, if the income is not sufficient, then a sufficient amount of principal.

My trustee shall not invade the principal on behalf of a principal beneficiary during my spouse's life.

This trust may be referred to as the "*name of trust* Trust."

____
[testator name]

TESTAMENT: EXAMPLE WITH TRUSTS

TRUST AFTER DEATH OF SPOUSE

After the death of my spouse, the trustee must pay out income from the trust, together with principal, to the extent my trustee may deem it desirable to do so, according to the following standards:

The trustee must provide my children with an education and a respectable, but not excessive, lifestyle according to my present standard of living. To that end, I direct that the trustee disperse a sufficient amount of income and, if the income is not sufficient, then a sufficient amount of principal, to provide each beneficiary with a good education, including not only a high school and college education, but such advanced or graduate degrees as my beneficiaries may have the aptitude for and interest in pursuing for the period normally required for such studies. Further, should the beneficiaries not have funds from this and other sources sufficient to provide for beneficiary's comfort, support, and maintenance, according to beneficiary's usual present standard of living, then the trustee must disburse income and, if the income is not sufficient, principal sufficient to enable the beneficiary to maintain that standard of living.

After the death of my spouse, the trust as to any beneficiary shall terminate as to that beneficiary when he or she attains the age of *desired age to end income payments* years.

The trustee will have all of the powers that may be conferred upon trustees under the laws of Louisiana, including, but not limited to, all of the powers that trustees are permitted to exercise under the provisions of Louisiana law as it may be amended in the future, including, but not limited to, the Louisiana Trust Code. The trustee will have the power to name a co-trustee or successor trustee.

The trust must pay a reasonable compensation to the trustee for services rendered and for the necessary expense of administering the trust. The trust must protect, save, indemnify, and hold harmless the trustee from any loss or liability arising out of the acts of such trustee, except for malicious and willful breach of the trustee's obligation. The trust must also pay reasonable costs, fees, and expenses to defend the trust and trustee from any suits or actions brought.

To the maximum extent permitted by Louisiana law, each beneficiary is prohibited from alienating any interest in the trust, voluntarily or involuntarily.

In the event of birth or adoption of any children by me in the future, the children must have the same and equal rights with the children above named, and jointly with them, without collation and subject to the trust provided or confirmed in this document; otherwise all provisions of this will must remain in full force and effect.

This trust will terminate as to all beneficiaries when the youngest of them reaches the *age of designated age* years. To the extent principal remains, the trustee is instructed to distribute it in equal shares and per stirpes to the principal beneficiaries.

[Other provisions of testament, such as naming a tutor and undertutor for minor children.]

Should any of the provisions of this testament, and the trust created or funded by it, be for any reason declared invalid, such invalidity shall not affect any of the other provisions and all invalid provisions shall be wholly disregarded in interpreting this will and trust.

____

[testator name]

IN WITNESS WHEREOF, I have signed on each page and declared this to be my Last Will and Testament, in the presence of the Notary Public and the competent witnesses hereafter named and undersigned, at Marksville, Louisiana, at the date written and after due reading of the whole.

DATE: _______________, 20____ ____

[TESTATOR]

In our presence the testator has declared or signified that this instrument is his testament and has signed it at the end and on each other separate page, and in the presence of the testator and each other we have hereunto subscribed our names this _____ day of _______________, 20____ at _________________, Louisiana.

WITNESSES:

_____________________________________ _____________________________________

Name: ______________________________ Name: ______________________________

____

Notary name: _______________________________, Notary Public

Notary ID or Bar Roll Number: ____________

My Commission is for Life

- -

Optional provisions:

Trust alternative 1:
A simple trust provision to add to any testament, if desired by testator

Add the following separate paragraph in the dispositive portion of the will (example):

As a particular bequest, I give and bequeath the sum of seven-hundred thousand dollars ($700,000.00) to Maria H. Caulfield, as trustee, to hold in trust and as fiduciary for these beneficiaries equally: my children Jennifer, Max and Stacy, and any other child of mine as a

____

[testator name]

result of birth or adoption of any children by me in the future. The trustee has the discretion to name the trust, name a co-trustee or successor trustee, administer and invest the trust for the benefit of my children, pay herself $2,500.00 per month compensation for the service, distribute income as necessary for the care, housing, feeding, and reasonable education of the beneficiaries, and retain accounting or legal professionals as needed to preserve, protect and manage the trust. When the youngest of my children reaches the age of 25, the trust will terminate and I direct the trustee to deliver the remaining property in equal shares and per stirpes to my children.

Trust alternative 2:
A very simple trust provision to add to any testament, if desired by testator

As a particular bequest, I give and bequeath the sum of two-hundred thousand dollars ($200,000.00) to my spouse Rachel Stein, as trustee, to hold in trust for the benefit of our son Kevin, until he reaches the age of 25; at such time the trust will terminate and I direct the trustee to deliver the remaining property, if any, to Kevin.

ADDITIONAL OPTIONAL PROVISIONS AND CLAUSES

Testamentary Provisions and Additional Clauses

Optional provisions a testator may want to add into a testament to achieve certain permissible goals. Some are quite common such as naming a tutor (guardian) for minor children in case the testator dies before they reach 18. Some are fairly unusual, such as disinheriting a child under age 24, but they can be done. None of these suggested clauses should automatically be included in a client's will; it is up to the client to decide which, if any, is appropriate for their needs.

A more complete list of 19 things a testator may lawfully do in a testament is found in Michele Childress, Louisiana Notary Exam Outline to the 2024 Study Guide 156-58 (2024), and permissible provisions are discussed in more detail in C. Alan Jennings et al., Fundamentals of Louisiana Notarial Law and Practice 481-92 (2024).

A provision to include a testamentary trust within a will is found elsewhere in this collection. In addition, related but not actually a testamentary trust, is a Pour Over provision to an already existing (inter vivos) trust, below.

A provision to designate who shall manage the remains of the deceased would mirror that in our collection as a separate notarized declaration (see that file, "Affidavit, disposition of remains"). It may be included with similar language as a clause in a will; however, it may be advisable for this to be done as a separate document (perhaps in addition to, but consistent with, a testamentary clause), if only because the remains will be dealt with before a succession is openedw2 or the will's validity is determined. In either form, the person may describe their preference as to how the remains will be treated, but the only binding part is the designation of who is to manage this decision.

Appointment of attorney for the estate

I name, designate and appoint *name* to be attorney for my executor and for my estate.

Appointment of executor

I name, designate and appoint *name* to be executor for my estate [, with full seizin and without bond *if testator intends*]. In the event that *name* is unable or unwilling to serve in that capacity, then in that event and only in that event, I name and designate *name of alternate* as alternate executor of my estate [, with full seizin and without bond. My executor shall serve as an independent executor [*if testator intends*].

Appointed executor to be authorized to act as independent administrator without bond

My executor(s), including any substitute or successor executor, may act as an independent administrator under the provisions of Louisiana C.C.P. art. 3396.2. The independent administrator shall have all of the powers allowed by law and is expressly relieved from the obligation to provide bond or other security.

Appointed executor to be authorized to act as independent administrator with bond

My executor(s), including any substitute or successor executor, may act as an independent administrator under the provisions of Louisiana C.C.P. art. 3396.2. The independent administrator shall have all of the powers allowed by law, but otherwise is expressly not relieved from the obligation to provide bond or other security as the law or judicial mandate would require.

Appointment of tutor (married parent)

In the event that my spouse, *name of spouse*, has predeceased me or if we perish in a common disaster, I desire and specifically designate that *name of tutor* be appointed tutor of my minor children, *names of minor children*, if the children are minors at the time of our deaths. I further designate that *name of undertutor* be appointed undertutor of the minor children.

Appointment of tutor (single parent)

To the extent the law permits, I desire that *name of tutor* be appointed tutor of my minor children, *names of minor children*, if the children are minors at my death. I further desire that *name of undertutor* be appointed undertutor of the minor children.

Birth or adoption after signing

In the event of the birth or adoption of any children after the date of execution of this last will and testament, then my testament will not be rescinded or revoked, but the legacies contained in it of *names of children in will*, must be made to *names of children*, and any children born to me or adopted by me after the date of execution of this will, in equal portions, subject to the same provisions, terms and conditions as the bequests made to *names of children.*

Collation, dispensation from (freeing legatee from repaying previous debt from their share)

All donations inter vivos which I have made to my children *[or, more broadly, legatees]* are intended as extra portions and collation must not be required of any of my children *[or legatees]*.[1]

Debts

I demand that there must be charged against and paid out of my estate all just debts, including funeral and administration expenses, owing or payable with respect to my estate.

Disinheritance of forced heir or someone who may become a forced heir at testator's death

For *state a reason listed in Civil Code art. 1621(A) [and preferably cite to and quote that specific provision; plus certainly at some place in the testament express the reasons, dates, facts, or circumstances justifying disinherison or else the action may lose its statutory presumption of validity]*, it is my intention and I do disinherit *name of person disinherited*, so that they are deprived of their *legitime [or 'of any inheritance']*. In the event that my request to disinherit *name of person* is not honored or is contrary to the laws of Louisiana, then, and only then, I leave and bequeath to *name of same person* the minimum forced portion of my estate legally required

[1] Under LA C.C. art. 1232, such dispensation from collation (forgiving a claw-back of debt) may be made in a will, but also can be done as a separate declaration made in authentic form. Further, "Unless expressly stated to the contrary, a declaration of dispensation from collation made in the last will and testament of the donor shall be effective as a dispensation from collating donations made both before and after execution of said testament."

under Louisiana law.[2]

Forced and disposable portions

I leave and bequeath to my children, *names of children,* an amount of property equal to the value of their forced portion of my estate under Louisiana law in effect at my death, in equal portions, *[optional: ...subject to the usufruct, for life, granted in favor of my [named] spouse.]*

— Disposable portion

I leave and bequeath to *name*, in full ownership, the disposable portion of my estate.

Forgiving an unworthy successor

Because *name* and I have reconciled and reconstituted our relationship, I forgive them and release them from an allegation they are an unworthy successor based on conduct occurring, and known to me, prior to the execution of this testament, and I affirmatively release this successor from the burden of proving forgiveness in a proceeding related to my estate.

General legacy

I leave and bequeath to *name(s) of person*, an undivided *amount of percent*% interest in and to all of the immovable property of which I die possessed.

OR

I leave and bequeath to *names of persons*, in equal shares, my *describe property*.

Joint legacy (avoiding the common law phrase "share and share alike")

I give and bequeath to *name* and *name* the amount of $*dollars* [*or other named property*].

No-contest (*in terrorem*) clause, to prevent challenges to the testament

If any person shall, in any manner, directly or indirectly, attempt to contest or oppose the validity of this testament, including any codicil to this testament which leaves this instrument remaining at least partly in force, or commences, continues, or prosecutes any legal proceedings to set this testament or such a codicil aside, then such person shall forfeit his or her legacy, cease to have any right or interest in the property, and, for purposes of this testament, be deemed to have predeceased me."

---

[2] Although it is common and sometimes thought of as "clever" to leave "$1" to a child meant to be disinherited, experienced estate attorney Paul Rabalais points out (in his excellent YouTube series) that the effect of this is to make the person a legatee, giving them standing to be part of the succession and receive all notifications and play a role in the proceedings, possibly delaying them or making them more expensive; we add that it may also trigger an ethical duty by the executor or estate attorney to that child, now that they are a named legatee to the estate, that would not exist if they were intentionally and entirely omitted.

In addition, regardless of forced heirship, it may be best to specifically name someone who is meant to be omitted and affirmatively say they are omitted, to preclude any dispute about whether the person was left out in error. Moreover, if they could possibly be a forced heir at the time of death, merely saying they are disinherited is not enough, given the requirements of C.C. art. 1621 above of specific reason for disinherison and factual support.

ADDITIONAL OPTIONAL PROVISIONS AND CLAUSES

Particular legacy

I leave and bequeath to *name* my (im)movable property *describe a specific property.*

Particular legacy of classes or groups

I leave and bequeath to *name* my (im)movable property *describe property of collection or grouping of things such as all the paintings in the lake house.*

Pour Over trust provision

I leave and bequeath *property* to the trustee of my trust, *already-existing trust name (set up inter vivos)*, for the benefit of and as a fiduciary to the beneficiary(ies) named in that trust.

Pour Over trust provision with Spendthrift provision preventing creditor access

I leave and bequeath *property* to the trustee of my trust, *already-existing trust name (set up inter vivos)*, for the benefit of and as a fiduciary to the beneficiary(ies) named in that trust, on condition that the property or funds generated by that property may not be assigned, sold, alienated, transferred, mortgaged, pledged, pawned, encumbered, borrowed against, used as collateral or otherwise subject the property to seizure, foreclosure, repossession, garnishment, attachment or other action by creditor(s) to collect any debt whether related to the property or not.

Preferred legacy (in the event the estate cannot pay all gifts)

I leave and bequeath to *name* the amount of $*dollars*, the legacy to be paid in preference to all others.

Simultaneous death of spouse

In the event, and only in the event, that my spouse, *name of spouse*, and I perish simultaneously in a common disaster, or if there is insufficient evidence to determine otherwise, it will be presumed that I survived my spouse, and in that event, and only in that event, I expressly revoke and rescind any and all bequests previously made to my spouse, *name of spouse*, and do leave and bequeath to my children [*or other successor legatee*], *names of children or other(s)*, in full ownership, all the property of which I die possessed, per stirpes and in equal portions.

Taxation

I direct that any and all federal and/or state taxes assessed, owed and/or charged, including, but not limited to, Louisiana inheritance and estate transfer tax and/or federal estate tax, arising out of the legacy made to *name* will be solely borne by my estate.

Universal legacy of entire estate

I leave and bequeath to my child [*or spouse or named legatee*], *name of child, spouse or legatee*, all of the property of which I die possessed, both movable and immovable, tangible and intangible.

ADDITIONAL OPTIONAL PROVISIONS AND CLAUSES

Universal legacy of residuary estate

I leave and bequeath to my child [*or spouse or named legatee*], *name of child, spouse or legatee*, the remainder of all of the property of which I die possessed, both immovable and movable, tangible and intangible.

Usufruct

I leave and bequeath to my spouse, *name*, the usufruct over all of the community property of which I die possessed, *until remarriage or for life*...

OR

I leave and bequeath to my spouse, *name [or other person]*, the usufruct, for *length of usufruct in years*, over all of the *community and/or separate property* of which I die possessed...

Additional optional terms for either of above: I expressly grant to my spouse, *name*, as usufructuary, the right to sell, mortgage, lease or otherwise dispose of all assets subject to the usufruct, whether the assets are consumable or nonconsumable things. Such disposition will not require the consent of the naked owner. The usufruct must not terminate upon disposition and must attach to the proceeds and any reinvestment of the proceeds.

My spouse, *name*, will have the power and authority to convert any or all property which is not productive of income into producing property and to convert any or all nonconsumable property into consumable property.

I grant to my spouse, *name*, every power that a usufructuary may have under the laws in effect at the time of my death or that may be allowed by any subsequent law.

OR

I expressly provide that there will be no usufruct established in favor of my spouse or any person upon any property, community or otherwise, that I may have or bequeath from my estate.

Vulgar (permissible) substitution

Pursuant to Louisiana Civil Code art. 1521, I specifically provide that if any legatee provided for in this testament does not survive me by a period of *up to six months*, then all of my property must devolve as if such heir or legatee had predeceased me.

OR

Pursuant to Louisiana Civil Code art 1521, I specifically provide that if *specific legatee* is unable or unwilling to accept their legacy provided in this testament, then I bequeath that property to *back-up person*.

BUT NOT (prohibited substitution):

I leave the ruby necklace with the fleur dis lis chain my maternal grandmother gave me to my wife Nancy on condition that, at her death, she bequeath it to our daughter Janet.

CODICIL: AMENDING A PREVIOUS TESTAMENT

CODICILS, ADDITIONS & REVOCATION

This version is used when a previous will exists that expresses the desires of the testator and has not been amended since; this is the first codicil. Otherwise, if there are previous codicils, remove the sentence confirming "no other codicils" and specifically name the other codicils, for example by date. Either declare that previous codicils remain in force and are not revoked, or revoke those codicils while still making it clear that the will itself is not revoked. For example, if a previous codicil is itself being amended in this act, the previous codicil should be revoked to make clear this replaces it.

This version actually alters, changes, or edits the language of the previous will. This sample has one such alteration but additional paragraphs may be added, for further edits or to add additional legacies (adding new paragraph numbers to the previous will). See next file in this collection if instead there are only additions and no edits to the previous will (or to see an example of additional paragraphs that can be combined with the edits in this sample).

This example changes a previous paragraph that had appointed different executors. The same structure can be used to replace a previous legacy or other provision in the will with a different one, e.g., replacing a legacy that had given the 2018 Kia Sorento to Jack but is now giving it to Jane. The edit can be as finely made as stating that in paragraph IV of the will, strike "one-third" and replace it with "one-fourth," if that is clear; but it is advisable to give more context (e.g., "as to my house on Elm St.," so that the alteration is uncontroversially obvious.

As with any notarial testament, it is always advisable to have a signature line at the bottom of the page, even of ones that appear to have the main signature line elsewhere on the page. The notary cannot know whether in fact the codicil will wind up on two pages when printed and then it would not fully comply with the requirement that the testator sign on each other separate page, having only signed on one of the two. This is especially likely to happen if there is more than one paragraph added.

STATE OF LOUISIANA

PARISH OF ____________________ *[where it is signed]*

CODICIL TO LAST WILL AND TESTAMENT

OF

____

I, ___________________________________, do hereby make this codicil to my last will and testament which is dated __________________ [*date of previous will*], and is expressly not revoked but continues in force, subject to the addition(s) below. I confirm that no other codicils to my last will and testament have been made previously.

[Testator Name], __________________________

CODICIL: AMENDING A PREVIOUS TESTAMENT

1.

I hereby amend Article III (3.1) by replacing the existing paragraph with new paragraph as follows:

I name and appoint my daughter Jane Jones as independent executor of my estate with full seizin and without the necessity of posting bond. Should Jane Jones be unable or unwilling to serve, then I appoint my son Jack Jones to be my independent executor with full seizin and without the necessity of posting bond.

All the other provisions of my Last Will and Testament are to remain in full force and effect.

____
[Print name], Testator .

In our presence the testator has declared or signified that this instrument is his or her codicil, that it is the intention to make this amendment to his or her last will and testament, that the codicil does make those changes, additions or deletions which he or she desires to make, and that the testator has signed it at the end and on each other separate page, and in the presence of the testator and each other we have hereunto subscribed our names this ____ day of _____________, 20____.

WITNESSES:

____
Print Name: _____________________________

____
Print Name: _____________________________

____
Print Name of Notary: __________________________________, Notary Public
Notary ID or Bar Roll No.: _______________
My Commission is for Life

[Testator Name], ____________________________

CODICIL: ADDING PARAGRAPHS

This version is used when a previous will exists that expresses the desires of the testator and has not been amended since; this is the first codicil. Otherwise, if there are previous codicils, remove the sentence confirming "no other codicils" and specifically name the other codicils, for example by date. Either declare that previous codicils remain in force and are not revoked, or revoke those codicils while still making it clear that the will itself is not revoked.

This version merely adds property and legacies to the previous will. It does not alter, change, or edit the language of the previous will other than to add onto it. This sample has one such addition but additional paragraphs may be added, for further legacies. See previous example in this collection if instead there are alterations or edits to the previous will.

As with any notarial testament, it is always advisable to have a signature line at the bottom of the page, even of ones that appear to have the main signature line elsewhere on the page. The notary cannot know whether in fact the codicil will wind up on two pages when printed and then it would not fully comply with the requirement that the testator sign on each other separate page, having only signed on one of the two. This is especially likely to happen if there is more than one paragraph added.

STATE OF LOUISIANA

PARISH OF ___________________ *[where it is signed]*

CODICIL TO LAST WILL AND TESTAMENT

OF

____

I, __________________________________, do hereby make this codicil to my last will and testament which is dated _________________ [*date of previous will*], and is expressly not revoked but continues in force, subject to the addition(s) below. I confirm that no other codicils to my last will and testament have been made previously.

1.

I hereby add Paragraph ___ [*insert new paragraph number, should be different than old paragraph number because this adds and should not overlap with an existing one in the will*], do hereby leave the property located at 123 Main Street, Denham Springs, to *donee/legatee name.*

____

[Print name], Testator

[Testator Name], ___________________________

CODICIL: ADDING PARAGRAPHS

In our presence the testator has declared or signified that this instrument is his or her codicil, that it is the intention to make this amendment to his or her last will and testament, that the codicil does make those changes, additions or deletions which he or she desires to make, and that the testator has signed it at the end and on each other separate page, and in the presence of the testator and each other we have hereunto subscribed our names this _____ day of ____________________, 20____.

WITNESSES:

____

Print Name: ____________________________

____

Print Name: ____________________________

____

Print Name of Notary: ________________________________, Notary Public

Notary ID or Bar Roll No.: _______________

My Commission is for Life

[Testator Name], ______________________

REVOCATION OF A PREVIOUS TESTAMENT

This version is used when a previous will exists that is now being revoked in its entirety. This revocation of a testament may be done in testamentary form or, as in this template, by authentic act. But revoking or changing individual legacies, or editing an existing will, must be done in testamentary form and cannot be validly done by authentic act. See LA C.C. art. 1608. For examples of such modifications or edits, see the previous "codicils" in this section.

This act revokes the will but does not replace it. This leaves the testator either in the position of being intestate or having an even earlier testament left intact, restored to validity (the earlier revocation is itself revoked, under art. 1609). For revocation and replacement, a new testament should be executed that includes the phrase "revoking all prior wills and codicils."

STATE OF LOUISIANA

PARISH OF ____________________

REVOCATION OF PREVIOUS LAST WILL AND TESTAMENT
OF

____

BEFORE ME, the undersigned notary, duly commissioned and qualified in the state and parish aforesaid, and in the presence of the two witnesses whose names are hereunto subscribed, PERSONALLY CAME and appeared the undersigned appearer, who declared unto me:

I, __________________________________, do hereby revoke in its entirety my last will and testament which is dated ________________ [date of previous will], in this authentic act which is expressly a "revocation of entire testament by testator" under Louisiana Civil Code article 1607(2), or as amended.

THUS DONE, SIGNED AND PASSED on the _____ day of ________________, 20____, in ______________, Louisiana, in the presence of the undersigned competent witnesses who have signed their names together with the appearer and me, notary, after due reading of the whole.

WITNESSES: APPEARER:

________________________________ ______________________________
Print Name Print Name

____
Print Name

____

Print Name of Notary: ____________________________________, Notary Public
Notary ID or Bar Roll No.: ________________
My Commission is for Life

SUCCESSION BY AFFIDAVIT (SMALL SUCCESSION)

SMALL SUCCESSION AFFIDAVITS

STATE OF LOUISIANA

PARISH OF ____________________

AFFIDAVIT OF SMALL SUCCESSION OF *NAME OF DECEASED*

On __________________, 20_____, BEFORE ME, the undersigned notary public duly qualified in the above parish and state, personally came and appeared:

____
Affiant 1

and

____
Affiant 2[1]

(hereafter individually and collectively referred to as "Affiant"), both of whom are of the age of majority,[2] who after being duly sworn, did depose and say that:

1. Affiant 1 is *the surviving spouse, or a major heir*, in relation to the Deceased. Affiant 2 is *a major heir, or third party knowledgeable of the facts stated herein*, in relation to the Deceased.
2. The Deceased died on _______________, year of _____. A certified copy of the Deceased's certificate of death is attached hereto.[3]
3. The Deceased's parish of domicile at the time of death was: __________________, at address: ____.
4. The Deceased died intestate.[4]

---

[1] At least two affiants should appear and sign. A surviving spouse, if any, must be a party to this affidavit, joined by at least one major heir. If no surviving spouse exists, two major heirs may appear and sign. If there is only one major heir and no surviving spouse, this affidavit must also be signed by a second person who has actual knowledge of the matters stated herein (e.g., a close friend of the decedent, an in-law, or a neighbor). A "major heir" is an heir of the deceased who is at least 18 (see next footnote). The notary or attorney should make a diligent effort to get all major heirs to sign this affidavit.

[2] If an heir who would otherwise appear is not of the age of majority, a natural tutor may execute this affidavit on behalf of the minor child without needing a judicial appointment or court order.

[3] If the deceased owned immovable property, this instrument cannot be filed until 90 days after the death.

SUCCESSION BY AFFIDAVIT (SMALL SUCCESSION)

5. The marital status of the Deceased at the time of death was: *single, married, or widowed.* The marital history of the Deceased was: *insert here.*

6. The surviving spouse's current domicile is: ______________________________ ______________________________ *[full address, or N/A].*

7. The names, relationship to the Deceased, and last known addresses of all of the heirs of the Deceased and the percentage of inheritance to which they are entitled:[5]
(1.) ______________________________
____
____
(2.) ______________________________
____
____
(3.) ______________________________
____
____
(4.) ______________________________
____
____
(5.) ______________________________
____
____
(6.) ______________________________
____
____

[4] This form applies the procedure and requisites of Code of Civil Procedure article 3432. A somewhat different form (and attachment) is used if the small succession falls under article 3432.1, if the decedent died with a will. In such a situation, see the fillable PDF in this collection that can be readily adapted to comply with article 3432.1.

[5] If more than 6, attach a supplementary list. It's best to note whether decedent's parents survived decedent and whether decedent ever adopted children. For the version used where the decedent died testate, it may also be useful to note whether any heirs are 24 or over and whether any have mental or physical disabilities.

SUCCESSION BY AFFIDAVIT (SMALL SUCCESSION)

8. Any heir not signing this Affidavit either (1) could not be located after the exercise of reasonable diligence, or (2) was given 10 days' notice by U.S. mail of Affiant's intent to execute this "Affidavit of Small Succession" and thereafter did not object.

9. The properties owned by the Deceased at the time of death, both movable and immovable, are more particularly described below:

[Here, insert full legal description of all movable and immovable property, show the value of each item, and include whether property is separate or community, and whether it is subject to a usufruct.][6]

10. The aggregate value of the above-described property(ies), located in Louisiana, at the time of the Deceased's death was less than $125,000.[7]

11. The above properties, under the intestacy laws of the State of Louisiana [OR say, if so: *under a valid judgment of the State of __________ entitled to full faith and credit*] are owned by ____________________________, ____________________________, and ____________________________, in undivided interests if more than one heir.

12. There is no need for an administration of this estate.[8]

13. Affiant understands and affirms under penalty of perjury that if Affiant is an heir, Affiant accepts the succession of the deceased, including the Deceased's debts. Affiant further acknowledges and affirms under penalty of perjury that Affiant executes this document after having read the document line-by-line, that Affiant understands the legal significance of this document, that the information contained in this Affidavit is true, correct and complete to the best of Affiant's knowledge, information and belief, and that Affiant executes this document knowingly, freely and voluntarily and without any coercion or reservation whatsoever.

14. Affiant understands that Louisiana Code of Civil Procedure article 3434: (1) instructs all banks, financial institutions, trust companies, warehousemen or other depository, or any person having property in his possession or under his control, upon receipt of a multiple original of this Affidavit, to pay or deliver any money or property of the deceased, as more particularly described herein, to the heirs of the deceased and the surviving spouse, if any, in the percentages listed herein; (2) instructs any domestic or foreign corporation, and the transfer agent for such corporation, upon receipt of a multiple original of this Affidavit, to transfer any stock or registered bonds in the name of the deceased and described herein, to the heirs of the deceased and surviving spouse, if any, in the percentages listed herein; and (3) provides that receipt of such money or property by the

---

[6] More particularly, state (1) property description (2) whether the property is separate or community property, (3) whether a legal usufruct of the surviving spouse attaches to the property, (4) the value of the property, and (5) list of the heirs and their respective proportionate shares of the property.

[7] This monetary limitation is not applicable if the death was over 20 years ago, dated to the time of filing of this affidavit. If so, state that fact in this paragraph instead of the monetary value being under $125,000. Where the monetary limit does apply, note that it is the gross estate value, not considering a reduction by any debts.

[8] Alternatively, if chose *under a valid judgment* in 11, say: "This estate was fully administered by ___________, a court of competent jurisdiction outside of Louisiana."

heirs named herein constitutes a full release and discharge of the payor for the payment of money or delivery of property made under the provisions of said article 3434.

15. The making of or swearing to a false affidavit is punishable by civil and criminal penalties under the law of Louisiana.

THUS DONE, SIGNED AND PASSED this _______ day of _________________, 20____, at _________________________, Louisiana.

____

Affiant 1 name, Affiant

____

Affiant 2 name, Affiant

____

Notary Name: ____________________________________

Notary ID or Bar Roll No.: _______________

My Commission is for Life

SUCCESSION BY AFFIDAVIT, ALTERNATE

STATE OF LOUISIANA

PARISH OF ____________________

AFFIDAVIT OF SMALL SUCCESSION OF *NAME OF DECEASED*

On this ____ day of ______________, 20____, BEFORE ME, the undersigned notary public duly qualified in the parish and state above, personally came and appeared:

____

Affiant 1

and

____

Affiant 2[1]

(hereafter individually and collectively referred to as "affiants"), both of full age of majority, who, after being duly sworn, did depose and say that in accordance with Louisiana Code of Civil Procedure articles 3421 to 3434, affiants make this affidavit of succession.

SECTION I

[Name of decedent], referred to as "decedent," died on *[date]* and was then domiciled in *[parish of decedent's domicile]*, Louisiana.

SECTION II *[choose one:]*

_______ The decedent died intestate; or

_______ The decedent died testate, left no immovable property, and the dispositions in the testament are the same as if the decedent had died intestate.

SECTION III

Decedent was married: (to *[name of decedent's spouse]*, with whom decedent was living and residing at the time of decedent's death), or (first to *[name of decedent's spouse in first marriage]*, from whom decedent was divorced on *[date of divorce]* in proceedings number _________ of the _________ judicial district court for ___________ Parish, Louisiana in the matter entitled _________ vs. _________, and secondly unto *[name of decedent's spouse in*

[1] For who must appear and other directives, including attachments, see C.C.P. 3421 *et seq.* and our previous example of small succession, which is somewhat more detailed than this form.

second marriage], with whom decedent was living and residing in ____________ Parish at the time of decedent's death).

SECTION IV

Of the marriage between decedent and *[name of decedent's spouse]*, ____ number of children were born, to wit:

[Name of decedent's child], born on date ____________, 20____, and, *[name of decedent's second child]*, born ____________, 20____, No child was born of decedent's marriage with *[name of decedent's spouse]*. The decedent had no other children. Decedent never adopted anyone, nor was decedent ever adopted by anyone.

SECTION V

The decedent left only the following described property, all community property, acquired during the marriage with *[name of decedent's spouse]*, which affiants list together with its value on the date of death:

Property Description	Fair Market Value	Decedent's One-half Interest

Less: Present value of usufruct of surviving spouse, age _______ *[Valuation factor]* $ _____

Valuation of naked ownership: $ _____

Value of inheritance—each child: $ _____

SECTION VI

The names, relationship to the Deceased, and last known addresses of all of the heirs of the Deceased and the percentage of inheritance to which they are entitled: (1.) ____

____

____

SUCCESSION BY AFFIDAVIT, ALTERNATE

(2.) ____

____

____

(3.) ____

____

____

(4.) ____

____

____

(5.) ____

____

____

(6.) ____

____

____

Any heir not signing this Affidavit either (1) could not be located after the exercise of reasonable diligence, or (2) was given 10 days' notice by U.S. mail of Affiants' intent to execute this "Affidavit of Small Succession" and, thereafter, did not object.

THUS DONE, SIGNED AND PASSED this _______ day of _________________, 20____, at _________________________, Louisiana.

____
Affiant 1 name, Affiant

____
Affiant 2 name, Affiant

____

Notary Name: ____________________________
Notary ID or Bar Roll No.: ______________
My Commission is for Life

SUCCESSION INVENTORY BY APPRAISERS

SUCCESSION INVENTORY & DESCRIPTIVE LIST (FOR SUCCESSIONS IN COURT)

INVENTORY BY APPRAISERS, SWORN TO NOTARY (SEE ALSO NEXT CHAPTER):

STATE OF LOUISIANA

PARISH OF ___________________

***Name of Notary,* Notary Public**
SUCCESSION OF *Full Name of Decedent*
INVENTORY OF SUCCESSION PROPERTY

Date
Address

BEFORE ME, the undersigned duly commissioned and qualified Notary Public came and appeared the undersigned

APPRAISERS:

Appraiser 1:
Name:
Identification Presented:
Address:
City:
State:
Zip:
Parish:
Phone:

Appraiser 2:
Name:
Identification Presented:
Address:
City:
State:
Zip:
Parish:
Phone:

Witness 1:
Name:

SUCCESSION INVENTORY BY APPRAISERS

Identification Presented:
Address:
City:
State:
Zip:
Parish:
Phone:

Witness 2:
Name:
Identification Presented:
Address:
City:
State:
Zip:
Parish:
Phone:

Interested persons attending:

Name:
Capacity/Interest:
Identification presented:
City:
State"
Zip:
Parish:
Phone:

Name:
Capacity/Interest:
Identification presented:
City:
State:
Zip:
Parish:
Phone:

COMMUNITY PROPERTY

List and fully describe each item of property, assigning the fair market value to each item and designating the property to be community property.

REAL ESTATE

Legal description *Fair Market Value*

SUCCESSION INVENTORY BY APPRAISERS

Legal description *Fair Market Value*

Legal description *Fair Market Value*

Fair market value $

CHECKING ACCOUNTS

Checking account number _________ of the _________Bank, _________ branch, in the name or names of _________, amount on deposit on date of decedent's death—$_____.

Checking account number _________ of the _________Bank, _________ branch, in the name or names of _________, amount on deposit on date of decedent's death—$_____.

Checking account number _________ of the _________Bank, _________ branch, in the name or names of _________, amount on deposit on date of decedent's death—$_____.

SAVINGS ACCOUNTS

Savings account number _________ of the _________homestead, _________ branch, in the name or names of _________, amount on deposit on date of decedent's death—$_____.

Fair market value $_____

STOCKS AND BONDS

Certificate number _________ of _________, representing _________shares of stock, in the name or names of _________, dated _________.

Fair market value $_____

CERTIFICATES OF DEPOSIT

Certificate of deposit number _________ of the _________bank, _________ branch, in the name or names of _________, dated _________, in the amount of $_____.

Fair market value $_____

UNITED STATES TREASURY BILLS

United States treasury bill, CUSIP number _________, in the amount of $_____, trade date _________, maturity date _________, in the name or names of _________, original of which is held in safekeeping in _________ Bank, as evidenced by receipt number _________, Account Number _________, dated _________.

Fair market value $_____

SUCCESSION INVENTORY BY APPRAISERS

UNITED STATES SAVINGS BONDS

United States savings bond number _________, series _________, in the amount of $_____, issue date _________, in the name or names of _________.

Fair market value $_____

MUTUAL FUNDS

_________ shares of stock in _________ trust/fund/account, account number _________, of _________ stock brokers, in the name or names of _________.

Fair market value $_____

AUTOMOBILES

One _________*year*, _________*make*, _________*model*, _________*body style, e.g., two-door* automobile, bearing vehicle identification number _________, Louisiana title number _________, registered in the name or names of _________.

Fair market value $_____

HOUSEHOLD FURNITURE AND EFFECTS

MOVABLE PROPERTY LISTING

Room: _________________________ Prepared by: ______________________________

Description	Location	Item FMV
___________________________	___________________________	__________
___________________________	___________________________	__________
___________________________	___________________________	__________
___________________________	___________________________	__________
___________________________	___________________________	__________
___________________________	___________________________	__________
___________________________	___________________________	__________
___________________________	___________________________	__________
___________________________	___________________________	__________
___________________________	___________________________	__________
___________________________	___________________________	__________
___________________________	___________________________	__________
___________________________	___________________________	__________
___________________________	___________________________	__________

Total Community Property $_____

SUCCESSION INVENTORY BY APPRAISERS

SEPARATE PROPERTY

List and fully describe each item of property, assigning the fair market value to each item and designating the property to be separate property.

Description	Location	Item FMV
______________________	______________________	________
______________________	______________________	________
______________________	______________________	________
______________________	______________________	________
______________________	______________________	________
______________________	______________________	________
______________________	______________________	________
______________________	______________________	________
______________________	______________________	________
______________________	______________________	________
______________________	______________________	________
______________________	______________________	________
______________________	______________________	________
______________________	______________________	________

Total Community Property $_____

Total separate property $_____

And there being no further property of the decedent to be listed on this Descriptive List, _________*I or we* close this descriptive list by the following recapitulation of the whole.

RECAPITULATION

COMMUNITY PROPERTY

Real Estate	$..
Checking Accounts	$..
Savings and Homestead Accounts	$..
Stocks and Bonds	$..
Certificates of Deposit	$..
United States Treasury Bills	$..
United States Savings Bonds	$..
Mutual Funds	$..
Automobiles	$..
Household Furniture and Effects	$..
Other Property	$..
Total Community Property	$..
Decedent's One-Half Interest in Community Property	$..

SUCCESSION INVENTORY BY APPRAISERS

SEPARATE PROPERTY

Real Estate	$..
Checking Accounts	$..
Savings and Homestead Accounts	$..
Stocks and Bonds	$..
Certificates of Deposit	$..
United States Treasury Bills	$..
United States Savings Bonds	$..
Mutual Funds	$..
Automobiles	$..
Household Furniture and Effects	$..
Other Property	$..
Total Separate Property	$..
Total Estate of Decedent	$..

____
Appraiser 1

____
Appraiser 2

SWORN TO AND SUBSCRIBED BEFORE ME this _______ day of ___________________, 20____

____

Notary Name: ________________________________
Notary ID or Bar Roll No.: ______________
My Commission is for Life

SWORN DESCRIPTIVE LIST FOR COURT

STATE OF LOUISIANA

PARISH OF ___________________

SWORN DETAILED DESCRIPTIVE LIST

BEFORE ME, the undersigned duly commissioned and qualified Notary Public, came and appeared the undersigned

Names of surviving spouse and child or children of majority age who, first being duly sworn, deposed that, in accordance with the provisions of Louisiana R.S. § 47:2408(A) and Louisiana Code of Civil Procedure article 3136, appearers present to the Court the following detailed descriptive list of all the items of property comprising the Succession of *name of decedent*, showing the fair market value of each item at the date of death of decedent, *name of decedent*:

COMMUNITY PROPERTY

[List and fully describe each item of property, assigning the fair market value to each item and designating the property to be community property.]

REAL ESTATE—PARISH

[Property description]

Fair market value $_____

CHECKING ACCOUNTS

Checking account number _________ of the _________Bank, _________ branch, in the name or names of _________, amount on deposit on date of decedent's death—$_____.

Savings and Homestead Accounts

Savings account number _________ of the _________homestead, _________ branch, in the name or names of _________, amount on deposit on date of decedent's death—$_____.

Fair market value $_____

STOCKS AND BONDS

Certificate number _________ of _________, representing _________shares of stock, in the name or names of _________, dated _________.

Fair market value $_____

SWORN DESCRIPTIVE LIST FOR COURT

CERTIFICATES OF DEPOSIT

Certificate of deposit number _________ of the _________bank, _________ branch, in the name or names of _________, dated _________, in the amount of $_____.

Fair market value $_____

UNITED STATES TREASURY BILLS

United States treasury bill, CUSIP number _________, in the amount of $_____, trade date _________, maturity date _________, in the name or names of _________, original of which is held in safekeeping in _________ Bank, as evidenced by receipt number _________, Account Number _________, dated _________.

Fair market value $_____

UNITED STATES SAVINGS BONDS

United States savings bond number _________, series _________, in the amount of $_____, issue date _________, in the name or names of _________.

Fair market value $_____

MUTUAL FUNDS

_________ shares of stock in _________ trust/fund/account, account number _________, of _________ stock brokers, in the name or names of _________.

Fair market value $_____

AUTOMOBILES

One _________*[year]*, _________*[make]*, _________*[model]*, _________*[body style, e.g., two-door]* automobile, bearing vehicle identification number _________, Louisiana title number _________, registered in the name or names of _________.

Fair market value $_____

HOUSEHOLD FURNITURE AND EFFECTS

Miscellaneous household furniture and effects located in the residence of decedent, at _________*[street address]*, _________, Louisiana.

Fair market value $_____

Total Community Property $_____

SWORN DESCRIPTIVE LIST FOR COURT

SEPARATE PROPERTY

[List and fully describe each item of property, assigning the fair market value to each item and designating the property to be separate property.]

Total separate property $_____

And there being no further property of the decedent to be listed on this Descriptive List, _________ *[I or we]* close this descriptive list by the following recapitulation of the whole.

RECAPITULATION

COMMUNITY PROPERTY

Real Estate	$..
Checking Accounts	$..
Savings and Homestead Accounts	$..
Stocks and Bonds	$..
Certificates of Deposit	$..
United States Treasury Bills	$..
United States Savings Bonds	$..
Mutual Funds	$..
Automobiles	$..
Household Furniture and Effects	$..
Other Property	$..
Total Community Property	$..
Decedent's One-Half Interest in Community Property	$..

SEPARATE PROPERTY

Real Estate	$..
Checking Accounts	$..
Savings and Homestead Accounts	$..
Stocks and Bonds	$..
Certificates of Deposit	$..
United States Treasury Bills	$..
United States Savings Bonds	$..
Mutual Funds	$..
Automobiles	$..
Household Furniture and Effects	$..
Other Property	$..
Total Separate Property	$..
Total Estate of Decedent	$..

SWORN DESCRIPTIVE LIST FOR COURT

Signed by appearers:

____
[Name of surviving spouse]

____
[Child of majority age]

____
[Child of majority age]

____
[Child of majority age]

SWORN TO AND SUBSCRIBED BEFORE ME this _______ day of ___________________, 20____, at __________________________, Louisiana.

____
Notary Name: __________________________________
Notary ID or Bar Roll No.: _______________
My Commission is for Life

SWORN DESCRIPTIVE LIST, VERSION BY LOUISIANA SUPREME COURT

APPENDIX 30.0A: SWORN DETAILED DESCRIPTIVE LIST (BLANK)

______________________	____ JUDICIAL DISTRICT COURT
Petitioner	
	DOCKET NO. _______________
Versus	
	PARISH OF _______________
______________________	
Defendant	STATE OF LOUISIANA

SWORN DETAILED DESCRIPTIVE LIST

BEFORE ME, the undersigned notary public, came and appeared __________________ who, after being duly sworn, declared that the following *Sworn Detailed Descriptive List* contains all of the community assets and debts, reimbursement, and accounting claims existing between the parties as of the _____ day of _______________, 20____.

Date of Marriage: ______________________________
Date Petition for Divorce Filed: _________________
Date of Judgment of Divorce: ___________________

I. COMMUNITY ASSETS

Property Description	Possessed By	Value
Immovable Property		
1.		
2.		
3.		
4.		
5.		
Banking & Other Financial Accounts		
1.		
2.		
3.		
4.		
5.		
6.		
7.		
Household Furniture & Movables		
1.		
2.		
3.		
4.		
5.		
6.		
7.		
8.		
9.		
10.		
11.		
12.		
13.		
14.		
15.		
Other		
1.		
2.		
3.		
4.		
5.		

6.		
7.		
8.		

II. <u>COMMUNITY DEBTS</u>

Debt Description	Value
1	
2.	
3.	
4.	
5.	
6.	
7.	
8.	

III. <u>REIMBURSEMENT CLAIMS</u>

Nature of Claim	Claimed By	Value
1.		
2.		
3.		
4.		
5.		
6.		
7.		
8.		

IV <u>PROPERTY CLAIMED TO BE SEPARATE</u>

	Property Description	Possessed By	How Acquired	Adjudication by the Court
1.				
2.				
3.				
4.				
5.				
6.				
7.				
8.				
9.				
10.				

____
Signed by Petitioner

SWORN TO AND SUBSCRIBED BEFORE ME, notary public, on this _____ day of _______________, 20____ at _________________________, LA.

____
Notary Public

Print name: ______________________
Bar Roll #:________________________
My commission expires: ______________

Revised July 1, 2017

AFFIDAVIT OF DEATH, DOMICILE AND HEIRSHIP

MISCELLANEOUS ACTS

STATE OF LOUISIANA

PARISH OF ____________________

AFFIDAVIT OF DEATH, DOMICILE AND HEIRSHIP[1]

BEFORE ME, the undersigned duly commissioned and qualified notary public came and appeared the undersigned

Affiant 1 and *Affiant 2*,

both persons of the full age of majority and residents and domiciled in ______________ Parish, Louisiana, who, after being duly sworn by me, notary, did depose and say:

That affiants are well acquainted with *name of decedent*, and with decedent's family, and that the following facts are within affiants' personal knowledge:

That *name of decedent*, died *say intestate or testate*, on *date of decedent's death*, in ______________ Parish, Louisiana. At the time of decedent's death, decedent was a resident of and domiciled in ______________ Parish, Louisiana.

That decedent was married *number of times*, as follows:

First, unto *name of decedent's first spouse*, from whom decedent was divorced on _____________, 20____, *date of judgment*, by judgment of the _________ Judicial District Court in and for _____________ Parish, Louisiana; and

Second, unto *name of decedent's second spouse*, with whom decedent was living and residing at the time of decedent's death.

Of the union between decedent and decedent's first spouse, the following children were born: *list children and dates of birth*.

Of the union between decedent and decedent's second spouse, no children were born.

No other children were born to, adopted by, nor filiated to decedent.

---

[1] This is *not* the "affidavit of heirship" used for titled movables to gain early ownership outside of succession for cars, trucks, and boats. That is found in the chapter on Movables.

AFFIDAVIT OF DEATH, DOMICILE AND HEIRSHIP

That the decedent did not, within one year prior to the date of decedent's death, dispose of any of decedent's property for an inadequate consideration.

____

[Name of Affiant number 1]

____

[Name of Affiant number 2]

SWORN TO AND SUBSCRIBED BEFORE ME this _______ day of ________________,
20____, at _________________________, Louisiana.

____

Notary Name: ___________________________________
Notary ID or Bar Roll No.: _______________
My Commission is for Life

AFFIDAVIT: DISPOSITION OF REMAINS

A person may designate someone to deal with the disposition of their remains. This designation may be made in a clause in a notarial will (though not an olographic will) or in a separate notarized document, as here. It is often advisable to do so in a separate notarized document so that the possible delay in dealing with testamentary and succession issues does not delay dealing with the decedent's remains.

It can be done as a straightforward designation or in the form of a simple affidavit, as suggested here. In this way, the appearer is an "affiant" and the person appointed to deal with the matter is an "agent." It is allowable that this agent be the same person as the executor, and the form can be adapted accordingly.

The version that is a separate notarized designation is, by statute, not required to be an authentic act—merely notarized. If witnesses are not available, the form below can be adapted to omit those. Nevertheless, the forms suggested by funeral homes typically include two witness lines. Out of an excess of caution—for the agent not to have to spend energy at a time of tragedy persuading morticians that they have misunderstood Louisiana law—it seems advisable to mimic their expectation by including witnesses if possible.

Whether done in a notarial testament or in a notarized statement, the designation is not really of how the remains will be handled (cremation, where buried, donation to medical science, etc.), but rather of who will deal with the matter. (This is why it can be treated similarly to an agency relationship or power of attorney). The affiant typically designates an agent who is amenable to enforcing their wishes. Nevertheless, it is appropriate to go ahead and spell out those wishes as "directives," for guidance and clarity, even if they may not be legally enforceable the way it is true for who is appointed. This form accommodates those preferences.

The original can also be duplicated as a true copy, which may be given to the agent for safe-keeping.

STATE OF LOUISIANA

PARISH OF ____________________

DISPOSITION OF REMAINS AFFIDAVIT

BEFORE ME, the undersigned duly commissioned and qualified Notary Public came and appeared the undersigned

Name of Affiant

I, *name of affiant*, being of sound mind, hereby nominate and appoint *name of agent*, whose contact information is:

Address of Agent: ____

____

Telephone: ____

to serve as my Agent regarding my funeral and the disposition of my remains pursuant to Louisiana R.S. 37:876.

My Agent shall have the authority and power to control the arrangements for my funeral and the disposition of my remains. The Executor of my estate, if different from my Agent, shall notify my Agent of this appointment in a timely manner and shall advise my Agent of the financial means available to carry out the funeral and disposition arrangements.

In the event *name of primary agent* should predecease me or be unable or unwilling to serve as my Agent, I nominate and appoint to be my successor agent the following:

Address of Agent: ____

____

Telephone: ____

MY DIRECTIVES ARE AS FOLLOWS (select one [*preferably by INITIAL*] and add instructions, such as funeral home, spread at sea, etc.):

_______ My remains are to be **cremated**.

____

____

____

_______ My remains are to be **buried**.

____

____

____

_______ My remains are to be **as stated below**.

____

____

____

Regarding any ceremony or event to commemorate my death:

____

____

____

AFFIDAVIT: DISPOSITION OF REMAINS

A true copy of this appointment shall have the same effect as an original.

WITNESSES:

____
Print witness name

____
Print witness name

AFFIANT:

____
Print name of Affiant

SWORN TO AND SUBSCRIBED BEFORE ME, this ______ day of ____________________, 20_____, in the presence of the above competent witnesses and me, Notary, at ___________________, Louisiana.

____

Notary name: __________________________________

Notary ID or Bar Roll No.: _______________

My Commission is for Life

11 • PROCÈS VERBAL AND NOTARIAL INVENTORIES

STATE OF LOUISIANA

PARISH OF ____________________

PROCÈS VERBAL OF OPENING OF A SAFE DEPOSIT BOX

______________________ BANK ______________________________ BRANCH

______________________ BOX NO. ______________________________ RENTOR

BE IT KNOWN and remembered that on this _____ day of _________________, 20_____, before me, a Notary Public duly commissioned and qualified, personally came and appeared ____ ____________________________, agent of ____________________________bank, and ___ ______________________of __________________________, "Locksmith," who did declare to me, Notary, in the presence of the undersigned competent witnesses, as follows:

That rental payments on the above referenced Safe Deposit Box are contractually overdue and that the bank has caused to be sent proper demand by certified mail to the last known address of the Rentor, and that the letter has been returned as undeliverable and/or the Rentor has not responded thereto, and that at least thirty (30) days have elapsed since the return of the certified letter, and that to date, rental payments on the Safe Deposit Box have not been brought current; and,

Further that said bank officer did state that after due notice and in accordance with the rules and regulations of ________________________ Bank and the agreement entered into with the Rentor, that s/he has authorized the above referenced safe deposit box to be forced open in the presence of me, Notary, and the contents therefore removed, examined, and inventoried by me.

Now, I, Notary, do declare the contents of the box are fully described herin, and constitute the entire effects of Rentor found in said Safe Deposit Box, to-wit:

Insert detailed inventoried list of safe deposit box, or refer here to Exhibit A.

And further, I, Notary declare that the contents were then placed in a package which was sealed, dated, and marked with the Rentor's name, and placed in the hand of said bank officer who declared that the package is now and shall be retained at the general risk of collection of rental payments against Rentor personally and/or against the contents formerly deposited in the Safe Deposit Box.

PROCÈS VERBAL OF OPENING SAFE DEPOSIT BOX

IN WITNESS WHEREOF, I have signed together with the appearers and the undersigned competent witnesses on the day and date above first mentioned all after due reading of the whole.

THUS DONE, READ AND PASSED on the _____ day of _________________, 20____, in _____________________, Louisiana, in the presence of the undersigned competent witnesses, who have signed their names together with the parties to this act and me, notary, after due reading of the whole.

WITNESSES:

____________________________	______________________________
Print Name	BANK OFFICER
____________________________	______________________________
Print Name	LOCKSMITH

____

Notary Name: ______________________________

Notary ID or Bar Roll No.: ____________

My Commission is for Life

PROCÈS VERBAL OF OPENING SAFE DEPOSIT BOX

EXHIBIT "A"
INVENTORY OF SAFE DEPOSIT BOX

Bank/Banking office: ____

Address: ____

____

Safe Deposit Box No.: ____________________

Registered in name of: ____

Contents of Box:

____

____

____

____

____

____

____

____

____

Page _____ of _____ pages *[add pages if necessary]*

Attached to and made part of the Procès Verbal dated this ______ day of _________________, 20____, by *Notary Public Name*, Notary Public, *Notary ID No.*

I, *Notary Public Name*, Notary Public in and for _______________ Parish, State of Louisiana, do hereby certify that I was present when the above-numbered Safe Deposit Box was opened and the above-listed contents were removed and inventoried by me in the presence of the undersigned official of the bank named above; and that the contents were deposited with said bank for safekeeping, in the presence of the undersigned bank official:

Bank Official:

____

Name: ________________________________

____

Notary Name: ___________________________

Notary ID or Bar Roll No.: ______________

My Commission is for Life

NOTICE OF TAKING INVENTORY

NOTICE OF TAKING INVENTORY BY NOTARY

[Upon request, the notary is required to send notice to the interested party(ies), such as an heir requesting notice, as follows. The request may be sent by ordinary mail, but priority mail is a better option.]

Name of interested party

Address of interested party

Date

Dear Interested Party <insert actual name>:

I hereby notify you that I, <insert your name>, Notary Public, will proceed to take an inventory of the property of <insert decedent's name; or that of spouse/interdict/minor>, located at <insert decedent's address or location of property>, on the <insert date of inventory> at <insert time>.

Signed,

____

<Notary name>, Notary Public

OATH OF APPRAISERS

STATE OF LOUISIANA

PARISH OF ______________________ *[where signed]*

OATH OF APPRAISER(S)

BEFORE ME, the undersigned duly commissioned and qualified Notary Public came and appeared the undersigned, who took the following oath:

We, the undersigned Appraiser(s). do solemnly swear (or affirm), that we will act faithfully in performing the duties entrusted to us appraisers appointed to appraise the property pointed out to us as belonging to the Succession [or Divorce/Interdiction/Tutorship] of ___________________________ [insert name of decedent/spouse/interdict/minor here].

____
[Name of Appraiser 1]

____
[Name of Appraiser 2]

SWORN TO AND SUBSCRIBED BEFORE ME
this ______ day of __________________, 20____

____,
NAME: ___________________________________, Notary Public,
Notary ID or Bar Roll No.: _____________
My Commission is for Life

PROCÈS VERBAL OF SUCCESSION INVENTORY BY NOTARY

Procès Verbal of name of decedent/spouse/interdict/minor   State of Louisiana

______________________________ [name of Notary Public]   Parish of ____________________

Procès Verbal of Inventory

I, the undersigned notary public, duly appointed by the Court in the matter of the Succession [or Divorce/Interdiction/Tutorship] of ______________ [name of decedent/spouse/interdict/minor; and the docket number of the succession or proceeding], Parish of ________________, State of Louisiana, proceeded to take a public inventory of all of the property belonging to the Succession [or Divorce/Interdiction/Tutorship] of [name of decedent etc.], located in the Parish of ________________ ____________, in the presence of ____________________________ and ____________________ ____________, two undersigned competent witnesses, and assisted [if necessary] by the following named appraisers, who were, upon request, duly notified of the inventory: __________ [names of those appraising the inventories] __________.

The manner in which the inventory was taken was by commencing the inventory at _____ [location] _______, the last residence of the decedent [or other party], at _____ [date and time] _____ ____________, by proceeding to list the contents of said residence, inventorying the contents of each room, and then aggregating the contents, as follows:

Room #1 *[describe room]*

Movable Property *[give description and fair market value of each item of movable property]*

[Note: The notary takes the inventory, but does not evaluate the property. The appraiser evaluates the property and gives that valuation to the notary to incorporate into the procès.]

Room #2 *[describe room]*

Movable Property *[give description and fair market value of each item of movable property]*

Property owned in whole or in part by third parties

Movable Property *[give description of any property on premises owned in whole or in part by any third parties]*

Immovable Property *[give description and fair market value of each item of immovable property]*

PROCÈS VERBAL OF SUCCESSION INVENTORY BY NOTARY

RECAPITULATION

1. Aggregate value of all movable property: ________________________
2. Aggregate value of all immovable property: ________________________
3. TOTAL VALUE OF THE ESTATE: ________________________

There being no other property pointed out to me, Notary Public, I close this inventory at ____ ________ [time] on _____________________ [date], in the presence of the undersigned witnesses and of the appraisers [if any], who have all sworn and signed together with me and in the presence of each other, after due reading of the whole.

WITNESSES:	APPRAISERS:
________________________________	________________________________
[print name]	[print name]
________________________________	________________________________
[print name]	[print name]

INTERESTED PERSONS ATTENDING [if any]:

____

[print name]

____

[print name]

____

[print notary name], Notary Public

Notary ID or Bar Roll No. ____________

My Commission is for Life

AFFIDAVIT OF APPOINTED NOTARY

[For a detailed and helpful example of a fictional Procès Verbal and Affidavit of Appointed Notary, as filled out, see Jennings et al., Fundamentals of Louisiana Notarial Law and Practice (ch. 26).]

STATE OF LOUISIANA

PARISH OF ______________________ *[where signed]*

AFFIDAVIT OF APPOINTED NOTARY

BEFORE ME, the undersigned duly commissioned and qualified Notary Public, came and appeared the undersigned affiant, ______________________ [name], Notary Public, appointed to inventory, who after being duly sworn, does hereby depose, affirm and state the following:

1. I am a Notary Public commissioned in the Parish of _______________ with jurisdiction in the following parishes: ________________________ [or "with statewide jurisdiction," if so].

2. I accepted service of [name of Order appointing administrator and taking of inventory; and Order appointing this notary to inventory dated ____________, 20___], containing notice of my appointment as notary to take and file an inventory of the property of the Succession of _____________ [or for case name of divorce, interdiction, or tutorship].

3. The notice of my appointment as notary was served upon me on ______________, 20___, by __________________, attorney for the Succession [or for the stated case name].

4. Thereafter I took the Inventory as follows: [detailed account (using multiple paragraphs from "a." to however many needed), of process of how inventory was done, including:

a. appointment of and names of appraisers for the purpose of appraising specified property;

b. opening proceedings, and commencing the taking of inventory, at the specified location;

c. filing with Court on named date(s) of Oath(s) of Appraiser of specified appraisers;

d. conducting inventory and, after receiving reports by appraisers, preparing the Procès Verbal pursuant to Code of Civil Procedure Art. 3133 and closing the proceedings at a specified time, date, and location;

AFFIDAVIT OF APPOINTED NOTARY

e. filing on specified date with the Court of a Petition Filing Inventory containing the Procès Verbal of Inventory; and of filing certified copy of this with collector of revenue pursuant to C.C.P. Art. 3134]

5. I attach to this affidavit a copy of my Petition Filing Inventory containing the Procès Verbal, an invoice rendered to the administrator for my professional services of taking the inventory and completing the Petition Filing Inventory and of submitting the return to the Court and collector of revenues, along with my related expenses.

6. I affirm and declare that I have fulfilled all my duties and responsibilities as the court-appointed notary to take inventory in this matter.

7. I aver that I am entitled to a fee of $__________ for my professional notarial services as commissioned by the Court and on behalf of the public trust, along with expenses of $__________ incurred for [stated activity, such as copying costs, notary fee for this affidavit before a second notary, filing fees, or records searches], for a total of $___________.

WHEREORE AFFIANT PRAYS that [he/she] be discharged and relieved of any further duty or responsibility related to the appointment and commission of the Court in the above named matter.

____

[Name of notary conducting inventory], Affiant

SWORN TO AND SUBSCRIBED BEFORE ME
this ______ day of ________________, 20____

____

[Name of second notary, only for this affidavit],
Notary Public, Notary ID or Bar Roll No.: _____________
My Commission is for Life

12 • POWER OF ATTORNEY AND LIVING WILL

POWER OF ATTORNEY: GENERAL & SPECIAL

STATE OF LOUISIANA

PARISH OF ______________________ *[where the instrument is signed]*

GENERAL POWER OF ATTORNEY[1]

BE IT KNOWN that on __________________, 20_____ *[date]*, before me, a notary public duly qualified in and for the above state and parish, and in the presence of the named and undersigned competent witnesses,[2] personally came and appeared:

Name of Principal, a person of the age of majority and a domiciliary of _______________ Parish, Louisiana, "Principal," who declared under oath that they comprehend generally the nature and consequences of the disposition that they are making; that they have been married but once, and then to *spouse name*, to whom they remain married and with whom they reside, and whose

---

[1] This is a "general" power of attorney (POA) because it authorizes a variety of powers and tasks in the agent, rather than just one or two very specific transactions, such as "selling my house" or "picking up prescriptions for me" (in which case it could be called a "special power of attorney" though just "power of attorney" is fine). It is advisable to use the generic term "power of attorney" rather than the subset of "mandate" or "procuration" both because those terms may wind up being inappropriate (though not invalidating) for the act as actually executed, and because most clients understand the general term and have not heard of the Louisiana versions. The difference is explained in a footnote at the end, here, but can be avoided by using the umbrella term "power of attorney." If it is preferred to use one term or the other, it can be substituted on this form, though then the drafter should try to match it up correctly with the signing process actually used (noted in that footnote).

This form is one of the more sweeping and broadly stated versions available and should be understand to place significant trust in the agent (for that reason it is often used from one spouse to another where they are already sharing access and responsibilities, or in favor of a trusted child). The agent in all instances acts as a fiduciary but may cause substantial harm if they are not trustworthy. Principal should understand that this typical form has immediate effect upon execution; although it can be revoked by principal, in the meantime agent may act under it and wield wide powers. This version is in contrast to one made *conditional* on (only becoming effective on) the disability of principal (found later in this chapter), since this one is immediately implemented. But it can be physically retained by principal until such time as they feel it is appropriate to start using it.

[2] This form is structured as an authentic act and thus references two witnesses. Technically, a POA only has to be an authentic act if the powers it is authorizing (and used for) are themselves performed under an authentic act (such as a donation or certain mortgages). A POA has to be in the form of the act it is empowering. If the drafter is sure that it is not being used for an act requiring authentic form, the references to "two witnesses" and the witness lines themselves may be removed. However, it is strongly advised to complete the POA as an authentic act if that is possible, both because you may be wrong about whether it's empowering something that must be in authentic form, or just because some recipients of the form do not know the Louisiana rule and will not accept it unless it has witnesses in addition to the notary. There seems to be no value in teaching our law's fine points to hospitals or brokerage houses when the main goal is to get the form accepted where it is intended to be.

principal address is *address*; and who declared that they appoint *Name of Agent*, "Agent,"[3] to be their agent, representative and attorney-in-fact, with full power and authority to act for, in the name of and on behalf of Principal, to do all acts necessary or deemed by Agent to be appropriate to represent principal including, but not limited to, the following enumerated powers.

ARTICLE I DURABILITY[4]

This Agency is "durable" and shall not be deemed revoked by my disability or incapacity. In the event that I am interdicted, or declared incapacitated for any reason, then I appoint my Agent herein as my curator or guardian over both my person and my property.

ARTICLE II PROHIBITED POWERS[5]

Notwithstanding the breadth of powers granted to my Agent in this Agency, my Agent shall not have or exercise, because of or arising out of this act, any of the following powers:
Life Insurance. Any power or incident of ownership over any policy insuring my Agent's life.
Gifts. Any power or authority over any irrevocable trust created by Agent, if I am a trustee or beneficiary of that trust. Nor shall my Agent have any power over any property my Agent may have donated to me.
Powers. Any power or authority to appoint any of my property to my Agent, to my Agent's estate, to my Agent's creditors, or to the creditors of my Agent's estate. My Agent shall have no power or authority to disclaim any assets on my behalf if the result would cause them to pass directly or indirectly to my Agent or his or her estate in any one calendar year. My Agent shall have no power or authority to discharge any of my Agent's legal obligations out of my property, including any obligation of support which my Agent may owe to others unless my Agent and I are equally obligated to render such support.

ARTICLE III PROPERTY

"Property" means all of my interests in property whether movable, immovable, real, personal, corporeal, incorporeal, tangible, intangible and mixed, wherever located, however acquired,

---

[3] It is also permissible to name and appoint co-agents, though the unintended consequence may be that they are always required to act together and unanimously (if stated in terms of "and") or may act independently and perhaps inconsistently (if in terms of "or" and stating independent authority). Even with such independent multiple agents, it is possible and perhaps desirable to name a primary decision-maker (a tie-breaker), as is stated on our "POA, healthcare power of attorney."

This is different from appointing a successor or back-up agent in case the named agent is unable or unwilling to serve, which may be advisable. In any of these situations, if desired, the appearance clause can be adapted to provide for the added agents, or specifying in the event of disagreement, whose decision controls.

[4] Although the power of attorney in Louisiana is durable unless stated otherwise (meaning it does not terminate upon the incapacity of principal), the forms here are expressly stated to be "durable," in compliance with other states' understandings. If the POA is necessary in a state outside of Louisiana, the inherent "durability" would not be evident to a non-civilian. Again it is better to be clear as to the intention than to assume the recipient understands Louisiana law. Plus this extra paragraph serves as a readily adapted statement for when principal actually wishes that their POA terminate if they are incapacitated; then describe it as "non-durable" and delete the "not" in "shall not be deemed."

[5] These are some of the powers which principal may wish to withhold from agent, but are not required to be. The key in all instances is implementing the understanding and legally valid wishes of principal.

whether owned by me now or hereafter acquired by me or on my behalf by Agent or by third persons. With regard to Property, Agent may:

General Powers. Have all of the powers that may be conferred upon agents under applicable law. If a question shall arise as to whether Agent has a particular power, this Agency shall be liberally construed as granting such power. Should future changes in the law expand the powers of agents, my Agent shall have those expanded powers.

Additional Powers. Without limiting my Agent's powers granted by the preceding paragraph, if those powers do not include the following, my Agent shall also have all of the following powers:

Purchases and Sales. To purchase, sell, exchange, convey, partition or otherwise acquire and dispose[6] of Property, at public or private sale for such purposes and upon such terms, including sales on credit, with or without security in such manner, and at such prices as my Agent may determine. My Agent may purchase U.S. Government bonds redeemable at par in payment of federal estate taxes.

Options. To grant options affecting Property for such purposes and periods, upon such conditions, in such manner, and at such prices as my Agent may determine; to exercise them for such price and on such terms and conditions as my Agent may see fit.

Operation of Businesses; Changes in Corporate Structure. To continue to operate or participate in the operation of any of my business interests, so long as my Agent may deem it advisable, to change the nature of the business, or enlarge or diminish the scope of its activities, to dissolve or liquidate it, or to participate in any incorporation, change, merger, consolidation, reorganization, dissolution or liquidation. To participate in any plan of liquidation, reorganization, consolidation or merger involving any company or companies whose stock or other securities may be subjected to any plan of reorganization or with any protective committee and to delegate to such committee discretionary powers with relation thereto and to pay a proportionate part of the expenses of such committee and any such assessments levied under such plan; to accept and retain new securities received by my Agent pursuant to any such plan; to exercise all conversion, subscription, voting and other rights of whatsoever nature pertaining to such property; and to pay any amount or amount of money my Agent may deem advisable.

Partnerships. To cause my Agent (on my behalf) to become a partner in such partnerships as my Agent may see fit, whether as a limited or general partner, or partner in commendam; to continue me or my Agent as a partner in any partnership in which I may be a partner or possessed of the right to become a partner; to consent to the continuation of any partnership that might otherwise terminate even though the articles of partnership may not provide for continuation.

Leases. To lease or give options to lease all or any part of any immovable property I may own for such price, and on such terms and conditions, for such purposes and at such rentals as my Agent may see fit; to enter into, amend or extend all kinds of leases including but not limited to all kinds of predial leases, surface leases, and oil, gas and mineral leases, with or without pooling provisions.

Oil, Gas and Other Minerals. To sell, lease, exchange, partition or otherwise alienate oil, gas or other minerals and interest therein, and the right to explore for them, or options for any of these, by such instruments, in such forms, for such bonus, rentals or other considerations, and for such

---

[6] In a POA the power to "convey" or "transfer" property does not include the power to "donate," unless that is expressly stated (e.g., adding "donate" to this list and "Donations" to its heading). Because of the risk of self-dealing or losing a valuable property without receiving a value in return (as would happen with a "sale"), principal should consider whether this power is wise to include in this provision.

terms and periods as my Agent may see fit. To invest in, to acquire and retain for so long a period as Agent may see fit, oil, gas and mineral leases and rights in and to oil, gas and other minerals either in the form of mineral interests, royalties or other proprietary or working interests, whether productive when acquired or nonproductive when acquired, whether or not speculative in nature, with or without pooling provisions, to explore or to contract for mineral exploration and to drill and to enter into pooling, unitization, repressurization, and any other type of agreement relating to the development, operation and conservation of mineral property.

Servitudes and Easements. To create servitudes or easements on any immovable property I may own for such purposes and periods, upon such conditions, in such manner, and at such price as my Agent may determine.

Borrowing. To borrow money by obligation either unsecured or secured, in such amounts, for such terms, at such rates of interest or without interest, and in such manner as my Agent may think desirable and to secure such loans by mortgage, pawn or pledge of Property or otherwise, and to mortgage or pledge Property for any period of time my Agent shall think desirable.

Lending. To make loans of Property to such persons, firms, partnerships, corporations, or political subdivision, including businesses or business interest in which my Agent may be personally interested for such purposes and for such periods, in such amounts and at such rates of interest, with or without security, and subject to such other terms as my Agent my determine.

Exchanges. To exchange Property for other property or to give options to exchange Property upon such terms as my Agent may deem advisable.

Retention of Property. To hold and retain Property in the form received so long as Agent deems advisable, and to purchase and retain securities or other properties, although of a kind or in an amount that would not ordinarily be considered suitable, whether or not such property is productive of income and even though it may not be prescribed or authorized by law.

Improvements. To raise any buildings or other structures as my Agent may consider expedient; to improve or develop immovable property; to erect, alter, or repair any buildings or other structures and to make any other kind of improvements my Agent may deem proper, to received, accept, hold, use, control, administer, build upon, manage or otherwise improve, repair, divide or subdivide all or any Property in the manner and to the extent my Agent may deem advisable.

Agents and Employees. To employ or retain such employees, independent contractors, agents and advisors as my Agent may deem necessary, to assist in performing any duties of my Agent, including, but by way of illustration only, investment advice, management advice, and for any other purposes my Agent considers advisable, and to determine reasonable charges for such services and to make payment out of Property.

Mutual Funds. To acquire and retain for so long a period as my Agent may see fit the shares, preferred or common, of investment companies, or investment trusts, whether of the open-end or closed-end type, and without notice to anyone, to participate in any common trust fund or pooled investment fund.

Life Insurance. To insure the life of any other person on whose life I may have an insurable interest. Life insurance shall be in such amounts as my Agent may determine, and in such forms as my Agent may deem wise by term insurance, ordinary life insurance, stated period payment insurance, endowment insurance or any other kind of life insurance. Proceeds of life insurance shall be made payable to any beneficiary or contingent beneficiary designated by my Agent. My Agent may elect any option provided by any policy. My Agent may surrender any of such policies at any time and obtain the cash surrender value, or may borrow against such value, or may exercise any other right of an owner of the policy.

Custody and Location of Property. To keep all or any part of the Property at any place in Louisiana or elsewhere within the United States or abroad with such depositories or custodians at such places as my Agent shall deem necessary or advisable, and to have the power to hold securities in the names of nominees.

Powers of Attorney. To give such powers of attorney, general or special, with or without power of substitution, in connection with the exercise of other powers as my Agent may deem advisable.

Retirement Plans. To create and contribute to an Individual Retirement Account (IRA) or employee benefit plan (including self-employed plans) for my benefit; to select payment options under plans in which I participate, and to change options I have selected. To make and change beneficiary designations, to make voluntary contributions, to "roll-over" plan benefits into other retirement plans, and to borrow money and purchase assets from plans and to see assets thereof, if authorized by any such plan.

Accounts. To establish accounts of all kinds (including checking, investment, money market and savings), for me with financial institutions, including banks, thrift institutions, brokerage firms, and credit unions. To modify, terminate make deposits to and write checks on or make withdrawals from and grant security interests in all accounts in my name or upon which I or my Agent are authorized signatories (except accounts held by me in a fiduciary capacity), whether such account was established by me or for me by my Agent. To negotiate, endorse or transfer any checks or other instruments with respect to any account; to contract for any services rendered by any bank or other institution.

Safe Deposit Boxes. To contract with any institution for a safe deposit box or a storage facility in my name. To have access to all safe deposit boxes or facilities in my name or to which I am an authorized signatory (except in a fiduciary capacity) whether or not the contract for such safe deposit box was executed by me (either alone or jointly with others) or by my Agent in my name. To add to and remove from the contents of any safe deposit box or facility and to terminate contracts for such boxes and facilities.

Legal Proceedings. To institute, supervise, prosecute, defend, intervene in, abandon, compromise, arbitrate, settle, dismiss, and appeal from any and all judicial or administrative proceedings, actions, suits, hearings, attachments, or sequestrations involving me in any way, including claims by or against me arising out of property damages or personal injuries suffered by or caused by me or under circumstances causing the loss to be borne by me; and to hire legal representation related to any of these matters.

Trusts. To execute trust instruments on my behalf as settlor or co-settlor, whether or not I am a beneficiary. To make gifts in trust on my behalf to trusts created by my Agent or to others trusts. To provide that a trust shall be revocable or irrevocable, and interests in the trust to be spendthrift or freely alienable. To serve as trustee of any other trust created by or for my benefit. To add any trust on my behalf. To withdraw or receive the income or principal and to request or demand such withdrawals of any trust.

Fiduciary Offices. To renounce any fiduciary office to which I may be appointed or elected, including (but not limited to) executor, administrator, personal, representative, trustee, tutor, curator, guardian, attorney-in-fact, or officer or director of a corporation. To render such accountings of my activities as may be required.

Taxation. To represent me in all tax matters including federal income, gift, property, estate and excise taxes. To prepare, sign, and file federal, state or local income, gift and other tax returns, of all kinds, including joint returns, FICA returns, payroll tax returns, claims for refunds, requests for extensions of time, petitions to the U.S. Tax Court or other courts regarding tax matters, and all other tax-related documents, including consents and agreements under Section 2032A of Internal Revenue Code, consents to split gifts, closing agreements, and any power of attorney form required by the Internal Revenue Service or any state or local taxing authority with respect to any tax year from 2010 and forward; to post bonds, receive confidential information and contest deficiencies determined by the Internal Revenue Service or any other taxing authority. To exercise any elections I may have under federal, state or local tax law; and generally to represent me or obtain professional representation for me in all tax matters and proceedings of all kinds and for any period before any taxing authority. To engage, compensate and discharge attorneys, accountants and other tax and financial advisors and consultants to represent or assist me in connection with any tax matter involving or in any way related to me or any Property in which I have or may have any interest or responsibility.

Gifts and Donations.[7] To make gifts or other gratuitous transfers either outright or in trust (including the forgiveness of debt and the completion of any charitable pledge), to such person or organizations as my Agent shall select.

Support. To continue to support any person I have undertaken to support or to whom I may owe an obligation of support. Support may include payment of real property taxes, payments on loans secured by my residence, maintenance of my residence, food, clothing and shelter, medical, dental and psychiatric care, normal vacations and travel expenses, education (including vocational and trade schools, training in music, stage, arts and sports, special training provided at institutions for the mentally or physically handicapped, preparatory, undergraduate and graduate or professional study in any field at public or private universities, colleges or other institutions of higher learning) including payments for tuition, books and incidental charges made by the educational institutions, travel costs to and from such institutions, room and board, and a reasonable amount of spending money. If I have been legally separated or divorced from my spouse, any support provided to such spouse by my Agent shall be limited to such support as may be required by law.

Miscellaneous Agreements. My Agent may enter into any and all kinds of agreements on my behalf, whether or not specifically described in this paragraph.

ARTICLE IV HEALTH CARE[8]

I give my Agent all powers regarding the following health care matters that I could exercise on my own behalf, if capable of doing so. My Agent may:

Medical Records. Have access to any medical information in any form regarding my physical or mental condition (notwithstanding any statutory protections of medical privacy and expressly waiving any claims or protections under them, as relates to my Agent's access), and to execute such consents as may be necessary to obtain it.

---

[7] This broader provision to donate and forgive debts should be deleted if the power to "donate" is not included in the list of authorized conveyances above.

[8] Although it is permissible and common for health care provisions to be included in a general power of attorney, many institutions will not honor them if they are not provided in a separate and focused document. It is usually advisable, if health care decisions are an important concern of principal, to enumerate them in a separate POA ("health care power of attorney" or "medical mandate"), as provided later in this chapter. As with the power to donate, health care powers must be expressly and specifically authorized.

Professionals. Retain, compensate and discharge any health care professionals my Agent deems necessary to examine, evaluate or treat me, whether for emergency, elective, recuperative, rehabilitative, convalescent or other care.
Institutionalization. Admit me to any health care facility recommended by a qualified health care professional, whether for physical or mental care or treatment, and remove me from such institution at any time, even if contrary to medical advice.
Treatment. Consent on my behalf to tests, treatment, medication, surgery, organ transplant or other procedures, and to revoke that consent, even if contrary to medical advice.
Chemical Dependency. Consent on my behalf to a course of treatment for chemical dependency, whether suspected or diagnosed, and to revoke such consent.
Pain Relief. Consent on my behalf to pain relief procedures, even if they are unconventional or experimental, and even if their use may risk addiction, injury or foreshortening my life.
Releases. Release from liability any health care professional or institution that acts on my behalf in reliance on my Agent.

ARTICLE V PERSONAL CARE

I give my Agent all powers regarding the following personal care matters that I could exercise on my own behalf, if capable of doing so. My Agent may:
Home Care. Provide for my continued maintenance and support. As nearly as possible, I desire to maintain my accustomed standard of living. My Agent shall provide me with a suitable place to live, by maintaining me in my family home (residence, apartment or other), paying principal interest, taxes, insurance and repairs as necessary. My Agent may retain or discharge domestic servants, attendants, companions, nurses, sitters, or other persons who provide care for me and my home. My Agent may authorize purchases of food, clothing, medical care and customary luxuries on my behalf.
Religious Needs. Continue my affiliation with my church, keeping me accessible to its clergy, members and other representatives, continuing and renewing any pledge made by me whether for capital, operations or other purposes, and generally to assist me in maintaining my church relationships to the extent my health permits.
Companions and Recreation. Hire, discharge, direct and compensate such companions as may be necessary for my health, recreation, travel and general wellbeing.
Funeral Arrangements. Arrange and contract for my funeral including appropriate arrangements and instructions for my funeral service or memorial service, including purchase of a burial plot or other appropriate disposition of my body. My Agent shall comply with such known written instructions as I may have or leave.
Curator or Guardian. Nominate on my behalf any person my Agent deems qualified (including my Agent) as my curator, undercurator, curator ad hoc, guardian, or conservator or any other fiduciary office I have a right to nominate or designate; to waive and bond on my behalf and to grant to that fiduciary or representative any powers that I might extend on my own behalf.
Institutional Care. If recommended by my physician, my Agent may contract for institutional health care (hospital, retirement facility, assisted living, memory care, nursing home, hospice or other) on my behalf. If reasonably advised that my return home is unlikely because of my condition, my Agent may sell, exchange, lease, sublease or dispose of my home and such of its contents as are no longer useful to me and are not specifically bequeathed in my will, all on such terms as to price, payment and security as my Agent deems reasonable.

ARTICLE VI REFUSAL OF MEDICAL TREATMENT

I do not wish my life prolonged artificially through extraordinary or heroic means if my condition is terminal.[9] Even over the objection of members of my family, my Agent may:
Withdraw or Withhold Life Support. If two licensed physicians (one of whom is my attending physician) have personally examined me and my attending physician has noted in my medical records that my condition is terminal and irreversible, my Agent may sign on my behalf any documents, waivers or releases necessary to withdraw, withhold or cease any procedure calculated only to prolong my life, including the use of a respirator, defibrillator, cardiopulmonary resuscitation, surgery, transplant, dialysis, blood transfusion, antibiotics, and anti-rheumatic and pressor or inotrope drugs.
Nourishment. Refuse or discontinue intravenous or parenteral feeding, misting, and endotracheal or nasogastic tubes, if advised that no undue pain will be caused to me.
Declaration. Contemplating that my medical care may be rendered in Louisiana, or that Louisiana law might otherwise apply, I have executed a Declaration Concerning Life-Sustaining Procedures ("Declaration") pursuant to Louisiana Revised Statutes 40:1151 and following as amended, a copy of which is attached.[10] By executing that Declaration I do not intend to limit or reduce the powers over my person elsewhere granted to my Agent in this agency, but rather to convey to my Agent such additional powers as are necessary to make or carry out the terms of that Declaration.

ARTICLE VII INCIDENTAL POWERS

To enforce exercise of the powers granted in this document and to the extent I could act on my own behalf if capable, my Agent may:
Proceedings. Institute or defend any lawsuit or administrative proceedings on my behalf.
Advisors and Employees. Hire, compensate, instruct and discharge attorneys, accountants, appraisers, experts, consultants or other advisors, employees or independent contractors my Agent deems necessary.
Modifications. Amend this document as may be necessary to exercise the powers granted herein.
Communications. Open, read, respond to and redirect any written communications directed to me; represent me before any postal authority, messenger service, or information service relevant matters.
Important Documents. Disclose, copy or deny access to any document; exercise my privilege of confidentiality and generally to care for and protect all information relevant to me in any form.
Pets. Provide continuing care for my pets or other animals owed by me or in my care, and contract and pay for their welfare.

---

[9] If in fact principal does not. This is not a decision that should be buried in a form or assumed one way or the other for the client. This Article may be adapted accordingly and would ideally be consistent with the Declaration Concerning Life-Sustaining Procedures noted below.
[10] If such a Declaration has not been executed or is not attached, this paragraph should be omitted or edited.

ARTICLE VIII THIRD PARTIES

To protect third parties who deal with my Agent under powers granted in this Agency, third persons may rely on my Agent's act or signature with the same force and effect as though I were personally present and acting for myself. Accordingly:

Notice of Amendment or Revocation. No person dealing with my Agent on my behalf shall be charged with any amendment to this Agency or its revocation until actual notice thereof is delivered to the third party.

Reliance. Until they receive actual notice that this Agency has been amended or revoked, third persons may assume that my Agent is acting within the scope of powers granted by me in this Agency, and that this Agency remains effective. No person who deals with my Agent shall be responsible for the Agent's proper application of funds or property.

Information. Persons who receive requests for information from my Agent are authorized to furnish it, as and when requested. I release them from any and all legal liability for furnishing the information my Agent requests. If that information is privileged, I waive the privilege. My Agent may disclose that information to such others as my Agent may deem appropriate.

ARTICLE IX MISCELLANEOUS PROVISIONS

Expenses. My Agent shall be entitled to reimbursement for all costs and expenses reasonably incurred on my behalf.

Nomination. I nominate my Agent to serve as my curator, undercurator, guardian, conservator and in any similar fiduciary capacity consonant with the powers granted in this Agency. If not permitted to nominate my Agent, I nevertheless make the strongest recommendation that my Agent be qualified for all such offices. Likewise, I nominate my Agent as tutor, undertutor or guardian of the person and property of my minor children,[11] or if not permitted to nominate, I make a similar strong recommendation that my Agent be appointed.

Release. I release and discharge my Agent and my Agent's heirs, successors and assigns from any and all liability to me, my heirs, successors and assigns arising out of any acts or omissions of my Agent, except for willful misconduct or gross negligence. My Agent shall have no responsibility to make my property productive of income, to increase the value of my estate or to diversify my investments.

Applicable Law. This instrument shall be governed by the laws of Louisiana.

Revocation, Removal, Amendment and Resignation. This Agency may be amended or revoked by me. My Agent may be removed by me at any time by written document delivered to my Agent. If this Agency has been recorded in the public records,[12] the act of revocation, amendment or removal shall be filed or recorded in the same manner. My Agent may resign by

---

[11] Principal may not in fact want to appoint agent in a role regarding their minor children, as the trust and talents for this agency may be different from appointment as a child's tutor. The "Likewise" provision may be deleted.

[12] Powers of attorney are effective upon proper execution and most need not be filed in the registry. (They *may* be, especially if that facilitates public notice or efficient reference to it when multiple acts are conducted under it.) In fact it is common for a POA to be used only directly with the original in hand (or multiple originals, or true copies), to be provided to the bank, hospital, etc., or attached to an instrument executed under it such as an Act of Sale. If the POA is filed, any revocation or modification should be, too, for public notice that the agent may be carrying a document which on its face seems powerful but has since been withdrawn or changed. Filing a revocation or modification may also be done even if the original was not filed, again for public notice purposes, especially if the originals cannot be retrieved and destroyed.

written resignation delivered to me or, if I am incapacitated or interdicted, by delivery to any person with whom I am residing or who is responsible for my care.

THUS DONE AND PASSED at ____________________, Louisiana, this _____ day of __________________, 20____, in the presence of the undersigned competent witnesses who have signed their names together with the principal and me, notary.

WITNESSES: PRINCIPAL:

________________________________ ________________________________

Print witness name *Print name of principal*

____

Print witness name

____

Notary name: ________________________________

Notary ID or Bar Roll No.: ________________

My Commission is for Life

The undersigned accepts the appointment created by this power of attorney to act as the principal's true and lawful agent, representative and attorney-in-fact.[13]

________________________________ DATE: _________________, 20_____

Print Name of Agent, Agent

---

[13] This POA is written as a "procuration," because it is a unilateral appointment by principal with only principal in the appearance clause. Agent may sign the acceptance at a different time and place (and possibly accepting years later), though it is common for both parties to sign at the same time and establish the agency immediately. It may also be written as a bilateral agreement, or "mandate," if both parties appear in the appearance clause and the main signature block has a line for agent; in that event there should be a statement in the body of act that the named person appears and accepts the appointment as agent, and the conclusion should state "with the principal an agent and me, notary," and then remove the acceptance of agency as a separate statement.

However, ultimately it makes little difference other than arrangement, because once agent has signed in either place, at any time before principal has died or withdrawn the act, it essentially becomes a mandate, because agent is accepting the terms of the appointment and making it mutual. This is why the generic term "power of attorney" is appropriate whether agent appears at the outset as with bilateral acts, or signs at the end in a separate statement (as here). The act is immediately effective upon acceptance.

GENERAL POWER OF ATTORNEY (VERSION 2)

STATE OF LOUISIANA

PARISH OF ____________________

GENERAL POWER OF ATTORNEY[1]

BE IT KNOWN that on ________________, 2024, before me, a notary public duly qualified in and for the above state and parish, and in the presence of the named and undersigned competent witnesses, PERSONALLY CAME and appeared:

Name of Principal, a person of the full age of majority and a resident and domicliary of ________________ Parish, Louisiana, "Principal," who declared under oath that they comprehend generally the nature and consequences of the disposition they are making, that they have been married but once, and then to *spouse name*, to whom they remain married and with whom they reside, and whose principal address is *address*;

And who declared that they appoint *Name of Agent*, "Agent," to be their agent, representative and attorney-in-fact, with full power and authority to act for, in the name of and on behalf of Principal, to do all acts necessary or deemed by agent to be appropriate to represent Principal including, but not limited to, the following:

Business and Affairs. To conduct, manage and transact the business and personal financial matters of Principal, of every nature and kind and without any exception whatsoever.
Correspondence. To open all letters, telegrams, deliveries and other correspondence addressed to Principal and to answer same in Principal's name.
Banking. To make and endorse and to accept and to pay promissory notes, drafts and bills of exchange; to sign checks drawn on and to draw money out of any bank, credit union or other financial institution or other account whatsoever in which funds may be on deposit in the name of or for the account of Principal; to deposit checks, drafts and bills of exchange in any account standing in the name of Principal; and to deliver to any such financial institution any promissory notes or other instruments for collection. To open, manage, operate, renew, or close any account at any such financial institution in the name of Principal; to deposit funds therein or withdraw all or part thereof; including certificates of deposit, checking, savings, money market or any other type of account or any Treasury notes or bills; the foregoing being illustrative and without limitation of the generality of this power.
Securities. To sell, purchase and transfer shares of stock, bonds, or any other securities of any corporation or any other legal entity, whether private or public and whether registered in the name of Principal or not, and to receive and receipt for the sale price thereof; to receive and receipt for all dividends, coupons or other distributions due or to become due thereon; and to deliver, pledge and pawn said shares of stock or bonds. To attend meetings of the stockholders of any corporation or holders of any securities of any legal entity in which Principal may be interested and to vote in the name of Principal on all questions and matters that may be submitted

[1] See detailed notes, explanations and cautions in the prior POA, a general power of attorney with notes.

or considered at such meeting. To receive all documents and notices and to exercise all rights and to fulfill all obligations of Principal regarding any security of any type, value or nature.
Loans. To borrow money in Principal's name from any bank or other financial institution; to make, issue and endorse any promissory note in the name of Principal, to renew the same from time to time; to deliver, pledge and pawn the same; and to waive and renounce any prescription accrued thereon.
Property: Sale, Purchase, Lease, Mortgage, Pledge. To sell, mortgage, encumber, pledge, purchase, lease, or grant servitudes pertaining to immovable (real) or movable (personal) property, although not described herein as permitted by Louisiana Civil Code Article 2997 on such terms and conditions as determined by Agent and to execute such documents to effect such acts and receive or pay amounts pursuant to such acts.
Mineral Rights. To execute mineral leases and other contracts, including unitization and pooling agreements, for the exploration and development of oil, gas, salt, sulfur and other minerals in and under any property of Principal or in which Principal may have an interest, on such terms and conditions and for such consideration as Agent may deem proper, and to receive and receipt for the bonuses, rents and proceeds thereof; to execute mineral and property deeds or leases either selling, buying or leasing mineral or royalty rights; and to execute all division orders or other agreements of every nature and kind whatsoever in connection with or relative to said acts.
Judicial Proceedings. To appear before all courts and to prosecute, defend, or compromise and settle by agreement, arbitration, or otherwise; to accept service of process on behalf of Principal; to sign all pleadings and do all things necessary; to obtain writs of attachment, sequestration and injunction; and to take appeals and, in any such instances, to furnish and sign on behalf of Principal the requisite security and bonds.
Successions To represent Principal judicially and otherwise, whether as heir, legatee, creditor, executor, administrator or otherwise, in all successions or estates in which Principal is, may be or may become interested, including any acceptance or renunciation thereof; to apply for the administration thereof and to demand, obtain and execute all orders, decrees and tax returns as Agent may deem proper; and to settle, compromise and liquidate Principal's interest therein and to receive and receipt for all property and effects to which Principal may be entitled in respect of said successions or estates.
Agents and Proxy. To act for Principal and be Principal's substitute in all instances in which Principal has been or may be appointed the agent of others; and to vote proxies of others issued in the name of Principal and to execute proxies in favor of others issued in the name of Principal and to execute proxies in favor of others to vote in the name of Principal.
Claims. To demand and obtain and to recover and receipt for sums of money, goods, properties and effects to which Principal is now or may be hereinafter entitled, and to that end to compromise and adjust all accounts and other obligations and to give good and sufficient discharge and acquittance therefor.
Creditors' Meetings. To attend meetings of creditors in which Principal may be interested and to vote in Principal's name on all questions and matters that may be submitted to or considered at such meeting.
Donations. To transfer without cause or consideration (i.e., donate inter vivos or grant gratuitously, or waive compensation for) any asset of Principal to any person as determined by Agent. However, any such donation shall require the prior unanimous written consent of Principal's spouse and children who are not then serving as an Agent hereunder; or, if Principal

has no children at the applicable time, Principal's legatees or heirs who would inherit from Principal if Principal passed away on the date of the donation.

Tax Returns and Related Matters. To file any federal, state, parish or other tax returns (including but not limited to income tax returns); to apply for extensions of time to file tax returns; to file elections related to tax matters; to represent the Principal in connection with any matter relating to any taxes, to grant powers of attorney to any authorized representative and to take any action relating to any taxes, including but not limited to taxes of the United States and the State of Louisiana.

Medical Decisions. To make any and all medical decisions related to treatment of the physical and/or mental health of the Principal, including but not limited to consultation with and granting authorization to hospitals, doctors, nurses and other medical personnel to take appropriate action regarding the physical and/or mental health of the Principal, and to appoint one or more physicians to examine the Principal when required by Principal's agreement to determine if the Principal is mentally or physically capable to perform those activities and functions that are conditioned by Principal's agreement on the Principal's mental or physical health. The authority does not authorize the Agent to make the decision related to withhold life sustaining support measures as defined in LA R.S. 40:1151.1 *et seq*. or to consent to the commitment of Principal to an institution of mental health without following the procedures prescribed by LA R.S. 28:1 *et seq*.

Insurance. To exercise any right, option or privilege available to Principal regarding any policy of insurance of any type, including life insurance or annuities, and including but not limited to the right to surrender the policy, make a policy loan, change the beneficiary, make a claim, receive payment on any claim, elect settlement or disbursement options, receive any check or draft, and endorse, collect and receive the proceeds of same.

General. To do and perform each and every other act, matter or thing whatsoever as may be appropriate in Agent's discretion as if such act, matter or thing were or had been particularly stated herein.

Durable. This power of attorney does not terminate upon the disability or incapacity of Principal and should be consider a "durable" power of attorney.[2]

Substitute Agent. Principal hereby grants the Agent in office the power to appoint and remove a substitute Agent, which appointment shall be by authentic act.

Liability of Agent. Agent shall be liable only for breach of duty to Principal committed in bad faith. Principal shall indemnify Agent and hold Agent harmless for all reasonable costs, fees and expenses regarding all matters hereunder, or legal actions brought by or against the Agent for which Agent is not liable within Agent's powers and duties as a fiduciary.

Reliance. This power of attorney executed by all appearers, may be filed and recorded with the Clerk of Court for the Parish of ________________ and registered in the conveyance records, and shall remain in effect as to third persons dealing with Agent until either such power or substitute power of attorney is revoked by notarial act and recorded as set forth above, and/or the third person receives actual notice of revocation. If any party who relies on this Power of Attorney delivers written notice to the Principal, this Power of Attorney shall remain in effect until such party receives written notice of revocation, notwithstanding recordation of revocation as stated above.

---

[2] Although the power of attorney in Louisiana is durable unless stated otherwise, the forms herein include a statement confirming this status, in compliance with other states' understanding and to avoid misunderstanding.

GENERAL POWER OF ATTORNEY (VERSION 2)

THUS DONE AND PASSED at ________________________, Louisiana, this _____ day of __________________, 20____, in the presence of the undersigned competent witnesses who have signed their names together with the said Principal and me, notary.

WITNESSES: PRINCIPAL:

___________________________ ______________________________

Print Name Print Name

____

Print Name

____

Notary name: ______________________________

Notary ID or Bar Roll No.: _______________

My Commission is for Life

ACCEPTANCE BY AGENT:

The undersigned accepts the appointment created by this power of attorney to act as the principal's true and lawful agent, representative and attorney-in-fact.

____________________________________ DATE: ______________, 20___

Print Name of Agent

GENERAL POWER OF ATTORNEY (VERSION 3)

STATE OF LOUISIANA

PARISH OF ____________________

GENERAL POWER OF ATTORNEY[1]

BE IT KNOWN that on ________________, 20_____, before me, a notary public duly qualified in and for the above state and parish, and in the presence of the named and undersigned competent witnesses, personally came and appeared:

PRINCIPAL NAME, of the full age of majority and domiciled in Jefferson Parish, residing at 717 Merry Lou Dr., River Ridge, LA 70123, who declares unto me that she has never married.

Herein referred to as "Principal," and who declares that Principal does, by these presents, make, name, constitute, and appoint:

AGENT NAME, domiciled in Escambia County, Florida, currently residing at 612 Awesome Lane, Pensacola, FL 32503,

To be my true and lawful agent and attorney-in-fact, herein "Agent," general and special, giving and by these presents granting unto the said Agent the full power and authority for Principal and in my name and behalf, to manage and conduct all of my affairs and to exercise all of my legal rights and powers, including all rights and powers that I may acquire in the future. My Agent's powers shall include, but not be limited to, the power to:

1. Open, maintain or close bank accounts (including, but not limited to checking accounts, savings accounts, and certificates of deposit), brokerage accounts, and other similar accounts with financial institutions.

    a. Conduct any business with any banking or financial institution with respect to any of my accounts, including but not limited to, signing checks, making deposits and withdrawals, obtaining bank statements, passbooks, drafts, money orders, warrants, and certificates or vouchers payable to me by any person, firm, corporation or political entity.

    b. Perform any act necessary to deposit, negotiate, sell or transfer any note, security, or draft of the United States of America, including U.S. Treasury Securities.

    c. Have access to any safe-deposit box that I might own, including its contents.

2. Sell, exchange, buy, invest, or reinvest any assets or property owned by me. Such assets or property may include income producing or non-income producing assets and property.

3. Purchase and/or maintain insurance, including life insurance upon my life or the life of any other appropriate person.

4. Take any and all legal steps necessary to collect any amount or debt owed to me, or to settle any claim whether made against me or asserted on my behalf against any other person or entity.

[1] See detailed notes, explanations and cautions in the first POA: general power of attorney with notes.

GENERAL POWER OF ATTORNEY (VERSION 3)

5. Enter into binding contracts and leases on my behalf.

6. Exercise all stock rights on my behalf as my proxy, including all rights with respect to stocks, bonds, debentures or other investments.

7. Employ professional and business assistance as may be appropriate, including attorneys, accountants, technology experts and real estate agents.

8. Sell, convey, lease, mortgage, manage, insure, improve, repair, or perform any other act with respect to any of my property (now owned or later acquired) including, but not limited to, immovables, real estate and real estate rights (including the right to remove tenants and to recover possession). This includes the right to sell or encumber my homestead legally described as: *[if applicable; otherwise add "N/A" or omit sentence]*

9. Prepare, sign, and file documents with any governmental body or agency, including but not limited to, my authorization to:

a. Prepare, sign and file income and other tax returns with federal, state, and local and other governmental bodies.

b. Obtain information or documents from any government or its agencies, and negotiate, compromise, or settle any matter with such government or agency (including tax matters).

c. Prepare applications, provide information, and perform any other act reasonably requested by any government or its agencies in connection with governmental benefits (including military and social security benefits).

10. Transfer any of my assets to the trustee of any revocable trust created by me, if such trust is in existence at the time of such transfer.

11. Disclaim any interest which might otherwise be transferred or distributed to me from any other person, estate, trust, or other entity, as may be appropriate.

12. Donate any movable or immovable property I now own or may own in the future, as well as accept any donations.

This Power of Attorney shall be construed as a General Power of Attorney; and should be construed as broadly as possible. The listing of specific powers is not intended to limit or restrict the general powers granted in this Power of Attorney in any manner.

Any power or authority granted to my Agent under this document shall be limited to the extent necessary to prevent this Power of Attorney from causing (i) my income to be taxable to Agent, (ii) my assets to be subject to a general power of appointment by Agent, and (iii) my Agent to have any incidents of ownership with respect to any life insurance policies that I may own on the life of Agent.

My Agent shall not be liable for any loss that results from a judgment error that was made in good faith. However, my Agent shall be liable for willful misconduct or the failure to act in good faith while acting under the authority of this Power of Attorney.

GENERAL POWER OF ATTORNEY (VERSION 3)

My Agent shall not be entitled to any compensation, during my lifetime or upon my death, for any services provided as Agent. My Agent shall be entitled to reimbursement of all reasonable expenses incurred in connection with this Power of Attorney.

My Agent shall provide an accounting for all funds handled and all acts performed as Agent, if I so request or if such a request be made by any authorized personal agent or fiduciary acting on my behalf.

This Power of Attorney shall become effective immediately. This Power of Attorney shall continue effective until my death and shall be durable during that time. This Power of Attorney may be revoked by me at any time by providing written notice to my Agent.

A true copy of this instrument shall have the force and effect of the original act.

AND NOW comes said Agent, who accepts this Power of Attorney and the appointment as Agent, and agrees to carry out its terms to the best of their ability.

THUS DONE AND PASSED at ________________________, Louisiana, this _____ day of __________________, 20____, in the presence of the undersigned competent witnesses who have signed their names together with the said Principal and me, notary.

WITNESSES: PRINCIPAL:

____________________________ ______________________________

Print Name Print Name

____

Print Name

____

Notary name: ______________________________

Notary ID or Bar Roll No.: ______________

My Commission is for Life

ACCEPTANCE BY AGENT:

The undersigned accepts the appointment created by this power of attorney to act as the principal's true and lawful agent, representative and attorney-in-fact.

_____________________________________ DATE: ________________, 20____

Print Name of Agent

GENERAL POWER OF ATTORNEY (VERSION 4)

STATE OF LOUISIANA

PARISH OF ____________________

GENERAL POWER OF ATTORNEY[1]

BE IT KNOWN that on __________________, 20 _____, before me, a notary public duly qualified in and for the above state and parish, and in the presence of the named and undersigned competent witnesses, personally came and appeared *Name of Principal*, a person over the age of majority and a resident of ___________________ Parish, Louisiana, herein "Principal," who declared under oath that they comprehend generally the nature and consequences of the disposition that are making, that they have been married but once, and then to *Spouse Name*, to whom they remain married and with whom they reside, and whose principal address is *address*;

And who declared that they appoint *Name of Agent*, "Agent," to be their agent and attorney-in-fact, with full power and authority to act for, in the name of and on behalf of Principal, to do all acts necessary or deemed by Agent to be appropriate to represent Principal including, but not limited to, the following:

1. Business and Affairs. To conduct, manage, and transact the business and personal financial matters of Principal, of every nature and kind without any exception.

2. Correspondence. To open all letters, emails, telegrams, cablegrams, facsimiles, emails, and other correspondence, electronic or otherwise, addressed to Principal and to answer same in Principal's name. This shall extend to all cellular devices and computer devices.

3. Banking. To make and endorse and to accept and to pay promissory notes, drafts, and bills of exchange; to sign checks drawn on and to draw money out of any bank, homestead, or other financial institution or other account in which funds may be on deposit in the name of or for the account of Principal; to deposit checks, drafts and bills of exchange in any account standing in the name of Principal; to deliver to any bank or other financial institution any promissory notes or other instruments for collection; to open, manage, operate, renew, or close any account at any bank or financial institution in the name of Principal; to deposit or withdraw all or part of the funds; including certificates of deposit, checking, savings, money market, or any other type of account or any Treasury notes or bills with the preceding list being illustrative and not limiting the generality of this power. Specifically, to contract with any institution to have access to all safe deposit boxes in Principal's name or to which Principal is an authorized signatory (except in a fiduciary capacity). To add or remove from the contents of any safe deposit box and to terminate contracts for such boxes.

4. Securities. To sell, purchase, and transfer shares of stock, bonds, or any other securities of any corporation or any other legal entity, whether private or public and whether registered in the

[1] See detailed notes, explanations and cautions in the first POA: general power of attorney with notes. This is one of the more complete versions, and one with a clause expressly including email and electronic correspondence.

name of Principal or not, and to receive and take receipt for the sale price of the securities; to receive and take receipt for all dividends, coupons, or other distributions due or to become due on the same; and to deliver, pledge, and pawn the shares of stock or bonds. To attend meetings of the stockholders of any corporation or holders of any securities of any legal entity in which Principal may be interested and to vote in the name of Principal on all questions and matters that may be submitted or considered at such meeting. To receive all documents and notices and to exercise all rights and to fulfill all obligations of Principal regarding any security of any type, value, or nature.

5. Loans. To borrow money in Principal's name from any bank or other financial institution; to make, issue, and endorse any promissory note in the name of Principal, and to renew the same from time to time; to deliver, pledge, and pawn the same; and to waive and renounce any prescription accrued on the same.

6. Property: Sale, Purchase, Lease, Mortgage, Pledge. To sell, mortgage, encumber, pledge, purchase, lease, protect, or grant servitudes pertaining to immovable (real) or movable (personal) property, including but not limited to vehicles, contents of residence, and all personal property although not described in this instrument as permitted by Louisiana Civil Code article 2996 on such terms and conditions as determined by Agent and to execute such documents to effect such acts and receive or pay amounts pursuant to such acts.

7. Mineral Rights. To execute mineral leases and other contracts, including unitization and pooling agreements, for the exploration and development of oil, gas, salt, sulfur, and other minerals in and under any property of Principal or in which principal may have an interest, on such terms and conditions and for such consideration as Agent may deem proper, and to receive and take receipt for the bonuses, rents and proceeds of the same; to execute mineral and property deeds or leases either selling, buying, or leasing mineral or royalty rights; and to execute all division orders or other agreements of every nature and kind in connection with or relative to the acts.

8. Judicial Proceedings. To appear before all courts and to prosecute, defend, or compromise and settle by agreement, arbitration, or otherwise; to accept service of process on behalf of Principal; to sign all pleadings and do all things necessary; to obtain writs of attachment, sequestration, and injunction; and to take appeals and, in any such instances, to furnish and sign on behalf of Principal the requisite security bonds.

9. Successions. To represent Principal judicially and otherwise, whether as heir, legatee, creditor, executor, administrator, or otherwise, in all successions or estates in which Principal is, may be or may become interested, including any acceptance or renunciation of the same; to apply for the administration of the succession or estate and to demand, obtain, and execute all orders, decrees, and tax returns as Agent may deem proper; and to settle, compromise, and liquidate Principal's interest in the same and to receive and take receipt for all property and effects to which Principal may be entitled in respect of the successions or estates.

10. Agents and Proxy. To act for Principal and be Principal's substitute in all instances in which Principal has been or may be appointed the agent of others; and to vote proxies of others

issued in the name of Principal and to execute proxies in favor of others to vote in the name of Principal.

11. Claims. To demand and obtain and to recover and take receipt for amounts of money, goods, properties, and effects to which Principal is now or may be in the future entitled and to that end to compromise and adjust all accounts and other obligations and to give full and sufficient discharge and acquittance for the same.

12. Creditor's Meetings. To attend meetings of creditors in which Principal may be interested and to vote in Principal's name on all questions and matters that may be submitted to or considered at such meeting.

13. Donations. To transfer without consideration (i.e., donate) any asset of Principal to any person as determined by Agent. However, any such donation will require the prior unanimous written consent of Principal's spouse and children who are not then serving as an agent; or, if Principal has no children at the applicable time, Principal's legatees or heirs who would inherit if Principal passed away on the date of donation.

14. Tax Returns and Related Matters. To file any federal, state or other tax returns (including, but not limited to, income tax returns); to apply for extensions of time to file tax returns; to file elections related to tax matters; to represent Principal in connection with any matter relating to any taxes; to grant powers of attorney to any authorized representative; and to take any action relating to any taxes, including, but not limited to, taxes of the United States and the State of Louisiana.

15. Medical Decisions. To make any and all medical decisions related to treatment of the physical and/or mental health of Principal, including, but not limited to, consultation with and granting authorization to hospitals, doctors, nurses, and other medical personnel to take appropriate action regarding the physical and/or mental health of Principal, and to appoint one or more physicians to examine Principal when required by Principal's agreement to determine if the Principal is mentally or physically capable to perform those activities and functions that are conditioned by Principal's agreement on the Principal's mental or physical health. This authority does not authorize the agent to make the decision related to withhold life sustaining support measures as defined in Louisiana Revised Statutes § 40:1151.1 *et seq.*, or to consent to the commitment of Principal to an institution of mental health without following the procedures prescribed by Louisiana Revised Statutes § 28:54 *et seq.*

16. Insurance. To exercise any right, option, or privilege available to Principal regarding any policy of insurance of any type, including life insurance or annuities, and including, but not limited to, the right to surrender the policy, make a policy loan, make a claim, receive payment on any claim, elect settlement, or disbursement options, receive any check or draft, and endorse, collect and receive the proceeds of same.

17. General. To do and perform each and every other act, matter or thing as may be appropriate in Agent's discretion as if such act, matter or thing were or had been particularly stated in this instrument.

18. Substitute Agent. Principal grants the agent in office the power to appoint and remove a

substitute agent, which appointment will be by authentic act subject to the provisions of Section 21, below.

19. Liability of Agent. Agent will be liable only for breach of duty to Principal committed in bad faith. Principal will indemnify agent and hold Agent harmless for all reasonable costs, fees and expenses regarding all matters in this contract, legal actions brought by or against Agent for which Agent is not liable within the standard specified in this section.

20. Limitation of Authority. Anything herein to the contrary notwithstanding, this power of attorney shall be construed and the authority herein granted shall be limited so that:

a. None of the above income earned or attributable to the properties covered by this power of attorney shall be taxed to Agent; and

b. The properties covered by this power of attorney shall not be included in the gross estate of Agent or taxed in Agent's estate as a general power of appointment as said term is defined in Section 2041 of the Internal Revenue Code of 1986, as amended. In this regard, no power created herein shall be exercisable by any agent in its own favor, or in favor of the agent's estate, the agent's creditors or the creditors of the agent's estate.

21. Reliance. This power of attorney and any substitute power of attorney executed pursuant to Section 18, above, may be filed and recorded with the clerk of court for ________________ Parish and registered in the conveyance records, and will remain in effect as to third persons dealing with Agent until either the power or substitute power of attorney is revoked by notarial act and recorded as set forth above, and/or the third person receives actual notice of revocation. If any party who relies on this power of attorney delivers written notice to Principal, this power of attorney will remain in effect until the party receives written notice of revocation, notwithstanding recordation of revocation as stated above.

A true copy of this act shall have the force and effect of the original act.

Principal avers that Principal understands the full import of this designation and is emotionally and mentally competent to make this appointment and grant these powers and authorities.

AND NOW COMES said Agent, who accepts this power of attorney and the appointment as agent, and agrees to carry out its terms to the best of their ability.

THUS DONE, SIGNED AND PASSED at ______________________, Louisiana, this _____ day of _________________, 20____, in the presence of the undersigned competent witnesses who have signed their names together with the said Principal and me, notary.

WITNESSES:	PRINCIPAL:
____________________________	____________________________________
Print Name	Print Name
____________________________	
Print Name	

____

Notary name: _________________________________

Notary ID or Bar Roll No.: ______________

My Commission is for Life

ACCEPTANCE BY AGENT:

The undersigned accepts the appointment created by this power of attorney to act as the principal's true and lawful agent, representative and attorney-in-fact.

____________________________________ DATE: __________________, 20____

Print Name of Agent

THE FOLLOWING TWO PAGES (304-305) ARE THE OFFICIAL "MILITARY POWER OF ATTORNEY" FORM PURSUANT TO 10 U.S.C. 1044(b).
NOTE: It is not editable but can be filled out by hand or typewriter.

GENERAL POWER OF ATTORNEY

PREAMBLE: This document is a MILITARY POWER OF ATTORNEY prepared pursuant to Title 10 United States Code, Section 1044(b), and executed by a person authorized to receive legal assistance from the military. Federal law exempts this power of attorney from any requirement of form, substance, formality, or recording that is prescribed for powers of attorney by the laws of a state, the District of Columbia, or a territory, commonwealth, or possession of the United States. Federal law specifies that this power of attorney shall be given the same legal effect as a power of attorney prepared and executed in accordance with the laws of the jurisdiction in which it is presented.

KNOW ALL PERSONS BY THESE PRESENTS: That I, ____, currently residing at ____, do hereby appoint ____ my true and lawful attorney-in-fact to manage and conduct all my affairs and act in all matters in my name and on my behalf. Such acts shall include the authority:

1. To lease, sell, use, establish title to, register, insure, transfer, mortgage, maintain, manage, pledge, exchange, or otherwise dispose of or encumber any and all of my property, real, personal, or mixed, including motor vehicles of any kind, and to execute and deliver good and sufficient deeds or other instruments for the lease, conveyance, mortgage, maintenance, or transfer of the same.

2. To buy, receive, lease, accept, or otherwise acquire in my name and for my account, property, real, personal, or mixed upon such terms, considerations, and conditions as my attorney-in-fact shall deem appropriate.

3. To transact all of my business on my behalf, including entering into contracts and the making of such investments as my attorney-in-fact shall deem sound.

4. To institute and prosecute, or to appear and defend, or to settle, any claims or litigation involving my interests or me. This authority shall include, but not be limited to, the authority to present a claim against the United States for damage to or loss of personal property.

5. To prepare, execute, sign, and file all tax returns and to receive and negotiate all tax refund checks.

6. To execute all documents needed for the travel of my family members and transportation or storage of my property, as authorized by law and military regulations; to sign for and clear government or other quarters in the best interests of my family members and in accordance with law and military regulations.

7. To demand, act to recover, and receive all sums of money which are now or will become owing or belonging to me, and to institute accounts on my behalf, and to deposit, draw upon, or expend such funds of mine as are necessary in furtherance of the powers granted herein. This authority shall include, but not be limited to, the authority to receive, endorse, cash, or deposit negotiable instruments made payable to me and drawn upon the Treasurer, or other fiscal officer or depository, of the United States.

8. Generally, to do, execute, and perform any other act, deed, matter, or thing, that in the opinion of my attorney-in-fact ought to be done, executed, or performed, in conjunction with this power of attorney.

NOTWITHSTANDING any language to the contrary in this instrument, my attorney-in-fact is specifically NOT granted the following powers:

a. To cancel or change the beneficiary of any policy of life insurance owned by me.

b. To exercise any rights or powers with respect to any person, matter, transaction, or property in my name or in my custody as a trustee, custodian, personal representative, or other fiduciary capacity for someone else.

I hereby give and grant unto my attorney-in-fact full power and authority to do and perform each and every act and matter concerning my estate, property, and affairs as fully and effectually to all intents and purposes as I could do legally if I were present.

I hereby authorize my attorney-in-fact to indemnify and hold harmless any third party who accepts and acts under or in accordance with this power of attorney.

I intend for this power of attorney to be a DURABLE power of attorney. This power of attorney will continue to be effective if I become disabled, incapacitated, or incompetent. All acts done by my attorney-in-fact hereunder shall have the same effect and inure to the benefit of and bind myself and my heirs as if I were competent, and not disabled, incapacitated, or incompetent.

GENERAL POWER OF ATTORNEY

I shall be considered disabled or incapacitated for purposes of this power of attorney if a physician, based on that physician's examination, certifies in writing at a date subsequent to the date on which this power of attorney is executed, that I am disabled from or incapable of exercising control over my person, property, personal affairs, or financial affairs. I authorize the physician who so certifies to disclose my physical or mental condition to another person for purposes of this power of attorney. A third party who accepts this power of attorney, endorsed by proper physician certification of my disability or incapacity, is held harmless and fully protected from any action taken under this power of attorney.

I hereby ratify all that my attorney-in-fact lawfully shall do or cause to be done by this document.

This power of attorney shall become effective when I sign and execute it below. Unless sooner revoked or terminated by me, this power of attorney shall become NULL and VOID on ____________________________________, 20____ (*expiration date*).

Notwithstanding my inclusion of a specific expiration date herein, if on the above-specified expiration date, or during the sixty (60) day period preceding that specified expiration date, I should be or have been determined by the United States Government to be in a military status of "missing," "missing in action," or "prisoner of war," or if I should be or have been properly certified, in writing, by a physician to be disabled from or incapable of exercising control over my person, property, personal affairs, or financial affairs, then this power of attorney shall remain valid and in full effect until sixty (60) days after I have returned to United States military control following termination of such status or sixty (60) days after I have recovered from such disability unless sooner revoked or terminated by me.

All business transacted hereunder for me or for my account shall be transacted in my name, and all endorsements and instruments executed by my attorney-in-fact for the purpose of carrying out the foregoing powers shall contain my name, followed by that of my attorney-in-fact and the designation "attorney-in-fact."

IN WITNESS WHEREOF, I sign, seal, declare, publish, make, and constitute this document as and for my power of attorney at Marine Corps Base Camp Pendleton, California on ____________________________________, 20_____ (*today's date*)

____

Signature of Grantor

ACKNOWLEGEMENT

With the United States Armed Forces
At Marine Corps Base Camp Pendleton

On this the _______ day of ______________________________, 20______, before the undersigned officer, personally appeared ____, satisfactorily proven to be (a) serving in or retired from the Armed Forces of the United States, or (b) a lawful dependent of a person serving in or retired from the Armed Forces of the United States, or (c) a person serving with, employed by, or accompanying the Armed Forces of the United States outside the United States and outside the Canal Zone, Puerto Rico, Guam, and the Virgin Islands, and to be the person whose name is subscribed to the within instrument and acknowledged that he or she executed the same. And the undersigned does further certify that he or she is at the date of this certificate an officer of the Armed Forces of the United States having the general powers of a notary public under the provisions of Section 936 or 1044(a) of Title 10 of the United States Code (Public Law 90-632 and 101-510).

AUTHORIZED TO ACT AS A NOTARY PUBLIC UNDER THE PROVISIONS OF SECTION 1044a OF TITLE 10 OF THE UNITED STATES CODE AND SECTION 1183.5 OF THE CALIFORNIA CIVIL CODE. NO SEAL REQUIRED BY LAW.

____

Signature of Notary

Name of Officer and Position:
Grade and Branch of Service:
Command or Organization:

SPECIAL POWER OF ATTORNEY FOR BANKING

STATE OF LOUISIANA

PARISH OF ____________________

SPECIAL POWER OF ATTORNEY (BANKING)

BEFORE ME, the undersigned notary, duly commissioned and qualified in the state and parish aforesaid, and in the presence of the two witnesses whose names are hereunto subscribed, PERSONALLY CAME and appeared:

Principal's name[1]

Who declared unto me:

I do make, appoint, nominate, and authorize *Agent's name,* to act as my true and lawful agent and attorney in fact ("Agent"), with full power and authority to act for me, individually, and in my name, place and stead, with reference to the transaction of any and all business related to or connected with my bank accounts at ______________________________ Bank *[or Credit Union, Savings & Loan, etc.]*, ______________________________________ (Address), ______________________________ (City), _______________ (State) , ________ (Zip Code) hereinafter "Bank" or "Institution," including, but not limited to, the following:

- Making deposits, transfers and withdrawals to or from any of my bank accounts at Bank.
- Writing, making and endorsing checks, drafts and other instruments in connection with my bank accounts at Bank.
- Opening new checking, savings, money market, certificates of deposit, IRAs or other accounts in my name and maintaining same.
- Approving and authorizing automatic withdrawals from my accounts.
- Using electronic means of transactions, computer access to my accounts, or a banking app in connection with my accounts at Bank.
- Executing signature cards for accounts maintained or opened by my Agent in my name.
- Performing any and all other matters relating to, or in connection with, my accounts at Bank.

I direct that the above-related powers and authority of my said Agent shall be so exercisable and effective regardless of the fact that I may be mentally or physically incapacitated or incapable of understanding or unable to express myself or act in my own behalf at the time of any action on my behalf by said Agent. Such incapacity, whether mental or physical, that I may exhibit shall not in any way interfere with the authority of my Agent herein to act fully on my behalf according to the terms hereof. In other words, this Power of Attorney shall not be affected by the subsequent disability, incompetence or incapacity of the Principal.

---

[1] Appearance clause, which may vary depending on the nature and content of the act; but in this instrument usually it is satisfied by principal's name. More completely, this would establish they are of the age of majority, their parish of domicile, and street address.

SPECIAL POWER OF ATTORNEY FOR BANKING

And I do hereby undertake to ratify and confirm, all and singular, the acts heretofore performed and to be hereinafter performed by my said Agent, acting in my name and on my behalf.

Bank shall honor this Power of Attorney until and unless Bank receives written notice of revocation of same signed by me. Bank is hereby indemnified and shall be held harmless by the undersigned for any and all actions taken by my Agent regarding my accounts at Bank, regardless of whether within the intended scope of this Power of Attorney or not; therefore, Bank shall have no liability for the actions of my Agent or for following the directions of my agent in connection with my bank accounts at Bank.

This act and the authority under it shall be effective immediately upon acceptance by Agent.

A true copy of this instrument shall have the same effect as an original.

THUS DONE AND PASSED at ________________________, Louisiana, this _____ day of __________________, 20____, in the presence of the undersigned competent witnesses who have signed their names together with the said Principal and me, notary.

WITNESSES:

____

Print Name

____

Print Name

PRINCIPAL:

____

Print Name

____

Notary name: _________________________________

Notary ID or Bar Roll No.: _____________

My Commission is for Life

AGENT'S ACCEPTANCE:

The undersigned accepts the appointment created by this power of attorney to act as the principal's true and lawful agent, representative and attorney-in-fact.

_______________________________ DATE: __________________, 20____

Print Name of Agent

SPECIAL POWER OF ATTORNEY FOR REAL ESTATE

STATE OF LOUISIANA

PARISH OF ____________________

SPECIAL POWER OF ATTORNEY

BE IT KNOWN that on __________________, 20____, before me, a notary public duly qualified in and for the above state and parish, and in the presence of the named and undersigned competent witnesses, personally came and appeared:

Name of Principal, a person of the age of majority and a resident of Tangipahoa Parish, Louisiana ("Principal"), who declared under oath that they have been married but once, and then to *Spouse name*, to whom they remain married and with whom they reside, and whose principal mailing address is *address*; and who declared that they appoint *Name of Agent*, of the age of majority and a domiciliary of St. Tammany Parish, whose primary mailing address is 12345 U.S. Hwy. 190, Mandeville, LA 70471 ("Agent"), to be their agent, representative and attorney-in-fact, with full power and authority to act for, do and perform all the things and acts specified herein and in the numbered paragraph(s) indicated below.

Principal further authorizes and empowers said Agent to do and perform every act, matter and thing, whatsoever, as shall or may be required and necessary in order to effectuate the purposes for which this power of attorney is granted, enumerated below, as fully and with like effect as if Principal has been personally present and had done any such thing, performed any such act, and/or signed any such document, deed, contract, note, application or other such agreement; Principal hereby ratifying and confirming any and all things done by said Agent and adopting them as Principal's own act and deed.

Here, describe the powers granted by the power of attorney. Usually, "sell/purchase the hereinafter described immovable property and appear before any notary and execute an act of sale, transferring and conveying with full warranty of title, the following property ("Property"): Legal description stated here (or attached, then state here that it is attached to this act). Municipal address, if one exists.

Principal further expressly stipulates that any ambiguities which may arise in the interpretation hereof shall be liberally construed so as to effectuate the purposes and to validate all things done by Agent. Whenever used herein, the singular number shall include the plural, and the masculine gender shall include all genders. Said Agent shall also have full power of substitution and revocation, hereby ratifying and confirming and agreeing to ratify and confirm all and whatsoever the said Agent shall lawfully do or cause to be done by virtue hereof.

1. The purpose for which this power of attorney is granted is:
   _____ Applicable
   _____ Not Applicable

SPECIAL POWER OF ATTORNEY FOR REAL ESTATE

To direct, instruct, authorize and permit Agent to sell and deliver the hereinafter described real estate, and/or all of Principal's rights, title and interest therein, with warranty of title and with subrogation of all actions of warranty, unto any person, firm or corporation or association, for such price and on such terms and conditions as Agent may deem proper, to pay and discharge any and all charges, expenses and encumbrances in connection therewith, and to receive and receipt for the selling price.

2. The purpose for which this power of attorney is granted is:

_____ Applicable
_____ Not Applicable

To direct, instruct, authorize and permit Agent to purchase hereinafter described real estate for the price and sum of $ ___________ cash, and $ ___________ to be evidenced by Principal's promissory note and secured by vendor's lien and/or mortgage on such real estate.

3. The purpose for which this power of attorney is granted is:

_____ Applicable
_____ Not Applicable

To direct, instruct, authorize and permit Agent to borrow from any person, firm or corporation, the total sum of $ ____________, said loan to be evidenced by Principal's promissory note and secured by vendor's lien and/or mortgage on the hereinafter described real estate, or Principal's undivided interest therein.

In the event that paragraphs 2 and/or 3 hereinabove shall be applicable, Principal does hereby expressly authorize Agent

(a) To execute the necessary sale and resale or act of mortgage to create a vendor's lien in favor of any building and loan association, and/or to execute any act of sale and/or mortgage, conventional mortgage, or any form of mortgage required to obtain mortgage loan insurance or loan guarantees from the Veterans Administration or Federal Housing Administration, on such form and on such items and conditions as the lender shall require, the said instrument to contain all usual state security clauses, including by way of example but not limited to confession of judgment, waiver of appraisement, and waiver of homestead exemption from seizure.

(b) To make, execute and deliver in Principal's name a promissory note in the amount of the credit portion of the purchase price or the amount of the loan, said note to be payable at such maturity and at such rate of interest and on such terms and conditions as Agent shall deem proper; Agent may increase or decrease the amount of note, not to exceed ten percent (10%).

(c) In the event that any loan is obtained from a building and loan association, to subscribe to shares of stock in said association and to pledge same to secure the loan, and to agree to comply with all the provisions of the charter, by laws and rules and regulations of such building and loan association, and all other things as such building and loan association shall require.

(d) To obligate Principal jointly and in solido in the event that there are other borrowers or purchasers.

THUS DONE AND PASSED at _______________________, Louisiana, this _____ day of __________________, 20____, in the presence of the undersigned competent witnesses who have signed their names together with the said Principal and me, notary.

WITNESSES:	PRINCIPAL:
____________________________	____________________________
Print Name	Print Name
____________________________	
Print Name	

____

Notary name: ______________________________

Notary ID or Bar Roll No.: ____________

My Commission is for Life

AGENT'S ACCEPTANCE:

The undersigned accepts the appointment created by this power of attorney to act as the principal's true and lawful agent, representative and attorney-in-fact.

______________________________ DATE: __________________, 20____

Print Name of Agent

SPECIAL POWER OF ATTORNEY FOR REAL ESTATE, SIMPLE

STATE OF LOUISIANA

PARISH OF ____________________

SPECIAL POWER OF ATTORNEY

BEFORE ME, a notary public duly qualified in and for the above state and parish, and in the presence of the named and undersigned competent witnesses, personally came and appeared:

Name of Principal, a person of the full age of majority and a domiciliary and resident of Cameron Parish, Louisiana ("Principal"), who declared under oath that they have never been married, and whose principal mailing address is 222 Maple St., Cameron, LA 70631, and who declared that they appoint:

Name of Agent, of the full age of majority and a domiciliary of Washington Parish ("Agent"), whose primary mailing address is 908B Washington St., Franklinton, LA 70438, to be their agent, representative and attorney-in-fact, with full power and authority to act for, do and perform all the things and acts specified herein, to act for Principal and in Principal's name, place and stead, to appear before any notary public and execute an act of sale,[1] conveying with full warranty of title, the following described property, to-wit:

ONE CERTAIN LOT OF GROUND, *here, put legal description (or attach to this act, then state here that it is an exhibit)* ... WITH ANY **IMPROVEMENTS THEREON ... BEARING THE MUNICIPAL NO.** *here, put the municipal number, if any; if none, state that fact.*

The sale of the said property shall be for the consideration and upon the terms and conditions as the said Agent shall, in their discretion, deem proper. Principal further declares that they do authorize their agent and attorney-in-fact, Agent, to incorporate in such instrument such terms, conditions and agreements as the said Agent shall deem meet and proper in their sole and uncontrolled discretion; to sign all papers, documents and acts necessary in order to convey the hereinabove described property; to receive and receipt for the proceeds thereof and to do any and all things Agent, in their sole and uncontrolled discretion, deems necessary or proper in connection therewith.

The said Principal does further declare that they do hereby give and grant unto the said agent, Agent, full and complete power to perform any and all acts necessary and proper in the premises as fully as Principal could do if they were personally present and acting for self. Principal also

[1] This is a simple special power of attorney that authorizes only a specific transaction, a sale—primarily, that the agent appear at a real estate closing in place of an absent principal (as is common, especially once the terms are fixed so that only the final signings remain). This form is adaptable, as other or further transactions and powers may be added to it in later paragraphs.

agrees that any action taken by Agent pursuant to this mandate shall constitute acceptance of this mandate.[2] A true copy of this act shall carry the full force and effect of the original.

THUS DONE AND PASSED at _______________________, Louisiana, this _____ day of _________________, 20____, in the presence of the undersigned competent witnesses[3] who have signed their names together with the said Principal and me, notary.

WITNESSES:	PRINCIPAL:
___________________________	______________________________
Print Name	Print Name
___________________________	
Print Name	

____

Notary name: _________________________
Notary ID or Bar Roll No.: ___________
My Commission is for Life

---

[2] In this version, the agent's use of the instrument in action equals an acceptance. There is no need to have the agent sign it, unlike other versions. This may be useful if the agent is not present at the time of signing this act, though they don't have to be in any event. This form is truly unilateral until those actions take place (a "procuration"), as the agent may not even know for some time they have been appointed and only agree to it by using the instrument to complete the sale. Even so, it is advisable to have the agent formally accept in writing, such as a statement clearly accepting the appointment in a separate writing or at the end of this document (and this simple special POA may be adapted accordingly).

[3] Because most acts of cash sale need not be in authentic form, the POA authorizing an agent to sign at a closing does not technically require two witnesses, so the witness block and references (here and in preamble) to "undersigned witnesses" may be removed if the principal is sure that the transaction will be a straightforward cash sale. However, the prudent course is to have this instrument witnessed in case the actions taken do require authentic form after all, such as that it turns out principal is a buyer to a sale with vendor's lien, and the terms of the credit sale include a confession of judgment clause. If principal wishes to restrict the powers to a cash sale with no possibility of financing it, even in part, that limitation can be stated in this act and references to witnesses removed.

SPECIAL POWER OF ATTORNEY FOR REAL ESTATE, DURABLE

STATE OF LOUISIANA

PARISH OF ____________________

SPECIAL POWER OF ATTORNEY

Be it known that on _________________, 20____, before me, a notary public duly qualified in and for the above state and parish, and in the presence of the named and undersigned competent witnesses, personally came and appeared:

Name of Principal, a person of the age of majority and a resident of ______________ Parish, Louisiana, "Principal," who declared under oath that they have been married twice, first to *Ex-spouse name*, from whom they are divorced, and then to *Spouse name*, to whom they remain married and with whom they reside, and whose principal mailing address is *address*; and who declared that they appoint *Name of Agent*, of the age of majority and a domiciliary of ______________ Parish, "Agent," whose primary mailing address is *mailing address*, to be their agent and attorney-in-fact, with full power and authority to act for, do and perform all the things and acts specified herein

1. To sell, exchange, donate, transfer, or convey any property, including stocks, bonds, notes, bills or any other security, belonging to Principal or any interest in them and to receive the price or other consideration for it.
2. To purchase, acquire by exchange or otherwise acquire any property, for and in the name of Principal and to make payment out of Principal's funds or assets.
3. To encumber, mortgage, pledge, pawn or otherwise grant any security interest in any property of Principal, whether to secure obligations of Principal or any other person or entity.
4. To create servitudes, building restrictions, or other real rights, easements and covenants of any kind that burden, benefit or otherwise affect any property of Principal.
5. Agent is authorized to make, sign and execute in the name of Principal all agreements, contracts, and instruments that may be necessary or convenient in Agent's sole discretion to carry out transactions entered into by Agent for Principal or to enable Agent fully to exercise the powers granted and to include any terms, conditions and provisions that Agent deems appropriate and to bind Principal as fully as though each instrument had been signed by Principal in person.
6. The agency created by this power of attorney is "durable" as provided by La. Civil Code Article 3026 and will not be deemed revoked by Principal's disability or incapacity. This power of attorney will be revoked only by subsequent writing.
7. Principal agrees to ratify and confirm all actions that Agent shall take pursuant to this power of attorney.
8. The term "property" means all kinds of property, whether movable, immovable, real, personal, mixed, corporeal, incorporeal, tangible or intangible.

SPECIAL POWER OF ATTORNEY FOR REAL ESTATE, DURABLE

THUS DONE AND PASSED at ________________________, Louisiana, this _____ day of __________________, 20____, in the presence of the undersigned competent witnesses who have signed their names together with the said Principal and me, notary.

WITNESSES: PRINCIPAL:

______________________________ ______________________________

Print Name Print Name

____

Print Name

____

Notary name: ______________________________

Notary ID or Bar Roll No.: _____________

My Commission is for Life

AGENT'S ACCEPTANCE:

The undersigned accepts the appointment created by this power of attorney to act as the principal's true and lawful agent, representative and attorney-in-fact.

______________________________ DATE: _____________________, 20___

Print Name of Agent

POWER OF ATTORNEY FOR HEALTH CARE

STATE OF LOUISIANA

PARISH OF ____________________ *[where the instrument is signed]*

HEALTH CARE POWER OF ATTORNEY[1]

BE IT KNOWN that on ________________, 20_____ *[date]*, before me, the undersigned notary duly commissioned and qualified in the state and parish aforesaid, and in the presence of the two witnesses whose names are hereunto subscribed, PERSONALLY CAME and appeared:

Name of Principal, here also "Appearer," a person of the full age of majority and a resident and domiciliary of the Parish of _______________, State of Louisiana, hereinafter sometimes referred to as "Appearer" or "Principal," appearing[2] for the purpose of granting a power of attorney for health care, as follows:

A. Designation of Health Care Agents. I reside at ______________________________ ____________________. My home/cell telephone number is (_____) _____-________. I name the following individuals as my Health Care Agents, with each of them having full power to act without the concurrence of any of the others.[3] All these individuals are collectively referred to as my "Agent." In the event of a disagreement among the individuals named as Health Care Agents relative to action to be taken herein, the decision of my First Health Care Agent, below, shall be determinative and final.

---

[1] This form is adapted from one approved by, and generously made available to the public by, the Louisiana State Bar Association. All footnote annotations are our own. It may also be called a "Medical Mandate" in Louisiana. See the annotations for "General Power of Attorney" example for an explanation of this and many other important details, including why such forms use two witnesses (as is true of the bar association's form).

After execution (including agent's acceptance), the client should provide copies to anyone who may need copies of the POA and retain the original of this form in personal papers. The notary is advised to provide a few multiple originals or certified true copies just in case a recipient demands to keep an original. Filing in the registry of the clerk of court is not typical for a medical mandate like this, whose use may be immediate and direct. A different form is conditional upon principal's disability and is explained in the file for "POA, Conditional."

[2] The appearance clause may be expanded depending on the nature and content, for example, specifying that principal is "a married man" and to whom (if so), or otherwise clarifying the relationship between principal and agent so that the POA is more likely to be accepted on its face.

[3] The desirability or disadvantages of appointing multiple co-agents with independent authority (as here, the default in the state bar's form), or using "and" to require they all concur, are noted in annotations for "POA, General Power of Attorney." This version helpfully names a primary decision-maker. If one agent is named, this clause can be edited to name a successor agent(s) as back-up in case the first is unable or unwilling to serve.

POWER OF ATTORNEY FOR HEALTH CARE

1. **First Health Care Agent**: ___________________________________
Address: ____
Cell Phone: (_____) _____-________
Home Phone: (_____) _____-________
Work Phone: (_____) _____-________

2. **Second Health Care Agent**: _________________________________
Address: ____
Cell Phone: (_____) _____-________
Home Phone: (_____) _____-________
Work Phone: (_____) _____-________

3. **Third Health Care Agent**: ___________________________________
Address: ____
Cell Phone: (_____) _____-________
Home Phone: (_____) _____-________
Work Phone: (_____) _____-________

4. **Fourth Health Care Agent:** _________________________________
Address: ____
Cell Phone: (_____) _____-________
Home Phone: (_____) _____-________
Work Phone: (_____) _____-________

B. Effective Date. By this document I intend to create a durable power of attorney effective upon, and only during, any period of incapacity in which, in the opinion of my Agent and attending physician, I am unable to make or communicate a choice regarding a particular health care decision. If I am a "qualified patient" as defined in Section 1299.58.2(8) of Title 40 of the Louisiana Revised Statutes or any amendment or replacement thereof or similar statute of another jurisdiction and I have executed a Declaration Relative to Life-Sustaining Procedures ["Living Will"], then such Declaration shall prevail to the extent that it is not inconsistent herewith.

C. Agent's Powers. My Agent shall have full authority to make decisions for me regarding my health care. In exercising this authority, my Agent shall follow my desires as stated in this document, my Living Will, or otherwise known to my Agent. Prior to making any decision, my Agent shall attempt to determine my desires. If I am unable to communicate in any way and my Agent cannot determine the choice I would want made, then my Agent shall make a choice for me based upon what my Agent believes to be in my best interests. My Agent's authority to interpret my desires is intended to be as broad as possible, except for any limitations I may state below.

1. Accordingly, unless specifically limited by Section 2 below, my Agent is authorized as follows:

a. To consent, refuse, or withdraw consent to any and all types of medical care, treatment, surgical procedures, diagnostic procedures, medication, and the use of mechanical or other procedures that affect any bodily function, including, but not limited to artificial respiration, nutritional support and hydration, and cardiopulmonary resuscitation;

b. To have access to my medical records and information, including health information and protected health information as defined by the Health Insurance Reportability and Accountability Act of 1996 (HIPAA), and regulations adopted pursuant thereto, to the same extent that I am entitled to, including the right to disclose the contents to others;

c. To authorize my admission to or discharge from (even against medical advice) any hospital, nursing home, residential care, assisted living, hospice case, or similar facility or service;

d. To contract on my behalf for any health care related service or facility on my behalf, without my Agent incurring personal financial liability for such contracts;

e. To hire and fire medical, social service, and other support personnel responsible for my care;

f. To authorize, or refuse to authorize, any medication or procedure intended to relieve pain, even though such use may lead to physical damage, addiction, or hasten the moment of (but not intentionally cause) my death;

g. To take any other action necessary to do what I authorize here, including but not limited to granting any waiver or release from liability required by any hospital, physician, or other health care provider; signing any documents relating to refusals of treatment or the leaving of a facility against medical advice; and pursuing any legal action in my name, and at the expense of my estate to force compliance with my wishes as determined by my Agent, or to seek damages for the failure to comply.

2. Statement of Desires, Special Provisions, and Limitations.

a. Life Sustaining Procedures. With respect to any "life-sustaining procedures," I have made provisions in a separate Living Will, dated even date herewith, and I direct that my Agent follow the directions provided therein.

b. Diagnostic Tests.[4]

_____ I do not wish to have diagnostic tests performed on me unless they are clearly related to making me well.

_____ I wish to have any diagnostic tests performed that both my Agent and my attending physician deem necessary.

[4] The client should make a choice between the two competing options. Ideally, have the client *initial* the choice rather than just using a check or X, as some medical providers prefer the assurance that a choice was deliberately made by principal. Similar deliberation and marking should be used on the remaining blanks. Be careful that the client does not quickly initial every blank.

c. Experimental Treatment and/or Surgery.

_____ I am aware of the risks involved with unknown, aggressive medical treatments, and I direct my Agent to consent to any experimental treatment or surgical procedure which may improve my condition.

_____ I do not wish to undertake treatments or undergo surgeries which have not been shown to offer meaningful, measurable results. I recognize that by refusing such treatment I may be significantly decreasing my life expectancy or eliminating the possibility of my recovery.

d. Blood Transfusions.

_____ I authorize any blood transfusions deemed necessary by my physician to restore me to health or improve my condition. I am aware of the risks associated with blood transfusions, including, but not limited to contracting blood-borne diseases such as AIDS or hepatitis, and, if possible, I would like to be transfused with my own blood or blood from a known donor.

_____ I understand the risks involved with withholding transfusions, including potentially hastening death, but, for religious reasons or otherwise, I do not consent to any blood transfusions.

e. Organ Donation.

_____ I do not want to make an organ or tissue donation and I do not want my Agent or family to do so.

_____ Pursuant to Louisiana law, I hereby give, effective upon my death,

_____ any needed organ, tissue or parts; or

_____ the following part or organs listed:

____
____ for

_____ any legally authorized purpose.
_____ transplant or therapeutic purposes only.
_____ research or education only.

f. Amputation.

_____ I understand the risks involved with amputating a limb and authorize my Agent to consent on my behalf to any such amputation which will significantly improve my medical condition.

_____ I do not consent to any amputation. I understand the risks involved with refusing to allow such an operation, including infection and bodily deformation, and choose to seek other treatments, even if they are significantly less likely to improve my life.

g. Cardiopulmonary Resuscitation.

_____ If my heart has stopped beating and there is no reasonable expectation of my recovery, I consent to a physician's Do Not Resuscitate order.

_____ If my heart has stopped beating, I wish to employ all means of medical treatment which will restore me to life.

h. Pain Relief.

_____ If I am in pain or significant discomfort, I want to be given appropriate medication to relieve such pain. In the event that I am in severe pain, I wish to receive sufficient medication to ease my discomfort, even if such dosages may shorten my expected life span.

_____ I do not wish to receive medication to relieve pain caused by terminal illness or any other debilitating disease. I understand that such wish may significantly affect my comfort and cause unnecessary suffering on my part, but, nevertheless, I withhold consent.

i. Clinical Trials.

_____ I am willing to participate in clinical trials.

_____ I do not consent to any participation in clinical trials.

_____ My Agent may give consent or refuse to allow participation in clinical trials.

j. Psychotropic Medications.

_____ I do not wish to receive psychotropic medications unless, in the opinion of my Agent, such administration is necessary to preserve my life.

_____ If I am diagnosed as having a psychoneurotic disorder, I am willing to be administered such psychotropic medications as my attending physician recommends.

k. Electroconvulsive Treatments.

_____ I do not wish to receive electroconvulsive treatment.

_____ I am willing to accept such electroconvulsive treatment as my attending physician recommends.

l. Pacemaker/Defibrillator.

_____ My Agent is authorized to order the disabling of any pacemaker/defibrillator that may have been installed in my body.

m. Autopsy.

_____ I do not consent to an autopsy.

_____ I consent to an autopsy.

_____ My Agent may give consent to, or refuse, an autopsy.

3. Protection and Third Parties Who Rely on my Agent. No person who relies in good faith upon any representations by my Agent or Successor Agent shall be liable to me, my estate, my heirs or assigns, for recognizing the Agent's authority.

4. Administrative Provisions.

a. I revoke any prior power of attorney for health care. This provision is not intended to revoke a general power of attorney or financial power of attorney I may have previously or subsequently made. In the event this instrument is inconsistent with a general or other power of attorney I have made that includes health care provisions or appoints a different agent for health care decisions, this instrument shall control.

b. This power of attorney is intended to be valid in any jurisdiction in which it is presented. A copy of this power of attorney is intended to have the same effect as the original.[5]

c. My Agent shall be entitled to receive from any of my medical providers any privileged information, including information which is privileged under the HIPAA Regulations.

d. My Agent shall not be entitled to compensation for services performed under this power of attorney, but my Agent shall be entitled to reimbursement for all reasonable expenses as a result of carrying out any provision of this power of attorney.

e. The powers delegated under this power of attorney are separable, so that the invalidity of one or more powers shall not affect any others.

f. This health care power of attorney is revocable in whole or in part by me. If I so choose, I can verbally, physically, or in writing, cancel this directive.

This power of attorney/medical mandate takes effect immediately. A true copy has the same effect as an original.

THUS DONE AND PASSED at ______________________, Louisiana, this _____ day of __________________, 20____, in the presence of the undersigned competent witnesses who have signed their names together with the said appearer and me, notary.

WITNESSES:	APPEARER:
______________________________	______________________________
Print witness name	*Print name of appearer/principal*
______________________________	
Print witness name	

____

Notary name: ______________________________

Notary ID or Bar Roll No.: ____________________

My Commission is for Life

ACCEPTANCES:[6]

[5] Some medical providers will not honor a plain photocopy despite this statement. It is emphasized in a final provision that "true copies" are the same as originals, a directive that is more likely to be honored.

[6] These are not required to be signed at the same time as the original act by principal, though they often are, to complete the mandate and have it be fully effective. Instead, the agents may sign at different times and places. Although the agents may sign in counterparts, that may be confusing to an inexperienced health care provider, who may interpret multiple copies of the original as inconsistent. It is advisable to either have all agents sign their acceptances on the same original, or prepare separate acceptances to be attached to one original. The original and

POWER OF ATTORNEY FOR HEALTH CARE

The undersigned each accepts the appointment created by this power of attorney to act as the principal's true and lawful agent, mandatary, representative and attorney-in-fact.

FIRST HEALTH CARE AGENT:

________________________________ DATE: _________________, 20____

Print Name of Agent, Agent

SECOND HEALTH CARE AGENT:

________________________________ DATE: _________________, 20____

Print Name of Agent, Agent

THIRD HEALTH CARE AGENT:

________________________________ DATE: _________________, 20____

Print Name of Agent, Agent

FOURTH HEALTH CARE AGENT:

________________________________ DATE: _________________, 20____

Print Name of Agent, Agent

---

attachments can be returned to the notary to then prepare multiple true copies (though signing and stamping on the principal's part rather than any signature page that was signed out of the notary's presence). This process is one reason why it is often convenient to have principal and agent sign together before the notary.

POWER OF ATTORNEY FOR HEALTH CARE, ALTERNATE

STATE OF LOUISIANA

PARISH OF ___________________

HEALTH CARE POWER OF ATTORNEY[1]

BEFORE ME, the undersigned Notary Public and witnesses personally came and appeared:

___________________________, ("PRINCIPAL"); and ______________________________

and _____________________________ (each individually "AGENT," who may act without

notice or consent of any other AGENT.)

ARTICLE 1 HEALTH CARE

I give my Agent all powers regarding the following health care matters that I could exercise on my own behalf, if capable of doing so. My Agent may:

1.1 Medical Records. Have access any medical information in any form regarding my physical or mental condition, and to execute such consents as may be necessary to obtain it; consent to the disclosure of my medical information to others.

1.2 Professionals. Retain, compensate and discharge any health care professionals my Agent deems necessary to examine, evaluate or treat me, whether for emergency, elective, recuperative, convalescent or other care.

1.3 Institutionalization. Admit me to any health care facility recommended by a qualified health care professional, whether for physical or mental care or treatment, and remove me from such institution at any time, even if contrary to medical advice.

1.4 Treatment. Consent on my behalf to tests, treatment, medication, surgery, organ transplant or other procedures, and to revoke that consent, even if contrary to medical advice.

1.5 Chemical Dependency. Consent on my behalf to a course of treatment for chemical dependency, whether suspected or diagnosed, or to revoke such consent.

---

[1] This version has immediate effect. To instead make it conditional upon the principal's disability, so that it goes into effect in the future if at all, insert conditional language found in the "health care power of attorney, conditional," This is different from a later declaration establishing disability, also found in this chapter. Making a medical mandate (or any POA) conditional is not related to the issue of its "durability," i.e., whether it terminates once the principal lacks capacity. Instead, making one conditional defines that the act *begins* on capacity.

1.6 Pain Relief. Consent on my behalf to pain relief procedures, even if they are unconventional or experimental, and even if their use may risk addiction, injury or foreshortening my life.

1.7 Releases. Release from liability any health care professional or institution that acts on my behalf in reliance on my Agent.

1.8 Release of Medical Information. Obtain medical information of any kind or type from my healthcare providers and/or insurance carriers or government agencies. My intention is that my Agent shall have the ability to obtain medical information and that this grant of authority shall comply with the Privacy Act so that my healthcare providers, my insurance companies or government agencies shall release my healthcare information to my Agent and/or discuss my medical needs with my Agent.

1.9 Representation. Represent me in any dealings with Medicare, Medicaid, Social Security or other medical, government or financial aid agency or my insurance carriers.

1.10 Execution of Documents. Execute on my behalf any documents related to the powers of conferred herein, including but not limited to hospitalization, institutional care, medical treatment, Medicaid, Medicare, Social Security, or any other medical, governmental or financial aid agency.

1.11 HIPPA. I do hereby authorize disclosure of protected health information (PHI) maintained on me to an Agent, pursuant to 45 CFR 164.508(c)(1)(iv). I hereby direct my medical providers to release copies of any and all medical records including, without limitation, reports, notes, correspondence, diagnostic studies, and any other records, to Agent, and to provide to Agent, verbally and/or in writing, information regarding my diagnosis, prognosis, condition and treatment or proposed treatment.

1.12 Medical Records. Have access to any medical information in any form regarding my physical or mental condition, and to execute such consents as may be necessary to obtain it. This includes, but is not limited to the disclosure of protected health information (PHI) maintained on Principal to Agent pursuant to 45 CFR 164.508(c)(1)(iv). Furthermore, Principal intends for Agent to be treated as Principal would be with respect to Principal's rights regarding the use and disclosure of Principal's individually identifiable health information, protected health information (PHI) or other medical records. This release authority applies to any information governed by the Health Insurance Portability and Accountability Act of 1996 ("HIPAA"), 42 USC 1320d and 45 CFR 164-164. In addition to the above, Principal authorizes any physician healthcare professional, dentist, health plan, hospital, clinic, laboratory, pharmacy or other covered health care provider, any insurance company and the Medical Information Bureau, Inc. or other health care clearinghouse that has provided treatment or services to Principal or that has paid for or is seeking payment from Principal for such services, to give, disclose and release to my Agent, without restriction, all of Principal's individually identifiable health information and medical records regarding any past, present or future medical or mental health condition, to include all information relating to the diagnosis and treatment of HIV/AIDS, sexually transmitted diseases, mental illness and drug or alcohol abuse. The authority given Agent shall supersede any prior agreement that Principal may have made with any health care providers to restrict access to or disclosure of Principal's individually identifiable health information. The authority given Agent has no expiration date and shall expire only in the event that Principal revokes the authority in writing and deliver it to Principal's health care provider.

ARTICLE II PERSONAL CARE

Principal grants Agent all powers regarding the following personal care matters that I could exercise on my own behalf, if capable of doing so. My agent may:

2.1 Home Care. Provide for my continued maintenance and support. As nearly as possible, I desire to maintain my accustomed standard of living. My Agent shall provide me with a suitable place to live, by maintaining me in my family residence or apartment (home), paying principal, interest, taxes, insurance and repairs as necessary. My Agent may retain or discharge domestic servants, attendants, companions, nurses, sitters or other persons who provide care for me and my home. My Agent may authorize purchases of food, clothing, medical care and customary luxuries on my behalf.

2.2 Institutional Care. If recommended by my physician, my Agent may contract for institutional health care (hospital, retirement facility, nursing home, hospice or other) on my behalf.

2.3 Religious Needs. Continue my affiliation with my church, keeping me accessible to its clergy, members or other representatives continuing and renewing any pledge made by me whether for capital, operations or other purposes, and generally to assist me in maintaining my church relationships to the extent my health permits.

2.4 Companions and Recreation. Hire, discharge, direct and compensate such companions as may be necessary for my health, recreation, travel, and general wellbeing.

2.5 Funeral Arrangements. Arrange and contract for my funeral including appropriate arrangements and instructions for my funeral service or memorial service, including purchase of a burial plot or other appropriate disposition of my body. My Agent shall comply with such known written instructions as I may have or leave.

ARTICLE III REFUSAL OF MEDICAL TREATMENT

Principal does not wish his/her life prolonged artificially through extraordinary or heroic means if my condition is terminal. Even over the objection of members of my family, my Agent may:

POWER OF ATTORNEY FOR HEALTH CARE, ALTERNATE

3.1 Withdraw or Withhold Life Support. If two licensed physicians (one of whom is my attending physician) have personally examined me and my attending physician has noted in my medical records that my condition is terminal and irreversible, or I am diagnosed as being in a profound comatose state with no reasonable chance of recovery, my Agent my sign on my behalf any documents, waivers or releases necessary to withdraw, withhold or cease any procedure calculated only to prolong my life, including the use of a respirator, cardiopulmonary resuscitation, surgery, dialysis, blood transfusion, antibiotics, antiarrhythmic and pressor drugs or transplants.

3.2 Nourishment. Refuse or discontinue intravenous or parenteral feeding, misting, and endotracheal or nasogastric tubes, if advised that no undue pain will be caused to me.

3.3 Declaration. Contemplating that my medical care may be rendered in Louisiana, or that Louisiana law might otherwise apply, I may have executed a Declaration Concerning Life-Sustaining Procedures ("Declaration" or "Living Will") pursuant to Louisiana Revised Statues 40:1151 *et seq.* as amended. By executing that Declaration I do not intend to limit or reduce the powers over my person elsewhere granted to my Agent in this agency, but rather to convey to my Agent such additional powers as are necessary to make or carry out the terms of that Declaration.

Initial one:

_____ This power of attorney confers upon Agent the authority to revoke, rescind or terminate any Living Will I have executed or make any decision contrary to the language or spirit of any Living Will I have executed.

_____ This power of attorney does *not* confer upon Agent the authority to revoke, rescind or terminate any Living Will I have executed or make any decision contrary to the language or spirit of any Living Will I have executed.

Initial one:

_____ This power of attorney confers upon Agent the authority to execute or consent to "Do Not Resuscitate" orders on my behalf.

_____ This power of attorney does *not* confer upon Agent the authority to revoke, rescind or terminate any "Do Not Resuscitate" order(s) I have executed or make any decision contrary to the language or spirit of any "Do Not Resuscitate" order(s) I have executed.

3.4 Amputations. Decide, at the Agent's discretion, to authorize or refuse to authorize the amputation of any of my limbs or other body parts.

ARTICLE IV MISCELLANEOUS PROVISIONS

4.1 Expenses. My Agent shall be entitled to reimbursement for all cost and expenses reasonably incurred on my behalf, but shall not otherwise be entitled to compensation for services rendered.

POWER OF ATTORNEY FOR HEALTH CARE, ALTERNATE

4.2 Release. I release and discharge my Agent and my Agent's heirs, successors and assigns from any and all liability to me, my heirs, successors and assigns arising out of any acts or omissions of Agent, except for willful misconduct or gross negligence. Agent shall have no responsibility to make any property productive of income, to increase the value of my estate or to diversify my investments.

4.3 Applicable Law. This instrument shall be governed by the laws of Louisiana.

4.4 Revocation, Removal, Amendment and Resignation. This agency may be amended or revoked by me. My Agent may be removed by me at any time by written document delivered to my Agent. If this agency has been recorded in the public records, the act of revocation, amendment or removal shall be filed or recorded in the same manner. My Agent may resign by written resignation delivered to me or, if I am incapacitated or interdicted, by delivery to any person with whom I am residing or who is responsible for my care.

4.5 General Power of Attorney. This health care power of attorney shall be separate and distinct from any other general or special power of attorney which I may give and shall not revoke any such power of attorney. In the event such power of attorney includes health care provisions or an appointment of an agent for health care matters or medical decisions, the instrument, provision and appointment herein shall control.

4.6 Durability; Curatorship. This power of attorney shall not terminate in the event of Principal's incapacity, disability or other condition making express revocation impossible or impractical. Further, in the event Principal is declared incompetent or in any proceedings in connection thereto, Principal designates Agent to act as, and be appointed, curator.

A true copy of this act shall carry the full force and effect of the original power of attorney.

THUS DONE AND PASSED at ________________________, Louisiana, this _____ day of __________________, 20____, in the presence of the undersigned competent witnesses who have signed their names together with the said appearer(s) and me, notary.

WITNESSES: PRINCIPAL:

____________________________ ______________________________

Print Name Print Name

____

Print Name

____

Notary name: __________________________

Notary ID or Bar Roll No.: ____________

My Commission is for Life

POWER OF ATTORNEY FOR HEALTH CARE, ALTERNATE

ACCEPTANCES:[2]

The undersigned each accepts the appointment created by this power of attorney to act as the principal's true and lawful agent, mandatary, representative and attorney-in-fact.

FIRST HEALTH CARE AGENT:

________________________________ DATE: ________________, 20____

Print Name of Agent, Agent

SECOND HEALTH CARE AGENT:

________________________________ DATE: ________________, 20____

Print Name of Agent, Agent

[2] These are not required to be signed at the same time as the original act by principal, though they often are, to complete the mandate and have it be fully effective. Instead, the agents may sign at different times and places.

POWER OF ATTORNEY FOR HEALTH CARE, CONDITIONAL

This is a "conditional health care power of attorney," which does not have immediate effect like most powers of attorney do but rather becomes effective only once the principal can no longer take care of their needs. It may never be used, or even accepted by the appointed agent. It is often called a "conditional procuration" since it is not intended to acted upon for years and may not be accepted by the agent for some time, after the disability finally occurs. Once the agent accepts the appointment, it is essentially a "mandate," so this form avoids the naming issue by terming it a "health care power of attorney" making it appropriate whether the agent signs almost immediately (or along with the principal, as is often true), or instead signs the form years later once its condition is met.

A conditional power of attorney is not limited to health care decisions. It is allowed, and often actually preferred, to make any form of a POA into one without immediate effect but used only when the principal is incapacitated. The bolded paragraph can be inserted into any special or general power of attorney, or other preferred forms for medical decisions, to turn it into a conditional one. Although the boldface may be removed, it does set apart what is most distinctive about this form of POA.

Later, when the agent is ready to use this authority because the condition is apparent, a separate document must be executed to establish the disability; a conditional POA is not automatically effective even when the disability is obvious and uncontroversial. The agent will need to couple this POA with the later document establishing disability to be able to use this POA (or a similar general or special one to which the bolded paragraph is added). That document is the "POA, declaration establishing disability" found elsewhere in this collection.

Although the original health care POA is not technically required to be in authentic form, it is advisable to have two witnesses since a medical provider may expect that. Regardless, the declaration establishing disability must be an authentic act.

CONDITIONAL HEALTH CARE POWER OF ATTORNEY

FROM: **ROBERT JONES** **STATE OF LOUISIANA**

TO: **SUSAN SMITH** **PARISH OF JEFFERSON**

Declaration made this _____ day of __________________, 20____, before me, the undersigned Notary Public in and for the Parish of Jefferson with statewide jurisdiction for the state of Louisiana, and in the presence of the undersigned competent witnesses, personally came and appeared:

ROBERT JONES, "Principal," a widower of the full age of majority and a resident of and domiciled in the Parish of Orleans, who declared unto me that he has been married but once, to Carol Jones, from whom he is widowed, and who further declared that he hereby names, constitutes, and appoints:

SUSAN SMITH, currently a resident of and domiciled in the County of Maricopa, State of Arizona, with contact telephone information of 480-555-4244 and 480-555-7011, as "Representative" and "Agent":

To make health care decisions on Principal's behalf, including but not limited to the right to arrange for and consent to medical and surgical procedures as authorized under LA R.S. 40:1151, as it may be amended, or any other applicable Louisiana law, as well as decisions concerning therapeutic treatment and the administration of drugs and other medications; and to make decisions including but not limited to medical expenses, nursing home residence, and insurance claims.

This power and authorization will become effective conditioned upon the establishing under R.S. 9:3890 of the disability of Principal. This will be established by authentic act executed by two

medical doctors[1] averring that due to infirmity Principal is unable to make or communicate reasoned decisions regarding the care of his person.

Principal expressly confirms that Agent shall have the authority to make health care decisions, including the authority to make declarations pursuant to R.S. 40:1151.2 authorizing the withholding or withdrawal of life-sustaining procedures in accordance with the requirements of R.S. 40:1151 *et seq.*, or as they may be amended.

Principal expressly grants his Agent the full authority to make decisions for him regarding his health care. The Agent is authorized to:

• Consent, refuse, or withdraw consent to any and all types of medical care, treatment, surgical procedures, medication, and the use of mechanical or other procedures that affect any bodily function, including but not limited to artificial respiration, nutritional support, and hydration, and cardiopulmonary resuscitation;

• Authorize, or refuse to authorize, any medication or procedure intended to relieve pain, even though such use may lead to physical damage, addiction, or hasten the moment of but not intentionally cause, death;

• Authorize admission to or discharge, even against medical advice, from any hospital, nursing care facility, or similar facility or service;

• Take any action necessary to making, documenting, and assuring implementation of decisions concerning Principal's health care, including, but not limited to, granting any waiver or release from liability required by any hospital, physician, nursing care provider, or other health care provider, signing any health care documents relating to refusals of treatment or the leaving of a facility against medical advice, and pursuing any legal action in Principal's name, and at the expense of Principal's estate to force compliance with his wishes as determined by Agent, or to seek actual or punitive damages for the failure to comply.

• Consent to the donation of all or any of his tissue or organs for purposes of transplantation.

Principal further authorizes any physician treating him to release to Agent any and all protected health records, HIPPA or otherwise protected, or any information which would be necessary for her to make an informed decision relative to his treatment and/or withdrawal of treatment or life support equipment. If the protected health information described herein is disclosed to and/or received by persons or organizations that are not health plans, covered health care providers or health care clearinghouses who are not subject to federal health information privacy laws, they may further disclose the protected health information, and it may no longer be protected by federal health federal health privacy laws. Principal further affirms that he has read the above and authorizes the disclosure of the protected health information as stated herein.

Principal further releases the physician(s) from any and all liability from any wrong disclosure or delivery of his protected health information or medical records to Agent and/or to any other treating physician or health care provider. This authorization is voluntary and is valid until revoked. Principal also confirms that a certified copy or notarized True Copy of this document has the same effect as the original.

ALTERNATE AGENT AND REPRESENTATIVE: In the event Susan Smith is not available or is unable or unwilling to serve as Agent, Principal hereby appoints JOHN T. THOMPSON to act as his

[1] Alternatively, the principal may choose that the declaration establishing their disability require certification by the attending physician and the agent. If so, this paragraph replaces "two medical doctors" with "the attending physician and the said Agent, ..."

POWER OF ATTORNEY FOR HEALTH CARE, CONDITIONAL

Agent and Representative, with all the powers enumerated herein. His contact telephone number is 480-555-7001.

THUS DONE AND PASSED on the _____ day of _________________, 20____, at the Parish and State aforesaid, and in the presence of the undersigned competent witnesses, who hereunto sign their names and me, Notary, after due reading of the whole.

I understand the full import of this designation and I am emotionally and mentally competent to make this appointment and grant these powers and authorities.

____

ROBERT JONES, Principal

Witness: ____

Printed Name: ____

City, Parish, and State: ____

Witness: ____

Printed Name: ____

City, Parish, and State: ____

____

[Print Name], Notary Public

Notary ID or Bar Roll No.: _____________

My Commission is for Life

AGENT'S ACCEPTANCE:

The undersigned accepts the appointment created by this power of attorney to act as the principal's true and lawful agent, representative, and attorney-in-fact.

____

SUSAN SMITH

Date: __________________, 20____

DECLARATION ESTABLISHING DISABILITY, FOR CONDITIONAL POA

STATE OF LOUISIANA

PARISH OF ____________________

DECLARATION ESTABLISHING DISABILITY[1]

BEFORE ME, the undersigned notary public, duly commissioned and qualified in and for the parish and state aforesaid, and the undersigned competent witnesses, personally came and appeared the undersigned:

____, physician, and

____, physician,

Who, after being duly sworn, do hereby each declare and state:

1. I am licensed to practice medicine by the Louisiana State Board of Medical Examiners.

2. I am asked to certify or declare the disability of a Principal to a conditional power of attorney; the Principal's name is ____. I understand that the power of attorney becomes effective upon establishing this disability in an authentic act made pursuant to Louisiana Revised Statute 9:3890, or as amended, which requires this statement from two physicians, as stated in the Principal's power of attorney.[2]

3. I have personally examined the Principal.

4. I declare that, due to infirmity, the Principal is unable consistently to make or to communicate reasoned decisions regarding the care of the Principal's person or property.

---

[1] This form is used to accompany and put into effect a "conditional procuration" (or "conditional power of attorney") made under LA R.S. 9:3890. That act is conditioned upon establishing the principal's disability as established (in this version) by two Louisiana physicians in an authentic act. It can also be executed in counterparts, i.e., signed as two separate authentic acts (using this one form as written but printed twice and executed separately by each declarant doctor, each with two witnesses before a notary).

[2] An alternate version under R.S. 9:3890(C) has this declaration made by the attending physician and the agent, if the original power of attorney so provides. In that case, this declaration may be adapted to be signed by attending physician and agent jointly on one form, or in separate statements each affirming their particular statements of fact confirming the necessary prerequisites under R.S. 9:3890. See file "POA, healthcare power of attorney, conditional" and notes.

DECLARATION ESTABLISHING DISABILITY, FOR CONDITIONAL POA

THUS DONE AND SIGNED at ____________________ *[city]*, Louisiana, in the presence of the undersigned witnesses and me, notary, after due reading of the whole.

____

Name of Physician 1, Declarant

____

Name of Physician 2, Declarant

WITNESSES:

____

Print witness name

____

Print witness name

SWORN TO AND SUBSCRIBED BEFORE ME
This _____ day of ___________________, 20____

____

[*print name*], Notary Public
Notary ID or Bar Roll No.: ____________
My Commission is for Life

REVOCATION OF ENTIRE POWER OF ATTORNEY

POWER OF ATTORNEY: REVOCATION, AGENCY RESIGNATION & VERIFICATION

STATE OF LOUISIANA

PARISH OF ____________________

REVOCATION OF POWER OF ATTORNEY[1]

BEFORE ME, the undersigned notary, duly commissioned and qualified in the state and parish aforesaid, and in the presence of the two witnesses whose names are hereunto subscribed, PERSONALLY CAME and appeared:

Principal's name.[2]

Who declared unto me:

I, ________________________________, Principal of an original Power of Attorney, hereby immediately revoke in its entirety the document titled **Durable Power of Attorney** *[or other name of instrument]* that I previously executed on ________________, 20____, which appointed *Agent's name(s)* as Agent(s). I hereby notify said Agent(s) and any other interested persons and institutions that all portions of said document are revoked.

This revocation takes effect immediately. A true copy has the same effect as an original.

THUS DONE AND PASSED at ______________________, Louisiana, this _____ day of _________________, 20____, in the presence of the undersigned competent witnesses who have signed their names together with the said Principal and me, notary, after due reading of the whole.

WITNESSES:	PRINCIPAL:
____________________________	______________________________
Print Name	Print Name

[1] This is the form for a principal to revoke completely a previously executed POA. Principal should provide copies of this instrument (ideally, true copies) to all agents and anyone who may have originals or copies of the power of attorney that may be relied upon. Principal should retain the original of this form in their personal papers. This form should be witnessed, especially if the original POA was witnessed. This notice should be filed even if the original POA was not filed for registry (giving notice to third parties that any agent no longer acts for principal even if they hold a POA in hand), though it is immediately effective without filing. If the original POA was *required* to be filed to have effect on third parties, a revocation or modification must also be filed, LA C.C. art. 3027.

[2] Appearance clause, which may vary depending on the nature and content of the act; but in this instrument usually it is satisfied by the principal's name. More completely, this would establish they are of the age of majority and their parish of domicile.

REVOCATION OF ENTIRE POWER OF ATTORNEY

____
Print Name

____

Notary name: ____________________________________

Notary ID or Bar Roll No.: _______________

My Commission is for Life

REVOCATION OF AGENCY BY PRINCIPAL

STATE OF LOUISIANA

PARISH OF ____________________

REVOCATION OF AGENCY APPOINTMENT IN POWER OF ATTORNEY[1]

BEFORE ME, the undersigned notary, duly commissioned and qualified in the state and parish aforesaid, and in the presence of the two witnesses whose names are hereunto subscribed, PERSONALLY CAME and appeared:

Principal's name.[2]

Who declared unto me:

The undersigned Principal executed a Power of Attorney dated ________________, 20____, and appointing *Agent's name* as agent and attorney-in-fact; and now Principal, hereby undersigned, revokes that appointment effective immediately. All other provisions of the Power of Attorney remain applicable, valid, and effective, and any successor agents or co-agents therein appointed may serve or continue to serve as so provided. Agent and all parties reliant on this Power of Attorney have been notified of this revocation of appointment.

This revocation takes effect immediately. A true copy has the same effect as an original.

THUS DONE AND PASSED at ______________________, Louisiana, this _____ day of _________________, 20____, in the presence of the undersigned competent witnesses who have signed their names together with the said Principal and me, notary.

WITNESSES:	PRINCIPAL:
____________________________	______________________________
Print Name	Print Name
____________________________	
Print Name	

---

[1] This is the form for principal to withdraw authority from an agent without revoking the POA itself (a different form does that). Principal should provide copies of this instrument (ideally, true copies) to anyone who may have originals or copies of the power of attorney that may be relied upon. Principal should retain the original of this form in their personal papers. It is advisable to have this form witnessed, especially if the original POA was witnessed. This notice should be filed even if the original POA was not filed for registry (giving notice to third parties that agent no longer acts for principal even if they hold a POA in hand), though it is immediately effective without filing. If the original POA was *required* to be filed to affect third parties, the revocation must also be filed.

[2] Appearance clause, which may vary depending on the nature and content of the act; but in this instrument usually it is satisfied by the principal's name. More completely, this would establish they are of the age of majority and their parish of domicile.

____

Notary name: ___________________________________

Notary ID or Bar Roll No.: ______________

My Commission is for Life

RESIGNATION OF AGENCY BY AGENT

STATE OF LOUISIANA

PARISH OF ____________________

RESIGNATION OF AGENCY IN POWER OF ATTORNEY[1]

BEFORE ME, the undersigned notary, duly commissioned and qualified in the state and parish aforesaid, and in the presence of the two witnesses whose names are hereunto subscribed, PERSONALLY CAME and appeared:

Agent's name.[2]

Who declared unto me:

The undersigned is named as Agent/Attorney in Fact for *Principal's name*, in a Power of Attorney dated __________________, 20_____; and now Agent, hereby undersigned, declines to act in that capacity effective immediately. Principal and all parties reliant on this Power of Attorney have been notified of this resignation.

This resignation takes effect immediately. A true copy has the same effect as an original.

THUS DONE AND PASSED at ______________________, Louisiana, this _____ day of __________________, 20____, in the presence of the undersigned competent witnesses who have signed their names together with the said Agent and me, notary.

WITNESSES:	AGENT:
____________________________	____________________________
Print Name	Print Name
____________________________	
Print Name	

____

Notary name: ____________________________

Notary ID or Bar Roll No.: ______________

My Commission is for Life

---

[1] This is the form for an agent to resign or withdraw from serving. They should provide copies of this instrument (ideally, true copies) to anyone who may have originals or copies of the power of attorney that is being resigned and relied upon. The agent should retain the original of this form in their personal papers. Although it not technically required that there be two witnesses (or perhaps, for that matter, that this notice be notarized, as no one can be forced to serve as agent), and so that block and mention of witnesses in the preamble may be removed, it is nonetheless advisable to have this form witnessed if the original POA was witnessed. Also consider filing this notice if the original POA was itself filed for registry, though it is immediately effective without filing.

[2] Appearance clause, which may vary depending on the nature and content of the act; but in this instrument usually it is satisfied by the agent's name. More completely, this would establish they are of the age of majority and their parish of domicile.

AFFIDAVIT OF VALIDITY BY AGENT (ATTACH TO POA)

STATE OF LOUISIANA

PARISH OF ____________________

AFFIDAVIT OF VALIDITY BY AGENT

BEFORE ME, the undersigned duly commissioned and qualified Notary Public, came and appeared the undersigned

____

Agent and Relationship to Principal (Spouse, Descendant, Friend, etc.)

Who, after being first duly sworn, did say:

1. Attached is a true, correct, completed, and unaltered copy of a Power of Attorney dated __ ____________, 20____, granted to me as agent and attorney-in-fact from ____ (Principal's name).
2. Principal, on the date of this Affidavit, is alive and has not given any notice to Agent of changes or termination of the Power of Attorney. Principal was mentally competent at the time the Power of Attorney was executed.
3. In consideration of the authority for which the parties may rely on this Power of Attorney, Agent agrees to indemnify and hold harmless the parties in reliance on this act from and against any and all losses, costs, damages, causes of action (including attorneys' fees) and any other expenses incurred by such reliance.

____

Signature of Agent Date

____

Address City State Zip Code Telephone

____

Tax ID Number/SSN Date of Birth

SWORN TO AND SUBSCRIBED BEFORE ME this _______ day of __________________, 20____

____

Notary Name: ________________________________

Notary ID or Bar Roll No.: ______________

My Commission is for Life

LIVING WILL

DECLARATION OF LIVING WILL (RE LIFE-SUSTAINING PROCEDURES)

STATE OF LOUISIANA

PARISH OF ____________________

DECLARATION OF LIVING WILL

Declaration made this date: ________________________, in the year ________:

I, _________________________________, being of sound mind, willfully and voluntarily make known my desire that my dying shall not be artificially prolonged under the circumstances set forth below and do hereby declare:

If at any time I should have an incurable injury, disease or illness, or be in a continual profound comatose state with no reasonable chance of recovery, certified to be a terminal and irreversible condition by two physicians who have personally examined me, one of whom shall be my attending physician, and the physicians have determined that my death will occur whether or not life-sustaining procedures are utilized and where the application of life-sustaining procedure would serve only to prolong artificially the dying process, I direct (**initial one only**):

_____ That all life-sustaining procedures, including nutrition and hydration, be withheld or withdrawn so that food and water will not be administered invasively.

_____ That life-sustaining procedures, except nutrition and hydration, be withheld or withdrawn so that food and water can be administered invasively.

I further direct that I be permitted to die naturally with only the administration of medication or the performance of any medical procedure deemed necessary to provide me with comfort care.

_____ I choose to have Blood/Blood Products withheld or withdrawn (**Initial only if applicable.**)

In the absence of my ability to give directions regarding the use of such life-sustaining procedures, it is my intention that this declaration shall be honored by my family and physician(s) as the final expression of my legal right to refuse medical or surgical treatment and accept the consequences from such refusal.

I understand the full import of this designation and I am emotionally and mentally competent to make this appointment and grant these powers and authorities.

Signed:

____

City, Parish, and State of residence: ____

The declarant has been personally known to me and I believe declarant to be of sound mind.

_______________________________ _______________________________

Witness 1 name: ________________________ ***Witness 2 name:*** ________________________

LIVING WILL, STATE FORM

LIVING WILL
STATE FORM IN ONE PAGE

13 • BUSINESS ORGANIZATIONS

ASSUMED & TRADE NAME OF BUSINESS

The "assumed name" is also called the "DBA," what the entity is "doing business as." An affidavit of assumed name must be filed with the Clerk of Court of the parish of principal place of business. See LA R.S. 51:281, prohibiting operating other a name other than the owner's, unless they file this disclosure.

The form below can be readily adapted to all situations requiring public disclosure (through filing with the parish) of assumed name, notably a sole proprietorship, LLC, or partnership (but a corporation does not need to file an assumed name). Ultimately, 51:281 requires disclosure of "real full name of the person owning, conducting, or transacting the business," and that person's mailing address.

Although "trade name" is commonly used for a variety of meanings, also including a "DBA," technically it is something that is registered with the Secretary of State only, and does not fulfill the parish-level disclosure requirement for an assumed name. (See form in this collection for trade name.) The intention of "trade name" is to protect the name against others using it, while the parish-based "assumed name" is to disclose true ownership to the public (the real LLC name behind the publicly used name). For example, Saturn Convenience Store may be the assumed name of Houghton Northwest LLC, as owned by its member Harold R. Houghton.

Registering a trade name with the state can protect the "brand" for 10 years at a time. It is optional. But filing an affidavit of assumed name with the parish is mandatory.

Many parishes have their own form affidavit for an assumed name. Confusingly, some of these forms say "trade name," such as that at Jefferson's and Tangipahoa's websites. But all of these are intended to be the assumed name filed with that parish.

STATE OF LOUISIANA

PARISH OF ____________________

AFFIDAVIT OF ASSUMED NAME FOR BUSINESS

BEFORE ME, the undersigned duly commissioned and qualified Notary Public came and appeared the undersigned

____, OWNER(S),

who after being duly sworn, did depose and say

That they are operating a business under the assumed name(s) of

____,

ASSUMED NAME (PARISH)

whose owner's mailing address is: ____

____

in the Parish of ________________________.

____

OWNER NAME: ______________________________

SWORN TO AND SUBSCRIBED BEFORE ME this ______ day of __________________, 20____

____

Notary Name: _____________________________

Notary ID or Bar Roll No.: _____________

My Commission is for Life

TRADE NAME (STATE)

Nancy Landry Secretary of State	**APPLICATION TO REGISTER TRADE NAME TRADEMARK OR SERVICE MARK** **(Pursuant to R.S. of 1950, Title 51, Chapter 1, Part VI as amended)**	
	Enclose $75 filing fee Make remittance payable to Secretary of State *Do Not Send Cash*	**Return to: Commercial Division P.O. Box 94125 Baton Rouge, LA 70804-9125 (225) 925-4704 www.sos.la.gov**

STATE OF ____________________

PARISH/COUNTY OF ____________________

Check One: ( ) Trade Name ( ) Trademark ( ) Service Mark

Check One: ( ) Original Filing ( ) Renewal

1. Name of person(s), Corporation, Limited Liability Company or Partnership applying for registration:

   ____

2. If applicant is a corporation, list state of incorporation: ____________________

3. Full street address and P.O. Box address, city, state, and zip of applicant: ____

4. Name of trade name, trademark or service mark to be registered. If logo is included, please describe. If the LOGO of your trade name, trademark or service mark is part of your registration, attach two copies of design.

   ____

   ____

5. Type of business or list of goods or services to which the trade name, trademark or service mark is applied:

   ____

6. Enter class(es) in which trademark or service mark is registered:
   (Class list on reverse side. There is a $75 registration fee for each class number registered.)

   ____

7. Date trade name, trademark or service mark first used by applicant ____________________
   Month, Day, Year

8. Date trade name, trademark or service mark first used in Louisiana ____________________
   Month, Day, Year

I, the applicant, am the owner of the trade name, trademark or service mark sought to be registered and no other person, firm, association, union or corporation has the right to such use in such class, either in the identical form hereinabove described, or in any such resemblance thereto as may be calculated to deceive, and the facsimiles or counterparts herein filed are true and correct.

Sworn to and subscribed before me, the undersigned Notary Public, on this date: ____________________

The below named person swears that he is the applicant, or an authorized representative of the applicant, named in the foregoing application, and that the facts alleged in said application are true.

NOTARY NAME MUST BE TYPED OR PRINTED WITH NOTARY #

____
Applicant or Authorized Representative

____________________ Notary Signature

____________________ Title

TRADE NAME (STATE)

INSTRUCTIONS

1. Trade Name - a word or group of words, name, symbol, device or any combination thereof used by a person to identify his business, vocation or occupation and distinguish it from the business, vocation or occupation of others. Trademark - any word, name, symbol, device or any combination thereof adopted and used by a person to identify goods, made or sold, and to distinguish them from goods made or sold by others. Service Mark - a mark used in the sale or advertising of services to identify the services of one person and distinguish them from the services of others.

2. Fill in the full name of the individual(s), corporation, partnership or limited liability company who is the owner of the trade name, trademark or service mark being registered.

3. Give full municipal and mailing address of the person(s) listed in No. 2.

4. List the trade name, trademark or service mark exactly as you intend to use it in your business. If a logo is included, please describe.

   NOTE: Our System stores logo registration documents in black-and-white only. Registrations submitted with full-color or grayscale logo graphics will be rejected. You must provide a black-and-white PDF of the logo with supporting text that sufficiently describes the unique elements of the logo.

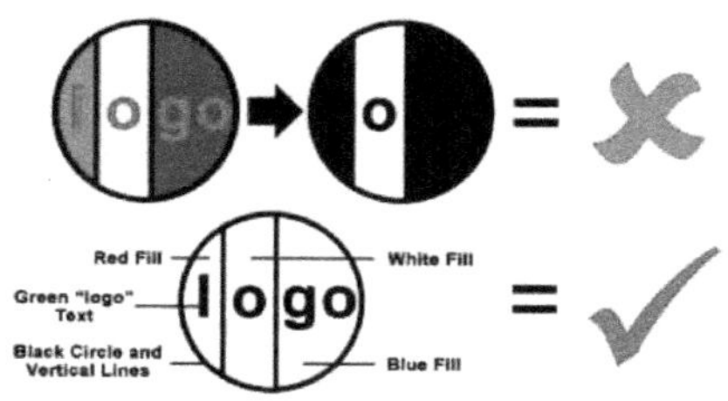

5. Describe the type of business, such as "restaurant" or "retail grocery store" etc. If you are registering a trademark or service mark, list goods or services to which the name is applied, such as "cosmetics", "baker goods", "fishing equipment", etc.

6. No. 6 applies only to trademarks and service marks. Write the class number(s) under item 6. Check the list of classes set out below which describe the category of goods (trademarks only) or services (service marks only) being registered. If goods or services are registered in more than one class, you must pay a registration fee of $75 for each class registered.

7. List the month, day and year when you first started using the trade name, trademark or service mark in business.

8. List the month, day and year when you first started using the trade name, trademark or service mark in Louisiana. The trade name, trademark or service mark must actually be in use on the date of this application. If you have not started actual use of the trade name, trademark or service mark, you can reserve the trade name, trademark or service mark for 120 days by sending a letter and $25 fee to the Secretary of State asking that it be reserved.

9. The affidavit must be notarized. Show the name of the applicant, the name of the person authorized to make the application and his title. The application must be signed by the applicant or the designated authorized representative.

NOTE: The certificate of registration shall be issued if the Secretary of State finds that the trade name is distinguishable from or not the same as a trade name, limited liability company name, or corporate name already in use in this state, or that the trademark or service mark is distinguishable from or not the same as a trademark or service mark already in use in this state which is registered in the same class.

The said classes are as follows:

A. Goods (Trade Marks)

1. Chemicals
2. Paints
3. Cosmetics & cleaning preparations
4. Lubricants & fuels
5. Pharmaceuticals
6. Metal goods
7. Machinery
8. Hand tools
9. Electrical & scientific apparatus
10. Medical apparatus
11. Environmental control apparatus
12. Vehicles
13. Firearms
14. Jewelry
15. Musical instruments
16. Paper goods & printed matter
17. Rubber goods
18. Leather goods
19. Nonmetallic building materials
20. Furniture & articles not otherwise classified
21. House wares & glass
22. Cordage & fibers
23. Yarns & threads
24. Fabrics
25. Clothing
26. Fancy goods
27. Floor coverings
28. Toys & sporting goods
29. Meats & processed foods
30. Staple foods
31. Natural agricultural products
32. Light beverages
33. Wines and spirits
34. Smokers' articles
35. Miscellaneous

B. Services (Service Marks)

36. Insurance & financial
37. Construction & repair
38. Communication
39. Transportation & storage
40. Material treatment
41. Education & entertainment
42. Miscellaneous
43. Advertising and business

ARTICLES OF INCORPORATION (CORPORATION)

INCORPORATION OR ORGANIZATION OF BUSINESS ENTITY

STATE OF LOUISIANA

PARISH OF ______________________

ARTICLES OF INCORPORATION

BEFORE ME, the undersigned duly commissioned and qualified Notary Public, came and appeared the undersigned subscribers herein, of full age of majority, who declared to me, Notary, that availing themselves of the provisions of the Louisiana Business Corporation Law (Louisiana R.S. § 12:1 *et seq.*), they do hereby form, organize and constitute themselves, as well as all such other persons who may hereafter join or become associated with them or their successors, into a business corporation under and in accordance with the following Articles of Incorporation:

ARTICLE I

NAME

The name of the Corporation is *corporation name*. The taxpayer identification number of the Corporation is *TIN*.

ARTICLE II

PURPOSE

The Corporation's purpose is to engage in any lawful activity for which corporations may be formed under the Louisiana Business Corporation Law.

ARTICLE III

STOCK

The Corporation has authority to issue _________ *number of shares* shares of common stock without par value.

ARTICLE IV

INCORPORATORS

The Incorporators' names and post office addresses are:

Name	Address
Incorporator 1	*Incorporator 1's address*
Incorporator 2	*Incorporator 2's address*

ARTICLE V

PREEMPTIVE RIGHTS

Shareholders shall have preemptive rights.

ARTICLE VI

DIRECTORS

The business affairs of the corporation shall be managed by the Board of Directors. The number of directors shall be such number, not less than _____ nor more than _____, as may be designated in the by-laws and if not designated, as may from time to time be elected by the shareholders, except that when all of the outstanding shares are held of record by fewer than ______ *[lower number above]* shareholders, then there need be only as many directors as there are shareholders, but this shall not prevent a greater number of directors as aforesaid. Any director absent from a meeting of the Board of Directors, or any committee thereof, may be represented by any other director who may cast the absent director's vote according to his or her written instructions, general or special.

ARTICLE VII

SPECIAL MEETINGS

Special meetings of shareholders may be called by the president or by a majority of the Board of Directors.

ARTICLE VIII

ISSUANCE OF STOCK

Without any necessity of action by the shareholders, previously authorized but unissued shares of stock of the corporation may be issued from time to time by the Board of Directors, and any and all shares so issued and paid for, shall be deemed full paid stock and not liable to any further assessment or call, and the holder of such shares shall not be liable for any further payment thereon.

ARTICLE IX

CUMULATIVE VOTING

In the election of directors, each shareholder of record shall have the right to multiply the number of votes to which he or she is entitled by the number of directors to be elected, and to cast all such votes for one candidate, or distribute them among any two or more candidates.

ARTICLE X

CONSENTS OF SHAREHOLDERS

Whenever the affirmative vote of shareholders is required to authorize or constitute corporate action, the consent in writing to such action signed only by shareholders holding that proportion of the total voting power on the question which is required by law or by these Articles of Incorporation, whichever requirement is higher, shall be sufficient for the purpose, without necessity for a meeting of shareholders.

ARTICLE XI

REVERSION

Cash, property or share dividends, shares issuable to shareholders in connection with a reclassification of stock, and the redemption price of redeemed shares, which are not claimed by the shareholders entitled thereto within one year after the dividend or redemption price became payable or the shares became issuable, despite reasonable efforts by the corporation to pay the dividend or redemption price or deliver the certificates for the shares to such shareholders within such time, shall, at the expiration of such time, revert in full ownership to the corporation, and the corporation's obligation to pay such dividend or redemption price or issue such shares, as the case may be, shall thereupon cease; provided that the board of directors may, at any time, for any reason satisfactory to it, but need not, authorize (1) payment of the amount of any cash or property dividend or redemption price, or (2) issuance of any shares, ownership of which has reverted to the corporation pursuant to this article, to the entity who or which would be entitled thereto had such reversion not occurred.

THUS DONE AND PASSED IN MULTIPLE ORIGINALS in ____________________ *city*, ________________ Parish, State of Louisiana, on the date of _________________, 20___.

______________________________ ______________________________

Incorporator 1 Witness (print name)

______________________________ ______________________________

Incorporator 2 Witness (print name)

____

Notary Name: _______________________________

Notary ID or Bar Roll No.: ____________

My Commission is for Life

STATE OF LOUISIANA

PARISH OF ______________________

AFFIDAVIT OF REGISTERED AGENT

On _______________, 20___, BEFORE ME, a Notary Public in and for the State and Parish aforesaid, personally came and appeared *name of registered agent for corporation*, whose post office address is *mailing address (not a P.O. Box)*, who is to me known to be the person, and who, being duly sworn, acknowledged to me that they do hereby accept appointment as the Registered Agent of *name of corporation*, which is a Corporation authorized to transact business in the State of Louisiana pursuant to the provisions of the Title 12, Chapters 1, 2, and 3.

____

REGISTERED AGENT

SWORN TO AND SUBSCRIBED BEFORE ME this ______ day of __________________, 20_____

ARTICLES OF INCORPORATION (CORPORATION)

____

Notary Name: ________________________________

Notary ID or Bar Roll No.: ____________

My Commission is for Life

INITIAL REPORT OF *[NAME OF CORPORATION]*

Name of corporation hereby makes its initial report as follows:

1. The registered office of the corporations is:
2. The name and mailing address of the registered agent of the corporation is:
3. The name and mailing address of the directors are:

Date: ________________, 20____

____

Incorporator 1

____

Incorporator 2

WHAT FOLLOWS ON PAGES 349-351 IS THE STATE'S ARTICLES OF INCORPORATION FORM AND INSTRUCTIONS, FROM THE SECRETARY OF STATE'S WEBSITE.

"AND LIKE TO SAVE LABOR, STATE FORM IS THERE."

Nancy Landry
Secretary of State

ARTICLES OF INCORPORATION
R.S. 12:1-202

Domestic Business Corporation
Enclose $75 Filing Fee
Make remittance payable to Secretary of State
Do Not Send Cash

Return to: **Commercial Division**
P.O. Box 94125
Baton Rouge, LA 70804-9125
Phone: (225) 925-4704
Web Site: www.sos.la.gov

STATE OF ______________________

PARISH/COUNTY OF ______________________

1. The name of this corporation is: ______________________

2. The corporation is formed for the purpose of: (check one)
   a. ( ) Engaging in any lawful business or activity for which corporations may be formed under this Chapter.
   b. ( ) ______________________
   (use for limited corporate activity)

3. The duration of this corporation is: (may be perpetual) ______________________

4. The number of shares which the corporation shall have authority to issue is: ______________________

5. The name and address of each incorporator is: ______________________

6. The street address, not a post office box only, of the corporation's initial registered office is: ______________________

7. The street address, not a post office box only, of the corporation's initial principal office is: ______________________

8. The name and street address, not a post office box only, of the corporation's initial registered agent is: ______________________

9. The names and street addresses of the corporation's initial directors are: ______________________

10. The protection against liability of directors and officers that is provided by R.S. 12:1-832 is accepted unless, otherwise, specified below:

    a. ( ) rejected ______________________
    (statement of rejection)

    b. ( ) limited ______________________
    (statement of limitations)

11. Other provisions: ______________________

SS399 Rev. 01/24

Incorporator Signature: ______________________________

On this _____ day of _________________________ 20___, before me, personally appeared ______________________________________,
to me known to be the person described in and who executed the foregoing instrument, and acknowledged that he executed it as his free act and deed.

____
Notary Signature, Printed Name, and Notary/Bar Roll Number

WRITTEN CONSENT TO APPOINTMENT

I hereby acknowledge and accept the appointment of registered agent for and on behalf of the above named corporation.

Registered agent(s) signature(s):

____

____

Sworn to and subscribed before me, the undersigned Notary Public, on this date: ______________________________

____
Notary Signature, Printed Name, and Notary/Bar Roll Number

INSTRUCTIONS

NOTE: A corporation is a complex form of business structure. This form contains only the minimum provisions required by law to be set forth in Articles of Incorporation. Additional provisions may be advisable or necessary, depending on the specific needs of each corporation. Consideration should be given to the advantages and disadvantages of incorporating, and the legal and tax consequences. You are strongly advised to seek legal advice from an attorney, and tax and other business advice from an accountant.

1. File the Articles of Incorporation, which contains a Written Consent to Appointment (both portions signed before a notary), and the requisite $75 filing fee with the Secretary of State's office.
2. The Articles of Incorporation may be delivered to the Secretary of State's office in advance, for filing as of any specified date (and any given time on such date) within 90 days after the date of delivery. Requests should be made in writing and must be submitted along with the Articles of Incorporation.
3. Please call the Internal Revenue Service at (800) 829-4933 for information to obtain a corporation's federal tax identification number.
4. If the Articles of Incorporation are filed within five (5) working days (exclusive of legal holidays) after acknowledgement, the corporate existence shall begin as of the time of such acknowledgement.

SS399 Rev. 01/24

ARTICLES OF ORGANIZATION (LLC)

STATE OF LOUISIANA

PARISH OF ______________________

ARTICLES OF ORGANIZATION
OF
[NAME OF LLC]

BEFORE ME, the undersigned duly commissioned and qualified Notary Public, came and appeared the undersigned, a person of the legal age of majority, for the purpose of forming a limited liability company under the Louisiana Limited Liability Company Law (Louisiana Revised Statutes § 12:1301 *et seq.*), who now hereby makes, signs and acknowledges these articles of organization of the *name of LLC*.

ARTICLE 1

The name of the limited liability company shall be: *name of LLC*.

ARTICLE 2

This limited liability company is formed for the purpose of engaging in any lawful activity for which limited liability companies may be formed under the Louisiana Limited Liability Company Law.

ARTICLE 3

The limited liability company shall be managed by its managers.[1] No member in such capacity has the authority or power to act for or on behalf of the limited liability company, to do any act that would be binding on the limited liability company, or to incur expenditures on behalf of the limited liability company. The managers are authorized to manage the business and affairs of the limited liability company, including without limitation the authority to do the following without the approval of the members:

(1) Sell, exchange, lease, mortgage, pledge, or otherwise transfer all or substantially all of the assets of the limited liability company.
(2) Incur indebtedness by the limited liability company in other than the ordinary course of business.
(3) Alienate, lease, or encumber immovable property of the limited liability company.
The affirmative vote of a majority of the managers shall be required for any act of the managers. Each manager shall be entitled to a single vote on all matters for which managers may vote. Unless otherwise authorized by a majority of the managers, no manager has the authority or power to act for or on behalf of the limited liability company, to do any act that would be binding on the limited liability company, or to incur expenditures on behalf of the limited liability company even if such action is in the ordinary course of business of the limited liability company. Limitations on the authority of the managers to bind the limited liability company are contained in a written operating agreement.

---

[1] This paragraph may be modified to allow management by members, as the needs of the organization dictate.

ARTICLES OF ORGANIZATION (LLC)

ARTICLE 4

As per Louisiana R.S. § 12:1305(C)(5), the following members or managers acting alone may execute certificates that establish the membership of any member, the authenticity of any records of the limited liability company, or the authority of any person to act on behalf of the limited liability company, including, but not limited to, the authority to take the actions referred to in Louisiana R.S. § 12:1318(B): *Names of authorized individuals*, the _________ *members or managers, etc.* of the company. Any person dealing with the limited liability company shall be entitled to rely conclusively on the certificates.

ARTICLE 5

The operating agreement and all amendments to it shall be in writing. In the event of a conflict between the articles of organization and the operating agreement, these articles of organization shall govern.

ARTICLE 6

The term of the Company shall be perpetual. [*OR* The term of the Company shall begin on this date and shall continue for a period of ______ *number of years if not perpetual* years.]

THUS DONE AND PASSED IN MULTIPLE ORIGINALS in ______________________ *city*, __________________ Parish, State of Louisiana, on the date of ___________________, 20____.

____
Organizer

____
Witness [print name]

____
Witness [print name]

____
Notary Name: _______________________________
Notary ID or Bar Roll No.: _____________
My Commission is for Life

STATE OF LOUISIANA

PARISH OF _______________________

ACKNOWLEDGMENT

On _______________, 20____, *date*, before me, the undersigned authority, duly commissioned and qualified in and for the state and parish set forth above, and in the presence of the undersigned competent witnesses, personally came and appeared *name of organizer*, who, having been duly sworn, declared that he executed the foregoing articles of organization as his free act and deed and for the purposes and considerations set forth in the instrument.

_________________________________ ______________________________
Organizer Witness

____
Witness

SWORN TO AND SUBSCRIBED BEFORE ME this ______ day of __________________, 20_____

____

Notary Name: ______________________________
Notary ID or Bar Roll No.: ____________
My Commission is for Life

INITIAL REPORT OF *[NAME OF LLC]*

LLC name hereby makes its initial report as follows:

Complying with the requirements of the Louisiana Limited Liability Company Law, the undersigned organizer of this company makes this initial report of the company.

1. The location and municipal address of the company's registered office is: *municipal address of company's registered office, but cannot be a P.O. Box*
2. The full name and municipal address of its registered agent are: *name and municipal address of agent, not a P.O. Box*
3. A notarized affidavit of acknowledgment and acceptance signed by each registered agent is attached to this document.
4. The names and municipal addresses of the initial members *[managers, if the company is managed by managers]* are: *names and municipal addresses of members or manager, not a P.O. Box*

Date: ___________________, 20_____

____
Organizer

ARTICLES OF ORGANIZATION (LLC)

STATE OF LOUISIANA

PARISH OF ____________________

AFFIDAVIT OF ACCEPTANCE OF APPOINTMENT BY DESIGNATED REGISTERED AGENT

BEFORE ME, a duly commissioned and qualified Notary Public, came and appeared the undersigned

____

NAME OF AGENT

Who, after being duly sworn, acknowledged that they do hereby accept appointment as the registered agent of *name of LLC*, which is a limited liability company authorized to transact business in the state of Louisiana pursuant to the provisions of the Louisiana Limited Liability Company Law.

____

Agent

SWORN TO AND SUBSCRIBED BEFORE ME this ______ day of __________________, 20_____

____

Notary Name: ____________________________

Notary ID or Bar Roll No.: ____________

My Commission is for Life

CERTIFICATE OF AUTHORITY TO ACT FOR LLC

AUTHORIZATIONS TO APPEAR OR ACT FOR BUSINES ENTITY

STATE OF LOUISIANA

PARISH OF ____________________

CERTIFICATE OF AUTHORITY[1]

BEFORE ME, the undersigned duly commissioned and qualified Notary Public, came and appeared the undersigned

NAME OF LLC, Limited Liability Company (TIN __-______), a Louisiana limited liability company whose articles of organization were filed with the Secretary of State on *date*, having a permanent mailing address of *address*, *city*, LA, *zip code*, appearing herein and through, represented by *name of member*, Member, duly authorized by Unanimous Written Consent of the Members, an original of which is attached hereto and made a part hereof,

Who, after being first duly sworn, deposed and said:

The undersigned (the "Member") hereby certifies that the Members are all of the members of *NAME OF LLC*, L.L.C. (the "Company"), or all of the members or managers of the Company required by the Company's articles of organization or operating agreement or contract to transact the Company's business and to grant the authority granted herein. The undersigned Member hereby certifies that the Company is a limited liability company or domestic limited liability company, as such terms are defined in LA R.S. 12:1301, organized under the laws of the State of Louisiana and registered with the Louisiana Secretary of State in accordance with LA R.S. 12:1301 *et seq.*, or a foreign limited liability company authorized to do business in the State of Louisiana pursuant to a certificate of authority issued by the Louisiana Secretary of State in accordance with LA R.S. 12:1342 *et seq.*

The Members hereby authorize, name, constitute and appoint *NAME OF MEMBER OR MANAGER* (referred to as "Authorized Individual") for and in the name and on behalf of the Company to sign on behalf of the company for *name reason for issuance of certificate (purchase of vehicle, sale of real estate, hiring of manager, etc.)*. This Certificate of Authority shall be valid until *name end date of validity of authority*.

Further, Authorized Individual is hereby authorized and empowered to appear before a Notary Public to sign and execute on behalf of the Company any and all documents necessary to

---

[1] This is one version of a "certificate of authority" that authorizes a person to act or sign documents on behalf of an LLC. It is the analog of a corporation's "corporate resolution" or an unincorporated association's "statement of authority" (the latter uses similar language but must be in authentic form). Take note that an unrelated "certificate of authority" may refer to one of the documents a new LLC must file with the Secretary of State as part of the incorporation and registration process. The one here is used for an ongoing LLC to act through others.

For LLC, corporations, and partnerships, see also a standardized form provided by the Louisiana Office of Financial Institutions, found later in this chapter.

CERTIFICATE OF AUTHORITY TO ACT FOR LLC

perform said acts. The Company and all members thereof shall be bound by all instruments, documents, agreements and other writing executed by the Authorized Individual.

Further, that any and all action taken by Authorized Individual in connection with this Certificate of Authority is hereby ratified and confirmed.

All persons, firms or corporations shall be entitled to rely on the authority granted herein to the Authorized Individual unless or until written instructions to the contrary signed by the Members are received by them.

____
Affiant

SWORN TO AND SUBSCRIBED BEFORE ME this ______ day of __________________, 20_____

____

Notary Name: ______________________________

Notary ID or Bar Roll No.: ____________

My Commission is for Life

CORPORATE RESOLUTION TO ACT FOR CORPORATION

CORPORATE RESOLUTION[1] OF

____

(Name of Corporation)

RESOLVED, that it is desirable and in the best interest of this Corporation that it act through appointed and authorized agents to accomplish its purposes; that the *title of corporate officers or other representative* are hereby authorized to *action(s) which the corporate officers are entitled to take*; that said officers are hereby authorized to perform on behalf of this Corporation any and all such acts as they may deem necessary or advisable in order to comply with the applicable laws of any such states, and in connection therewith to execute and file all requisite papers and documents, including, but not limited to *actions which must be taken to accomplish the goals of this resolution* or the doing by them of any act in connection with the foregoing matters; and the execution by such officers of any such paper or document, or the doing by them of any act in connection with the foregoing matters, shall conclusively establish their authority therefore from this Corporation and the approval and ratification by this Corporation of the papers and documents so executed and the action so taken.

CERTIFICATE

The undersigned hereby certifies that s/he is the Secretary of ________________________,
a corporation organized and existing under the laws of the State of _________________; that the foregoing is a true and correct copy of a resolution duly adopted at a meeting of the Board of Directors of said corporation held on the _____ day of _________________, 20___, at which meeting a quorum was at all times present and acting; that the passage of said resolution was in all respects legal; and that said resolution is in full force and effect.

Dated this _____ day of _________________, 20____.

Signed,

[CORPORATE SEAL]

____

Secretary's printed name

[1] See also a standardized form, next in this chapter, in a PDF. The state's PDF form can be used for LLCs, partnerships, and corporations.

CERTIFICATE OF RESOLUTION FOR ALL BUSINESS ENTITIES, STATE FORM

CERTIFICATE OF RESOLUTION

Use this form to designate additional authorized individuals to act on behalf of the Licensee.

Each person listed in the initial application as a director, manager, member, partner, sole proprietor, 10% or greater equity owner and/or executive officer (CEO, CFO, COO, President, EVP, Secretary, Treasurer, or individuals of similar status or function) will be considered authorized to prepare, execute, verify, and present to the Office of Financial Institutions ("OFI") a written application for licensure, registration, documents or subsequent changes in the licensee's records with OFI. Therefore, anyone listed in the initial application is not required to file this form.

This is to certify that at a meeting of the ☐ Board of Directors/or ☐ Members/ or ☐ Partners of

____
Full legal name of applicant/company

organized under the laws of the State/Commonwealth of ______________________________ held at

______________________, ______________________, __________, __________
Street address City State Zip Code

on the ______________ day of ______________________ 20____, the following resolution was

duly and legally presented and adopted, to wit:

It being the desire and purpose of ____
Full legal name of applicant/company
to be licensed or registered and maintain such license or registration, BE IT RESOLVED, that

______________________________who is the ______________________________
Name of additional authorized representative Title of additional authorized representative

of this ☐ limited liability company, ☐ corporation, ☐ limited partnership, or ☐ general partnership is in his/her official capacity, hereby authorized and directed to prepare, execute, verify, and present to OFI all requisite papers and documents, including, but not limited to, applications, reports, and licensing forms or subsequent changes in the licensee's records with OFI.

____
AUTHORIZED SIGNATURE
(If corporation, this form must be signed by the Secretary)

____
Print Name

TITLE : ______________________________

DATE: ______________________________

14 • OFFICE OF THE NOTARY AND MISCELLANEOUS

OATH OF OFFICE

STATE OF LOUISIANA **PARISH OF** ____________________

I, ______________________________ do solemnly swear (or affirm) that I will support the
(Print or Type Name)
constitution and laws of the United States and the constitution and laws of this state and that I will faithfully and impartially discharge and perform all the duties incumbent on me as **notary public/exofficio notary/deputy Clerk**
(circle one)

for the ______________________________
(Parish name if notary public/agency name if ex-officio or deputy clerk)

according to the best of my ability and understanding, so help me God.

(Circle One) Mr. Ms. Mrs. Miss

____
(Signature)

(Officials authorized to administer oaths: governor, secretary of state, clerks of court, notaries public, judges, justices of the peace)

Sworn to and subscribed before me this _____ day of ______________, _____.

____
(Signature)

____
(Printed name of official administering oath – ID number if applicable)

ATTENTION: An address and telephone number must be provided for public record.

Residence Mailing Address:

____

____

Telephone: ______________________

Office Mailing Address:

____

____

Telephone: ______________________

1. File an Oath of Office with: Secretary of State, P.O. Box 94125, Baton Rouge, LA 70804-9125.

2. File a duplicate Oath of Office with the parish Clerk of Court within one month after the oath is administered. In Orleans Parish file with the Clerk of Civil District Court. See La. R.S. 42:162 for more information.

SS 408N - Oath of Office for Notary Public

Nancy Landry
Secretary of State

COMPLAINT ALLEGING UNAUTHORIZED EXERCISE OF NOTARIAL POWERS

La. R.S. 35:601 *et seq.*

RETURN COMPLETED FORM TO:
Secretary of State Notary Division,
P.O. Box 94125
Baton Rouge, LA 70804

Parish of ______________________________

Before me, the undersigned authority came and appeared the undersigned complainant, who in accordance with the provisions of La. R.S. 35:603, and being duly sworn, did depose and say that

____ ______________________ is in violation of the
Printed name of subject of complaint **Notary ID# if known**

following provision(s) of La. R.S. 601 *et seq.* (UNAUTHORIZED EXERCISE OF NOTARIAL POWERS)

Violation(s): check all that apply

_____ Commission or authority to exercise notary function is statutorily or judicially suspended.
_____ Commission or authority to exercise notary function is statutorily or administratively revoked.
_____ No longer validly commissioned.
_____ Commission in retirement status under provisions of R.S.35:202(G)
_____ No longer validly possessed of the office or position from which authority to exercise notarial functions were derived.
_____ Convicted of a felony and has not been pardoned.
_____ Not authorized by law to exercise that particular notarial function.
_____ Violated any provision of any law governing the office of notary or the exercise of notary authority.
_____ Abandoned his commission.
_____ Failed to pay over money entrusted to him in his official capacity as a notary public.
_____ Failed to satisfy any final judgment rendered against him in his official capacity as a notary public.
_____ Not authorized to exercise notarial powers.

Complainant's statement to include details of violation(s), its nature, the dates, time(s), address(es) where violation(s) occurred and address of subject of the complaint. (attach additional page(s) if necessary):

____

____

____

____

Complainant name: ____ **Phone:** ______________________

Complainant address: ____________________________________ **City, State, Zip:** ______________________

____
Signature of Complainant

Sworn to and subscribed before me this ____ day of ___________, 20___

____
Signature of notary

____ ________________
Printed name of notary La. Notary ID#

INDEX

ABOUT THE AUTHORS

MICHELE CHILDRESS is an attorney licensed in Louisiana, since 2002. She received her notary commission that same year. She earned her B.A. from Loyola University–New Orleans and her J.D. degree from Loyola as well. She is a member of the Louisiana Bar Association with 22 years of experience in law and legal research. She is the author of *Louisiana Notary Exam Outline to the Study Guide: A Simpler Summary of the Official Book*. She has also edited and produced modern editions of Joseph Story's classic *Commentaries on the Constitution of the United States* and Woodrow Wilson's *Constitutional Government in the United States*.

Michele is a commissioned Louisiana notary who, along with her husband Alan, previously owned a notary/shipping service in Jefferson Parish. They have performed thousands of notarial acts covering a wide range of subjects and formats. They offer remote prep seminars for the notary exam, live and recorded, through the website *ChildressNotary.com*, as well as a seminar called "I Passed – Now What?" Michele is a panelist sharing practical advice with newly commissioned notaries as part of the annual convention of the Louisiana Notary Association.

STEVEN ALAN CHILDRESS is a senior professor at Tulane Law School, holding the Conrad Meyer III Professorship in Civil Procedure. He has taught Torts, Evidence, and Legal Profession at Tulane since 1988, in addition to visiting positions at Loyola and GW. He also teaches the Louisiana Notary Law class in Tulane's School of Professional Advancement. He has lectured for Continuing Legal Education on notary practice, legal ethics, and evidence law, as well as teaching Louisiana Bar Review for a decade.

Alan earned his law degree from Harvard and a PhD in Jurisprudence from Berkeley. He clerked in Shreveport for the federal court of appeals, then practiced law in California. He is a member of the California and D.C. bars, holding his law licenses there, and the Louisiana Notary Association. He co-authored the three-volume treatise *Federal Standards of Review* and edited three books on legal ethics. More recently, he wrote *Louisiana Notary Exam Sidepiece to the Study Guide, Louisiana Notary Exam Sample Questions and Answers*, and the introductory guide, *Become a Notary Public in Louisiana*.

If you have suggestions or corrections to this guidebook, please email them to *quidprolaw@gmail.com*.

Visit us at *www.quidprobooks.com.*

www.ingramcontent.com/pod-product-compliance
Lightning Source LLC
LaVergne TN
LVHW080924210926
848485LV00004B/725